DIALOGISM

NEW DIRECTIONS IN MATHEMATICS AND SCIENCE EDUCATION
Volume 15

Scope

Mathematics and science education are in a state of change. Received models of teaching, curriculum, and researching in the two fields are adopting and developing new ways of thinking about how people of all ages know, learn, and develop. The recent literature in both fields includes contributions focusing on issues and using theoretical frames that were unthinkable a decade ago. For example, we see an increase in the use of conceptual and methodological tools from anthropology and semiotics to understand how different forms of knowledge are interconnected, how students learn, how textbooks are written, etcetera. Science and mathematics educators also have turned to issues such as identity and emotion as salient to the way in which people of all ages display and develop knowledge and skills. And they use dialectical or phenomenological approaches to answer ever arising questions about learning and development in science and mathematics.

The purpose of this series is to encourage the publication of books that are close to the cutting edge of both fields. The series aims at becoming a leader in providing refreshing and bold new work—rather than out-of-date reproductions of past states of the art—shaping both fields more than reproducing them, thereby closing the traditional gap that exists between journal articles and books in terms of their salience about what is new. The series is intended not only to foster books concerned with knowing, learning, and teaching in school but also with doing and learning mathematics and science across the whole lifespan (e.g., science in kindergarten; mathematics at work); and it is to be a vehicle for publishing books that fall between the two domains—such as when scientists learn about graphs and graphing as part of their work.

Dialogism

A Bakhtinian Perspective on Science and Learning

By

Wolff-Michael Roth
University of Victoria, Canada

SENSE PUBLISHERS
ROTTERDAM / BOSTON / TAIPEI

A C.I.P. record for this book is available from the Library of Congress.

ISBN 978-90-8790-862-1 (paperback)
ISBN 978-90-8790-863-8 (hardback)
ISBN 978-90-8790-864-5 (ebook)

Published by: Sense Publishers,
P.O. Box 21858, 3001 AW Rotterdam, The Netherlands
http://www.sensepublishers.com

Printed on acid-free paper

Contents

Preface

In this book, I take a 38-minute conversation in one classroom—which has as its topic the production of a hierarchically organized map of science concepts—as 'excuse' for an extended reflection on language, learning, language development, linguistic transformation, and the learning paradox. Specifically, I focus on three learning paradoxes insufficiently attended to in the learning sciences generally and in science education more specifically: (a) how learners can intend to learn what they do not know and which therefore cannot serve as the object of their intentions; (b) how persons can learn something new when their current understandings and therefore their grounds and means for learning are inconsistent (contradictory) with what they are supposed to learn; and (c) how the subject matter disciplines are both reproduced and transformed over time given that today's experts themselves have come to school yesterday uninstructed about science. The answers to these paradoxes can be found in an approach to language with a dialectical materialist foundation that Mikhail Bakhtin called *dialogism*. By analyzing the unfolding speech during concept-mapping task in a high school physics course, I show how change in language—and therefore learning—arises without being intended from the very fact that students speak. Bakhtin postulates that any language changes that occur over millennia can be understood when every speech act is theorized as a creative act transforming the language system as a whole all the while reproducing it. This is a position consistent with that taken by the philosopher Edmund Husserl on the historical development of the sciences, or the position Martin Heidegger takes on language. In each case, the author suggests genetic mechanisms *internal to* the phenomenon as the reason for change. In Bakhtin, this change is the very consequence of dialogism, the non-self-identical nature of each and every word even and precisely when it is uttered two or more times in a sequence.

One of the questions one might have concerning language is the manner in which it is reproduced and, more importantly, how it is transformed and therefore produced anew. It is only when we understand how language slowly changes over time both individually and collectively that we get a real theoretical handle on language and that we come to a perspective that overcomes the simplistic view of language as a tool that people deploy to make the contents of their minds available to others. The entire book implements this program in unfolding issues that we need to know about language. While the reader moves from chapter to chapter and within each chapter, from the beginning to its end, I introduce what is required thereby slowly building up the new perspective as a whole.

In this book, I propose taking a radically different approach then the one taken by the different forms of constructivism, all of which are based on the same Kantian metaphor of the rational Self that constructs itself, where the construction of the starting Self remains in the analytic blind spot. I propose to tackle the learning paradox in terms of a perspective on language that considers it to be a non-self-identical phenomenon. I take the Bakhtinian position—which is the one other language philosophers also take today (e.g., Derrida)—that language ('the word') is different from, and therefore stands in a dialogical relation with, itself. This non-self-identical nature immediately implies that language changes, and it does so at microgenetic, ontogenetic, and cultural-historical scales, just as the Russian psychologist Lev S. Vygotsky predicted it. I show how language is the ground, the tool, and the material (object) of and for the learner. It is precisely because of these multiplicities that we get to the emergence of new possibilities, new structural relations in what we can say about something that we cannot even envision before we actually have the language that allows us to do it. We learn language in the way we become acquainted with, and competent in, a new workplace, that is, by participating with others whose complicity we need and who need our complicity in making the place for what it is. That is, we do not learn by *constructing* or *reconstructing* our understanding. We do not learn by abandoning or eradicating what we currently know. We do not learn by receiving information, which we would not understand because our receivers (i.e., listeners, audiences) cannot be tuned in the right way prior to instruction. Rather, we learn by participating in taking up positions in the world, and language specifically—and communication generally—is but and aspect of taking up positions in ways that are intelligible by and defensible to others.

The implications for method are that we do not need to look for mental activity between the ears and underneath the skin. We find anything 'mental' in society and societal relations, for the structure of 'mental' activity is as social as that of its external objectification. Any word, because of its concrete material form, exerts an effect on social|mental[1] activity: It begins to structure internal life as much as it structures external life and gives both a more defined and stable expression. The recommended Bakhtinian implications for the study of language are as follows. We need to analyze first the forms and types of verbal interaction in relation to the concrete conditions where it is realized in concrete form. We then analyze the forms of distinct utterances, acts of single utterances in close relation with the situation of which they constitute irreducible moments, that is, the categories of speech acts. We finally examine language in its usual form. It is in the same order that language actually evolves. First, the social relations evolve. Second, communication and verbal interactions evolve in

---

1. To create dialectical notions, I use the Sheffer stroke '|'. It corresponds to a logical NAND (not and) operation. If, as in the instance of agency and passivity, we have two mutually exclusive terms, that is, they are alternately true or false, the resulting statement agency|passivity—which can also be written as 'NOT (agency AND passivity)'—is always true precisely because it embodies an inner contradiction.

the context of social relations and speech acts evolve within verbal interaction. Third, the evolution is reflected in the changes of forms of language.

Having gotten us off the ground, I elaborate in chapter 2 a foundation for my work with language. I elaborate on the problematic of the learning paradox, which, to me, is the main unacknowledged problem of much of current learning research. In the subsequent chapters 3–6, I use one concept-mapping session to introduce my way of thinking about language, learning, speaking, and thinking that I have developed in the course of reading not only Marxist scholars such as Bakhtin and Vygotsky but also in the course of reading late-20th-century philosophers, such as Paul Ricœur, Jacques Derrida, Hélène Cixous, and others. Where necessary, I draw on other philosophers as sources for evolving a different understanding of knowing and learning and, therefore, for articulating a solution to the learning paradox that other researchers have few if any means of properly tackling.

For the purpose of introducing and discussing my argument about learning the language (dialect, idiom) of science, I draw on the transcription of one concept-mapping session that I have used for an article written and published while I was a high school teacher.[2] To allow readers to 'verify' the analyses presented here, I provide the entire transcript in the Appendix. In this appendix, readers also find transcription conventions, a description of the study site, and glossary of physics terms involved in these students' talk. During the session, the students repeatedly but briefly talked about non-science issues. I took note of the importance of these sections with respect to theorizing learning only recently. I also verified repeatedly the accuracy of the transcription and, despite the deterioration of the sound on the original VHS tape, some improvements to the transcript were made, in some instances requiring the insertion of a line (also numbered using the alphabet). That is, all inserted lines should be read as the preceding numerical line to which letters from the alphabet are added (e.g., turn 175a).

Throughout this book, I refer to 'the teacher' rather than using the pronoun ('I') and the possessive adjectives ('me', 'my', 'mine') to facilitate the presentation and to avoid the possible confusion between me, the author and analyst, and me, the teacher teaching the class nearly 20 years ago.

In this book, I frequently draw on foreign language versions of books and articles. I do so for the very reasons that I am writing this book, that is, for reasons of the special nature of language and the contradiction in translation, which is one of translating the untranslatable. I do so because, as a native (fluent) speaker of German and French, I can render what is said in the way I read and understand it rather than in the official translation, which often change the very sense of what is said and written. In any event, there are in many cases multiple translations of the same works that differ in essential ways. For example, I have three versions of Martin Heidegger's *Sein and Zeit* ('Being and Time'), one original and two different English translations; I also

---

2. Wolff-Michael Roth and Anita Roychoudhury, 'The Social Construction of Scientific Concepts or The Concept Map as Conscription Device and Tool for Social Thinking in High School Science', *Science Education*, Vol. 76 (1993), 531–57. A companion article focused on more structural aspects of the interactions from which the concept maps sprang forth. See Wolff-Michael Roth and Anita Roychoudhury, 'The Concept Map as a Tool for the Collaborative Construction of Knowledge: A Microanalysis of High School Physics Students', *Journal of Research in Science Teaching*, Vol. 30 (1993), 503–34.

have Georg Wilhelm Friedrich Hegel's *Phänomenologie des Geistes* ('Phenomenology of Spirit', 'Phenomenology of Mind') in the original and in two different English translations; and I have a French and an English translation of *Marksizm i filosofiîa îazyka*, which in the English translation (*Marxism and the Philosophy of Language*) is attributed to 'Valentin N. Vološinov', but in the French translation (*Le marxisme et la philosophie du langage*) is attributed to 'Mikhail Bakhtine' with some editing help from 'V. N. Volochinov'. In the French version, the translator adheres to de Saussure's terms *signification* (signification) and *sens* (sense), on the one hand, and *theme*, on the other hand. In the English translation, a new word, *meaning* is introduced to translate sometimes sense, sometimes signification, and sometimes theme. It is not surprising that one of the foremost scholar on poetics and a commentator on Bakhtin, Tzvetan Todorov, remarks that the translations of Bakhtin's work are often poor, contradictory, not in the least because individuals not familiar with the system of thought have accomplished them. 'Translations do exist, but I am not sure we should derive any solace from that fact. Having practiced the craft of translator myself, I shall refrain from taking my colleagues to task for occasional lapses that, in any case, are unavoidable. However, what I find alarming in this instance is that Bakhtin has been translated by individuals who did not know or did not understand this system of thought, though I will concede that this is not an easy matter. . . . The same Russian word is not translated in the same way by the various translators, a fact that may cause the Western reader undue and uncalled-for difficulty'.[3] Thus, I could ascertain that the English translation of *Marksizm i filosofiîa îazyka* contradicts itself within a few paragraphs. On the one hand, it states that the utterance 'What time is it?' has a different meaning each time it is used. On the other hand, two paragraphs later, it states that 'meaning' is that which is reproducible in all instances of repetition. In the French translation, sense or signification of the expression 'What time is it?' is the same, but its *theme* is a function of the cultural-historical situation.[4]

In reading multiple translations, I have come to note that with respect to Russian translations into English, distinctions are made in the former language—as in the German language that gave birth to dialectical thinking (G.W.F. Hegel, Karl Marx, Friedrich Engels)—that are not carried over into English translations. For example, in Russian and German there are two terms denoting very different entities, both of which are translated into English as *activity*. This cannot but lead to theoretical confusion. My German colleague Reinders Duit often talked to me about how the three concepts of heat (energy), temperature, and entropy have evolved from one and the same ancient term through a process of unfolding. The separation of the intensive property *temperature* from the extensive property *heat* accorded between the 17th and 18th century, the *entropy* concept was created during the 19th century. Nowadays no science teacher or professor would accept students to confuse the three terms and the conceptual terrain these cover, though way back when one term was used to cover the

---

3. Tzvetan Todorov, *Mikhail Bakhtin, The Dialogical Principle* (Minneapolis: University of Minnesota Press, 1984), xii.

4. Mikhail Bakhtine [V. N. Volochinov], *Le marxisme et la philosophie du language: essaie d'application de la méthode sociologique en linguistique* (Paris: Les Éditions de Minuit, 1977); Valentin N. Vološinov, *Marxism and the Philosophy of Language* (Cambridge, MA: Harvard University Press, 1973).

entire terrain even scientists confused them. Similarly, to give a more accurate presentation of the thinking of a foreign-language philosopher, we need to ascertain that the translation of key theoretical terms makes the same kind of distinctions in the target language (here English) as are made in the source language. Russian and German texts in cultural-historical theories make a distinction between social and societal, but English texts use the term social to cover the terrain of both. Clearly the two terms are not identical, for if learning is societally mediated, then there is a political dimension (society as unjust, marked by inequities along gender, race, class, culture, etc.) that is not present when learning is socially mediated.

Across his works, Mikhail Bakhtin elaborates a theory of signs that he had appropriated from the Swiss linguist Ferdinand de Saussure. The French translation of Bakhtin (V. N. Vološinov) retains the Saussurean distinctions and conceptualizations (e.g., 'sense' and 'signification'), whereas the English translation attempts to take different terms (e.g., 'sense', 'meaning', and 'signification') and thereby makes a mess of what Bakhtin was and is all about. I therefore abstain from using the term 'meaning' unless where I really need it, and then I place it in quotation marks. Moreover, readers of Bakhtin will note that he often engages in repetition and difference in and through his writing. I will draw on the same technique and return to the same statements repeatedly, which not merely repeat but actually augment and transform the argument I make.

Victoria, BC
March 2009

1

Getting Talk (and Learning) Off the Ground

How does one (cognitive) structure generate a new (cognitive) structure that is more complex than the starting one? Or to put it in educational terms, how does one aim at learning something when one *cannot know* what it is that one is aiming at because what is to be learned is the outcome of the instructional process? This problem, which has been named the *learning paradox,* challenges constructivist and constructionist approaches to learning.[1] It is a problem that did not have a solution when Carl Bereiter first articulated its extent and it continues to be an unattended problem in much of the current learning sciences and science learning literatures. The problem exists not only for those attempting to understand learning at school but also for those who want to understand how learning at cultural-historical scales can generate more *complex* (rather than more extensive) ways of understanding than the currently existing ones. The history of thought has shown that dialectical and dialogical approaches have the potential to provide useful solutions because the contradictions that are expressed in paradoxes are inner features and one-sided expressions of more complex unities. Thus, Karl Marx shows in *Capital* that 'value', because of its inner contradiction of 'use-value' and 'exchange-value' that are enacted in every commercial act, constitutes a driver in the economic *perpetuum mobile* that has led to capitalism as observable in his 19th century England. Mikhail Bakhtin uses a similar approach to theorize the development of language generally and the development of literary genres more specifically. And in more recent years, Jacques Derrida, Jean-Luc Nancy, and other philosophers propose a slew of concepts on the same principle, including *différance*, *khôra*, and *syncope* as non-self-identical concepts/phenomena that have development as an inherent effect.

In this book, I show that the general approach to language developed by Mikhail Bakhtin[2] with his specific concept of the dialogic nature of the word, which is the linguistic (structural) equivalent to Karl Marx's dialectic of value, offers precisely such a

---

1. Carl Bereiter, 'Toward a Solution of the Learning Paradox', *Review of Educational Research,* Vol. 55 (1985), 201–25.
2. Mikhaïl Bakhtine [V. N. Volochinov], *Le marxisme et la philosophie du langage: essaie d'application de la méthode sociologique en linguistique* (Paris: Les Éditions de Minuit, 1977).

materialist dialectical framework that allows us to understand how the learning paradox is overcome in praxis. In the course of unfolding the issues of language and learning in the face of the learning paradox, I show that the ideas of Lev S. Vygotsky about
the irreducible relation between the development of thinking and speaking and modern philosophical conceptions of language align with one another to produce a new
perspective that overcomes some of the problems in current educational thought about
how students learn (e.g., constructivism, conceptual change). In particular, the current
study shows that the (radical, social) constructivist way of theorizing learning cannot
help us out of the learning paradox and therefore constitutes an unhelpful way of
thinking about learning or about participating in social (societal) encounters.

Getting Started

One question poses itself now: How do we get off the ground in such a chicken-and-
egg situation? More specifically, if we assume that you, the reader, read this book
because you want to learn something, how can I, the author, assist you given that you
do not know what it is that you will know once you are done reading the book? We
know that pragmatically there does not appear to be an issue, because people *do* learn.
The question I raise here is this: How do students learn if they *cannot* aim at what they
are supposed to learn because conceiving of and framing the aim requires them to
know beforehand what they are *going* to learn and what they are going to know only
in the future? In other words, how can learners aim at something that they can articulate only after they already know what they are supposed to learn intentionally? Or, to
translate the issue once more, how can a reader learn a language (vocabulary, dialect,
idiom) that is required to formulate its own purpose? (Readers should take note that I
have expressed the 'same' question in three very different ways and that I have therefore translated an English question into another English question supposed to be the
same.) To get us off the ground, I invite you into one of my physics classes, where I
use a particular technique, concept mapping, to assist students in bringing together all
the main concepts that are contained in a unit or textbook chapter. (See more on the
background of this study in the Appendix.)

The three 12th-grade physics students sit around a hierarchically ordered set of
concepts written onto slips of paper (Fig. 1.1). They have arrived at this configuration
during the preceding 32 minutes. This is their capstone task of a unit on the quantum
nature of light—they have previously done a unit on the wave nature of light—and the
concept words on the paper slips are those that appear in bold-face in the relevant
chapter of their main textbook for the course (on desk, forefront of Fig. 1.1). Their
teacher, having read a number of texts on language in science and in particular Jay
Lemke's *Talking Science* and Bruce Gregory's *Inventing Reality: Physics as Language*, has made it a practice to finish each unit (chapter) with this form of task. This
task allows students to talk about the relationship between the major concepts presented in the textbook, which they are to learn according to the official, provincial
curriculum guideline. We enter the session near the end of the concept-mapping task,

Fig. 1.1. Three students toward the end of their concept-mapping task in the process of 'transcribing' the hierarchically ordered terms on movable paper slips onto a sheet of paper, adding linking words. The students are Miles (left), Ralf (center), and Ken (right).

while the students, close to the conclusion of the lesson, are in the process of transcribing the configuration of concept words onto an 11-inch-by-17-inch sheet of paper. They are also asked to link relevant pairs of concepts with pencil lines and write a linking word (a verb) such that statements can be read off the map in top down, horizontal fashion, or bottom-upward direction (the latter case requiring an arrow head). Among the paper slips there are two that are imprinted with 'WAVES' and 'DIFFRACTION', respectively.[3] The following fragment from the transcript (see the full transcript of the entire session in the Appendix, beginning p. 294) has been extracted from near the end of the lesson. In the fragment, the three students discuss the question which word (verb) they should use to link the two concept words.

Fragment 1.1 begins with Ken's (right in Fig. 1.1) question whether they can connect WAVES and DIFFRACTION (turn 482), two of the terms to be mapped. Ralf (center, Fig. 1.1) responds that they can connect 'it' 'to all' (turn 483). Ken then utters, 'can alter matter waves, put "can alter"' (turn 484).[4]

Fragment 1.1
```
482 K: can we connect the waves to diffraction?
483 R: we can connect it to all.
484 K: can alter matter waves; put can alter;
485 M: diffraction can alter; affects; diffraction affects;
```

Fragment 1.1 looks like the transcript of a simple, everyday, mundane exchange concerning the question of how two concept words are to be linked. In fact, however, we can only say that Ken asks a question, that Ralf provides a response, and that Ken

---

3. When capitalized, such as PHOTON or WAVE, the terms refer to the printed concept words; when the words are spoken, they appear in normal type, often with quotation marks.
4. The transcription conventions can be found in the Appendix, p. 294.

then proposes a connecting word and therewith a proposition because of the particular relation between these turns. There is an internal dynamic to the conversation that does not allow us to break it into individual utterances but, to understand the dynamic how utterance enchains with utterance, developing until the participants no longer pursue the topic, we have to take, as a minimum, two consecutive turns as one whole unit. This unit cannot be further divided because any part would be dependent on all other parts of the unit and on the unit as a whole. This is so because 'an utterance is a link in the chain of speech communication, and it cannot be broken off from the preceding links that determine it both from within and from without, giving rise within it to unmediated responsive reactions and dialogic reverberations'.[5] Because this linkage, the turn 483 actually has a double function, it completes the turn pair (with turn 482) of which it constitutes the second part, allowing the effect of the preceding utterance to be witnessed in the setting; and it offers the beginning of another turn pair unit (with turn 484), which is completed in the subsequent turn where a concrete way of connecting the term is offered. When a speaker speaks, the link between utterances does not yet exist but it comes about because any utterance is constructed taking into account possible responsive reactions. It is precisely for the sake of these reactions that the utterance, in essence, is actually created.

There is something else that should puzzle the reader. We, as Ralf has done before us, can hear Ken *ask a question*, 'Can we connect waves to diffraction?' What is the competence that allows us to hear a sound stream as a question? Note that the question mark in the transcript indicates that the pitch is rising toward the end. The transcriber, here I, has heard the utterance as a question and transcribed this hearing using a question mark. The grammatical structure of the utterance and the use of interrogatives are other clues that allow us to hear a question. However, what matters most *to* this *conversation and to* its *unfolding* is not what *we*, the analysts, hear but what the members to the situation are hearing and how they take the utterance up in their own subsequent discursive and practical actions.

Another mundane aspect of language can be observed in Fragment 1.1 that is important to Bakhtin's theorizing. In his second turn completion, Ralf, in saying 'we can connect' (turn 483), repeats part of Ken's utterance but inverts the first two words ('can we connect' [turn 482]). The words appear to be the same, but functionally they are different; and this different function is in part expressed in the different intonation that comes with the second articulation, accentuation, and accent. Ralf also brings in another part of Ken's utterance. But he does so indirectly by using what linguists have come to call a 'deictic term' or 'shifter'. Thus, in saying 'we can connect "it" to all', Ralf uses the deictic 'it' to bring into his utterance something Ken has said without actually repeating that something. Another instance of repetition is found within Ken's second turn, 'can alter'. But does repetition mean that the two instances, the first and the repeated are the same? I tend to take it with Bakhtin, who tells us that they are not: 'as an utterance (or part of an utterance no one sentence) *no one sentence*, even if it has only one word, *can ever be repeated*: it is always a *new* utterance (even if it is a

---

5. Mikhail M. Bakhtin, *Speech Genres and Other Late Essays* (Austin: University of Texas Press, 1986), 94.

quotation)'.[6] Elsewhere he provides an example from the work of Dostoevsky (the same example Lev Vygotsky uses to make a point about the difference between the 'meaning' of the same word) where six drunken workers utter the same ('unprintable') swear word. Even though uttered six times in a row, it is never the same word, because it is uttered with different intonation in each case. How can it be that the *same* word is different even though the repetition has occurred within a couple of seconds?

The first sketch of an answer is that the function of each occurrence changes in the repetition. For example, the function of 'can we connect' is to make salient (significant) the absence of a link between WAVE and DIFFRACTION. Furthermore, the order of the words is heard, among speakers of mundane English, to be marking the word sequence as a question. On the other hand, the function of 'we can connect' is to make a statement about one or more connections that can be done. In the first instance, the presence of a connection is queried, whereas in the second it is affirmed. In its second appearance, the utterance also has the function of making a link to the previous utterance. It serves as a (perhaps redundant) sign that *this* utterance pertains to the previous one and that these two utterances therefore constitute a pair. An interesting aspect is the change of the structural relation: the order of the words has been changed. Such syntactic changes are among the most under-analyzed features aspects of the creative production of speech and yet are among the most central to a theory of linguistic change both at the moment-to-moment level and at historical scales of language. These changes teach us a lot, according to Bakhtin, about how language is learned and how language changes at every conceivable time scale. I take it with Bakhtin who says that '[o]ur practical everyday speech is full of other people's words: with some of them we completely merge our own voice, forgetting whose they are; others, which we take as authoritative, we use to reinforce our own words; still others, finally, we populate with our own aspirations, alien or hostile to them'.[7]

In the present situation, the three students, members to the situation, speak. In speaking, they not only speak *about* the concepts but also, while speaking, they bring about the task context (the lesson, the session), which itself is part of the students' lifeworld as such. That is, students, in talking, also organize the societal situation that constitutes a context of their talk (who is talking, when), that is, to manage the task (e.g., ask questions when they are uncertain about something). There are therefore different dimensions to the talk. But this fact does not seem to astonish the students; they do not seem to take notice of this. They do what they do without taking time out and without giving any indication that they have to stop to *reflect about* or *interpret* what others are saying. Maurice Merleau-Ponty is right, therefore, when he says that the 'linguistic and intersubjective world no longer astonishes us, we no longer distinguish it from the world itself, and we reflect within a world already talked about and talking'.[8] That is, when people actually reflect then it is in a world that is already talked about and a talking world. We live in language; we speak out of language; and it is language that speaks through us. In this world, communication and the compre-

---

6. Bakhtin, op. cit. note 5, 108, emphasis added.
7. Mikhail Bakhtin, *Problems of Dostoevsky's Poetics* (Minneapolis: University of Minnesota Press, 1984), 195.
8. Maurice Merleau-Ponty, *Phénoménologie de la perception* (Paris: Gallimard, 1945), 214.

hension of others and their speech is possible *because* of the mutuality of intentions, which is available in my intentions and the speech/gestures of others as well my intentions and speech exhibited in the conduct of others. 'The sense of a [verbal, manual] gesture thus "understood" does not lie behind it, it fuses with the structure of the world that the gesture points out and that I take up in my own account, the world spreads itself all over the gesture'.[9] In speaking I say something, that is, returning to the etymological roots (Indo-Germanic *soq'', *seq'') I point, I mark: 'the being of language is speech as pointer'.[10]

Above, I write (think in public) about a repetition that occurs across two turns at talk. A second form of repetition, one that occurs *within* an utterance, is perhaps more difficult to understand as one that involves or produces a change. But a radical implementation of Bakhtin's program requires us to understand the two occurrences of the same word in the same utterance to be different. In the present instance, Ken utters 'put "can alter"' (turn 484) for a second time (turn 485), and when it is done, it occurs against its first occurrence as the ground. That is, when we hear 'can alter' again, it no longer has the same context and function as the first time, where it initially marks something as significant. This first instance may be glossed as 'one way of connecting matter waves and diffraction is by using "can alter", which then forms the statement "DIFFRACTION –can alter–› MATTER WAVES" on the sheet'. But when Ken utters 'can alter' for a second time, we can hear it as articulating his insistence, as in the gloss 'You don't seem to listen, I said, "put «can alter»"'. What matters for the unfolding of the conversation is not how we, researchers, *interpret* the statement or how the statement can be heard, but how the participants themselves are hearing it at the actual moment that the fragment is recorded. Therefore, to understand the conversation and its *inner dynamic*, we need to listen to how the participants hear, and we need to theorize the conversation from the perspective of the dynamic internal to it. Here, Miles at first repeats part of the proposed link, then utters a different verb, and repeats the new verb together with the subject ('diffraction') of the emerging predicative statement ('diffraction affects matter waves').

Fragment 1.2
```
484 K: can alter matter waves; put can alter;
485 M: diffraction can alter; affects; diffraction affects;
486 R: can alter?
487 M: [affects.]
488 K: [affects.]
489 R: diffraction affects matter waves?
```

In this situation, we observe the emergence of a new way of saying something involving the concept names 'diffraction' and 'matter waves'. Ken first utters 'can alter' as the connective verb. The subsequent utterance, which also constitutes the social evaluation of the previous one, first repeats the word but then substitutes another one, 'affects'. Miles repeats the verb himself. Ralf utters 'can alter?' with a rising pitch, as

---

9. Merleau-Ponty, op. cit. note 8, 216–17.
10. Martin Heidegger, *Gesamtausgabe Band 12: Unterwegs zur Sprache* (Frankfurt: Vittorio Klostermann, 1985), 242.

if producing what we may gloss as 'should we use "can alter"?' First Miles then Ken utters 'affects', each with a decreasing pitch, indicating a statement-type utterance. We may hear the first instance as 'let's use "affects" instead of can alter' and we may hear the repetition as, 'Yes, I agree, let's use "affects"'. Ralf confirms such a hearing by uttering the implied statement as a whole, 'diffraction affects matter waves'. But he also questions (hearable because of the pitch raising toward the end) whether this is the way the connection should be. Miles confirms (turn 490), and Ken then elaborates further (turn 491). This is not the way in which the proposition ultimately will be noted, as can be seen in Fig. 1.2. Rather, it will be fixed in a transformed way in which the subject and predicate are exchanged, 'Matter waves undergo diffraction'. It is another translation at the very heart of language, a self-quoting that transforms the language in and through use.

The new verb Miles proposes comes to be repeated three times in the following turns 487 to 489. But initially, Ralf utters with a rising intonation toward the end (marked in the transcript by the question mark) 'can alter?' Such rising intonation, even in utterances as short as this, (at least fluent) English speakers hear a question. That is, although one might have heard the repeated utterance of 'affects' as stating Miles' preference for this verb, Ralf can be glossed as asking whether he should use 'can alter' to predicate 'diffraction' with the expression 'can alter matter waves'. It might also have been heard as a preference for the first of the two verbs articulated in the preceding turn. Simultaneously, Ken and Miles utter 'affects'. But they thereby do not merely duplicate the verb Miles has already articulated repeatedly. As the period ('.') in the transcription indicates, both utterances are produced with a downward intonation, as we find this in factual statements of ordinary everyday talk. We can hear the utterances both as a negation of what has been offered as solution to the open problem in question form ('can alter?') and as an affirmation of the alternative ('affects'). This time, Ralf articulates the entire proposition that would result, 'diffraction affects matter waves', and he does so with a rising pitch allowing us to hear him utter a question glossed as 'Shall I put down "diffraction affects matter waves"?'

When one student uses another student's words (or that of the teacher or textbook) he does not merely replicate them (i.e., in precisely the same way). When a word is reactivated, earlier forms of sense enter the later forms, giving something new to the latter. In this way, the uttered word no longer stands on its own but it includes the existence of the first utterance as its contextual ground. This is precisely the point both Bakhtin and Vygotsky make when they retell the story Dostoevsky shares in his *A Diary of a Writer* entirely consisting of a single 'unprintable' word. In this story, it is the repetition and intonation that make all the difference; it is the 'modulation of voice that reveals psychological context within which a word is to be understood'.[11] For Bakhtin, expressive intonation is the carrier of social evaluation and value judgment.[12] Because the immediate situation and its most ephemeral aspects mediate the expressive intonation, no sound (only part of which we hear as a concept word) is ever going to be the same. More so, we not only hear the word, we also hear the expressive into-

---

11. Lev S. Vygotsky, *Thought and Language* (Cambridge, MA: MIT Press, 1986), 243.
12. Bakhtine, op. cit. note 2, 147–8.

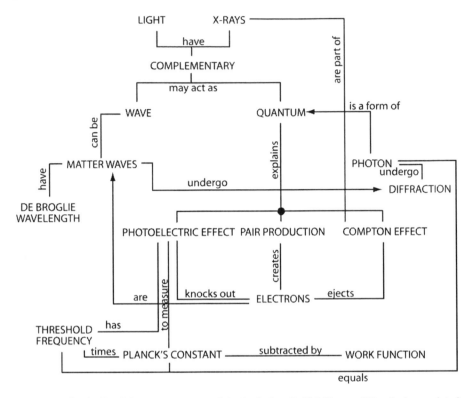

Fig. 1.2. A facsimile of the concept map as it looked when Ralf, Miles, and Ken had completed just following the bell that terminated the lesson.

nation and therefore the social evaluation that comes with it. It is in this way, therefore, that a word—which really refers to a communicative complex that encompasses expressive intonation, expressive gesture and body movement, body position and body orientation—can never be the same. It is in this sense that we have to understand the idea of the impossibility of ever exactly hearing the same word twice.

We note that in these fragments the speech is in telegrammatic brevity and full of ellipses. But the members to the setting apparently understand what is happening and what the others say. Moreover, they refer to, or rather mark, parts of this context that are immediately there (as the slips with the concept words) or once removed (something they or others have said in the immediate or recent past). The collective speech therefore takes a form that is characteristic of inner speech: 'Predication is the natural form of inner speech; psychologically, it consists of predicates only'.[13]

Over the minute that follows, there are more proposals without apparent agreement on one. Ralf eventually says 'give me another word', to which Miles responds by saying 'we gave you about six'. The three students ultimately settle on a new verb, 'undergo', which Miles suggests in the recording immediately after the two fragments but

13. Vygotsky, op. cit. note 11, 243.

which is different from the 'about six' that they have given Ralf before. Ultimately, the students complete their concept map (Fig. 1.2) slightly past the lesson bell. This map represents a summary and an account of the way in which these students articulate the concepts of their most recent textbook chapter. It also is a summary of the work that they have completed in this lesson, or perhaps better expressed, it is a trace that this work has left on the sheet of paper. This trace bears all the marks of the process, the written and verbal sources of texts that the students have produced, reproduced, and finally settled on as their solution to the problem of linking concept names in pair-wise fashion while giving expression to their hierarchical relation.

Throughout the fragments from the videotape and transcript presented above we can hear and see the three students evidently struggle with the production of but one small part of their ultimate result. They do so with words and sentences that may sound quite naïve to some readers' ears when they are compared to the language one can find in a high school and more so in a university textbook of physics. But naiveté does not mean lack of ability. We do know in fact that one of these students today is a science professor and another is an engineer with a Master's degree and vice-president of an innovation company. That is, despite their struggles observable in the materials presented, they have continued to evolve their competencies to participate in contexts where science-related language is used and produced. We may ask now, how is such development possible given the tentative beginnings in talking science observable here? I suggest that this requires us to take a different view on language and its development. Thus, we already see that the language employed evolves, as the students produce new ways of relating two terms, here through the repeated substitution of common verbs. In producing the map generally and the links specifically, these students use their everyday language, their vernacular, the competence of and for which they have brought with them to school, to manage both their interaction and the task. This, then, is the tenor that I take here in unfolding a different, Bakhtinian perspective on science language and learning.

Looking Back After Lift-Off

My text provides a first answer to the learning paradox. As you, my reader, have progressed from the beginning of this first chapter to this point, you have been exposed to the very processes that allow us to learn and to understand how learning occurs. With your familiar language competence, you have followed my exposition. Although some of what I am writing may have been unfamiliar to you, you have already had the potential for understanding this text within the horizon of your pre-reading competencies. Furthermore, what I am presenting here and how I present it presupposes its own intelligibility, for it would not make sense for me to write something that I know is inaccessible to my readers. I am also attempting to convince you. To strengthen my voice, I draw on direct and indirect quotes of certain authors, including Bakhtin and Vygotsky. I use their words, but for my own intentions, with my own inflections; and I do so in a context very different from theirs. As I deploy these words for my inten-

tion and thereby transform them, I also ready these words to be taken up again by you
and to resonate in ever-new ways with every new reader. As soon as you speak to
someone else, quoting Bakhtin or me, these words become further transformed, and
our pedagogical language as a whole changes. It changes even if we do not think
about changing it because the change is both inevitable and occurs without a special
effort. A special transformation occurs as you use your language to make my language—which really is also yours, or neither yours nor mine because it belongs to the
collective and to itself—the object of your inquiry. In so doing, we get a process of
enfolding, recursivity, and self-reference. It is precisely through this process of integrating self-reference that we can bootstrap into new forms of speaking and understanding. There is a history of related thought that allows us to understand how dialectical relations of self-reference lead to growth, learning, and development.

Already a little more than 200 years ago, the German philosopher Georg W.F.
Hegel asked himself the question how something like consciousness could ever get off
the ground and develop in the way (human) cultural history shows.[14] He thinks of an
ingenious process that basically takes the shape of an enfolding, producing a fold. It
goes about like this. The subject of consciousness, to make itself the object of an inquiry, has to externalize, objectify itself, and thereby differentiate itself from itself.
When it then engages with itself in objectified form, which appears as an 'other than
itself', it comes to understand itself in new ways because in reflecting, the objectified
self re-enters the subject, thereby subjectifying an objective form of its previous self.
More recently, the French philosopher Paul Ricœur has offered a similar process but
uses a language that readers may find more up-to-date and less arcane. Thus, when
someone interprets a text, the person has to draw on his/her practical understanding of
how the world works to provide an explanation of what the text says; but any such
explanation augments and develops practical understanding of the world. That is,
practical understanding precedes, accompanies, and completes explanation. It is the
prerequisite for anything like explanation to exist and occur. But in the process of
evolving an explanation, practical understanding is augmented, develops. We can
therefore comprehend this process of interpretation as an occasion in which practical
understanding folds over itself and, in the course, develops itself. It is the fold that
stands for the complexification of understanding.

Philosophers are not the only people concerned with how a system gets itself off
the ground and keeps on moving. Writers, too, have been faced with this problem. To
obtain change from the inside of his *Ulysses*, James Joyce does not operate *on* things.
Any artistic operation Joyce conducts is done *in* language, *with* language, and *on* language, that is, on things and on the way they are made available through the medium
of language. Joyce thereby achieves change from with in the system. Thus, 'in *Ulysses*, time is experienced as change but *from within*. The reader and the author move
towards a possession of time from inside the flow. If there is a law of the historical
process, it cannot be found outside the process itself, for the option is already deter-

---

14. Georg Wilhelm Friedrich Hegel, *Phenomenology of Spirit* (Oxford: Oxford University Press,
1806/1977).

mined from the individual point of view one holds within *the process*.[15] This, in the literary world, is the solution that Hegel proposes for the complexification of consciousness, which has to occur from within. This is also the solution I propose for learning on the part of science students, such as the ones who figure in the fragments particularly and in the entire lesson analyzed throughout this book more generally. It is the dialectic or rather the dialogic nature of language that belongs not only to these intellectuals and their intellectual lives but also to the entire evolution of our culture.

In the course of this book, I show how this process of language folding over itself, producing and reproducing itself, integrates itself over, leading to new, and developmentally more-advanced forms of language. I show how language is the ground, the tool, and the material (object) of engagement in such tasks as concept mapping. This very relationship of language to itself is the source of the autopoeisis of language and linguistic forms. These more advanced forms of language—syntactically, semantically—we hear as indicators of learning and development.

In this book, I am concerned with communication. Because I draw only on language and other communicative signs, both in the students' use and in my describing and theorizing, there is no need for me to get underneath students' skullcap and between their ears for theorizing what and how they know and how they learn. Focusing in this way on communication generally and language specifically comes with many advantages, including that it is objectively given for anyone overhearing a situation. We do not have to debate what a person *really thinks*, or the conception a person really has, because we focus on what happens collectively; and we understand from the irreducible collective situation what a person says and how others act, act upon and react to it, and therefore what forms of hearing have been enacted. Language therefore constitutes your (my reader's) and my common ground. We are *building on this ground* with materials *from this ground;* and this allows us to *get off the ground* and evolve new forms of language for talking about science language and science learning.

Communication in Setting

These first fragments and analyses presented here show how students mobilize what others have said. That is, they use direct and indirect speech (writing) and thereby, mobilize (transformed) texts that are attributed to authors other than themselves. For example, the students refer to a sentence or diagram in a textbook, they directly or indirectly report what the teacher has said, they relate—mostly by means of indirect speech—what some famous scientist has articulated, and refer to something someone else has contributed in the course of the task. The students also articulate what 'they' are or would be saying if they ordered the concepts in one rather than in another way. In this situation, therefore, the concept names specifically and the entire arrangement

---

15. Umberto Eco, *The Aesthetics of Chaosmos: The Middle Ages of James Joyce* (Cambridge, MA: Harvard University Press, 1989), 42.

generally constitute other aspects of the communicative event. They are both the signifier and the context that transact to produce the *theme*, the significance of the said in
this context. Because signification always and already exists, new words can find a
place in the world, and making sense of a new word means allowing it to have, or giving it a place in, a world that already exists and is shot through with significations.

The transcribed event provides evidence that students' language is what one might
describe in vernacular as 'choppy'. It is neither well formed grammatically nor does it
have much similarity with written statements, fully formed (written) arguments, and
the likes that educators and learning scientists often seek in their students' products.
However, the students here do not participate in a task that asks them to utter well
formed sentences only, which in fact might have inhibited them in doing what they
do. They are asked to order the concept names and arrange them hierarchically. *This* is
the object/motive of their task. They talk over and about their task, and this talk
changes in the process. Their task is to formulate simple statements of *subject–verb–
object* type (e.g., 'the player' 'kicks' 'the ball'), which also can be understood in the
form of the *subject–predicate* structure (e.g., 'the player' 'kicks the ball'), where the
predicate includes the verb of predication and the object. Predication is at the core of
both individual and collective development, because it reifies the first things (objects)
we know and that we know precisely because we predicate them.[16] Simple sentences
are the first predicative statements we make and that embody observation: 'The dog is
black', where 'the dog' is the object and 'is black' is its predicate. These simple observation sentences are the beginning, the basis of language, though a giant further
step is required in the evolution of language: *observation categoricals* that generalize
across many observations. The question of generalization also is at the heart of the
problem that the students here face, namely how to order the concept words with respect to each other. In chapter 7, I squarely address this issue in the context of the
question of the hierarchical relationship between two concept names, 'quantum' and
'photon'.

The language that serves these students as the ground, tool, and material (object) to
accomplish their talk occurs in some setting. In this triple function, language *itself*
imposes the conditions of its own production, of its own development, and of its own
refinement. There are other resources in a setting such as a classroom that interaction
participants can use for marking, re-marking, and remarking sense and that therefore
enable and constrain how something can be said, what is actually said, how it can be
heard, and how it actually is heard. Because important aspects of communication
therefore remain where they are—e.g., a drawing in a textbook on the table—to be
addressed or brought into communicative acts as the need arises, these aspects do not
have to be named. This allows talk to be elliptic because signification is distributed
across the context as a whole and can be marked in a variety of ways other than in
saying (i.e., pointing with prosody, hand, finger). As soon as someone points to such
an aspect, a drawing in a book or a configuration of words on the table, others can
mark or re-mark them as audience or in subsequent speech of their own. And everything done, heard, and said is understood (not reflectively, but in the form of *partici-*

---

16. Willard V. Quine, *From Stimulus to Science* (Cambridge, MA: Harvard University Press, 1995).

Fig. 1.3. All three students are clearly oriented toward the diagram and toward Ken's gesture while he proposes to link DIFFRACTION and MATTER WAVES and inscribing it with 'can alter'.

pative thinking that expresses the same orientations among the members in the group) to be part of the overall goal of completing the task and to produce the concept map. Thus, the students make ample use of verbal and gestural deixis. They do not talk about those things that go without saying, that is, that everyone already understands and knows others to understand.

The use of gestures, body movements, and body orientations renders communication more complex, on the one hand, but also makes it easy and less cumbersome to follow for participants. Take Fragment 1.3, which reproduces one of Ken's utterances in Fragment 1.1. In addition to the utterance, he first places his right-hand (RH) index finger onto the paper slip on which MATTER WAVES is printed (Fig. 1.3, bottom) while saying 'alter', and then, as he produces what we hear as 'matter waves', his index moves until it reaches DIFFRACTION (Fig. 1.3, top).

Fragment 1.3
```
484 K: can [alter] [matter waves;] [put can alter;]
          [((places and rests RH index on MATTER WAVE, as in
       Fig. 1.2, bottom))
                  [((moves RH index from MATTER WAVES to end
       at DIFFRACTION, as in Fig. 1.3))
                               [((returns to MATTER
       WAVES))
```

Here we see Ken move his index finger from one inscription to another, producing an ephemeral link. He not only gestures what we understand to be a link, currently as ephemeral as any verbal production, but he thereby instructs Ralf to draw an actual, lasting pencil link in the corresponding space of the sheet of paper. He also instructs his peer what to write on the link to be drawn: 'can alter'. He then utters 'put can alter' and, simultaneously, moves his index finger back to MATTER WAVES. This fragment therefore is in fact supporting the idea of making a pencil line from one term to the other, because there is not much sense in writing a term other than a concept name onto the map without also associating it with a line.

We note some interesting grammatical relations. Ken first points to MATTER WAVES and then moves his arm and hand until he touches DIFFRACTION. Grammatically this would mean that matter waves 'can alter' diffraction. But the utterance itself is constructed with 'matter waves' in the object position, that is, as part of the predicate that modifies and specifies the subject. The subject of the utterance is 'diffraction', which is pointed to subsequently. Clearly, however, his hand is moving upward on the sheet and to the right, which means that the order of the proposition would be, in terms of the rules for reading and constructing concept maps, from DIFFRACTION to MATTER WAVES. But in the second part of the utterance, the grammatical construction of the utterance, into which the words DIFFRACTION and MATTER WAVES are entered by means of a gestural pointing, does produce a grammar that is consistent with standard English to yield a proposition: DIFFRACTION 'can alter' MATTER WAVES. That is, we can actually understand the production in turn 484 as a repetition in which the speaker self-corrects before anyone else can actually intervene.

If we just consider this one turn on its own, it would make very little sense. That is, if one were to suppose that there is 'meaning' inherent in the word or utterance, there is very little that we would be able to draw from the statement. And yet, there is no indication from others that this communicative act is problematic. The two others, Miles and Ralf are, as can be clearly seen and heard, oriented toward the map and are in a position to perceive the pointing and the moving gestures. The entire production is part of a larger context in which students are asked to produce an orderly map, in which the printed terms are related hierarchically and connected by means of verbs to form propositions. It is precisely in the situation as a whole that we have to look for signification, which gives a specific never repeatable aspect to the utterance. This specific aspect-in-the-setting, Bakhtin refers to as *theme*. The available significations, that is, the preceding expressive acts and the setting as a whole, establish a common world between and including the speaking subjects, a sensible and experienced world to which the present and novel speech refers like a gesture of the head, body, or hand. Language is merely one way of taking up position in the world in which to mark, re-mark, and remark sense. There is therefore no 'meaning' attached to words or behind words. Students do not construct 'meaning'. Speakers mark, re-mark, and expand significations; and they may do so using a variety of means. Participative listeners attend to, re-mark and remark the precise sense-in-the-setting of the word. That is, words are but one way in which significations can be made salient for others and for oneself. This also means that from the Bakhtinian perspective I am taking here we cannot look at an utterance in itself but always have to look at its social evaluation. The social evaluation comes from the other. That is, we consider not only the saying (i.e., utterance) but the hearing (i.e., social evaluation available in response) that others enact as well. To understand a conversation in its uniqueness as an unfolding event, we have to make it a *social* phenomenon sui generis. As such, it cannot be reduced to and thought to be composed of the individual utterances. That is, individual utterances are not like elements that make a compound, the conversation.

This has immediate consequences, theoretically and methodically. Theoretically it means that we cannot attribute a word merely to speakers, for speakers address others and they do so with utterances that inherently are the utterances of others as well. Speakers have to (consciously or unconsciously) presuppose that their audience already is in a position to understand. That is, the intelligibility of the utterance *is presupposed* and therefore cannot be the utterance of the speaker alone—and in practical understanding it is that of the audience as well. In practical understanding, the word therefore always bestrides the speaker and the listener. This immediately implies a double relation that any utterance entertains. On the one hand, it is the completion of a turn pair and the social evaluation of the preceding turn; on the other hand, it is the beginning of a subsequent turn pair. Each utterance therefore is like a link in a chain, and we can understand it only in its dual relation to the preceding and the subsequent links that it connects. If we were to consider an utterance in itself, there would not exist any *inherent* link and therefore no conversation as a phenomenon sui generis, just talking heads spilling text independently of one another.

Methodically, the implication is that we have to analyze *turn pairs*, which constitute our minimum unit of analysis. Inherent in the idea of the unit is that there are no elements that make it. Any structure smaller than the unit is a *moment*, which cannot ever be understood on its own but only in its constitutive relations to all other moments and to the unit as a whole. Because in some cases, the participants make salient that some misunderstanding exists, it might take several turns to complete such a unit. For example, an utterance might offer up the first part of a question–answer unit, but, because the addressee does not understand, it may take several turns before the answer completes the unit. Science educators are already familiar with other turn-taking units, including the school-specific sequences whereby a teacher initiates, one or more students respond, and the teacher evaluates (sometimes better known by its acronym IRE). This unit might actually be longer than three turns at talk and therefore might be found spread over a long series of utterances (e.g., if a student where to say, 'What do you mean?' or when the students do not bring forth the sought for answer in the center slot between initiation and evaluation).

I begin this chapter with the framing of the key issue: How do we get out of the learning paradox? The learning paradox articulates the contradiction that exists because persons cannot intend learning something that still lies outside the horizon of their comprehension. Just as Christopher Columbus could not *intend* to discover the Americas—had he known them, he could not have discovered them because he already knew they existed—students cannot intend learning something that they do not already know, just as poets cannot make clear what they want to say until they have developed the language in which they succeed in saying the poem and making clear what they want to say. Or, to put it into conceptual change terms, if students do not know the target cognitive structure, how can they *intentionally* engage in constructing it? How, if you do not know the target structure can you construct an analogy, given that there are so many structures in the world that serves us as a source? How can you construct a specific structure if you do not and cannot yet have a plan or even the language to formulate such a plan? This is especially the case when students are required to engage in 'radical restructuring' of their 'conceptions', because what is taken to be their current, source conceptual structure is completely incompatible with the target conceptual structure. How can the students engage in *intentionally* construct a conceptual structure that is radically different from what they know right now and of which they know as little as Columbus knew of the Americas?

2

The Ground that Grounds

In this book, I am concerned with the puzzle of language, learning, and the learning paradox. Concerning the latter, I provide the beginning of a solution through a dynamic perspective on language that exists in the concept and phenomenon of dialogism. In this perspective, there is no phenomenon such as *the* language, for what we are after is in continuous flux. We therefore need a genetic approach to the study of language and speech. At best, we can produce an idealized language by fixing it at a particular instance in time. We then can arrive at something like the language of a novel such as *Ulysses*, which James Joyce conceived of as a 'total work, a Work-as-Cosmos', where 'the reference point is not the poet in his ivory tower but the human community and, ultimately, all history and culture'.[1] This requires a historical-genetic study of language, because, like literature, it is impossible to study it from the historical place of a particular culture, and it is even more fatal, to paraphrase Bakhtin, to encapsulate language in its own contemporaneity.[2] Bakhtin speaks in a similar way about the language and world of Rabelais[3] or about the poetics of and discourse in Dostoevsky's writings.[4] We cannot understand the language or the genre that these authors use independent of their cultural-historical positions. But, as articulated especially in his Marxist, sociological perspective on language, Bakhtin emphasizes that language generally, and genres such as the novel particularly, do change because of a mechanism *internal* to language itself: Change and renewal occur every time someone utters a word, a novel or poem being only one of the forms that an utterance can take. To know the effect of an utterance, whatever its form (a word, longer verbal utterance, poem, novel, or play), we always need the social evaluation to understand its role in the evolution of its cultural-historical situation. In the case of the spoken word, this evaluation occurs in the immediate situation, whereas in the written work the evalua-

---

1. Umberto Eco, *The Aesthetics of Chaosmos: The Middle Ages of James Joyce* (Cambridge, MA: Harvard University Press, 1989), 33.
2. Mikhail Bakhtin, *Speech Genres and Other Late Essays* (Austin: University of Texas Press, 1986).
3. Mikhail Bakhtin, *Rabelais and his World* (Bloomington: Indiana University Press, 1984).
4. Mikhail Bakhtin, *Problems of Dostoevsky's Poetics* (Minneapolis: University of Minnesota Press, 1984).

tion is produced during the reading of a piece of work and during the subsequent discussion of it in various public arenas (Internet, literary scholarship, marketplace).

Bakhtin's work on the evolution of literary genres is useful here, because it may enlighten us about the question concerning how complex forms—literary in his case—emerge from simpler ones that precede them. In the way Bakhtin views the evolution of the novel and other speech genres to be driven by the change in everyday language, I approach the change and complexification of students' science language as occurring in, with, and on the basis of their everyday vernacular that begins, accompanies, and completes the specific languages, genres, idioms or dialects that they learn in their subject matter classroom.

In this chapter, I articulate the background to the problematic that I address in and with this book. I begin by exhibiting some of the conventional approaches to language, before revisiting aspects of my very early work on language generally and on concept mapping in particular. I articulate and elaborate the learning paradox as an ontogenetic and as a cultural-historical phenomenon. I outline some of the context that comes with the particular perspective I take here on language, which takes Bakhtin's work as the ground but also draws on other, sympathetic and commensurable perspectives on language, such as those taken by pragmatic philosophers (Davidson, Quine, Rorty), philosophers of difference (Derrida, Nancy), or hermeneutic and phenomenological philosophers (Merleau-Ponty, Ricœur).

Conventional Approaches to Language

In this ever-too-brief section, I present the approach many educational researchers take in analyzing classroom conversations: Language as a means to make public private thought and thought structures or to take a stand and stance. I do not do so to set up a straw-person, which I then knock down. In fact, I am not so innocent myself. In the (now-somewhat-distant) past I have contributed, in and through my research, to the reproduction of this very view of language as a transparent window that I now undo in writing. I have used language—just as the work that I use in the following to exemplify problematic practices in the analysis of speech—as a transparent window into the minds of students, their intentions, and their knowledge and understanding. But my past understanding does not hold up in the face of the thousands of hours of transcripts that I have been analyzing. In this book, therefore, I both renounce the old position and offer a new, better and much improved one that does not lead to the logical contradictions within my earlier work. For the demonstration of how and why my new, Bakhtinian approach to language differs, I do need to provide some sample analyses to articulate the difference more concretely. I therefore take some randomly selected analyses from the literature to exemplify my point.

Language commonly is taken as a transparent window on the mind or as a medium more or less independent of the conceptual structures of the mind. This may not be surprising given that much research implements a Kantian constructivism and given the generally unarticulated fact that 'nowhere does Kantianism offer a theory of language, of the purity, or of the originality of language'.[5] As an example of how transparency works in a concrete case, take the following brief exchange between a conceptual change interviewer and a 15-year-old student named Jane.[6] The interview concerns the phenomenon of refraction (bending) when light moves from one medium, such as air (glass), into another medium, such as glass (water).

Fragment 2.1
```
Int.   Would you like to tell me what happens here to make it
       [the beam of light] bend?
Jane   Because it is going through different densities . . .
       it makes the light bend.
Int.   How does the density affect the beam to make it bend?
Jane   I'm not sure. Don't know.
Int.   Have you got any idea what happens here to make it
       bend?
Jane   The light slows down . . .
```

The interview subsequently continues, where we find another exchange.

Fragment 2.2
```
Int.   Any idea how that [bending] happens?
Jane   It might be or it might not be different densities in
       there [the glass block].
```

Based on these two fragments, the authors make two claims to support their conceptual change approach. First, they suggest that 'Jane demonstrated that the notion of refraction being related to light changing speed in media with different densities was intelligible to her'. They continue by suggesting that 'statements like, "I'm not sure" and "it might or might not be" indicated that she did not necessarily believe that this is how the world actually is and the concept was probably not plausible to her'.

We can make a number of observations. First, the authors reduce a complex phenomenon of interaction to two brief statements about what Jane finds 'intelligible' and about what she 'believes'. Readers can immediately ascertain, however, that Jane does not talk about intelligibility whatsoever. We see Jane and the interviewer engaged in exchanges about some topic and there is little evidence that the topic makes much sense to Jane at all. We do hear her say 'I'm not sure. Don't know' when the interviewer asks her how density affects the light beam to make it bend. Jane here articulates for us that she is not sure, and she then revises this statement to 'don't know'. Yet the authors claim that Jane 'demonstrated' that 'the notion of refraction being related to light changing speed in media with different densities was intelligible'. Jane says that she does not know what makes the light bend. The interviewer insists and Jane then offers up something, 'light slows down'. The authors do not tell us what comes after, so we do not know the appreciation of the comment that the interviewer

---

5. Jean-Luc Nancy, *The Discourse of the Syncope* (Stanford, CA: Stanford University Press, 2008), 87.

6. The following excerpts are taken from David Treagust and Reinders Duit, 'Conceptual Change: A Discussion of Theoretical, Methodological and Practical Challenges for Science Education', *Cultural Studies of Science Education*, Vol. 3 (2008), 297–328. All excerpts come from pages 304–5.

provides to Jane. We do not know, therefore, how, from a conversation-as-phenomenon-sui-generis perspective, that contribution mediates between Jane's preceding 'I'm not sure. Don't know' and what comes thereafter. It might be that the interviewer expresses appreciation that Jane has ventured something. We do not know whether Jane proffers 'light slows down' as a hypothesis, whether she repeats something she has heard in class; and we do not know whether she is mobilizing the expression for her own intention or whether she merely seeks to satisfy the interviewer by contributing to the conversation in such a way that the interviewer can proceed in his/her protocol.

Second, the authors do not attend to the fact that the interviewer offers up the connection between densities and changing speed in asking 'How does the density affect the beam to make it bend?' The syntactic construction of the sentence makes it such that something other than bending is the searched for answer. Had the interviewer asked 'How does density affect the beam?' a possible response is 'It makes it bend'. Here, however, bending is already part of the query so that the question—if the utterance is heard as such—attempts to elicit something else. The interviewer subsequently asks Jane whether she has an idea about 'how that happens', to which Jane responds, 'It might be or it might not be different densities in there'. Jane responds, and in responding assists the interviewer to get through his/her protocol and complete this part of a research project. There is nothing in this excerpt that allows us to say that Jane 'believes' or 'knows' anything about light refraction, density, and different speed *other than that she knows the words and short phrases*. Whether these sentences are partially her own is not known and it remains unknown whether she has any intentions other than doing what she does, that is, duly responding when she is asked.

Third, the authors claim that in saying 'I'm not sure' and 'it might or might not be' Jane 'did not necessarily believe that this is how the world actually is and the concept is probably not plausible to her'. Again, the authors put words into Jane's mouth and thoughts into her mind (see chapter 9 on putting words into someone's mouth and subsequently believing the other has actually said something to that effect). Jane does not tell us what the authors claim that Jane believes and that she finds something plausible or not. The authors thereby treat language as a medium that allows them to get at something that characterizes Jane—her knowledge, her beliefs—without actually saying so. This something is said to be in her mind. That is, the authors presuppose something to be in Jane's mind that makes her say what she says. And even when Jane acknowledges being uncertain and not knowing, the authors *attribute to her* knowledge and beliefs. What their analysis does is this: it turns Jane into a fixed entity, a person with a (at least momentarily) fixed mental structure that can be probed by asking the right questions. The authors leave out the competencies required of Jane to participate in this way and her express willingness to respond to questions and thereby to constitute the event for what it is planned, an interview. The *authors* rather than Jane pull together different aspects of an unfolding event and say that all of this can be attributed to Jane and her current knowledge and her set of beliefs.

In fact, there is little evidence that the authors work with the transcript by staying *right at* the words that people are saying. They read the transcript *through* their conceptual change framework independent of how Jane and the interviewer bring the session about and independent of what Jane formulates to be her intention, beliefs, or knowledge. The analysts force the interview onto the Procrustean bed of their conceptual change 'framework', without noticing that they may actually stretch or shrink the language and situation in the way that the mythical Procrustes stretched and shrunk his guests to make them fit his (previously adjusted) guest-bed. For example, Jane says that she does not know (the answer), and yet, the authors attribute to her knowledge. Jane herself says *she does not know*, whereas the conceptual change researchers attribute the (lack of) plausibility and intelligibility of an idea or concept to her.

To discourse and conversation analysts, including myself, such an approach is unacceptable.[7] We want to understand how the interview unfolds and how the participants sustain a topic, and thereby the event as a whole, over some time; and we want to know what the interaction routines are that allow participants to do what they do. We take the conversation to be an *irreducible* phenomenon the results of which cannot be attributed to individuals. It is irreducible because every turn completes a unit, provides us with the social appreciation of the preceding turn, and is a first part of the succeeding turn-pair unit, which itself is completed in a subsequent turn. Was the interviewer satisfied with Jane's utterance 'The light slows down'? If the interviewer moves on to a different topic, this may be clearly understood as an evaluation that the previous topic has been completed. The interviewer may provide further signs of completion of an interview section by fiddling with some papers to look for the next item on the interview protocol.

Conceptual change researchers are not the only individuals taking language as a transparent window into the mind. Even researchers who reference the work of Vygotsky analyze utterances as if these provided windows on the mind of the conversation participants. To exhibit common ways of analyzing transcripts, I randomly accessed a recently published article and analysis of knowing and learning in science classrooms.[8] In this article, even though the authors ground their work in Vygotsky, they provide analyses and make claims that ought not go without challenge because of issues that I problematize in this book. Take the following excerpt from a lesson in which the children were asked to classify, among others, toothpaste and the authors' interpretation.

Fragment 2.3
```
5 Terrance:   I think // I.
6 Joe: It's solid.
7 Terrance:   We think it's um gas.
8 Joe: A solid.
9 Kimberly:   Um I think it's a liquid.
```

---

7. In my lab during data analysis meetings, we call it 'going into someone's head'. There is a lot of laughter, for when challenged to provide proof for the assertion about what a person *really* thinks or intends, the person having made such a claim cannot ever provide it. We therefore challenge each other to stick with what is actually said rather than with something inaccessible behind it.

8. The quote and subsequent interpretations are taken from Maria Varelas, Christine C. Pappas, Justine M. Kane, Amy Arsenault, Jennifer Hankes and Begoña M. Cowan, 'Urban Primary-grade Children Think and Talk Science: Curricular and Instructional Practices that Nurture Participation and Argumentation', *Science Education*, Vol. 92 (2008), 65–95. The excerpts are from pages 74, 75, and 78.

The authors use this piece of transcript to claim that there are social and cognitive relationships interwoven. More particularly, they claim that 'Terrance first changes his mind from "I think" to "we think" signaling group agreement, but quickly Joe and Kimberly object to that'. They do not point us to any evidence that Terrance *consciously* revises what he has said; and we do not see evidence that he has done so *because of* what others have said in the meantime. Neither is there a direct relationship between words and thought nor is the relationship between the word and thought constant. This is so because 'the structure of speech does not simply mirror the structure of thought' because 'the simplest utterance, far from reflecting a constant, rigid correspondence between sound and meaning, really is a process'.[9] Unless a child in the situation was to say, 'I changed my mind' or some other child or teacher were to say, 'he changed his mind', we have little if any evidence that an actual change of mind has happened. And would such a 'change of mind' have to be modeled as a conceptual change, an opinion, or as declarative or procedural knowledge? We have to study the situated development of (cultural) thought in minute-to-minute, temporal, and historical fashion precisely because the syntactical organization and psychological organization do not tend to accord in the way generally assumed. Thus, only a cultural-historical theory can deal with this and similarly complex problem that the study of thought and speech constitutes, where the genetic method pertains not only to temporal scales of history and development (ontogenesis) but also to the moment-to-moment unfolding of thought.

The authors also claim that Joe and Terrance 'negotiate and argue about their ideas', as trying to 'argue about [their] position', contradicting themselves, changing their minds, or 'hold[ing] on to their reasoning'. There is no evidence that they actually negotiated or intended to do so. Rather, all we can hear (see) is that students articulate different categorical descriptors for the same substance (tooth paste). Another equally-to-be-justified description of what happens in the episode would be that the children *confronted* one another with their opinions. Already as s a high school physics teacher, while watching videotapes of my concept mapping lessons, I noted that students contributed to 'collaborative' sessions in the way seen above, clearly without learning in the situation. To assist them in learning from one another, I then modeled for them the practice of asking for explanations, elaborations, and justifications. I wrote large posters with these three words and actively reminded students not to put up with someone else merely making statements—as the children in the episode—but to *argue* each point, which requires individuals to elaborate their ideas, explicate, and justify them. The videotapes of subsequent lessons show that student learning does improve with the improvements in the interactional processes. That is, watching videos back then led me to the opposite conclusion than the one arrived at by Varelas and colleagues, students are making statements rather than arguing and engaging with ideas. The changes that occurred proved me right in the sense that students did come to learn more once they engaged in processes that I could recognize as arguing ideas.

The illustrated forms of analysis come with the danger that we allow thinking to be connected directly to words. Thinking, in this approach, first is taken to be hidden,

---

9. Lev S. Vygotsky, *Thought and Language* (Cambridge, MA: MIT Press, 1986), 219, 222.

secret, and private; subsequently it comes to be presented publicly in words, as if the person were 'spilling beans'. This is consistent with Kant's constructivist philosophy where reason can stand on its own, constructing itself from certain a priori givens. Language is needed so that others may understand us, as we understand ourselves— but this language is marked by 'the absence of tone, the absence of the seductive, contagiously affect-laden voice, the absence of the veiled voice'.[10] Many authors analyzing conversations in this manner do not generally attend to the unfolding evolution that occurs. They do so despite evidence in the literature that thought *emerges* from very fuzzy general seeds and then develops as it realizes itself in language and gesture; and they do so despite theoretical arguments that verbal articulation *mediates* and *transforms* thought. Researchers going about analysis in this manner do not heed the advice that '[n]o matter how they were interpreted, the relations between thought and word were always considered constant, established forever. Our investigation has shown that they are, on the contrary, delicate, changeable relations between processes, which arise during the development of verbal thought'.[11] When Kimberly comes to speak the situation no longer is the same as it was for Joe (line 6), who makes the first statement. It is an opening, and other statements do not *merely* occur, but they occur against the background of what has already been said. More so, Joe cannot know what others will say after him, and, in most everyday conversations, others (here Terrance and Kimberley) do not know what they will say 15 seconds, a minute, or an hour hence. Yet we know that conversations build on what has been said, and (university, funding) committees may arrive at classifications and at statements that are not even close to what anyone has come to the meeting with. In fact, committees at times come to conclusions quite opposite to what any single member has thought prior to the meeting.

At the end of *Thought and Language*, Vygotsky suggests that thinking and speaking hold the key to practical consciousness, which reflects the physical and social reality of persons in action. His precisely one-year-older contemporary Mikhail Bakhtin refers to understanding practical consciousness as *participative thinking*.[12] This concept fits into the non-reductionist approach that I take here. We participate in a world without having to reflect. This does not mean that we are like robots doing what we are programmed to do without thinking. Rather, it means that there is a lot of skill mobilized in making societal situations what they are, and each of us contributes in the collaborative work that brings society off in the way that we experience it. Therefore, our understanding is not mechanical and we understand societal situations *participatively*, as knowledgeable participants, rather than in a reflective way. We rarely stop and reflect in everyday life, we just jump in and engage and contribute to making the situation happen. Students such as Jane, Kimberly, Joe, or Terrence participate in a situation, which is not a box within which they find themselves but which is something that their action creates simultaneously while speaking about the topic. They 'know' what is happening not because they reflect or reflect upon the situation but because they have taken positions in this world and collaborate with others to make it

---

10. Nancy, op. cit. note 5, 78.
11. Vygotsky, op. cit. note 9, 254.
12. Mikhail M. Bakhtin, *Toward a Philosophy of the Act* (Austin: University of Texas Press, 1993), 8.

what it is: a(n) (un-) successful conceptual change interview or a(n) (un-) successful science lesson. To better understand participative-thinking-in-action and its relation to language, the analysis of situations in which speech features (conversations, lectures) therefore needs to take into account developments that occur at the microlevel—where they take this or that direction—as well as more global directions and developments (ontogenesis, culture). It is only by providing appropriate theories for the real-time, dialogical production of participative understanding, knowing, and learning that we can test them for their plausibility and fruitfulness.

Some readers may claim that the hearer of the talk (reader of the transcript) can understand what the speaker means. But this gets us precisely at the heart of the problem that hearers themselves are attuned to what the speaker means even if the speaker does not say as much. The degree to which the two forms of understanding overlap depends, as Vygotsky illustrates through an analysis of a scene from Lev N. Tolstoy's *Anna Karenina*, on shared culture and degree of familiarity between the interlocutors. How do we know that a speaker actually means what someone attributes him/her to mean? A talk may be characterized by stumbles, mumbles, pauses, non-grammatical production, and so on all of which are part of a non-fluent production. So what *does* a speaker think? How competent is s/he in the domain that s/he is to teach the students present in the classroom? The purpose of this book as a whole precisely is to develop and articulate a way of approaching talk that differs from the ways in which talk generally is analyzed, theorized, and explained in the (science education) research literature. My investigation takes a dialogical perspective on thought, which not only continuously changes but which also stands to language in an ever-changing relation. In so doing, I go beyond the giants on whose shoulders I stand in considering material forms other than language in which thought realizes itself and to which language bears a complex relation.

Revisiting 'The Social Construction of Scientific Concepts'

As articulated at the beginning of the previous section, I am not innocent and have contributed to the reproduction and transformation of linguistic analyses of school science lessons in the way I critique. Here I return to my research in which I first reported my work on concept mapping and in the context of which I recorded the videotape and produced the transcript that I use throughout this book. Prior to doing this work, I had begun my research career employing a neo-Piagetian information processing approach before moving on to constructivism. Very early on in my encounter with constructivism, I became familiar with an area of research that reported how science was really done rather than how science is described in the methods descriptions of research articles. This research area, generally referred to as the 'social studies of science', includes sociologists and social constructivists. I immediately found the studies and frameworks more interesting than the radical constructivist works that I had read in large part because of the trouble I found students to experience doing concept mapping on their own and the greater facility they showed when working on the task in groups. In particular, my observations as a teacher, which appeared to be consistent with a sociological or social constructivist perspective of learning in real classrooms, led me to evaluate the social constructivist perspective more favorably than the radical constructivist position. Perhaps not surprisingly, therefore, already more than a decade and a half ago I featured the results of my teacher-researcher studies regarding concept mapping in one of the first science education articles on the 'social construction' of scientific concepts.[13] The work was conducted in my high school physics classes where students completed concept-mapping tasks on a regular basis.

The article came during a turning point in the field of science education when some researchers moved away from the Piagetian stage and information processing theories in vogue just before that. The field had begun to explore, among others, radical constructivism as a suitable alternative paradigm. The role of sociocultural forces and mediating elements was new to the field. Today, however, the idea of the social construction of knowledge is probably uncontested, though precisely what it means in a context that continues to favor the focus on individual learning outcomes—e.g., testing, grades, career progress all are based on the individual as unit of analysis—remains to be shown. The question one might pose is whether individual or social construction as metaphors of learning continue to be useful in the face of other, alternative theories that have very different implications for science learning environments, curriculum design, research on science learning and instruction, and so on.

Language-based approaches have experienced an increase in popularity since Jay Lemke's early work in this direction.[14] However, the types of analyses he offers are highly technical and demand the deployment of functional grammars. One shortcoming of such analyses is the fact that few if any teachers of science will find functional analyses useful, especially in the here and now of the unfolding classroom. Moreover, one of the criticisms Bakhtin might have voiced about Lemke's approach is the apparently static form of analysis that focuses on stable patterns in language and on the thematic patterns of actor-process-location-classifier relations in sentences. For Bakhtin, the most important aspect of language is its change, the continuous change of the theme; and the stability of *a* language is only a figment, an image that results when a whole system is frozen in time at a single instant. Instead, we need to think of language as something living, something self-changing in the very moment that it realizes itself, including its grammar and thematic patterns. The writings of Jacques Derrida and Hélène Cixous, the founder of *écriture féminine*, are exemplary in this context, because the movement of language is available right in the text and brought about by means of the text.

My whole purpose in and with this book is to articulate an approach to science knowing, learning, and teaching that is grounded in the dialectical materialist, dialogi-

---

13. Wolff-Michael Roth and Anita Roychoudhury, 'The Social Construction of Scientific Concepts or The Concept Map as Conscription Device and Tool for Social Thinking in High School Science', *Science Education*, Vol. 76 (1993), 531–57. A companion article focused on more structural aspects of the interactions from which the concept maps sprang forth. See Wolff-Michael Roth and Anita Roychoudhury, 'The Concept Map as a Tool for the Collaborative Construction of Knowledge: A Microanalysis of High School Physics Students', *Journal of Research in Science Teaching*, Vol. 30 (1993), 503–34.

14. Jay Lemke, *Talking Science: Language, Learning and Values* (Norwood, NJ: Ablex, 1990).

cal language philosophy articulated by Mikhail Bakhtin and members of his circle and a kin ways of understanding thinking, speaking, and being in the world. One of their key concepts, dialogism, is sometimes taken up in the Western literature, but not in the way it was designed. Rather it is used to refer to situations that involve conversations, dialogues, in small groups or whole classes. But Bakhtin insists that dialogism is not the same as dialogue. The latter term refers to two or more individuals having a conversation, whereas dialogism refers to the non-self-identical nature of the word specifically and of language in general. In other words, dialogism is the idea that a word uttered as part of some conversation does not belong to the speaker, that it is not an expression of something that the individual spills from his or her mind into the public arena. Each signifying element that can be isolated within an utterance—as well as the utterance in its entirety—finds itself transferred to another context, an active context of a response. Signification therefore does not lie in the word or, for this matter, in the soul of the speaker or, to add the counterpart in the conversation, in the soul of the interlocutor. This is so because 'signification is the effect of the *interaction of speaker and recipient, imposing itself on the material of a given sound complex*'.[15] That is, the word, which has come to the speaker from the others, in speaking, is for the other and, in speaking, returns to the other: It bestraddles speaker and audience. In fact, one may also say that language uses speakers and audiences to reproduce itself as a social rather than as an individual phenomenon, a way of expressing the situation that is reminiscent of Martin Heidegger's expression 'Die Sprache spricht' (language speaks).[16]

In this book, I provide an alternative reading of the concept-mapping lessons that had founded my original social construction argument. I show that we can do learning science and science learning research as concrete human psychology and objective psychology that does not require to construe mental worlds but that finds all its data and evidence in social relations and the natural worlds that are available to and used by members to a setting. That is, I do not argue that there are no private thoughts or that there are no structures in mind. Rather, I show that we can go about our research in a very different way that takes into account everything that the members to a setting themselves make available to each other (a) to achieve the object/motives that orient what they do and (b) to go about the process of this achievement. Of interest in such an account are 'knowledge', 'thoughts', and 'intentions' only to the extent that members themselves make them available to and for one another. Only this is of interest because solely what *they* have and make available orients their every next move.

---

15. Mikhaïl Bakhtine [V. N. Volochinov], *Le marxisme et la philosophie du langage: essaie d'application de la méthode sociologique en linguistique* (Paris: Les Éditions de Minuit, 1977), 147.

16. Martin Heidegger, *Gesamtausgabe Band 12: Unterwegs zur Sprache* (Frankfurt: Vittorio Klostermann, 1985), 10.

The Learning Paradox

At the time when I originally started the research in my own classrooms, I was not yet thinking about the challenges that the learning paradox posed to educators. In fact, I had not yet heard the term at all, though I know today that Carl Bereiter had published his review article a few years before I began my classroom research. However, perhaps because I was transcribing all my videotapes word for word within a couple of days of recording them, I had the opportunity to see closely what was happening. I began to notice that students' talk was not so much rationalist and oriented toward a specific goal, namely what I had set out in my planning book following the provincially set learning objectives for my courses. Only a year after I began my classroom research on concept mapping, I read *Contingency, Irony, and Solidarity* by the American pragmatist philosopher Richard Rorty. It was then that I began to 'put my finger on' the phenomenon. I was particularly taken by a chapter entitled 'The Contingency of Language' in which the philosopher argues that linguistic changes are not the result of 'act of wills' but contingently emerge from the praxis of using language. In particular, he writes about how scientific language associated with the Copernican revolution changed as an emergent rather than a planned (constructed) phenomenon: 'After a hundred years of inconclusive muddle, the Europeans found themselves speaking in a way which took these interlocked theses [from telescopic observations] for granted'.[17] He further suggests that cultural changes do not result from applying criteria and that we should look neither within ourselves nor in the (material) world for finding decision-making criteria that mediate the emergence of a new idiom.

I was taken by this description, for it describes what I have been seeing. Students appear to *evolve* new ways of talking rather than *intend* to speak new languages. One word in particular was fit for denoting my observation: *muddle*. In my classrooms, the students clearly did not talk the way in which they talked outside, in the dorms, during the sports activities that we participated in together. They did not talk like physicists either, in the way I (the teacher) might have expressed myself about a particular phenomenon or in the way I might have contributed to a conversation concerning some concepts. I heard such 'muddle', a term I always used in a positive sense as a necessary language from everyday speak to science speak, in the dorms when 'the boys' in the residence I co-supervised discussed Stephen Hawking's *A Brief History of Time*. Later I came to prefer the term *Sabir*, because it does not have the same negative connotations as muddle. Sabir are hybrid languages that Mediterranean merchants spoke—bringing resources from any and every language that they could draw on—in and for making a deal. But I did not grasp the full implications of my observations. It was only through a continued interest in phenomenological studies that I investigated learning through the eyes of the learner and eventually came to understand the phenomenon that I now denote as the learning paradox.

---

17. Richard Rorty, *Contingency, Irony, and Solidarity* (Cambridge: Cambridge University Press, 1989), 6.

Ontogenetic Perspectives

One event in particular 'pushed me over the edge' and eventually allowed me to recognize the fundamental contradiction. During a stay in northern Germany as a fellow of the *Institute for Advanced Studies*, while analyzing videotapes featuring tenth-grade students in the process of learning about static electricity in a specially designed hands-on unit, I decided to put myself through an experiment in which I would closely record what I learned. One day I went on a trip along roads that I had never taken before and recorded, after returning home, everything I remembered to have seen. On the next day, I wrote down what I remembered from the previous day and then cycled the same one-hour circuit again, sometimes attempting to predict what I would see around the next corner and again noting into my research log everything I remembered once I returned home. I did this precise circuit for 20 days in a row. On the seventh day I had a striking experience. (I had many similar experiences over the three months of my fellowship.) I was close to home when I noticed two giant feed silos close to the road. I was flabbergasted. I had passed the same spot for six days in a row, intending to learn as much as possible about the way, and I had not seen these, what I now took to be impossible-to-miss towers in the landscape. My first thought was that I *could not have intended* finding the twin silos in my 'hands-on' course, because I did not know of their existence. Despite my 'hands-on' experience in their vicinity, I did not notice them. More so, I thought, if a teacher had given me a test about the towers after one of the first six days, I would have flunked miserably. The twin silos are nowhere in my research log until that seventh day when I first noticed them. And yet, to the teacher these silos would have existed as really and as impossible-to-miss as they existed for me within a fraction of a second after they began to exist for me.

This is not a singular experience. Just a few weeks prior to writing this paragraph, I am returning home from the university along a road that I have taken for more than ten years. All of a sudden I am struck. I see a church (Fig. 2.1), which evidently has been in this place for a considerable amount of time, certainly for longer than the ten years that I have been passing by here. Yet this is the very first time that I notice this church. Again, I could not have intended perceiving and learning about the church because I did not know it was there. Moreover, if I had taken a test related to the presence of this church, I would have flunked miserably. I have not seen the church previously, although I am a keen observer of the everyday world because of a deep concern for all aspects of knowing and learning around me. It is not that I have come by here *quickly,* by car, though I have done so, too: For the past 10 years I have been *cycling* along this road without seeing the church that so clearly sits right next to the road.

The learning paradox can be articulated in terms of the perennial question of how structures of new and higher complexity can emerge on the ground of less complex structures. As Carl Bereiter shows in his review article written more than 20 years ago, Piagetian and radical constructivism have not been able to provide answers to this fundamental quandary. Culture in itself cannot provide an account of this quandary, because even if adults helped children to achieve skills that they subsequently internalize, the question remains how this internalization would take place. As experiments

Fig. 2.1. An analogy for the learning paradox. For over ten years, I had passed this spot on the bicycle while going and coming from work without (consciously) noticing it. How could I have intended learning about the church given that I did not know if its existence?

in the cultural-historical tradition have shown, thought can emerge where there is no thought *when there are mediational processes that allow not only engagement and participation but also enable a reflexive turn in which these processes turn upon themselves.* Thus, the research conducted by the Russian psychologist Alexander Meshcheryakov shows that deaf-blind children, who heretofore merely vegetated, were able to develop normal levels of thought (and even attending university).[18] His experience shows that it is not sufficient to engage the children in some tasks but to allow them to become aware by reflexively turning upon the task and the tools involved. Thus, one of the ways in which the children become conscious of tools (objects) *as* tools (objects) is by allowing them not only to learn to eat with a spoon but also to explore the very spoon that they eat with. This is a nice analogy for the way in which I present language and language learning in this book, as a *recursive* system. It is not sufficient to allow students to engage in talk about something, they need to engage reflexively and recursively in talking about their talk, in using language for talking about and manipulating language. It is in this reflexive turn of language upon itself that it reaches higher levels of complexity.

When we look at the videotapes and through transcripts such as the ones I feature here (see, e.g., the transcript of one concept mapping task in the Appendix), we see students accomplish a task where there is no evidence at all that they engage in the planful and 'intentional' 'construction' of 'a specific piece of conceptual knowledge'. The verb 'to construct' is transitive and requires an object, something to be worked

18. Alexander Meshcheryakov, *Awakening to Life: On the Education of Deaf-blind Children in the Soviet Union* (Moscow: Progress, 1974).

with and the focus of the doing, and a motive/goal/intention that serves as an aim to be worked toward. The verb describes the work on a concrete object to transform it so it takes another, the intended form. However, the knowledge that the curriculum sets as the goal is unavailable to students, it is whatever students will have acquired *as a consequence* of the curriculum. There is no doubt that the students whom we follow in this book through one concept-mapping session—Ken, Miles, and Ralf—learn to speak physics while making a concept map. But they do not *construct* the new forms of language, because to do so they would need criteria for deciding whether one construction is better than another—like carpenters need plans so that they can decide which material and tool to use to make precisely the house that their customers want. In the acquisition of new knowledge, such criteria *cannot* exist because it is only with our new ways of talking that we evolve that we can specify what it is that we learned. But, and this may sound contradictory, the choice for which language to use—i.e., which language game to play—is not arbitrary either, because there is a path-dependence to the evolution of language where, to paraphrase Rorty, we loose the habit of using certain words and gradually acquire the habit of using others.

The concept of *construction* and the associate verb *to construct* are limited and limiting to attain a truly productive and generative way of thinking about learning generally and the learning paradox particularly. When I think about construction, I think about building homes and parts thereof—I recently finished an entire basement, including the walls, sound insulation, bathroom, and vapor and sound barriers. I am familiar with construction work. The builders constructing a house find themselves with clearly distinct raw materials that already have their intended uses. There is the concrete that is going to be used to pour a foundation, 2-by-4's to frame the walls and '4-by-8' sheets of plywood or particleboard to produce the shell; and there are beams and materials to build the rafters for making the roof, to be covered with some form of shingles. The builders know and therefore can intend the final product. They have a plan. They can have a plan because of their experience with the distance that exists between projected and real outcomes. They construct the building and, because they have a plan, they know when they have erred, and when they have to revise a job. They can assess the final product by comparing it to what is on the paper.

Students are in a situation very different from construction workers. Students do not construct knowledge and frameworks in the way the workers do. Students do not know what the outcome of their activity will be and therefore do not and cannot engage in the intentional construction of the target knowledge. They are not like architects either, who have certain fundamental elements that they put together to derive the plan for a building. This would not be learning *new* things but merely differentiating what is already known. Instead, students find themselves in the position of bricoleurs who take the materials at hand to see how they can solve with it the problem they have. They are involved in *creative* acts where they cannot know their creation until after it has occurred. In chapter 10 I further articulate a phenomenological perspective on the creative act of painting as an analogy for learning something new.

In his discussion of the contingency of language, Rorty also draws on the analogy between language ('vocabularies') and tools to articulate the major drawback that this analogy comes with. His conclusion underscores my point about the problem of the constructivist perspective. Thus, '[t]he craftsman typically knows what job he needs to do before picking or inventing tools with which to do it. By contrast, someone like Galileo, Yeats, or Hegel (a "poet" in my wide sense of the term—the sense of "one who makes things new") is typically unable to make clear exactly what it is that he wants to do before developing the language in which he succeeds in doing it. His new vocabulary makes possible, for the first time, a formulation of its own purpose. It is a tool for doing something which could not have been envisaged prior to the development of a particular set of descriptions, those which it itself helps to provide'.[19]

To further elaborate on the distinction between constructing something and building something as a bricoleur, let us look at drawing as an analogy. We can decide to draw/paint a horse. The two verbs are transitive, which means we have some vision of what the outcome will be, then take a pencil and paper and work toward producing such an image. We can compare the outcome to what we had intended or to a picture of a horse or even to a real horse. We may decide that our drawing is well done or needs revisions. On the other hand, we may doodle. But the verb 'to doodle' is an intransitive word and therefore can be done without an object. The result of such 'art' is something that emerges from unintended and conditioned movements, like a Jackson Pollock painting. Students therefore are more in the situation of a Jackson Pollock using paint to evolve a painting that he himself did not anticipate the outcome of. Not only Pollock but even the classical painters, when they were after creating a new way of looking at the world, could not tell beforehand what they needed to paint to make this new way of painting happen. It is only when they had painted that they could recognize that they had done something new.[20]

To understand learning we have to come to grips with the question of the horizon that separates that which is known from that which is unknown, that is, the horizon that separates the clearing and the darkness beyond. The very question of the intent to learn requires the acknowledgment of a world beyond the horizon of the clearing, a world that is not yet known but that can open itself so that we can see what is unseen (rather than the invisible). This horizon itself holds the key, because it implies as a priori the very knowledge about the unknown. The horizon *as* horizon generally is not thematic. When I recently read about some South American Aymara tribe where people point a finger over the back rather than toward the front when talking about the future[21], I realized the problem Westerners have of getting away from learning as a purely intentional act. We point forward and toward a horizon, and therefore, what we want to do is ahead of us. To the Aymara, however, the future is behind the back, so that they can think of the future as bringing that to view that unavoidably is unseen and cannot be anticipated. It is precisely the historical and phenomenological methods that make thematic those aspects of everyday life accessible to the non-scientific ground upon which any transformation into the scientific occurs. The same aspects serve as material that becomes what we subsequently name scientific; and it is the tool

19. Rorty, op. cit. note 17, 12.

20. Jean-Luc Marion, *The Crossing of the Visible* (Stanford, CA: Stanford University Press, 2004).

21. Rafael Núñez and Eve Sweetser, 'With the Future Behind Them: Convergent Evidence From Aymara Language and Gesture in the Crosslinguistic Comparison of Spatial Construals of Time', *Cognitive Science,* Vol. 30 (2006), 401–50.

with which the transformation is accomplished. Language, because it is the most important structure in our lives, plays an important role in the processes by means of which we overcome the learning paradox in any practical situation. The existence of language is made possible by the empathic community of human beings among each other, which has as its correlate the world of objects, and, therefore, an objective world.

Cultural-Historical Perspectives

When we theorize learning, it might help not to think about students in the world today but about the first time ever that a human being spoke or about the first time ever someone did geometry. How did language emerge if it takes at least two individuals to understand, the speaker and the listener? How did geometry get off the ground in a non-geometrical culture? How did science ever get off the ground in a cultural context through and through marked by traditional ecological knowledge (later Aristotelian thought) and, from the perspective of present-day science, through and through non-scientific? In the context of describing the crisis of the European sciences, Edmund Husserl suggests that a true science can only be founded when the original concepts are fixed in writing: 'In the first verbal collaborations of the beginning geometers lacked understandably the need for an *accurate fixation of descriptions for the pre-scientific ur-material and of the ways in which related geometrical idealities emerged and the for the latter relevant "axiomatic" statements*'.[22] Here the 'raw material' is understood as the way in which people understood geometry prior to the first formal geometry: their proto-geometric concepts. Husserl describes the situation how geometry can emerge from pre- and even non-geometric thought. He suggests that a science can emerge only on the condition that it is written down so that it can both be reflected upon and that its idealities can be reproduced infinitely into the future. The concept-mapping task puts the students in a situation similar to the one in which early geometers found themselves. Students are asked to produce a system of statements with given concept words on the basis of their pre-instructional language and beginning language. It is in and through the fixation of this 'ur-material' in a way that it preserves the very essence of talking science. The emergence of geometry talk from something that is non-scientific requires there to be processes that allow any form of non-scientific talk to turn into scientific talk, both on cultural-historical (phylogenetic) and on ontogenetic scales. This problem of the 'ur-constitution' of geometry therefore pertains in similar ways to all of the sciences. It also allows us to think about the 'ur-constitution' of structurally more advanced forms of talking and thinking about scientific phenomena.

How can the original sense of what is scientific about a science be recovered in the practices today? How is the 'ur-sense' maintained in the intentional history of sense?

---

22. Edmund Husserl, 'Die Frage nach dem Ursprung der Geometrie als intentional-historisches Problem', *Revue internationale de philosophie*, Vol. 1 (1939), 203–25, 218, original emphasis.

$$\nabla \cdot D = \rho; \quad \nabla \cdot B = 0; \quad \nabla \times E = -\frac{\partial B}{\partial t}; \quad \nabla \times H = j + \frac{\partial D}{\partial t}$$

Fig. 2.2. Four tiny little equations contain all the knowledge about electromagnetism known during the mid-19th century, which initially and in different form took James Clerk Maxwell an entire book to develop. The point is that for a physicist each symbol, each letter *can* but does not have to be unpacked.

The ur-materials that constitute the first scientific sense, the ur-premises so to speak, derive prior to all science from the lived-in world, which is not a merely material world surrounding the individual like a box but it is always and already a structured cultural world shot through with signification and, above all, a structured world that the individual co-constitutes.

The special problem that poses itself is how some of these students then become scientists themselves and, in so doing, contribute to reproducing the science all the while they are producing it anew, with new theoretical concepts and methods. There is the historicity of the sciences themselves; and the students generally (as members of society that makes science possible) and future scientists specifically develop and in their development both reproduce science and generate its renewal. In and through their participation, culture generally changes, and so does the culture of science specifically. That is, despite all the worries on the part of science educators generally and conceptual change theorists particularly, not only do new generations reproduce science as it has historically developed *but also* they produce new forms of science that we have not even thought about only a few years ago. But the same happens to all those forms of language that they term to be due to 'misconceptions'. This leads us to another question: How is it that recent generations do not have to reproduce the entire history of science, that they do not have to return to the basics to work their way through to current thinking, but pick up on forms of science that did not even exist some 100 years ago? Again, the approach I take here much better than the conceptual change perspective explains the continual transformation of science *all the while students struggle in school with developing forms of discourse that appear to have been those of the past.* Throughout this book I show how a concept word becomes more complex and contains or indexes other forms of talking like a black box.

Black boxes are used whenever a piece of machinery *or a set of commands is too complex.* In its place cyberneticians draw a little box about which they need to know nothing but its input and output. An example that I have always liked—about how language becomes simpler because new forms black box old forms—is that of the relationship between electric fields, magnetic fields, electric charges and currents, and magnetic poles. It took the physicist James Clerk Maxwell an entire book to develop the ideas and equations to show the relations that integrated everything physicists knew about electricity and magnetism during the mid-19th century. Today, one can find the key issues Maxwell developed in his book in any undergraduate textbook: four tiny equations (Fig. 2.2). A physicist can, but does not have to, unpack each symbol, each letter, and each equation. The beauty and efficiency lies in the fact that all the discourse of an entire book, the knowledge of an entire field during a particular historical period can now be expressed and used in four tiny equations that are an integral part of the physicist's, applied mathematician's, or engineer's language. Black boxes can be used without requiring acquisition or skills that are embodied on their inside. Black boxes therefore constitute one of the forms in which the language of a field becomes more complex. New generations do not have to learn the skills that are required on the inside of the black box, but they need to evolve the competencies to use the black box as a tool. In this way, new generations immediately operate with language and practices that are more complex than those of generations past. But black boxing does not get rid of the history that produces it, so that 'the curse of five thousand years of culture [comes to be] encrusted on each movement, each word'.[23]

In concept mapping, the students use language to evolve statements that they have never made before, that is, they use language to evolve language. Language as they find it today, which contains ancient forms of talking about things in new and more economic form, is the ground, the material, and the tool of concept mapping. New generations of students find a language in which today's forms of talking are encapsulated and do no longer have to be made explicit. Students are not, and do not have to be, asked to reproduce the science of Aristotle or Galileo but the science of today embodies their achievements in its very core. To understand learning both at ontogenetic and cultural-historical scales, we need to understand the real problem, which is one of *inner*-historic nature: the problem of the way in which sense itself comes about in the practical engagement with a world populated with others and with objects.

Scientific language therefore becomes increasingly complex as older forms of talking/writing come to be enfolded into new forms of talking/writing. There is an abyss unfolding between 'the essence of the new dimension and its relation to the old familiar field of life. Nowhere else is the distance so great from unclearly arising needs to goal-determined plans, from vague questionings to first working problems—through which actual working science first begins'.[24] Against this abyss all other difficulties in understanding the essence of learning are minor. This abyss has been discussed in the learning sciences literature under the term of *learning paradox*. How then can we get out of the learning paradox, out of any learning paradox? One process that lets us get off the ground as if we were lifting ourselves up at our own shoelaces is called *bootstrapping*. This method comes in various guises in different fields, including computing, physics, or business. The term is generally used to refer to processes that can unfold without external help, that is, to processes that are self-sustaining.

Bootstrapping

The term bootstrapping is used to denote the situation where a system develops into a structurally more complex one by its own structurally less complex means. It is a way

---

23. Eco, op. cit. note 1, 44.

24. Edmund Husserl, *The Crisis of European Sciences and Transcendental Phenomenology: An Introduction to Phenomenology* (Evanston, IL: Northwestern University Press, 1970), 120.

for overcoming the chicken-and-egg problem, which requires a chicken to lay the egg from which the chicken has come. The closest analogy for the present purposes may be one from computer programming, where the problem presents itself in the context of writing a compiler (assembler), a program that translates English-like instructions into machine-readable code, in the target language. That is, the challenge is to write a translator in the language that it is to translate into but that does not yet exist (i.e., the classical chicken-and-egg situation). *Literate Programming* is one approach that successfully deals with this chicken-and-egg situation of writing a program and its documentation simultaneously. In one example, CWEB, the programmer works with two languages simultaneously, TeX for formatting and C for programming. The typographic dimensions of TeX allow the exposition and explication of the program's structure, whereas C provides the tools for specifying the algorithm.

If the learning of a language at the individual and cultural levels is possible, then this possibility has to be *internal* to language. That is, change has to be possible from *within the perspective of the learners* and from within the language they use rather than as conceived by scholars. Change has to be possible and available as a transformation from within the consciousness of the speakers of (prescientific) language. Students themselves achieve the possibility of creating a ground for scientific language through the powers embedded and embodied in the language they use, in its own powers. And they do so through original self-reflection, which itself is a possibility of language. In the process, their ('naïve') language (and world) comes to be transformed into a phenomenon or, more accurately, into a universe of phenomena. The beginning of the process, of course, is necessarily one of experiencing, talking, and thinking in naïve self-evidence.

At the same time, the development of new forms of language (vocabularies, dialects, idioms) does not come from a simple fitting of old vocabularies. It is not a melding or fitting different pieces of students' everyday language. That is, the trial-and-error creation of a new, third vocabulary is not a discovery about how old vocabularies fit together but rather it has to be an evolution of something new that constitutes a creative transformation of what currently is available. This is also why an inferential process cannot reach a new language. We do not get to the new by starting with premises formulated in the old vocabularies. Creations such as new languages are not the result of successfully fitting together pieces of a puzzle but are the result of a creative endeavor where something new and unanticipated emerges.

In natural language learning—talking physics in a 12th-grade high school classroom being one of its local dialects—language is the material, the tool, and the ground upon which new forms of language are produced. It is only as a recursive system that language can transform itself. As learners, we are all thrown into the vernacular of our community, and its discourse generally is different from the discourse that characterizes the scientific discourses of textbooks. This local dialect of physics, characteristic of textbooks, cannot be reached from existing language by means of a simple, linear process—e.g., more or less sudden replacement of old forms of speaking by new forms of speaking. What we need to understand and theorize is how learners can and do bootstrap themselves from their everyday ways of talking into the local dialects of any field, here exemplified by the local dialect of high school physics. The transcripts (as the audio- and videotapes) that I use here generally and the introductory transcript fragments specifically provide evidence for the multiple functions that language has in learning processes: (a) there are speakers talking to organize what they do, that is, they use language to manage their collaboration; (b) at a second level, the students talk *about* their topic, here the concepts written on paper slips and the hierarchical relations between the concept words; (c) they make the situation one in which schooling is reproduced and transformed; and (d) all of this occurs in and out of language, which constitutes the very ground that makes all of the other functions possible.

A Dynamic Approach to Language, Culture, and Learning

Central to Mikhail Bakhtin's writing is the concept of *dialogism*. Sometimes taken literally, researchers use the term to refer to the fact that two or more people in a classroom engage one another in speaking: in a dialogue. But this is not at all what Bakhtin is concerned with. 'Dialogue is studied merely as a compositional form in the structuring of speech, but the internal dialogism of the word (which occurs in a monologic utterance as well as in a rejoinder), the dialogism that penetrates its entire structure, all its semantic and expressive layers, is almost entirely ignored'.[25] There is therefore an internal relation of the word to itself, an internal dialogism. This internal dialogism involves different moments of the word. These moments derive from the *dis*location or diastasis within the word, which allows the latter to stand both for itself and something else: a material thing and a pointer to or marker of something else.

The dialogism internal to the word, this inner contradiction, expresses itself in various phenomena—much like the inner contradiction of light expresses itself such that it sometimes has wave character and at other times it has particle character. These include the fact that there are different senses that a word can take, that a word can be defined and explicated in other words and this new text is said to pertain to the same topic, and that the same word takes different senses for different people (e.g., speaker and listener). This makes the word undecidable in at least two ways: (a) one cannot ever decide which of the possible (dictionary) senses is relevant until a specific situation is identified and (b) one cannot ever decide what the thing or phenomenon is, that is, in the utterance of the word, marked, re-marked, and remarked against the ground. That is, the undecidable is made from the exact superposition of the word's blind spot and its focal point, the center of its saying. Another effect of dialogism is the fact that the word encounters an alien aspect in the object, a thing that is different from but denoted by the word. A third effect is that each word is not only marked by who speaks but also by who listens. The word is directed toward another, with an anticipated effect made available in the response. That is, the word is a directed *answerword*, because it provokes an answer, it anticipates an answer, and it structures itself in the direction of an answer. I concur with Bakhtin who writes that there are two faces to each word in its double determination as coming from someone and being

---

25. Mikhail M. Bakhtin, *The Dialogic Imagination* (Austin: University of Texas, 1981), 279.

directed toward someone. It arises as *the interactional product of the speaker–listener conversation*. Active understanding of the word therefore is itself dialogic, because it projects the germ of a response.

The most profound aspect of this theory and the one least taken up in the educational literature is that of the non-self-identical nature of the word. The word cannot be identical with itself because it is dialogical *right at its heart*, and therefore constitutes difference as such. The contradictory nature of the word (language) has been taken up in philosophy during the latter part of the 20th century. For example, Paul Ricœur articulates for us to the enigma that one can always say the same thing differently and at the same time, the identical sense, which is to render two equivalent versions of the same statement, is forever unfindable.[26] Similarly, Jacques Derrida formulates the inner contradiction that derives from the dialogic nature of the word in two antinomic and incompossible propositions that are contradictory not only between themselves but also within themselves[27]:

1. *We only ever speak one language.*
2. *We never speak only one language.*

The incompossible nature of the two statements, which actually constitutes the very law of translation, comes from the facts that (a) if we speak only one language, no translation is necessary and (b) if we never speak only one language, then even our mother tongue cannot be pure. There is therefore an active division within language, within every word, that is the very source of dialogism. The incompossible pair of statements also throws into relieve a contradiction in Bakhtin's own writings generally and in his use of the word monologic particularly.

Bakhtin appears to contradict himself in simultaneously claiming that the word is dialogic and that there are monologic utterances. In the educational literature, the term of the monologic utterance is frequently applied to situations where teachers talk, as in a lecture, and students do not have opportunities for actively engaging in the conversation. Derrida elucidates the issue by combining the two points. First, there *appears to be* a monolingualism where all language becomes translatable, understandable, and therefore constitutes the hegemony of a *One*. Second, and completely consistent with Bakhtin, we never speak only one language, even in the single-word utterance. Thus, theorists of bilingualism make the point that there is no such thing as *the* language and no such thing as absolute monolingualism.

Dialogism leads us to understand the continual translation right at the heart of every language, dialect, or idiom. Thus, understanding involves at least two interlocutors at the heart of a speech community, which, though not completely foreigners with respect to one another, are other with respect to one another. This otherness requires an internal translation. We get to the same position if we think that an authentic understanding always has to be active and always already contains the design of a response. That is, at issue is that understanding is not just the utterance but, because of this additional design of a response that overlays itself and modifies the utterance, there is

---

26. Paul Ricœur, *Sur la traduction* (Paris: Bayard, 2004).

27. Jacques Derrida, *Monolingualism of the Other; or, The Prosthesis of Origin* (Stanford, CA: Stanford University Press, 1998), 7.

transformation and translation. In active understanding, each salient element of the utterance that is imbued with signification and the utterance as a whole are transferred into the active setting of the response. It is precisely the setting that reduces the polysemy of and inherent to the individual word to a specific, singular sense. This provides an explication why monolingualism always is the monolingualism of the Other, the listener, who reduces possible polysemy to a singular hearing. Within this new unit of the intellected utterance, there is a new form of polysemy, where what has been said can be heard in different ways. Here it is the setting that reduces the many different senses of the said and the ear of the other to the one sense that marks significance at the instant. But even in the setting, ambiguity that results from polysemy is not reduced to the *One*. We know this to be the case because of all the misunderstandings that we may experience on a daily basis whenever we intend to say one thing and others hear us say a different thing or when two different hearers hear us say a different thing simultaneously, that is, when they disagree about just what we have said.

The concept of monologism (monolingualism) is a contradiction, because every word is already dialogical and every utterance is spoken for the benefit of someone other as much as for oneself. The contraction is apparent in the fact that I have only one language, and this one never is mine. It is language that speaks, as much or more so than I. My own language is a language that I can assimilate because there is always something foreign in it. My language, the only one I hear myself speak and agree to speak, therefore always and already is the language of the Other, a language I have heard prior to speaking, a language I hear and speak simultaneously. That is, even if I mobilize the word of another for my own intentions, it remains the word of the Other, who not only is the source of my language but also the anticipated recipient. Any word, utterance, or language always and already bestraddles speakers and listeners, authors and audiences, and original works and their translations.

Signification and Theme

Bakhtin's theoretical framework is built upon concepts that he derives from the French-writing Swiss linguist Ferdinand de Saussure, whose main concept is that of the *sign*, consisting of the *signifier* (Fr. significant) and the *signified* (Fr. signifié). The two relate as *signification* (Fr. signification). The signifier is the vehicle, the material body of the sign; the signified the idea or concept that it stands for. A sign, in this approach, therefore has two planes, a material one and an ideational one. That is, a word *always* has two planes: There is always some material body that gives shape to the signifier and there is always the ideational plane that gives the word its sense. These two planes cannot be separated; they always exist together. This two-aspect nature of the sign fits well with the dialectical materialist approach underlying the writing of Bakhtin and the members of his circle. In a strong sense, there are no signs as individual pure entities that one might denote by the term 'sign'. For Bakhtin, there are only sign functions or significations and, as for Martin Heidegger, sign and signified arise together from the process of signification. At its lower limit, signification gives us the dictionary sense of a word, which can appear in the form of (a) a sound complex that we hear in a particular way, (b) traces of ink on paper or other material, or (c) some image.

This double nature of the sign (word) is the source of dialogism. It is the fundamental form of dialogism itself. Bakhtin constructs his approach to language on the model of Karl Marx's treatment of political economy in *Capital*. For Marx, there is a foundational phenomenon, commodity. A commodity embodies *value*. But experience shows that for one person a commodity has *exchange-value* whereas for the other person involved in a barter trade, the same commodity has *use-value*. Thus, a seamstress who has finished a shirt may use it to get some bread so that her family has something to eat for dinner. For the baker, on the other hand, the same shirt is use-value. For the other commodity involved in the trade, the relations are the reverse. The bread is exchange-value for the baker but use-value for the seamstress. There are therefore two sides to any commodity, and which side is realized *appears* to depend on the perspective. Now Marx says that commodity expresses itself as both use-value and exchange-value because it is *both at the same time*, it embodies an inner contradiction. It is like the light discussed by the students in this book, which exhibits wave character in some experiments and particle character in others.

Taking this approach concerning the double-nature of the word provides Bakhtin with the same possibilities that the contradictory nature of value offered to Marx. The inner contradiction is the source for development and change. Just as in Marx's *Capital* each barter exchange developed exchange forms until the capitalist economy of Marx's 19th-century England emerged, each utterance develops language in Bakhtin's system. The resulting change is the source of the development of any language including its genre, and, in fact, the development of the genres themselves. Languages continually renew themselves in the very process of speaking (writing), and as soon as they are no longer used, they become 'dead languages'. That is, language lives in use, and in use undergoes continuous and simultaneous death and rebirth—a major theme in Bakhtin's writings.

Opening any dictionary one will see that there is more than one sense in which a word can be read or heard. We can find the same material body (signified) participating in different settings with different significations or sign-functions. This gives the sign a spectral nature, because any signifier can be associated with different signifieds and therefore significations (sign-functions). Each time a word is mobilized for a particular intention that is itself a function of the setting it will realize a different possibility from the spectrum of significations. Thus, Bakhtin asks us to 'imagine the *intention* of such a word, that is, its *directionality toward the object*, in the form of a ray of light, then the living and unrepeatable play of colors and light on the facets of the image that it constructs can be explained as the spectral dispersion of the ray-word, not within the object itself . . . but rather as its spectral dispersion in an atmosphere filled with alien words, value judgments and accents through which the ray passes on its way toward the object'.[28] All of these possible significations are but potentialities. Once the signifier (word) is uttered in a social situation, the context mediates and

---

28. Bakhtin, op. cit. note 25, 277.

modifies the signification. In fact, in context, the signifier–signified relation together with all the other possible words constitute the *theme*. To Bakhtin, the theme constitutes the highest degree of the linguistic signifying capacity. In a strong sense, only the theme signifies in a determinate manner. Signification is the lowest degree of linguistic signifying capacity. Signification in itself means little by itself, it is but a linguistic potential, a possibility to signify. Therefore, 'no living word relates to its object in a *singular way*: between a word and its object, between the word and the speaking subject, there exists an elastic environment of other, alien words about the same object, the same theme, and this is an environment that it is often difficult to penetrate'.[29] The setting and the word form something like a piece of cloth, they constitute the woof and the weft that cannot be separated lest the cloth be destroyed. Theme as thematic unit implicates the speech context. That is, the thematic unity of an utterance is determined not only by the linguistic forms that enter its composition but also by the nonverbal aspects of the setting. Ultimately, therefore, what is marked, remarked, and remarked is the theme: it is what matters and drives the unfolding conversation.

Serious difficulties and problems in English-language scholarly circles derive from the fact that Bakhtin's term 'signification' that is of Saussurian origin is often translated into English by the term 'meaning' but also into other words. But clearly, the translation of Bakhtin's own definitions suggest that 'meaning is the lower limit of linguistic significance. Meaning in essence means nothing'. Signification, on the other hand, is a relation between the signifier and the signified, not a thing, the translation itself, which follows requests such as 'What do you mean by . . .?'.

The theme constitutes a dynamic and complex system of interdependent signs that parallels and refracts the conditions of a given instant. Thus, the 'utterance "what time is it?" has a different sense each time it is used and, consequently, according to our terminology, another theme that depends on the concrete historical situation" (historical at the microscopic scale) in the course of which it is uttered and of which it in fact constitutes an element'.[30] That is, the *theme* is the ideological parallel that refracts (rather than mirror-like reflects) the material world. In this way, each utterance, as thematic unit, becomes situated and, in fact, irreproducible. Theoretically, this would not be satisfactory to a dialectical materialist approach. Therefore, there also is something repeatable about the utterance, which is its sense, that is, the relation of the signifier (sound envelope, heard as word) and the signified. Signification, therefore, is the lower limit of the signifier–signified relation and describes the relationship between a word and its (dictionary) sense. The theme is indivisible, whereas the signification associated with an utterance can be analyzed into a sequence of significations related to the linguistic elements that make the utterance. This precisely is the kind of analysis that Jay Lemke provides us with in *Talking Science*, a compositional analysis of the various signifying elements within an utterance and in a complex of utterances. An informal thematic diagram a la Lemke would look like the concept map that my students produced as a result of their task (Fig. 1.2).

29. Bakhtin, op. cit. note 25, 276.
30. Bakhtine, op. cit. note 15, 142.

Considering the upper limit of linguistic signification (theme) takes us to investigate the sense of a given word under the conditions of a concrete utterance in a concrete setting. It is precisely here that we need careful, descriptively adequate ethnographic studies of the context, on the one hand, and the way in which interaction participants *themselves* hear what their interlocutors are saying. Rather than imposing external ways of hearing, to understand why a conversation develops as it does, we need to attend to how the participants themselves take up what others are saying and doing with their respective utterances. In each second turn, which also is a first turn for the turn that follows, an evaluation occurs for the purpose in the situation. There is acceptance, rejection, or even creatively mobilized uncertainty any one of which moves the conversation a bit ahead, continuously transforming language in the process.

Dialogism, Heterogeneity, Development

As a result of the dialogism within the word, there are other phenomena of doubling that occur. Any single word exists for a speaker not in one but in three aspects. First, it is a more or less neutral word of a language and therefore belongs to everybody and nobody ('language speaks'). Second, every word also is an *Other's* word. It is this generalized other from whom the word has come to me. The word therefore belongs to another person. It is filled with echoes of the utterances that others have produced, for millennia, with the echoes of their voices continuing to resound in the word. This aspect has been picked up in the feminist and critical literature, which has shown that specific words serve the reproduction of a patriarchic system and male-dominated society. Third, each word also is *my* word, for, since I am mobilizing it in a particular situation, within a particular orientation toward what to say, it is already imbued with my expression. This last type of word is the only one attended to in our field.

We can always say the same thing differently. This is what we do when we define words in dictionaries or, in everyday conversations, when we say what we really mean without having said so. We find, in this manner, on the inside of our own language community, the enigma of the same, the signification itself, the unfindable identical sense, which is supposed to render equivalent the two versions of the same thing. But such translations do not always provide the same content for it is precisely here that we find the origin of misunderstandings and miscommunication. The same word may mean differently and different words are taken to mean the same. But a word is never the same. A language therefore always is a mêlée of languages, always is a *Sabir*, containing both foreign languages and foreign words from the same language. Like in all mêlées, these languages are not identical with themselves. They are heterogeneous, they are hybrids, meaning the same with different words and meaning differently with the same words. In the more poetic words of the modern-day dialectical philosopher Jean-Luc Nancy, the continual working and reworking of language is expressed thus: languages 'cannot be added up. They encounter one another, mix with one another, alter one another, reconfigure one another. They culture and cultivate one another, prepare each other's ground, irrigate and drain another, plough one another or graft themselves on the other'.[31]

Having laid the ground that grounds the inquiry I evolve further the idea of the nature of language in learning over the course of the following four chapters. These four chapters take as their objects four consecutive parts of the conversation over and about the concept-mapping task. The first three parts constitute an opening, a six-minute conversation with the teacher, and the completion of the placement of the paper slips and its transcription onto paper up to the point where the students announced that they have finished. The fourth part consists of the moments when the students transcribe and finalize their map on paper. The corresponding chapter 6 develops language and learning issues while following the students through the final part of the session, the construction of the lines linking concept names and the choice of verbs written on the lines so that statements are produced.

---

31. Jean-Luc Nancy, 'L'éloge de la mêlée', *Transeuropéennes*, Vol. 1 (1993), 8–18, 13.

3

Beginning the Bootstrap

'Before born babe bliss had. Within womb won he worship. Whatever in that one case done commodiously done was. A couch by midwives attended with wholesome food reposeful, cleanest swaddles as though forthbringing were now done and by wise fore-sight set'.[1] In this chapter, I am concerned with how, in learning, we begin the apparently impossible task to learn something absolutely knew by pulling ourselves up at our own bootstraps in the way the famous Baron of Münchhausen had done in one of his outrageous tall tales. The bootstrap required to overcome the learning paradox has been of interest to philosophers and writers for a long time. Thus, James Joyce addresses this issue by writing one of the chapters of the *Ulysses* in a way that recapitulates the history of the English language in a description of a scene from a maternity ward in 1904 Dublin. But the birth of the child is preceded by something ('Before born babe bliss had'), as English is preceded by Latin, Anglo-Saxon, and Norman languages. We can trace these languages even further backward to get to their Indo-Germanic roots. But then, in our backward travel, there will be a time when language began, when a first person uttered a word. And this word, even though it has been the first, was a word already for two. Language, from the very beginning, is always and already possible not merely for one person, the one who utters it for the first time, but to all those who are its intended recipients and therefore have to understand it.

'Before born babe bliss had'. Today, any baby born always and already comes into a world shot through with significations, that is, ordered in thematic ways. Babies have barely emerged from the womb when parents 'talk' to them, reproduce and trans-form the babies' sounds, give them a finger to hold on to, take them on their shoulders to pat them, kiss them, rub noses with them, and so on. This world consists of sounds, gestures, body movements, body positions, and intonations (prosody) that those pro-duce who always already have been there 'before born babe bliss had'. As they par-ticipate in the socially and materially structured world, babies come to discern regu-larities, including the sounds that ultimately turn into words as babies learn to produce these themselves. There is no real beginning, because the world always and already is

---

1. James Joyce, *Ulysses* (New York: Random House, 1986), 315.

and children come to participate in it. Babies are born *into language* and, once they begin *using language*, speak *out of language*. These early beginnings therefore are the ground, the material, and the tools with and from which spring forth all subsequent developments. We cannot rid the children of these beginnings, of the experiences that mark them, and the mother's tongue that has become the very starting point of their lives. The mother's tongue will always remain the base layer of the palimpsest onto which all other tongues, dialects, and languages are grafted. This is the fundamental thesis Mikhail Bakhtin proposes for the development of great literature, which, in the case of François Rabelais, was expressed in a language that high culture and modern sensitivities might appreciate as abject. The original language (dialect, accent) is that to which the learning of all other languages (dialects, accents, tongues) refers us back, even and precisely when the other languages constitute another such language (English, French, German). We can always guess at what a word means only to find that there is a bottomless ground that exists before we ever awakened into consciousness.

It is this ground that allows us to found all other languages, dialects, and idioms and the learning thereof. Thus, when teachers or professors of physics introduce students to new idioms about and related to objects in the world, they have to use a language already intelligible to the latter, so that here, too, teaching and learning have to fall back onto some language other than the one to be learned. This is what has been referred to as translating from a language into itself.[2] This other language is the ground, which has to be transformed to become something new beyond itself, in a process that I denote by the term *bootstrapping*. At the beginning, students always bring the vernacular, this other language, to any task that they are asked to accomplish. This vernacular is, in many instances, the antithesis of the new idiom that students are to learn, such as when in the areas of mechanics, dynamics, or astronomy to which students bring vernacular forms that science educators have come to qualify as 'misconception' talk.

When students arrive in our classrooms, they are equally endowed with a history of experiences in the world, including language and other forms of communicative competencies that are the (back-) ground, the material, and the tools that constitute a beginning before the beginning of any lesson. But these lessons, especially lessons such as the one I take as the object of the present inquiry, provide opportunities for development of language. I therefore do not consider this language in terms of 'misconceptions' but rather the opposite perspective: *this language is the very possibility for learning to take place*. The transcript that I place at the center of this inquiry tells us about the emergence of a language about the complementarity of wave and particle models in describing quantum phenomena. It is a weaving together of talk from very different sources, involving propositions about different things in the situation, references to books, and the naming of specific physicists as having said this or that. Similarly, readers come to this book endowed with a history of experiences in the world, including language and other forms of communicative competencies related to learning generally and learning science more specifically. It is precisely these experiences that constitute the reader's ground and tool that work the materials that I present here.

---

2. Abdelkebir Khatibi, 'Incipits', in *Du bilinguisme* (Paris: Denoël, 1985).

Learning by concept mapping and learning by reading a book on the language in concept mapping together constitute kin (reflexive, recursive) processes. I therefore structure the following analyses such that they constitute a 'building up' of issues in the course of the unfolding analysis and, frequently, I return to the 'same' issues repeatedly only to take them to a new level. In the process, I also unfold the full perspective on language that we can derive from Bakhtin and like-minded scholars.

Starting to Map

'Before born babe bliss had'. Language puts language into play. Language begets language. 'The god of writing is thus at once his father, his son, and himself. He cannot be assigned a fixed spot in the play of differences. Sly, slippery, and masked, an intriguer and a card, like Hermes, he is neither king nor jack, but rather a sort of *joker*, a floating signifier, a wild card, one who puts play into play'.[3] Language is the origin, the generatrix, father and son, the more and the less complex. It is the beginning, and it is the development, without an end yet in sight.

The concept-mapping task requires students to produce a two-dimensional arrangement of a set of concept names. The dimensions express hierarchical relations such that concepts 'higher up' are more inclusive for the purposes at hand and those lower are more specific. Concept names appearing at the same level represent the same degree of inclusiveness. The students link the concept names writing verbs on lines between them and thereby produce a network of propositions. These propositions, however, are not yet their own. Students have to rely on the ways of talking that they are already familiar with. The new ways of saying things are subject to the task, are its results, and come to be embedded in the concept map itself. In the process, different forms of language come to be mobilized, directly or indirectly attributed to others. The sources include other participants, teacher, textbooks, and famous physicists. All this talk comes to be refracted in the task, comes to be refracted for the task, being both embodied in it directly and indirectly mediating the process of achieving some final product. But this listing—or any listing for that matter—does not exhaust the competencies with which the students come to the task. Although they do not have a conception of the end result, although the students do not have a mental structure that they externalize in the lesson (in the way concept mapping was originally conceived), the task presupposes that they understand the instructions, the sense of the words involved, how to work with others, how to understand others even in the face of apparent disagreements between the students involved.

Students never come to a situation empty, as blank slates (Lat., *tabulae rasae*). The present students have had many experiences during their 17 years prior to the lesson in which the students to the concept-mapping task are asked to produce the concept map as a scheduled means for reviewing and organizing the main concepts (Tab. A1, see page 291) in the present unit on the particle nature of light. The session follows a se-

---

3. Jacques Derrida, *Dissemination* (Chicago: University of Chicago Press), 93.

Fig. 3.1. The mapping task occurs in a setting filled with traces of their past lessons, including the computers, word-problem solutions, and diagrams. Ken and Ralf are about to begin.

ries of tasks that included laboratory experiments, reading assignments, textbook questions, end-of-chapter word problems, computer simulations, brief teacher presentations, and whole group discussions about quantum theory. At the time of this lesson, the classroom is littered with signs of past lessons, computers are spread throughout, and the chalkboard is filled with graphs, concepts, and calculations (Fig. 3.1).

When Ralf, Miles, and Ken arrive in the classroom on this day, there is an envelope with the 16 concept words, the same that are highlighted in the textbook chapter that is at the heart of the unit that they presently study. Ralf has spread the concept names in front of him on the table (Fig. 3.2a). Ken, already sitting at the table, watches him while Miles, in the background, is just about to join them. Although they have studied the unit on the quantum nature of light for two weeks, they do not yet know what they will end up with at the end of this lesson: a hierarchically ordered and linked set of concept words (Fig. 3.2b). A quick Google search using the terms 'concept map' and 'cognitive structure' provides ample evidence for the fact that many scholars think of these maps as corresponding to students' pre-existing 'mental structure' or as a 'mental structure' that evolves during the concept-mapping task. In this book, I approach the problem differently, as it is quite evident that in all sorts of situations people participate in conversations without ever having thought about the topic before. They therefore *cannot have* a mental structure that allows them to contribute to the conversation or to actively understand what others are saying, because, as it were, mental structure is the outcome, the end result of a constructive process. And yet: students not only can but also do engage in tasks for which they *cannot have* a mental structure. They do not even hesitate but, as this lesson shows, they begin as if producing something of which they do not yet know what it will ultimately look like.

Fig. 3.2. a. Beginning stage of the concept-mapping session. b. End stage of the session, which is completed when the students transcribe the map onto a sheet of paper, which also contains the connecting lines and linking words. Ken sits to the right, Ralf in the middle, Miles on the left from the viewer's perspective.

The recording begins with Ralf articulating not only the concept names but also the first initial connections, 'photoelectric effect is pair production' (turn 001). Linguists and philosophers of language parse such an utterance into two parts, a subject ('photoelectric effect') and a predicate ('is pair production'). The subsequent utterance shows that Ken apparently is not taking up the issue ('put that under quantum' [turn 002]) so that it is fruitless to ask what the 'meaning' of Ralf's proposition is—which can only be evaluated *in this setting* and requires that we have available a social evaluation in and with the subsequent utterance.[4]

Fragment 3.1
```
001 R: plancks constant is (??) ((mumbles)); photoelectric
       effect is is pair production.
002 K: put that under quantum.
003 R: what is quantum.
004 K: what quantum means; are light is a particle instead of
       waves
005 R: but that is quanta;
006 K: yea; its like this;
007 R: and its quanta, its the singular form.
008 K: yes i see what you mean. wave and quantum are an
       instant;
009 R: quantum is part of a wave and then, photon, photon and
       quantum is the same thing.
010 K: they are the same. no no; i am saying if we are going
       downward, this is going down, thats ((WAVE)) one, thats
       ((QUANTUM)) another theory, and this ((PHOTON)) is the
       third theory, it goes here ((below QUANTUM))
```

Ken's utterance, however, becomes the beginning of a problematic that Ralf states in the form of (what we can hear to be) a question, 'what is quantum?' (turn 003). Ken

---

4. A glossary of the physics concepts can be found in the Appendix, p. 292.

has the next turn, 'what quantum means'. By repeating Ralf's utterance almost identically, he provides an indication that what he says pertains to the utterance that it repeats. This also changes the function the utterance has, even if it consisted of precisely the same words. There is, however, a small change. Instead of uttering the statement 'what is quantum', Ken says 'what quantum means' (turn 004). The first change is in the position of the verb, which has traded place with the word 'quantum'. This change, which is a change in grammatical form, is required by the context if it is not the question form that is to be repeated. Thus, the change in grammatical structure signals the coming of a response to what the differently structured utterance proffered as a question. The second noticeable change is that from the auxiliary verb 'is' to the true verb 'means' (notice that the third person form is retained). Ken then produces an utterance that we may hear as a statement 'light is a particle instead of waves' (turn 004). The predicate logic of it identifies the subject ('light') as belonging ('is') to a group ('particle'); the utterance also excludes it as belonging to another group ('instead of') of entities, the name of which is also part of the set of concepts ('wave'). What Ken thereby achieves is a translation or rather an unpacking of the term 'quantum', which is now said to 'mean' 'light is a particle instead of a wave'. Here it is relevant to note that the curricular unit prior to the one on the quantum nature of light deals with its wave characteristics. Thus, in his utterance, Ken provides a context within which the term at issue ('quantum') separates out two aspects of a phenomenon ('light').

Ralf announces disagreement ('but' [turn 005]) and then articulates it, 'that is quanta'. 'That' is a shifter, an indexical term referring something in the context. This context may be the material setting so that 'that' refers to some entity or process. This context may be the preceding conversation so that 'that' refers to something that has been said and therefore is no longer present in its material form. Precisely what it is that 'that' refers to cannot be decided by an outside observer without access to the same kind of practical understanding that allows other members to disambiguate its target. What it is *in this situation* has to be found and therefore indicated by those present in the setting itself. The grammatical form of the predicate helps listeners in evolving their understandings: whatever 'that' refers to is said to belong to 'quanta'. If the listener can make the assumption that 'that' refers to the last statement made, its referent is 'light is a particle instead of waves'. Ralf thereby states that this referent is a translation of quanta rather than quantum as Ken has made it to appear. Ken indicates agreement, 'yea' and 'it's like this' (turn 006). Ralf utters what we can hear as an elaboration of his earlier statement and to the contrast it intends to make, 'it's quanta, it's the singular form'.

This talk resonates the language of the textbook through and through. There is also talk employed reflexively, talk about the word itself, its grammatical nature ('it's the singular form'). This, too, refracts the language that can be found in the textbook, where we find a marginal note printed in blue ink: 'The word quantum, plural quanta, comes from the Latin word *quantus*, which means "how much"'. We find in Ralf's utterance a translation into the reverse statement, rather than talking about one being the plural form of the other, he makes a statement about the second being the singular form of the former. He thereby refracts already existing discourse, which he has become familiar with while reading the book. Ken's utterance 'This is the third theory' (turn 010) articulates what photon stands for, it is a denominative function, it is the name for something else.

The question about what is quantum emerges. Turns 003–004 produce a question–answer pair concerning the nature of the term *quantum*. The second utterance articulates the sense of the term, light existing as a particle instead of in the form of waves. The next turn sequence (004–005) is a statement–contest pair, where Ralf joins Ken with the contrasting 'but' and an alternative statement, 'that is quanta'. 'That' refers the listener to something proximal in the preceding utterance, and the word *quanta* then is heard against the preceding word *quantum*. Ralf continues to elaborate reiterating that 'it's quanta' and whatever else is referred to 'is the singular form' (turn 007). Ken begins with an accepting adverbial 'yes', continues to formulate that he now understands ('I see') what the other means, and articulates what he hears the other to have meant without saying so: 'wave and quantum are an instant'. In the next utterance, quantum is articulated as part of a wave and photon and quantum as alternative expression for 'the same thing' (turn 009). The next turn begins with an affirmation ('they are the same') produced by repetition of the end of the preceding utterance, followed by a disavowal of what has been said, 'no, no', as if there had been a delay in the utterance, its repetition and the understanding. Ken articulates what he has been saying and is attempting to say: wave and quantum are different theories about light.

'Yes, I see what you mean' (turn 008). Ken then utters another proposition with 'wave and quantum' as the subject and 'is an instant' as the predicate. We do not know whether he has the intention of continuing, because, from a grammatical perspective, he might have said 'is an instant of' and then completed with another noun, such as 'light'. Ken is articulating what he is saying, what he has been saying or what he has meant to say. He also articulates what he hears Ralf to mean and then rearticulates it: 'wave and quantum are an instant'. That is, there is a difference between what they say and what they mean to say, and they then express what is meant thereby attempting to bridge the gap between the saying and the said.

How do we have to think about repeated words, which, precisely because they are repeated, also flag a need for repetition? In a repetition we hear the same sound envelope again, which allows us to identify the word as being the same. But it no longer is the same word because it does not have the same function, that is, to stay within a Bakhtinian framework, it no longer refers us to the same *theme*. The repetition does not reproduce *the same*, but it gains particular significance in that it has the first utterance as part of its background. The second time the word is said and heard is different because it has a different background. It 'means' differently because it has a different function. In my Bakhtinian framework, the second turn in a pair constitutes the social evaluation. Without this evaluation, we cannot understand participative thinking or the reigning theme. The most evident but also the most superficial aspects of social appreciation contained in a repeated word are articulated and communicated by means of intonation.

In the opening pages of this book I refer to Dostoyevsky's account of the six workers, who, after a night out, return home completely drunk. One of them uses a swearword, which, one individual at a time, the others repeat. But it is never the same word, because each utterance occurs against the background that includes the others preceding it, and each is uttered with a different intonation, expressing both appreciation for the previous utterances and constituting a new statement itself to be evaluated by the next utterance. In the concept-mapping sessions, repetition may function as an agreement when the social-evaluative part of the turn is pronounced with a descending pitch, as we would find it in a statement of a matter of fact (in the transcription, indicated by a semi-colon or a period). This is the case here, where Ken's utterance begins with a descending pitch on 'are the same'. But, uttered with a pitch that increases toward the end of the expression, it may actually raise a question.

The word, which already is the word of the other, is reproduced in the present situation for the purposes (intentions) at hand. When it is spoken again, it is the word of the first *in this situation*, which now comes to be refracted in the speech of the second person using it. The refraction also includes social evaluation and has particular functions, here to signal agreement. But this agreement, as the unfolding analysis (in this and the next three chapters) shows, may be opened up for renewed inquiry because it has not been and perhaps cannot be finalized.

There is another interesting phenomenon in this first fragment. Ralf is saying what they could say, 'quantum is part of a wave'; and he does so in saying it. In fact, Ralf continues the opening Ken makes in his re-articulation of what Ralf meant to say without saying so (turn 008). Ken initially repeats and thereby confirms Ralf's framing, but then changes ('No, no') and then states what he is saying (has said) without having said so. This is an interesting phenomenon that remains to be appreciated in the learning sciences literature. It is interesting because the use of the word 'mean' signals a transformation at the heart of language, as students hear what others mean to say but do not really say in these words. Or students tell others what they really mean to say with what they have said but not in the same way. This is a form of indirect discourse that allows speakers and hearers to transform, render in different words what has been said and thereby put their own voices into the saying of others. It is both a take-up of the speech of others and a transformation, occurring at the heart of language, which is translated into itself.

Talking (About) the Process

Human beings participate in activities, where I understand the term 'activity' as a cultural-historical process of production rather than as a task that children or students complete in a classroom. Thus, in the present situation, the three students participate in the activity of schooling, which is realized in and by their involvement of a particular task. Human beings also produce sound streams, which we hear and understand as words that take their place in life such that the language of real life and the life of real language are inseparable. This sound stream is a constitutive part of the activity (c, Fig. 3.3). This means that each, sound stream and activity, presupposes the other. A lesson comes about through talk, but the specific talk presupposes the lessons that it constitutes. As part of participating in cultural-historical activities, human beings learn

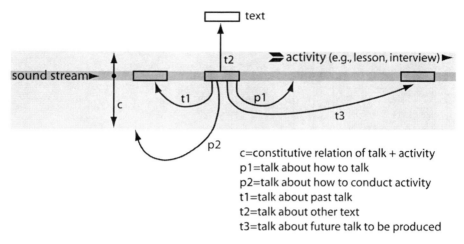

Fig. 3.3. The sound stream (left to right) has very different functions, as general and constitutive *ground* of the activity, as *tool* for talking about other aspects—including other talk, process)—and as *object*, when a text or stretch of talk is the content of talk.

to use this sound stream not just to constitute observation sentences, the human equivalents to birdcalls and the cries of apes, but to 'talk *about*' things rather than to signal situations. Participants in an activity may use language for orienting each other (a) to how they want to proceed (p1, Fig. 3.3), (b) to some text that they want to produce as a result of the activity (t3, Fig. 3.3), (c) to how the activity is presently going (p2, Fig. 3.3), (d) to what they have said before (t1, Fig. 3.3), or (e) to some other spoken or written text (t2, Fig. 3.3) produced within another activity system. Examples for all of these processes are provided as the text unfolds. There are other moments of the activity that are important, such as, for example, the concrete setting—building and room—within which the activity takes place and the furnishing available. All of this constitutes a system of signification within and constitutive of the activity of schooling. This system is recursive and self-referential, as shown in the arrows. Throughout this concept-mapping episode, there is evidence for these different functions of the sound stream for bringing off the session in the form we can observe it on the videotape.

In the following fragment, Ralf first talks about the process itself, 'What about this one?' and then articulates two concept words and a possible relation between them 'quantum *is part of* the wave'. We can gloss a possible hearing of the first part of the utterance as 'What do you think about this one?'. Here the 'this' is an index to the subsequent utterance 'quantum is part of the wave', associated with the movement of the hand that relates the two associated concept labels. Ralf does not state something about a concept but instead asks another individual to express himself about a proposition. Ralf's turn ends with an evaluation, 'quantum is the part that it's the end' followed by the exclamation, 'no, no'. In one and the same utterance, Ralf thereby brings together very different functions of language, a question about process, a proposal for the solution of the current task problem (building a concept map), and an auto-generated social evaluation marking the unsuitability of the offered proposition.

Fragment 3.2
```
011 R: what about this one. quantum is part of the wave.
       quantum is the part that its the end- no. no.
012 K: yea; its different; there is a wave theory,
```

'Yea, its different' (turn 012). In and through Ken's utterance, the turn pair 011–012 is completed. In and through this utterance, we come to know what at least one of the participants has heard, and therefore, we come to know the effect of the preceding utterance. This second part of the turn pair is an evaluation of what has been uttered before and is, according to Bakhtin, an integral part of its function in the conversation as a whole. It is the pair of turns that constitutes a link in the conversational chain. Each pair is a link, because it is implied in the previous pair and implies a subsequent pair. It is only through this second utterance that the sense of any individual word and the statement as a whole *in and for this situation* comes to be known to any third person. This third person may be another participant, but, in the present instance, it includes the analyst (who in this situation was actually present) and the readers of these lines, who are vicarious observers.

Shifters—verbal indexes including 'it', 'this', and 'that'—are used to make a previous utterance part of the present one without actually articulating it. In the statement, 'It's different', the student refers to something that the previous speaker Ralf has said and suggests that it is different. Using a shifter, the speaker in fact asks his listeners to dig through their retentions and find the relevant expression to be made present again. Simultaneously, here, too, there is a social evaluation at work, one in which the current speaker indicates the state of affairs to differ from what has been said before.

The videotape does not allow us to gauge the sense of Miles' comment in this situation, because neither Ralf nor Ken nor the teacher provides a second-turn part. The comment 'don't worry about it' stands alone and therefore has no perceivable role in the development of this conversation—at least not from what is observable in and at this instant. Ken then utters a proposition that has two parts and that can be parsed as 'electron *is* a particle' and 'electron is not a quantum' (turn 014).

Fragment 3.3
```
013 M: ((in the background)) ?? dont worry about it.
014 K: electron is a particle and not a quantum.
015 R: no; there is a wave theory and particle theory but,
016 K: but thats only one transmitted by waves.
017    (4.42)
018 R: quantum says that a wave has not a continuous band of
       energy.
019 M: yea, this should come in front because of those- are
       also discovered first.
```

Ralf contributes the social evaluation, 'no, there is a wave theory and a particle theory' and then begins a contrast 'but' (turn 015), which Ken appears to continue when he says 'but that's only one transmitted by waves' (turn 016). The repetition *makes it appear* as if he is continuing Ralf's utterance, which in fact constitutes the social evaluation of Ken's own previous utterance. A conversational chain link is joined to another conversational chain link. There is a longer pause, which comes to an end when Ralf utters something of an explanation, 'quantum says that a wave has not a continuous band of energy' (turn 018), which Miles acknowledges and evaluates in a positive manner, 'Yea'.

With the statement 'quantum says', Ralf articulates the content of the concept word (sign), the sense in which the term is to be taken. He unpacks the term. He is telling his fellow students and therefore also us, the observers, what the concept is really saying without him actually saying so. He thereby unpacks a bit of the network of significance relations that determine the life of language and the language of life in this instant. It is a translation of the term into a different language, which, here, is nothing but another such English.

'This should come in front because of those– are also discovered first'. In turn 019, Miles continues from his positive evaluation to make a statement that does not articulate a link between two concept words into a proposition but rather proposes an organization of the task where one of the concepts ('this') should be considered in a particular part of the hierarchy ('in front'). By following Miles' utterance with an 'and' in 'and this [LIGHT] is' (turn 020), Ken suggests that something is to be added. He simultaneously provides a positive evaluation of the preceding proposal, to which his own is to be added. Miles clearly marks understanding what Ken is proposing and suggests that this is not an option, 'no' explaining that they had 'screwed that up the last time' and then provides the alternative, 'wave goes on top'. Overlapping Miles, Ralf's utterance constitutes a positive evaluation by repeating the preceding utterance, 'wave goes on top', and then he compounds the positive evaluation by marking its correctness, 'that's right' (turn 022).

Fragment 3.4
```
019 M: yea, this should come in front because of those- are
       also discovered first.
020 K: and this ((LIGHT)) is,
021 M: no remember, we screwed that up the last time the wave
       goes [on top.]
022 R:      [wave go]es on top; thats right.
```

Those concerned with education in content-oriented subject matter, that is, educators concerned with the transmission, handing down, or reproduction of cultural knowledge generally are interested in content-related talk and therefore, with the way in which language is used to make statements within the subject matter domain. This tendency within the field of science education is so strong that research articles that do not squarely address students' content-related utterances may experience difficulties of being accepted in science education journals, 'because the article does not deal with science learning'. Here I take a different perspective. Content learning is only one of many dimensions in and of the fullness of life. There are many other life moments that prop up anything that we can recognize as content learning. Content learning cannot be abstracted from this fullness of life without penalty. This is quite evident in the area of conceptions and conceptual change research where, after years of exhibiting disattention to social or emotional moments of learning, researchers finally begin to consider the role of such phenomena in learning. But these dimensions are add-ons, external factors, which, like all factors, do not change the inner nature of the original phenomenon.

Among the neglected moments is talk about process by means of which, for example, the task comes to be structured, students assign themselves roles, and students produce comments about what has or has not worked in the past. Whereas science educators have often disregarded the role of these other concerns in learning and development, they are, from a cultural-historical perspective, central to the productive process and therefore also to any of its outcomes. That is, these moments are not only central to the productive endeavor, they also mark the product, which, in the present instance, is both the final concept map that the students will have produced at the end of the session and the traces their participation leaves in their bodies. (Not only physical labor but also mental labor transforms the body.) For Bakhtin, it is only out of such considerations of the fullness of life that we can understand individual moments of it, including knowing, conceptual understanding, and learning. Each of these dimensions constitutes, in a Bakhtinian perspective, only a *one-sided* expression of life as a whole. Thus, Bakhtin shows that we cannot understand the evolution of the novel genre by analyzing only novels. Rather, to understand the change in the novel genre we need to study the evolution of cultural life generally.

Although different dimensions in the topic of talk can be identified, all of it occurs in talk. Human beings are in language and speak out of language. There are no 'natural' boundaries within language so that 'different' issues are not naturally separated from other issues. There is therefore no conscious stepping from one issue into another. The change in the nature of topic occurs as a matter of fact and without particular attention and comment. The change an analyst might notice is not even treated as a change by the members to the setting. For example, in turn 014, Ken produces the proposition 'electron is a particle and not a quantum'. It is a statement about the nature of electrons, quanta, and particles. It is a content-related statement. On the other hand, in turn 21, Miles tells his peers that they should 'remember' for they 'screwed that up the last time' they had worked on a map with these terms. It is a comment about the process. When we read from turn 014 to turn 021, there is no marker that the students are aware of any change to have occurred. The conversation is simply unfolding and their talk produces topic, situation, and process simultaneously. We also note that the students use non-formal language characteristic of the fullness of life but that may not be admitted by a scientific journal, in a science textbook, or in to response to an examination question. Thus, Miles says that they 'screwed . . . up'. In chapters 8 and 9, I deal with the issue of the fullness of language and social life, especially their carnal and carnival moments. The tenor of the present argument is that once we take a more holistic perspective on language and life, then we can understand knowing and learning of one of the science domains. This domain, as any other domain, produces a reduced version of language, an idiom, and one that is made official and is turned into a canon to be observed: the idiom including physics concepts.

Dim Stirring of Thought

What follows in the unfolding conversation of the three students are utterances marked by their brevity and their apparent role in the structuring of reality before and containing them. When I first analyzed such talk nearly two decades ago, I was frustrated as a teacher, because I could not see the concept talk and grammatically well-structured sentences that the researchers of conceptions and misconceptions used as data in the science education literature. I thought that my students and I, their teacher, were deficient because of it. Today I understand the issue differently. Thus, I understand the abbreviated talk as a form of public 'inner' speech, in fact, a collective form of abbreviated speech normally characteristic of inner speech. We might, paraphrasing Vygotsky, articulate this inner speech as 'verbal thinking that announces a thought in its first stirring'.[5] In *Thought and Language*, Vygotsky is mostly concerned with individuals, though, admittedly, in the very last pages of this book he acknowledges that any consciousness, inherently enabled and mediated by language, is consciousness both for the self and for the other. He suggests that the word is a thing in human consciousness that is impossible for one person and only becomes a reality for two. Bakhtin takes the same position and suggests that the word always exists between two people and cannot ever be reduced to an individual. However, in *Thought and Language*, the 'stirring of a thought' and its subsequent development are discussed only from the perspective of the individual, who, in speaking, produces resources that mediate thought, and who, in thinking, produces resources for speaking. The two, thinking and speaking, are separate but mutually constitutive processes related by another process. This other process Vygotsky calls *word meaning*. Because of the inherent problem with the word 'meaning', I stay away from using it and, where appropriate, use Bakhtin's equivalent term *theme*.

In the current situation, the discussion of 'inner speech' has to be enlarged to the group level, for the students no longer think for themselves but they think together and for one another, and, in this, draw on language that always is the language from and for the other. Thought and ideas emerge at a collective level and are developed by the collective. To deepen this analysis, I take in chapter 7 the double perspective on the evolution of one concept from both individual and collective perspectives. Here, however, we continue to follow the group in its endeavor to get off the ground with their task.

Thinking with and for the others takes, in the present context, the abridged form of inner speech that Vygotsky has been writing about in *Thought and Language*. Vygotsky notes that inner speech is for the individual, whereas external speech is for others. Inner speech is essentially and purely *predicative* in nature and does not have the nor-

5. Lev S. Vygotsky, *Thought and Language* (Cambridge, MA: MIT Press, 1986), 217.

normal sentence structure. Inner speech is not external speech minus sound but has a very different structure and function. Nevertheless, because all higher cognitive functions are internalizations of previous societal relations, it can be observed in everyday situations. For example, pure predication is observed when in responses to questions ('Yes', 'No') or in affirmations. Thus, among several examples from the preceding conversation, we find Ken responding 'yea' (turn 006) to an utterance in which Ralf asserts something about a previously stated relation, 'but that is quanta' (turn 005). In this situation, the 'yea' is predicative, which is possible only because all participants understand that the utterance is related to the previous utterance. The full statement therefore might be glossed as 'yea, that is quanta' where the index 'that' is understood to the previously articulated situation. Ken's 'yea' is one such instance of predicative language here used both for his peers as much as for himself. The following Fragment 3.5, as many turns in the process of the production of the concept map, is full of predicative utterances, consisting of one-word statements or of sentences that are incomplete when measured against the standard grammar of written English.

Fragment 3.5
```
023  M: okay. photon.
024  R: in pair production are all the different things here,
025  K: they are different.
026  R: photoelectrons.
027  K: get all the;
028  M: i am so sweaty.
029  K: complementary?
030     (.)
031  R: complementary?
032  M: look around the guy
033  K: complementarity.
034  M: well what type? uh, jesus, we should put x=rays up here
         with the light, like that. should we put x=rays there?
035  R: yea, okay. work function (.) if work function (.)
         [photon and],
036  M: [we need    ] something,
037  R: quantum are the same.
```

From the perspective of written language, which some science educators champion to be a way of learning subject matter ('writing to learn'), there is little in Fragment 3.5 that can be compared to the normative language of scientific texts. However, it is clear that all the utterances have pragmatic function. There would be no sense to talk at all if whatever is said did not have a function in moving the event along. In talking, the students move this session forward, and what they say marks out sense *in* and, significantly, *for this situation*. Even though the students may not appear to be talking to on another, each utterance marks for others what an individual is attending to, such as when Miles utters 'okay, photon' (turn 023) or both Ken and Ralf say 'complementary' with an increasing pitch (turns 023, 031). In fact, we can hear this as an 'exchange', because Ken (incorrectly) reads aloud from one of the slips (COMPLEMENTARITY) 'complementary', which, because of the rising pitch can be heard as in the gloss 'so what do we do with this "complementarity"?' Ralf apparently repeats the utterance 'complementary'. But his repetition has a different intonation than the first utterance, and therefore its function is different. By saying 'photon and quantum are the same' (turns 035, 037), Ralf points out that one can be used in lieu of the other, one expressing the other, one as being synonymous with the other, or one can be translated by the other.

Although little appears to occur, we need to understand this part of the conversation as constitutive of the process from which the ultimate map and student learning emerges. I know first hand that these students will remember this particular session 18 months later, and they even remember particular accomplishments and parts of it. I understand these students as doing what Maurice Merleau-Ponty might describe as 'taking up a position in the world', a world that is itself becoming in and through their actions. They organize the setting; and language is one of the means by which they do so. But this does not necessitate that we seek the reasons for the language in a person's brain. For 'even as verbal speech may first become word in the brain of man and then become sound in his thought, although both are merely refractions of the true event because in truth language does not reside in man but man stands in language and speaks out of it'.[6] All three participants to the situation stand in language and speak out of language in the same manner. But, because they are at the beginning of their session, they are, to use an analogy, like persons in a dark room that they do not know. To be able to accomplish anything like producing a map, they need to grope, grope things, grope out, and grope their way. It is in and through all of this groping that they come to have a world, in which the final concept map is a constitutive part. In the process, they come to develop a language; and there is no longer a difference between knowing this language and knowing their way around this world. This is so because 'It is not the word name but the structure of the language that preserves the whole system of human practical actions with objects, actions in which objects speak for themselves, with their own voices. It is the structure of the language that reproduces the structure of the actual life of society'.[7] Because the students are starting completely 'in the dark' about what their final result will be, we cannot expect much more than a groping in and with language. Rather than deploring this language, as those concerned with getting students to reproduce scientific language in the 'right way' might do, I want us to celebrate it as the real competence it constitutes and exhibits in making a world where at the moment there is little else that they can go by.

It is this groping that constitutes the 'dim stirring of a thought', which, like a seed, lays the ground for something to emerge, though this initial language does not *determine* what will come thereafter and what will come forth as end product. But it is this dim stirring at the collective level, where words—in any case ideological and societal, even as inner speech—are for the other, mark engagement, raise questions, seek attention, and so forth.

In Fragment 3.5, there are two other aspects that require further attention. In turn 028, Miles utters 'I am so sweaty'. This statement apparently has nothing to do with the current task of mapping 16 concepts from a chapter on the quantum nature of light.

---

6. Martin Buber, *I and Thou* (New York: Simon & Schuster, 1970), 89.
7. Felix Mikhailov, *The Riddle of Self* (Moscow: Progress, 1980), 219.

Moreover, in turn 034, he says 'Jesus', a term often used as part of swearing. Both aspects of language and content are not normally discussed in the science education literature yet repeatedly turn up in the transcript exhibited here and in everyday life more generally. They are expressions of the life that the students currently experience. These terms should therefore deserve our attention even if the official ideology of schooling and of science education research bans such language and content as matters of interest or relevance. Bakhtin, however, makes repeated claims about the need to understand limited domains and their development in terms of the fullness of life, its carnal and carnival principles. I tend to these issues in chapter 8, providing a very different picture of what it means to transform (one's) language and to learn a new language, even if it is, for English speakers, but another idiom of English.

In Fragment 3.6, we are confronted with a new phenomenon: the name of a famous person is introduced to the conversation ('this one was, this one done by Planck' [turn 040]). The name is that of the German physicist Max Planck, who contributed in significant ways to the development of quantum theory. Here, Planck is credited with something that he has done. Although saying that someone has done something is different from saying that he has said something followed by indirect speech attributed to him, the very utterance of the name of a famous scientist has a function that we need to understand in its function on the unfolding of the conversation.

Fragment 3.6
```
038 M: no; this one ((points to PHOTON)) should be a bit
       lower.
039 R: why? its the same; they are exactly the same.
040 M: this one was, ((QUANTUM)) this one done by planck; and
       this ((PHOTON)) one,
041 R: yea; but this is essentially the same.
```

In the present situation, we do not know the function of this name, because the subsequent turns do not appear to take it up. In turn 041, Ralf says that 'this is essentially the same', where he repeats his own utterance in turn 039 almost identically, although he changes 'exactly the same' to 'essentially the same'. This may in fact soften the claim, because something that is *essentially* the same does not need to be *exactly* the same. Two plum trees are essentially the same, although they might look very differently in any concrete situation. I return to the issue of the function of naming physicists, which is similar to my own attributing phrases—in directly quoting or paraphrasing—to Bakhtin, Hegel, Heidegger, or Vygotsky.

Repetition and Difference: A First Return

One of the important aspects to both Vygotsky and Bakhtin is the repetition of words and longer utterances. In the work of both, the repeated word, though apparently the same, no longer is the same because it has a different function the second, third, and fourth time from the one it had when it was articulated for the first time. The function of a word, the theme it marks in any given situation, cannot be found in the word itself but in its relations to the other words and the situation as a whole. It can only be found in its role within the language of life, where language actually has a life and is inseparable from life. Take the following example. A repetition of the word 'complementarity' occurs in turns 045 and 046, and the same word is repeated in a one-word statement in turn 048. This fullness of life is also available here, when, in the turn following Ralf, Miles makes a statement about having played Frisbee. He then repeats the statement in turn 044 but adds 'so I'm so tired'. Although his two peers do not say anything in response, we do know that in subsequent instances there are repeated interactions where the results of his playing of Frisbee, the fact that he is sweating, comes up and plays a role in the unfolding event. All the references to sweat and having played Frisbee are analyzed in chapter 8.

Fragment 3.7
```
041 R: yea; but this is essentially the same.
042 M: because, i just came back from playing frisbee.
043 R: look at this here.
044 M: i just played frisbee, so i=m so tired.
045 K: complementarity?
046 T: complementarity?
```

The two utterances are not the same, for the second one is uttered after the first one has already been completed. The pitch rises as the sound unfolds and proceeds toward the end, allowing us to hear it as a question. The second utterance 'quotes' the first, takes it up again, this time being proffered by the teacher. It, too, is uttered with a rising pitch, which indicates a question. But the two questions are not the same. In the first instance, we can hear something as glossed by 'So what are we going to do with complementarity?' or 'What is complementarity?' The second utterance, however, we do not hear as if it has been said independently of everything else. Rather, we hear it as following a first occurrence, of which it also constitutes an evaluation. Moreover, this second time it also *projects* a new response. Thus, the second time we may hear it as 'So what about complementarity?' or as 'What is your question about complementarity?' Whereas the first utterance indicates a question related to the term, the second requests an articulation of what the problem is.

Fragment 3.8
```
047 R: was in the theory ((turns pages))
048 T: what did it have to do with bohrs principle?
       complementarity.
049 M: i can=t remember that at all.
050 R: i heard something about,
```

In this instance, the teacher uses the past tense to refer to the relation of 'it', to be heard as referring to 'complementarity', and Bohr's principle. That the 'it' is to be heard as a repetition of 'complementarity' becomes evident when the teacher rearticulates the concept name on a descending pitch, following the first part of the utterance that ends with 'principle' and on a rising pitch. It is something that has been talked about before or that the students and teachers read (together) somewhere else, 'What did it have to do. . .'. So the two concepts have been the topic in the classroom before and the teacher requests a re-articulation of the relation. Miles is the first to respond, suggesting that he 'can't remember that at all'. His use of 'that' points to something in the previous utterance that he cannot remember, the topic or theme of what is being articulated in and with language. The evaluation provides us with a clue to the fact that participants themselves hear turn 048 as a question to remember something ('what was it about') and the concomitant admission not to remember anything at all. The second response does articulate having heard something about it—leaving open what the 'it' or its referent is.

Repetition and difference is central to my thinking—here pertaining to the work of Bakhtin particularly but also to Vygotsky, but similarly addressed more recently in the writings of Jean-Luc Nancy, Jacques Derrida, and Giles Deleuze—of how cultural change is internal to culture. If the second utterance of a word not merely repeats it but constitutes a change, a new resource, a new function in the unfolding of culture, then there immediately exists a process internal to the cultural life of a language that makes language and life change. No longer required are forces, exceptional individuals, time, or other mechanisms that make cultures and societies change, but change is a result of the very existence of the phenomenon. The idea is a familiar one, having been associated with Heraclites and his statement about the river into which one cannot step twice. However, in philosophical thought, difference and repetition have come to be central only during more recent years. The following quote points us to the fullness of life situation that Felix Mikhailov, Maurice Merleau-Ponty, and Martin Buber take as their units for analyzing anything like language. 'Repetition is a condition of action before it is a concept of reflection. We produce something new only on condition that we repeat—once in the mode which constitutes the past, and once more in the present of metamorphosis. Moreover, what is produced, the absolutely new itself, is in turn nothing but repetition: the third repetition, this time by excess, the repetition of the future as eternal return'.[8]

This quote teaches us that introducing new words when the old ones available no longer suffice is but one of the outcomes of repetition and difference. In the following fragment, students query whether they may introduce additional terms to be included into the concept map and therefore into their language. But in its absolute novelty to the conversation, the concept word already has been pre-figured in the current talk so that it already constitutes a repetition in the way Deleuze proposes: as excess over, but already pre-figured in, a previous present. As such, the new concept word 'energy' would be an object of talk and linguistic material for producing the concept map. It would also be constitutive of the ground of the language that serves the students as the very constitution of the world that they are asked to navigate and structure. In Fragment 3.9, Ralf notes that there 'is no energy here'. Miles orients himself to the teacher and asks, 'can we add terms'. That is, the first statement is treated as articulating the lack of something, a 'term', to be included in building a map; and the second turn simultaneously asks for the addition of a term and thereby acknowledges its lack.

---

8. Gilles Deleuze, *Difference and Repetition* (New York: Columbia University Press, 1994), 90.

Fragment 3.9
```
051 M: okay threshold frequency. hey- we should put the work
       function; he can=t find it; put the work function and
       threshold frequency together because they are related;
       but,
052 R: there is no energy here. ((turning pages in book))
053 M: doc, can we add terms? (1.70) doc? (0.75) can we add
       terms?
054 T: yes you can.
055 M: yes (0.40) because we want the energy?
056    (0.34)
057 T: energy; yea.
```

Here, Ralf articulates what can be heard as a statement about the current state of affair: the absence of a paper slip with the term 'energy'. The statement is confirmed in the second part of the turn unit, when Miles queries the teacher ('doc' = Doctor, the teacher) whether they could add terms. Again, this is the first part of a sequence, the questioning nature of which is confirmed in the subsequent turn 054. Miles elaborates, 'because we want the energy', and the teacher completes the turn by affirming it: 'energy, yea' (turn 057). In this sequence of turns, we also see that the absence of the term energy is confirmed not only by several students in whose utterance the absence is affirmed, but also by the teacher who accedes to the request to add ('want') energy. The teacher first affirms that they can add, and then, in his next turn, utters on a falling pitch 'energy; yea'.

Here, too, we have a repetition of the term; and here, too, repetition changes the signifying relationship of the word to the lived context. Miles' utterance may be glossed by means of 'we need the term energy to build our concept map'. The teacher, in going next, produces the evaluation. It begins by ascertaining that the term in question is energy and ends with the statement 'yea', which here can be heard as 'you can add the term energy'. In fact, the utterance of 'energy' may have sufficed as an affirmation that they can add this term. But despite an affirmative intonation, uttering 'energy' alone might have been left uncertainty whether the term may or may not be added. The 'yea' not only completes the turn pair but also doubles up the affirmation. Here, too, the function of the first occurrence is that of articulating the required item for the teacher, and the function of the second occurrence is to ascertain that it is the term. This term then is articulated as one that may be added.

Finally, there is repetition within Miles' utterance. In the sound stream he produces, the words 'doc' and 'can we add terms' are produced twice. The second time, these evidently have a different function. The situation has changed. Why might Miles have repeated himself within the same utterance? It may sound commonsensical that a person repeats calling on someone if s/he has evidence that the person called upon has not heard. This is especially the case when, as here, there is a pause between the two, which means that the other has not responded within the 1 second that is normally realized as the maximum pause length between turns. Repetition here gives a different function to the particular words, and therefore to the signification in situation.

Repetition and difference are central to the understanding of linguistic development and, therefore, of learning. Linguistic development is contingent, as we cannot know what future forms of English, French, German, or Russian will look like or even whether they will die out (as ancient Latin) or whether they will live in multiply transformed ways, in the way that Latin resonates in modern languages, particularly Romance languages. Bakhtin's description of the development of genre here serves me as a proper analogy for thinking about language more generally. 'A genre is always the same and yet not the same, always old and new simultaneously. Genre is reborn and renewed at every new stage in the development of literature and in every individual work of a given genre. This constitutes the life of the genre. Therefore even the archaic elements preserved in a genre are not dead but eternally alive; that is, archaic elements are capable of renewing themselves. A genre lives in the present, but always *remembers* its past, its beginning. Genre is a representative of creative memory in the process of literary development. Precisely for this reason genre is capable of guaranteeing the *unit* and *uninterrupted continuity* of this development'.[9] That is, Latin is both dead, as language proper, and alive, in the Romance languages to which it has given rise. Aristotle's scientific language is dead, but it continues to live in the language of physics to this day.

We can understand the development of students' language in the same way: We consider their root genre to be the vernacular that they are familiar with, their everyday idiom. This idiom is transformed and transforms itself, as part of participation in schooling, to produce new forms of genre, some of which may be characteristic of, bear family resemblance with, the sciences, mathematics, or history. Because every scientist develops in this way, and because the sciences themselves historically developed out of the vernacular, the vernacular genre itself is the *foundation* of science, although much of the vernacular comes to be abstracted in the written forms that are employed in the (natural, social, mathematical) sciences. The vernacular is the ground, the material, and the tool for anything like scientific language to emerge at both at the collective and at the individual level. It therefore makes very little sense to aspire 'eradicating' some of the vernacular, the part expressing itself as 'misconceptions', because it constitutes an integral part of the vernacular taken as a whole. It is, to paraphrase Felix Mikhailov, not the word name that is related to the world but the structure of language as a whole.[10]

Teachers and Teaching

No cultural reproduction can be considered without thinking about the role of teachers. 'What is the role of the teacher?' 'Of course', readers might respond, 'they teach students so that the latter know and can repeat cultural-historically developed knowledge and skills'. Institutionally, teachers take an important role in society, contributing to the reproduction of its past acquisitions and accomplishments and, in so doing, to

9. Mikhail Bakhtin, *Problems of Dostoevsky's Poetics* (Minneapolis: University of Minneapolis Press, 1984), 106.
10. Felix Mikhailov, *The Riddle of Self* (Moscow: Progress, 1980).

the 'immortality' of society. How this occurs is a function of what one considers the process of learning to be. Within behaviorism, it does not matter what changes occur on the inside of learners (underneath their skulls, between their ears) as long as they do what others think they ought to do. The rat model, common in the biological and medical sciences, also has been (and sometimes still is) used in the social and psychological sciences. Teachers provide the stimuli and the rewards by means of which students are coaxed into exhibiting successful behavior.

Ideas about teachers and teaching have changed in and with the cognitive revolution largely taking place during the 1980s. In this approach, the uptake and the processing of information become important. Teachers are held responsible for providing the information and for teaching by whatever means the procedural skills that allow students to process the information they are also asked to retain ('store' in 'long-term memory'). The downfall of the research in this paradigm comes with the failure to heed the early theories of information processing, which point out that sender and receiver need to be tuned in the same way for information transmission to be possible. It is quite evident that students who do not know what is to be learned cannot be tuned in the same way that the teachers and textbook authors are. What is information to the teacher is nothing to the student, because, to paraphrase Richard Rorty, it is only when the students speak the language of the science that they understand the significance of the language itself generally and the significance of individual words in the constitution of the whole more specifically.[11]

Even more recently, conceptual change theory and constructivism have dominated science education. In conceptual change, the rational approach taken in the sciences, as shown in studies of the history of science, is believed to be the way in which students learn. It is held that there has to be *dissatisfaction* with current ideas for describing and theorizing the world, new ideas and theories have to be *intelligible* and *plausible*, and these new ideas and theories have to promise *fruitfulness* before the uptake of and reorientation to new concepts and theories occur. What the researchers in this domain do not realize is that dissatisfaction requires attunement to ideas that are not working and to possible new ways of understanding. However, even though another theory is intelligible and plausible, this does not guarantee its uptake. In the fullness of life, there is more involved than the rational decision between abstract alternatives.

To teach according to conceptual change principles, teachers are asked to disrupt students' ways of thinking, to 'eradicate' the old forms, and to facilitate the uptake of new theories. But, as I emphasize throughout this book, the vernacular language that students bring with them to school constitutes *all they have*, that is, the students' *ground on which to build, the material to be used in building, and the tools with which to build*. Moreover, in constructivism learners are said to 'construct' 'frameworks' that they test and then maintain or abandon according to the viability principle. But it is precisely the teacher-intended framework that students cannot see, hear, and grasp, because doing so requires the framework itself. This is the aporia: 'How and beginning with what do we form an image of that which we do not know?'[12] How can stu-

---

11. Richard Rorty, *Contingency, Irony, and Solidarity* (Cambridge: Cambridge University Press, 1989).
12. Michel Henry, *Incarnation: une philosophie de la chair* (Paris: Seuil, 2000), 120.

dents 'construct' something that they cannot have an image of and therefore cannot intend? Well, there we have another different framing of the learning paradox. I am not surprised that there has been a lot of confusion about what teachers are to do, especially because constructivism is a theory of learning, not of teaching. As a science teacher, before knowing many theories at all, I did not find radical constructivism a viable theory for understanding what is happening in my classroom and therefore never took to the theory.

Fused with ideas about knowledge of collectivities, social constructivism is to allow students to 'construct' knowledge together and then to 'construct' it for themselves. How this process is to occur has not been articulated to my knowledge, at least not very well. Especially how students are to construct something first together in the absence of having it already constructed individually has, to my knowledge, never been addressed. This question, however, goes to the heart of the learning paradox. Thinking about learning in terms of learning to speak a language by participating in speaking it—where the mother tongue generally and the vernacular more specifically already constitute a linguistic foundation—has become a fruitful idea to me, first as a teacher and subsequently as a researcher. So what is the role of the teacher when he, in this instance, begins to think about learning physics as learning to speak a language? I introduce some of the salient issues in the following first exchanges between the three students and their teacher and then make teacher–student conversation the central focus of chapter 4.

A first function of the teacher within this unfolding conversation can be gleaned from the end of the preceding Fragment 3.9. Here, after articulating the absence of a concept name (Ralf), Miles turns toward the teacher, names and thereby addresses him ('Doc'), and utters, 'Can we add terms'. Although uttered with a falling intonation—which would indicate a statement rather than a question—the teacher responds affirmatively, 'yes you can', thereby treating the statement as a question.

Grammatically, it would have been more appropriate to ask 'may we add a term?'. This is so because, in the query, the student already presupposes that he can and he seeks affirmation from the teacher that what he does is an indication of his ability. Pragmatically, this grammatical consideration is irrelevant, because in repeating part of the utterance, the teacher affirms that they 'can' (may) add a term to the set of 16 terms that they already have. Miles elaborates, 'because we want energy' (turn 055), which the teacher confirms to be the term in question, 'energy, yea'. Pragmatically, therefore, the student and the teacher achieve a four-turn request–permission sequence, in which the student asks permission, elaborates a reason for the request ('we want energy'), and in which the teacher signals permission by repeating this accord.

In this exchange, the participants do more work than simply requesting and giving permission. They also achieve, again, the institutional difference between someone who is asked for permission and the person who is asking for it. Control over the task thereby is conferred to the adult, and the younger person is constituted as subaltern. It is clear that Miles initiates the turn sequence and that therefore he plays an important role in the production of the particular relations between the different kinds of participants. This is clear in chapter 8 when I turn to some of the exchanges and actions between the three students themselves, in which the carnal and carnival nature of life comes to play. This carnival nature of relations generally is not observed between the adult (the 'teacher') and the teenagers ('the students') in this classroom. In its formality, these latter relations reproduce the formality of the subject matter. To this particular aspect of carnival and the formal I also turn to in chapters 8 and 9.

The conversation continues with two additional contributions that remind us of the carnal and carnival aspects of life, which, for the most part, are not apparent when 'serious students' engage in science lessons. Reading the transcript and viewing/hearing the recordings do not provide evidence that any 'code switching' or any other 'switching' is occurring. There is no evidence of strong or weak cultural boundaries that either students cross or that allow one culture to leak into another. Turns 058 and 059 can be taken to constitute evidence for the fullness of life in which students find themselves, and that does (is allowed to) appear because the students do not repress it at this instant. Not suppressing the fullness of everyday language may mean violating the restricted and restrictive genre of science, and this, too, is part of the analysis I provide in chapters 8 and 9. The simple presence of a teacher may mediate the presence of this language, therefore making invisible to researchers the real processes underlying the use and transformation of language in science conversations.

The three students then continue in the predicative manner that has characterized their language to this point. Ken utters 'the index, is not in it, yea, yea, okay'. Miles follows, 'we can put diffraction' (turn 062). Ralf, repeating the word and thereby making reference to the preceding utterance, says 'diffraction was in' (turn 062); and Miles follows through by uttering 'is kind of'. We can hear this turn as providing a link between the 'diffraction' in the preceding turn and something else. But Ken provides a negative evaluation, that is, he realizes an offer/proposal–rejection turn. The two then articulate in express form what the rumination turns out, 'diffraction is out of place' and 'it doesn't belong here' (which he repeats when Ken asks about its location 'where, diffraction'). Ken then completes his evaluation, 'no, yea' and elaborates it, 'photon can diffract of all sorts of thing' (turn 069).

Fragment 3.10
```
058 R: god, what a-
059 M: i am swimming in sweat in this- ((still turns pages))
060 K: the index, is not in it, yea; yea; okay.
061 M: we can put diffraction-
062 R: diffraction was in;
063 M: is kind of,
064 K: no.
065 R: ((mumbles something))
066 M: diffraction is totally out of place, it doesnt belong
       here.
067 K: where, diffraction?
068 M: i dont think it belongs here.
069 K: no, yea, photon can diffract off all sorts of things,
       cant they?
```

We do not know what this exchange might have evolved into if the teacher had not appeared at the table uttering what will be concretized as a question–response pair. A fact is that Ken uses both a negation ('no') and an affirmation ('yea'), the second immediately succeeding the first. Yet we can hear it as an affirmation in two consecutive predicative forms, as rendered in the gloss, 'No, it does not belong here' and 'Yea, I agree'. This hearing is further confirmed by the statement that Ken then produces, 'photon can diffract of all sorts of things', which might serve as a justification for diffraction to be associated with 'all sorts of things' (turn 069). Ken appends 'can't they' to his statement, thereby allowing uncertainty to enter. He offers the possibility to be wrong, though we do not know whether others agree or disagree because of the rupture in the conversation that occurs when the teacher approaches and engages with the students.

This interruption is itself the result of interactional turns, which may, but do not have to confirm, the different institutional status of a person who arrives in some place, interrupts an ongoing conversation, and begins a new topic. For whatever more or less legitimate reasons he might have had, the teacher proffers a question, 'have you got complementarity' (turn 070), which Ken concretizes by offering a response, 'no, it is not even in the index' (turn 071). In the second part of the two-turn unit, Ken states that that 'it is not even in the index' (turn 071). He does more than respond 'no, we don't have this term yet built in'. He gives, in fact, a description that he has already searched for the term in the index. Although the three have not been talking about complementarity, it does become the topic in and through the turn sequence that follows. Ralf does not appear to take up the new topic, as he produces another predication. Moreover, there is an evaluative element, 'it is *not even* in the index'. It is possible (though not necessary) to hear this utterance as a complaint that the teacher has included a term that is 'not even in the index'.

Fragment 3.11
```
070 T: ((Coming from another group)) have you got
       complementarity?
071 K: no; its not even in the index.
072 R: concept;
073 T: what was the whole chapter, what were the last two
       chapters about?
074    (2.46)
075 M: quantum, well, the last chapter about quantum and
       photon and,
076 T: yea, and that before?
077 R: oh, i think that is the duality of wave.
078 T: exactly.
```

The teacher then offers another first turn of a question–response unit, 'What was the whole chapter, what were the last two chapters about?' The teacher uses the past tense, 'What *were* the two chapters about?' (turn 073). The topic and its articulation are something to be recalled, the things have already been read and talked about. The teacher thereby asks for a repetition, for a reporting of the speech or its content of earlier conversations and readings. The unit is completed in the next turn, when Miles utters 'quantum, well the last chapter about quantum and photon' (turn 075). So in this turn, the two collaborate in articulating and in making public the theme of the last chapter. But there is more to it. The teacher not only offers a first part in a question–answer unit, he also completes a previously begun turn unit. Here, it is both a self-correction of the previous question and an evaluation of the two preceding student turns. These have not yielded the second part that the preceding utterance offered as a first part to the question–answer unit. That is, we could gloss the situation as one in which students do not answer the teacher's question. The teacher then engages in a repair sequence to articulate the question in a different way. This reading is confirmed in the next two turns at talk.

First, the teacher and Ralf together establish the topic of the preceding chapter, one of the two chapters that the teacher asks about, a question that is only partially answered when Miles suggests the thematic content of the latter of the two chapters. An evaluation follows. In fact, we have here a classical initiation-response-evaluation (IRE) sequence, where the teacher asks students to recall something (initiates), the students respond, and the teacher provides the evaluation ('exactly'). Second, Ken repeats Ralf's utterance, preceded by an expression of realization (recognition, surprise). We may gloss the possible hearing as 'Oh, yea, the duality of wave was the topic of the chapter'. Third, the teacher then articulates what the students are really mean by saying 'duality of wave'. He provides a gloss and therefore produces yet another way of saying what has been said differently: 'You are talking, complementary means that the two, that wave can have both, but not both at the same time' (turn 080). After a brief and partially overlapping interjection, the teacher notices that the issue at hand, complementarity, means 'either one or the other' (turn 082). In this, he also and further translates 'can have both, but not both at the same time'. The teacher therefore offers yet another way of saying 'the same thing' but in different words. Ralf completes the turn unit by articulating the implication of the previous statement, 'and you have to decide which one you want to use'. The teacher and students thereby realize a re-voicing, which is also a transformation, of the statement in their textbook, which states that 'to understand a specific experiment, one must use either the wave or the photon theory but not both'.

In turn 085, the teacher employs the indexical term 'that' to bring the preceding student utterance into his sentence without actually repeating it, and then provides a social evaluation by uttering the predicate 'is right'. However, in adding 'but it depends on your particular experiment' (turn 085), he qualifies that which precedes. That is, by saying 'which one to use depends on your particular experiment', he glosses the statement that one has to decide which of two options to use.

Fragment 3.12
```
079 K: oh. the duality of wave;
080 T: so you are talking, complementary means that the two::,
       that wave can have both, but not both at the same time.
081 K: ah; [so thats],
082 T:     [either  ] one or the other and complementarity
       means (.) either one or the other.
083 R: and you have to decide which one you want to use.
084 M: ah, okay.
085 T: yea, thats right, but it depends on your particular
       experiment
```

```
086 M: no, it should go-
087 K: no, go under light, perhaps
088 T: remember that you can show, you can do experiments that
       show wave [character ].
089 K:             [are x=rays].
```

'Remember' is an index to something that has been said-read-heard-seen before. It is a request to make present again, to re-present, and therefore to repeat something that has been present at some previous instant. It is a way of articulating the content of previous talk or the talk itself. It is a reminder of something that has been heard or read before and now is reproduced in indirect speech, 'remember that *you can show, you can do experiments that show wave character but the same experiment doesn't show both*' (turns 088, 090). The italic part of the teacher quote provided here is the reported speech, which constitutes a translation, a paraphrase, or some other translation in the teacher's own words of something that has been said or read in the past.

Fragment 3.13
```
089 K:             [are x=rays].
090 T: but the same experiment doesnt show both.
091 K: are the x=rays proven particles, are x=rays both energy
       and particles because complementarity- if thats proven
       as energy and the particle can go over this; but if its
       not, then we go with light.
092 T: why, why, for example, do you have x=rays and light?
093 M: because they are both waves, they can both travel in
       waves.
094 T: and they are both electromagnetic waves.
095 R: thats right.
096 K: actually, x=rays;
097 R: so thats a-
098 M: yea, so have i, let me think, this electron, electrons,
       have gotta go up by the photon, no-
```

In turns 092–094, we possibly observe a familiar pattern that has been described in the literature about turn taking, institutional roles, and the reification of structure: teacher initiation–student response–teacher evaluation (IRE). The sequence might be heard as an IRE sequence, as the teacher asks students why they have x-rays and light. In the present situation, however, it asks the students why they have the two terms at the same level. Miles provides an answer, 'because they are both waves' (turn 093). This turn pair can be heard as teacher question–student answer pair. But the next pair does not take the pattern student response–teacher evaluation, at least not in the often-reported form of a 'yes', 'no', 'right', '(in-) correct' statement. Rather, the second part of the pair begins with the conjunctive 'and' followed by a restatement of what the preceding student just said, 'they are both . . . waves' (turn 094). In this, the teacher—by *repeating* (part of) the student utterance in a descending pitch that makes the utterance a statement— can be heard as confirming the previous student answer. But there is more. The teacher adds the adjective 'electromagnetic'. The utterance therefore is not merely repeating what the student has said but actually transforming it in the process of repetition, adding another element that here takes adjectival form. The utterance has been transformed and the common nature of light and x-rays as electromagnetic radiation has been highlighted (in and as of being said). But the social evaluation now comes from a student, Ralf, who, following the teacher, says 'that's right' (turn 095). The teacher asks a question to which he does not yet have an answer, that is, why the students put the two at the same level (turn 092) and it is a student completing the sequence stating that the teacher is right in his understanding (assessment) of the situation. This, then, is clear evidence for the non-realization of an IRE sequence, which in fact constitutes a Bakhtinian *finalization*, but a truly dialogical inquiry, where the answer is not yet given in advance of uttering the question.

We can appreciate the events in this section in very different ways—and this may be an ethical rather than analytical issue. On the one hand, the teacher can be said to have done what he is paid for. He has engaged the students, leads them through a particular relevant topic, and monitors their ways of speaking about the topic of complementarity and the quantum mechanical nature of light. On the other hand, one can imagine other trajectories that this event might have taken, thereby turning it into a very different one indeed. For example, the teacher might have joined the group, listened, and then engaged with the students over the topics that are currently salient to them. On the other hand, he might have discovered trouble surrounding the paper slip inscribed with COMPLEMENTARITY and the utterance 'complementarity' while overhearing other groups and, for whatever pedagogical reasons, might have determined that an intervention then and there would (might) be propitious. Thus, rather than waiting for the students 'to spin their wheels' or 'to go down a blind alley', he might have decided to intervene even at the cost of interrupting their conversation, hijacking it, and shifting it to a new topic. In this, he would have reasserted and reified knowledge/power differences between school staff and school 'clients'. But because my concern here lies with understanding the events rather than measuring them against ethical standards external to the situation, I do not take the high road by conferring judgment. I stick with clearing the way for understanding how these students and their teacher produce the lesson. In the course of this lesson and as its result, students come to have experiences that they will subsequently remember for a long time. I will come to detect the changes in these students' language in the essays (on light, on physics as language) and examinations that they write in the weeks and months following this lesson. We do note that the conversational topic changes, from an initial intervention, which then develops into a conversation about various aspects surrounding the complementarity principle. It is in responding to the repeated teacher advances that the topic comes to be changed; and it is in and through the repeated query–response sequences that the traditional division of labor that exists in schools is reproduced.

Signification and Theme

One of the most abused terms in the literature on learning is 'meaning'. An important task that educators have yet to address, therefore, is the way we ought to understand the term. Educators often write or say something like 'students have to construct the meaning of a word', 'the word has meaning for a student', or 'a task is meaningful'. What the 'meaning' of 'meaning' is, however, remains without clarification.[13] If we were to follow Ludwig Wittgenstein, we would not look for the 'meaning' of words but we would be concerned with how words are used. If we were to do this with the statements just articulated, we would say that 'meaning' is something like a characteristic or a property that a word can have or cannot have. It is something that is not inherent in words but something that students can make. Something like a word or situation is meaning*ful* when it is full of 'meaning', 'has' 'meaning'. But all of this does not explain to us what 'meaning' is. Vygotsky does and simultaneously does not help to clarify the term. He writes about 'word meaning' as mediating between word and thought. Word meaning, according to Vygotsky, constitutes a unit that cannot be further broken down. It is an amalgamate: One cannot tell whether it is a speech phenomenon or a thought phenomenon. Thus, to 'understand another's speech, it is not sufficient to understand his words—we must understand his thought. But even that is not enough—we must also know its motivation. No psychological analysis of an utterance is complete until that plane is reached'.[14]

Vygotsky is in agreement with Bakhtin about the fact that both word and thought are developmental processes. The same is the case for the relationship between the two: *word meaning* itself develops. Word meaning therefore is not something constant, a specific property attached to a word, but something that changes together in and with thinking and speaking. These changes are observable at different temporal scales, from the turn taking at the micro-scale to time scales characteristic of individual development (ontogenesis) and to cultural-historical time scales. Turning away from the overused term of 'meaning', we may adopt Bakhtin's theory of the word. Accordingly, the word and the social situation are indissolubly related. A word therefore has different significations (senses) that a dictionary describes, and it is associated with something else that is particular to each and every situation, its thematic unity. Which of the different dictionary senses is associated with a particular word depends on the situation. Finding the signification of the word is a problem that speakers solve in pragmatic manner, or rather, it generally is a non-problem. We hear the utterance 'It is nice today' without having to ask ourselves which of the 44 different senses of 'nice' listed in the Oxford English Dictionary is relevant to the situation. The thematic unity of the situation collapses the signification into one, but it does not equally collapse what the function of the utterance is, whether it is meant sarcastically or ironically, whether it is a pick-up line or a rejection of an advance, and so forth. Bakhtin calls the dictionary senses that a word takes, thereby following Ferdinand de Saussure, its *significations*, which he defines as the lower limit of the signifying capacity of the word.[15] In this, Bakhtin therefore is very close to Wittgenstein: the sense

---

13. Using an ethnographic study of graph interpretation 'in captivity' and 'in the wild', I articulate the problematic nature of the concept of 'meaning'. See Wolff-Michael Roth, 'What is the Meaning of Meaning? A Case Study from Graphing', *Journal of Mathematical Behavior*, Vol. 23 (2004), 75–92.

14. Vygotsky, op. cit. note 5, 253.

15. Mikhaïl Bakhtine [V. N. Volochinov], *Le marxisme et la philosophie du language: essaie d'application de la méthode sociologique en linguistique* (Paris: Les Éditions de Minuit, 1977).

of a word is a function of its use in concrete situations. The sense is that which is reiterable across situations, which is precisely the reason why it can be defined in a dictionary way independent of any particular situation and often without examples.

The 'something else' associated with a word in situation, Bakhtin calls *theme*. It is irreducible and historically contingent; it is singular and 'once-occurring', to use another Bakhtinian concept. The theme is singular because 'content/sense abstracted from the act/deed can be formed into a certain open and unitary Being, but this, of course, is not that unique Being in which we live and die, in which our answerable acts or deeds are performed; it is fundamentally and essentially alien to living history'.[16] Thus, the theme is a reaction of a developing consciousness to Being, the world as it presents itself, itself in the process of becoming. The thematic unity makes salient the noted fact that the life of language and the language of life are indistinguishable. The theme, therefore, cannot be derived from an analysis such as the ones Jay Lemke provides in *Talking Science*, which, in its focus on structural relations, is in pursuit of the iterable parts of language in use. At this point, to paraphrase one of the most important modern philosophers, Donald Davidson, there is no difference between knowing a language and knowing your way around the world.[17] The theme constitutes authentic, active understanding of the situation as a whole. It is a concept only comprehensible within a dialogical approach, as the *theme* of an utterance already contains within it the sketch of the response, the next turn. The thematic unity, the situation as understood in and by a living consciousness, determines the particular sense that a word or utterance is taken to have in the moment. This particular sense is therefore not in the word (sound complex) or in the soul of the speaker or in the soul of the listener. The particular sense of the utterance *in this situation* has to be understood as the effect of the speaker–listener transaction on the given sound complex.

As articulated in the preceding paragraph, the theme in Bakhtin's work is equivalent to the *word meaning* in Vygotsky's work. It is the grasp of consciousness over the situation as a whole, including the motivation or rather, the collective motive that allows making sense of individual actions and goals at hand. Because the theme requires the active understanding of the participants, the relevant motive and goals are the collective ones. It is precisely for this reason that the sense or specific signification of a word is the lower limit of the signifying capacity of language, whereas the theme is the upper limit of the same process.

The thematic unity is given by the specific situation in which the students find themselves. Throughout the concept mapping sessions, the three articulate for others the sense in which some word or utterance should be taken. In each case, a translation is involved. In the first 100 turns at talk, students use the verb 'mean' four times, and they will use it 10 more times in the remainder of the session. Here, they generally use the verb to mark that they articulate a particular sense in which a word or expression is or is to be used. But there are other ways in which this is done as well. In Fragment 3.14, Miles queries 'What's pair production?' and Ralf, in uttering 'Pair production is

---

16. Mikhail M. Bakhtin, *Toward a Philosophy of the Act* (Austin: University of Texas Press, 1993), 8.
17. Donald Davidson, 'A Nice Derangement of Epitaphs', in *Truth and Interpretation* edited by Ernest Lepore (Oxford: Blackwell, 1986), 433–46.

when . . . it creates matter' (turns 107, 109), reifies the turn pair as a question–answer sequence as an assertion about the dictionary sense of the term.

Fragment 3.14
```
099 K: the electron- we=ll put-
100 R: momentum of the light, what do you think?
101 K: the electrons are,
102 M: wave, putting that over there
103 K: no; electrons are photoelectrons; so they are back
       there.
104 R: i see.
105 K: so its under photoelectric effect.
106 M: electrons, threshold frequency. whats pair production?
107 R: pair production is when,
108 K: compton effect by x=rays.
109 R: when it creates matter;
110 M: thats right, compton effect deals with x=rays that
       should be just up there. wait, compton effect is when
       it hits and it hits the electron, it hits the electron
       so the electron should be up here.
```

The students articulate what something means when they find a description such as 'it hits and it hits the electron' to the concept name 'Compton effect'. The named effect 'is when' the description provided is true. The lower limit of the relation between the two, the signifier and the signified is signification (i.e., the much-abused 'meaning') and the upper limit, which cannot be reduced to the utterance itself but to the *practical-understanding-in-context*, is the theme. Bakhtin asks us to focus on the understanding of an utterance but to do so sociologically, that is, to approach the utterance as something between and connecting speaker and hearer. Accordingly, only active practical understanding on the part of the listener can grasp theme. Active listening means orienting oneself toward practical understanding in context, which is always an understanding of how the world works including the language that is a constitutive part of it. To practically understand someone else's utterance therefore means that I have to orient myself with respect to the situation as a whole. It means that I have to situate myself in the presently relevant context.

A practical understanding of the situation including the relation of the utterance and words constitute the theme of the latter. Long ago I read an article in which the authors provide the example of children who know the dictionary sense of words but who, in concrete situations, use them inappropriately. I find the same phenomenon among graduate students who speak English as a foreign language, and who, looking up in dictionaries, frequently choose inappropriate words from among the possible translations of some word in their native mother tongue. That is, they select an inappropriate one from the list of possible senses; but in so doing, they miss the theme. Understanding the theme in which a word takes a constitutive part, however, means that a student practically understands the situation as a whole, and, conversely, practically understanding the situation as a whole also frames the thematic unity in which specific words have a place. In this case, a student is actually in a position to provide an alternative word or utterance that has the same function in this situation. Educators and educational researcher therefore often say that a student understands or knows (the 'meaning' of) the word.

This has implications for theorizing what some researchers call the 'construction of meaning'. In fact, students have to construct nothing. To practically understand the situation they have to be familiar with it; and familiarity with the situation provides a place for the word. It is not that students have to construct 'meaning', whatever this concept name might refer us to, but that they have to become familiar with the appropriate placement and use of words in concrete situations. Initially, a student might use the language of another, in direct speech, and subsequently, report what others have said or written in indirect speech. The utterances within which students use the word change; students therefore experience the different themes in which a word may be involved and have its place. Because whole situations are characterized by their motives, practical understanding of a situation therefore means that an individual can articulate appropriate intentions with respect to its unfolding. Educators like to quote or paraphrase Bakhtin in such instances in saying that students making use of words for their own intentions. We find evidence for a particular stage of such transformations in the following fragment, when Ken articulates the sense of the term 'Compton effect'.

The fragment begins with Miles' articulation of what the term 'deals with' and what it 'is' (turn 110). Ken announces the emergence of a contrast ('but there are'), but Ralf and Miles, respectively, take the next slots in the sequential order of turns. Ken then begins again, providing an articulation of the 'Compton effect' in his own words, that is, in words that have previously come to him from others but that he has become so familiar with that using or reflecting on them no longer requires any effort.

Fragment 3.15
```
110 M: thats right, compton effect deals with x=rays that
       should be just up there. wait, compton effect is when
       it hits and it hits the electron, it hits the electron
       so the electron should be up here.
111 K: but there are,
112 R: god, i forgot so much.
113 M: compton effect is right there.
114 K: compton effect is just when the x=rays. its like proven
       that x=rays act like particles also, like they are
       photons. so also the compton effect says that it allows
       the lower frequency to come through.
```

In turn 114, Ken no longer uses direct or indirect speech that reproduces the words of others (textbook, teacher) to articulate what the word name denotes and therefore what at least one of its senses might be. In the sciences, ambivalence and polysemy do not constitute appreciated features of language. The sciences constitute, as Bakhtin says, a monological form of knowledge; that is, there is a right, scientific way, and there are wrong, non-scientific ways.[18] There can be no debate. There exists therefore

---

18. Mikhaïl Bakhtine, *Esthétique de la création verbale* (Paris: Éditions Gallimard, 1984), 383.

a collective endeavor designed to reduce the polysemy of any term to such an extent so that there is only one sense left. In such an instance, the sense of a word would be 'clear' and 'unambiguous'. The textbook reads: 'Compton proposed that the incident X-ray photon was acting like a particle that collides with an electron in the metal'. Following an evaluation statement ('its like proven that'), Ken articulates some of the facts that can be parsed from the textbook sentence: 'X-rays act like particles' and 'X-rays are photons'. The textbook further states: 'the photon bounces off an electron, emerging with lower energy'. On the preceding textbook page we find the statement that 'these photons had a lower energy, they also had a lower frequency'. That is, the same photon emerges but at a lower energy and frequency. Now, in Ken's utterance we find these statements in a new form, that the Compton effect allows the 'the lower frequency to come through' (turn 114).

The nature of words as integral to themes rather than as determinable from the senses that a dictionary might provide can also be seen in the next fragment. Here Ralf again takes up the talk about the word 'complementarity' (turn 115). In this utterance, he states that 'to describe light you have to decide with complementarity'. He does not refer to a decision that they have to make at that instance, but rather describes a situation in which a researcher is forced to choose between two options ('with the complementarity'), which description (theory), to choose. That is, the researcher has to decide whether the phenomenon, here light, acts as a wave or acts as matter does. The decision described here therefore is not one on their present plane, but at a very different plane. He does not talk about his peers ('you') have to make a decision, but rather, some actor has to decide which of the two models (sub-theories) to employ.

Fragment 3.16
```
115 R: this one here- and to describe light you have to decide
       with the complementarity- if it acts like a wave or- as
       matter.
116 K: and thats where- that goes to [matter wave;  ]
117 M:                               [you know what] we should
       have light on the top; have, [have wave]-
118 R:                              [no; wave ] stays on the
       top.
119 M: [no, i know.]
120 R: [because its] the most general.
121 M: no, but if we have light on the top, we could put wave
       down here so we could have matter and all the way down,
       matter waves
       [we get particles]
122 K: [or we can make  ] our own, own [things up. ]
123 R:                                 [we can also]-
124 K: matter waves and energy waves- we can make our- a
       reason to make energy wave one-
125 R: ((mumbles)) light waves ((pause)) ((Ralf arranges))
126 K: because you already made the arrow up and not putting
       the wave on top.
127 M: thats what i said
128 K: so, wave is the most general, put that on top.
```

```
129 R: particle production; photoelectric effect; matter
       waves; ((reads from slips with these words))
```

The students go back and forth about 'matter waves' and 'waves'. Miles notes repeatedly what they should or could do (turns 117, 121). The actions he describes are on their plane, the one in which they live and actually make decisions. The students exhibit practical understanding of these differences, because if there were any misunderstandings salient, they would make this the topic of their talk. Alternatively, if there were undetected differences in individual practical understanding, these would be irrelevant to the unfolding conversation at this point in time. Only those resources matter to the conversation that the interaction participants actually make available to and for each other (as well as for and to themselves). Each person acts as if there is mutually shared understanding of each word until such a point that the differences are noted. One such situation of possible misunderstanding is addressed in Fragment 3.16. In turn 122, Ken utters an alternative to what has been said by using the contrastive 'or', which he follows up by saying 'we can make our own, own things up'. A reader who is not in the situation might read this turn in this sense: Ken articulates the liberty of making up relationships in their own way. Neither Ralf nor Miles appear to be responding, so that Ken, after uttering something about matter waves and energy waves, states a reason 'because you already made the arrow up and not putting the wave on top' (turn 126). Miles affirms that he has said that (see turns 117 and 121 where light is said to go on top and wave subordinated to it). In fact, he has said that already, as the past tense that he uses indicates. That is, rather than 'making things up', however you like them, he proposes to choose an alternate route. Light is currently on top of the hierarchy and there is an arrow upward from wave, which, according to the conventions, means that the link has to be read upward and against the hierarchy, the dispreferred option in this task.

Ralf reads the words printed on the paper slips, thereby reporting them again, uttering them for the situation at hand. What is the purpose of the reading? One way of hearing his reading is in terms of questioning what to do with word names. Simultaneously, he lets others know what he is attending to—which they can because they are all competent in perceiving the ink trace MATTER WAVES and the sound 'matter waves' as being 'the same'. The predicative form he employs leaves open and underdetermined the function of these utterances. But simultaneously, nobody asks the question about the event in which they participate. They thereby exhibit to each other that they understand the situation and all aspects of it, including the single-word utterance reading of individual labels. Each word constitutes a bridge between the individual and collective, communicating to others aspects of the situation, forms of attention, and also communicates the individual engagement even if the precise content of this engagement might not be known or available. What is important to the situation and what propels the event are the materials each student makes available for the other, including indications of their mutual understanding of the event and the current state of the task that their engagement pushes toward completion.

Miles begins the next fragment with the attempt to recall the name of the scientist who theorized matter waves and then utters 'What's this?', which Ken reifies as a question in articulating the scientist's name ('de Broglie', turn 131). In the course of the fragment, the students utter further concept names and repeatedly the name of another physicist, '[Max] Planck'.

Fragment 3.17
```
130 M: matter waves deal with this guy- whats his?
131 K: de broglie. ((figured on the page in Ralf's book))
132 M: okay, where are we gonna toss plancks constant?
133 K: it deals with practically all of them.
134 M: its gonna be on top, because its pretty important.
135 K: under complementarity.
136 R: its connected, see kinetic energy is either plancks
       constant times frequency or electrons or ((looks into
       book, p.713)) because kinetic energy (??)
 ((interlude on racism))
137 K: what is pair production up there?
138 R: its the creation of matter.
139 K: where would matter waves go, though?
140 R: matter waves is, for example, an electron if it travels
       or even when we=re-
141 K: no, i understand now, wouldnt it be right under this?
       complementarity theory because thats like quantum?
142 M: no, matter waves deal with this guys wavelength.
143 R: make it, lets do something here-
144 M: take ends here;
145 T: ((Comes out of background)) why would you for example
       single out wave to go on top?
```

The production of short utterances continues. Sometimes a student proffers a question and another one reifies it as such by completing a question–response sequence of turns (e.g., turns 137 & 138, 139 & 140, 141 & 142). In this instance, the inquiry is completely dialogic in its form, where questions are raised, and others respond to them; and all this moves the task ahead, develops practical understanding of the situation, the task, and the concept names involved. This part of the session ends when the teacher appears again at the table of this group after having, thus far, spent time with another group.

In reading along, careful readers may have noted the transcriber's (my) comment about the 'interlude on racism'. This note appears in the electronic transcript, which I produced in 1992 from the original, handwritten transcript produced in May of 1991. In the original there are several lines in which the students talk about and accuse each other of racism, quite apparently in a joking manner. At the time of my first analysis, I deemed irrelevant to science education this 'interlude' and several others that would occur. As a teacher-researcher, I had much more pressing concerns, for example, the fact that the language students use is so abridged, and that they use a language in which I could not discern any 'conception' however hard I tried. It would take me another decade of intensive research to note that this form of 'abridged' language is actually the norm and is not deficient at all. It would take me a second decade before I came to realize that the 'interludes' and 'off-topic talks' are as, if not more important to understand the learning of science in terms of language. But analyzing the tapes at the time allowed me to become sensitive to the fact that however abridged, students use the language *as a sufficient means* to communicate, frame problems, and find solutions. *There is nothing deficient about what they do and we, science educators, need to be able to appreciate the* productive *dimensions in such talk.* This talk is an aspect of situated communication, including other forms (e.g., prosody, gestures, body movements and positions), in which the situation as a whole provides the semiotic (sense-making) resources for getting done the job at hand. Today I realize the theoretical importance for attending to such 'interludes', because they can tell us a lot about the world as the participants, here the students, live and experience it. Because I am interested in better understanding learning as mediated by the fullness of life rather than in terms of the words laid out by some official curriculum guideline I address interludes together with instances of laughter, joking, and the references to carnal (bodily) matters in chapters 8 and 9.

Talking the Talk, Change, and the Self-Organization of Learning

In this book, one of my fundamental concerns lies with the learning paradox, whereby students cannot intend to construct the knowledge and 'meaning' specified in the curriculum and in teachers' planning books because the intention is a function of the knowledge students are to learn/obtain *as a result* and at the end of instruction. In this book, I suggest that this requires a bootstrapping process that lies outside the intention of the individual student or the teacher. In the ppresent chapter, I show how the concept mapping starts and introduces some fundamental concepts that I am working with. Inherently language is a dynamic phenomenon, which produces itself anew each time it is used. That is, change is inherent in praxis and in participation. Change is apparent even if precisely the same word names are produced again. The problem therefore is not change. Change is inevitable. Anticipating what will change and how it will change, however, is a very different question.

Repetition and difference play an important role in this conceptualization of language and linguistic phenomena. This is so not only since Gilles Deleuze's book of the same name, *Repetition and Difference*, but is embodied in a history of thought from the early Greek (Heraclites) to Friedrich Nietzsche and Mikhail Bakhtin. Friedrich Hegel and Karl Marx, too, contributed to the current-day understanding of difference in and for itself and its relation to repetition. Marx in particular saw development to occur when some abstract idea, like a seed, concretizes and particularizes itself and, in so doing, gives rise to the articulation of possibilities that themselves become seeds—or cells—to subsequent developments into different forms. It is an evolutionary principle that underlies this form of thinking, a diversification of forms beginning from a single ancestor. Language is but one of these phenomena, continually transforming itself in the very act of reproducing itself. The neat part of the idea is that because language never reproduces itself identically, transformation is introduced to its very nature. It is like the quintessential river of Heraclites, which is never the same. Even the scientific language changes, though scientists may think that their language is constant once it has achieved the correct form. The sciences transform themselves, the languages and genres they admit, despite themselves; and they do so because of the inner nature of speaking and working in and with a language as such.

A second major point of this chapter is that (spoken) language is not a phenomenon that can be theorized independently of the situation in which it is produced and reproduced in and as concrete utterance. Although dictionaries may list the different senses of any given word, the *particular* sense in which it is used in a concrete situation depends on the situation itself. Moreover, new senses not yet recorded in a dictionary may continuously spring up. That is, the dictionary sense is only the lower limit of the signifying capacity of language. What matters pragmatically is the upper limit, the theme, which figures fundamentally in the practical consciousness that parallels the material world constituting its dialectical and dialogical complement. This consciousness and the corresponding active, participatory, and therefore dialogical understanding refer us to both the relation between the material and ideal aspects of the world and to the relation between the members to the setting.

A third point I introduce in this chapter is the tension that arises for a teacher who espouses the knowing-a-language-is-knowing-your-way-around-the-world metaphor and dialogism as the fundamental process of knowing. How can such a position be reconciled with the declared goals of education generally and science education in particular? These goals are about inducting students into particularly limited forms of discourse (idioms) that are abstracted from the broader experience of life, its intentions, motives, goals, intentions, emotions, embodiment, and ambiguity, that is, from its carnal and carnival aspects. We do see in this chapter that even with the best of intentions, when a teacher is wedded to the idea of helping his students to be successful in their future, more monological forms of thinking and acting come to be reproduced. Here, the adjective 'monological' is used to note a single idea or a single sense rather than something pertaining to monologue, which, as I show in subsequent chapters, may be dialogical in character. I also show how the institutional position of the teacher do not have to be enforced by him (alone), but are collaboratively produced by ('willing', 'motivated') students.

In this chapter, I also refer to the collective endeavor that reduces polysemy—a phenomenon Bakhtin terms the dialogism—inherent in words. The fact that the natural sciences tend to reduce the word also means that they attempt to abstract it from its normal state of language as such. But this is next to impossible, as conceptual change researchers have found, because students continue to use everyday words and descriptions to talk about natural phenomena. Terms such as 'force', 'velocity', 'impulse', 'heat', 'temperature', and 'energy' are variably used in the English language, although they tend to have an extremely limited sense when used in physics or in other natural sciences. Not only are there different senses possible in everyday language, as opening any dictionary will show, but also there are innumerable and ever-changing, neverrepeating themes in which an individual word may find and take its place. We therefore need to understand learning science as learning how to speak a particular form of English (French, German, Russian), a particular idiom or dialect, that is, as an exception rather than the rule. From this perspective, I therefore do not think that speaking of 'code switching' is particularly useful when theorizing classroom conversations where students talk about physics (science) and about other things. When science students do speak about topics other than the sciences, we have to understand the situation in terms of a carnivalization of the situation, which essentially means opening up and increasing polysemy rather than eliminating it. Words and utterances are then used in a carnivalized way and relativize what they are presently doing and to recontextualize it in a more complete world. I return to these issues particularly in chapters 8 and 9.

4

Teaching is Translating

An integral part of the learning paradox is the relationship between teacher, who is already 'in the know' about the subject matter, and the student, who has not yet mastered its idiom. If we think the situation in terms of language, the teacher—physics, chemistry, biology, or earth sciences—speaks a specialty language, an idiom or dialect, particular to the field. However, in popular parlance and as a means to denigrate an article in the peer review process, specialty language is often referred to as *jargon*. Now students attend a course in some subject precisely to acquire its specialty language, its jargon, or perhaps dialect, idiom. But the student does not speak and understand the specialty language, the jargon, the language of the insider. How can they (we) learn another language, a specialty language, or a jargon if we do not already have the potential to understand it? For learning physics is not different from learning a language other than one's mother tongue. How does one learn German or French if one has grown up in the prairies of the US or Canada where English is the only language around? And how does the teacher have to speak to teach others this foreign language?

This analogy of people learning a language given that they already know another language may have a shortcoming in that it does not allow us to easily think the situation whereby in learning to speak a scientific dialect it is not only the language that we have to acquire but also an entire segment of the world that does not yet exist for us. Language speaks, which, when we attempt to understand language out of language, means that language points out ('to say' derives from the Indo-Germanic *sek̯-, to point, to notice, to see). We can think of the situation of a newborn baby, who eventually comes to speak a language. But it does not have another language as a starting point, which it could draw upon to interpret what is coming along its way. It comes to know the language and the world simultaneously in and through participation.

In the case of school or university students, the analogy of learning another language holds up. But a paradox remains, for the things of physics and their names go together. How do we come to know what 'phonons', 'quarks', 'baryons', and 'flavor' are? Knowing to use the words and knowing the situations in which it is useful to deploy them go hand in hand; there is no difference in knowing this language and in knowing one's way around a corresponding physics laboratory (office). How can we learn this language given that we do not know the things these word names denote, and knowing these things means knowing their names? The paradox arises from the fact that we can be spoken to only in a language that we already understand or have the potential to understand when we hear it for the first time. What happens in such a case is that 'each word of a difficult text awakens in us thoughts that belonged to us before, but its significations sometimes connect in a new thought that recasts them all'.[1] Merleau-Ponty suggests that in listening to others, in understanding there is therefore a taking up of others' thought through speech, a reflection in others, a power to think according to others that enriches our own thoughts. Speaking means is hearing; our speaking requires that we have always and already heard before.

Pragmatically, of course, people have always solved the problem of learning another language since, according to the Bible, the ultimate deity punished humans for their hubris of wanting to build a tower that reaches the heavens: 'God seeing what the people were doing, confused their languages and scattered the people throughout the earth'. But humankind coped so that there always have been translators, though the very fact of translation raises problematic issues because no two languages together with other cultural practices structure life and being in the world can exist in the same way. For some time now I have been thinking about the problem of teaching in terms of *Sabir*, the Portuguese variety of Lingua Franca, spoken in the Mediterranean and along the routes of Portuguese merchants outside the Mediterranean basin. The basis of this Lingua Franca is Romance, with inflections dropped and syntax simpler than that of the standard languages from which it drew. Because its vocabulary differed from place to place, meeting the particulars and needs of the contexts in which it was employed, it is advantageous to think of Sabir in the plural, not as *a* language but as a group of languages. In fact, philosophers of the late-20th century—including Jacques Derrida, Jean-Luc Nancy, and Paul Ricœur—ask us to think of every language as a multiplicity, which allows the translation of language into another version of itself.

Once we accept language as a multiplicity, which makes possible translations into another version of itself, teaching can then be understood as occurring at the boundary between two languages. The first language is that which students speak when they arrive in our courses, often their mother tongue. The second language (literally) is the disciplinary language of the subject matter, the specific dialect that makes this discipline different from all others. Thinking like this will allow us to anticipate an experience that anyone has had migrating to a foreign nation where another language is spoken. The resulting conversation contains words and grammar from both, adapted to the needs of all members to a setting. In the school (university) context, this means that the emerging *Sabir* suits the teacher, concerned with teaching students to learn a new language, and the students, who come with very different levels of competence in the language to be acquired. A dialogical relation therefore comes to exist at the very heart of the English (French, German) language, where the vernacular and the scientific dialect are continually translated into one another, giving rise to *Sabir*, which

---

1. Maurice Merleau-Ponty, *Phénoménologie de la perception* (Paris: Gallimard, 1945), 208.

literally means 'to know'. Speaking *Sabir*, we come to know; in speaking *Sabir*, we articulate our knowing and understanding.

Monological and Dialogical Talk

Concept-mapping tasks have been used for assessment purposes to find out what is in the students' minds. But the collaborative concept-mapping exercise may also be seen as a means for allowing students to learn by putting the concept names from a textbook chapter into relation. In the present instance, it is the capstone task in the unit on the wave and quantum nature of light. For this teacher, however, there exists a tension. Although he is concerned with allowing students to develop forms of talking with and about the concepts, he is also concerned with their well-being and future development. It is not, therefore, that students should evolve *any* form of language. Whereas he might have been able to live with such a situation, this is in the declared interest of *these* students and their parents, who have aspirations to go to college and university. Thus, the teacher wants students to develop discourse that others in the sciences would be able to find acceptable. Some of these students explicitly hold him accountable to those forms of discourse that are acceptable and 'true'. These students want to attain this discourse to be able to enter the university program of their choice.

When there is a truth, a form of language that is used as a measure toward which development is aimed, Bakhtin terms it monologic, characterized by one form of logic, ideology. By the term 'monological talk', he does not mean monologue, just as by the term 'dialogical talk', he does not mean dialogue. Rather, for Bakhtin at issue are ideas. If there is only one idea, often personified in the speaker or author, then he uses the adjective 'monological', thereby marking that there is *one* voice, *one* big idea. On the other hand, he uses the adjective 'dialogical' to characterize multiple ideas—in Dostoevsky often personified in and by different personalities—that 'battle it out', are confronted with each other, challenge each other, and transform one another. This is precisely the formulation that Jean-Luc Nancy uses to characterize what happens at the inside of a multiplicity, whether this multiplicity is a culture or a language.[2] The different voices work each other, transform one another: A multiplicity inherently is a dialogical phenomenon, a mêlée.

Many researchers confuse monological talk and monologue and, similarly, dialogical talk and dialogue. Dialogical talk may in fact be found within one and the same person, such as when Raskolnikov, the protagonist of Dostoevsky's *Crime and Punishment*, confronts very different ideas and very different voices in his opening internal monologue. Bakhtin notes, 'That was not a psychological evolution of an idea within a single self-enclosed consciousness. On the contrary, the consciousness of the solitary Raskolnikov because a field of battle for others' voices, the events of recent days . . . reflected in his consciousness, take on the form of a most intense dialogue with absentee participants . . . and in this dialogue he tries to "get his thought

---

2. Jean-Luc Nancy, 'L'éloge de la mêlée', *Transeuropéennes*, Vol. 1 (1993), 8–18.

straight"'.[3] This idea of the field of battle is precisely the one that Nancy refers to as the mêlée. In contrast, scientific discourse is one-sided, characterized by rhetorical seriousness, rationality, singular sense, and dogmatism. These are precisely aspects for which Bakhtin retains the use of the adjective 'monologic(al)'. It is in contrast to the carnival sense of the world, which is all encompassing, all of its parts in dialogical relations, generative, producing development and growth. The carnivalistic sense of the world is contradictory, sublating[4] any dualism one might think of. Whereas I deal with the carnival aspects of language in this classroom in chapters 8 and 9, I focus in this chapter on the monological discourse of the sciences and the tensions this creates for a teacher interested in teaching consistently with dialogism. Bakhtin's discussion of the evolution of the Socratic dialogue can teach us a lot about the two forms of talk and about teaching generally and the teaching of science more specifically. He writes that '[i]n Plato's dialogues of his first and second periods, the dialogic nature of truth is still recognized in the philosophical worldview itself, although in weakened form. Thus the dialogue of these early periods has not yet been transformed into a simple means for expounding ready-made ideas (for pedagogical purposes) and Socrates has not yet been transformed into a "teacher". In the final period of Plato's work that has already taken place: the monologism of the content begins to destroy the form of Socratic dialogue. Consequently, when the genre of the Socratic dialogue entered the service of the established, dogmatic worldviews of various philosophical schools and religious doctrines, it lost all connection with a carnival sense of the world and was transformed into a simple form of expounding already found, ready-made irrefutable truth; ultimately, it degenerated completely into a question-and-answer form for training neophytes (catechism)'.[5]

It is not difficult to create a link between Bakhtin's description of Socrates the teacher, expounding ready-made, irrefutable truth and the aims of current schooling, to achieve high scores on international comparisons and high-stakes examinations, where the standard answers *constitute truth* for the purposes at hand. We can understand the carnival sense of the world as what geneticists call the 'wild type', the typical form of an organism, strain, gene, or characteristic as it occurs in the natural world. Scientific discourse is a mutation in which much of the wild type has been abstracted and only specific characteristics have been retained, though the fundamental aspects of language—e.g., phonetics, syntax, and semantics—are retained. Characteristically, the genetically modified animals not only differ in their genetic make up, but, as a well-known researcher working with knock-out genes recently told me, they have been inbred to such an extent that behaviorally they are incomparable to their wild kin even if the mutation has nothing to do with this behavior. This 'wild type' language and human behavior is what I am interested in (see chapters 8 and 9) as the 'natural form', which, in some instances, is accessible to us in situation where only the domesticated ('disciplined') forms of language ought to be present.

---

3. Mikhail Bakhtin, *Problems of Dostoevsky's Poetics* (Minneapolis: University of Minnesota Press, 1984), 88.

4. The verb 'to sublate' means both to overcome and to keep, store.

5. Bakhtin, op. cit. note 3, 110.

The dialogical means of seeking truth is counterposed to the official monological means of science teaching. When the truth to be arrived at is unknown, the inquiry is dialogical, but when the truth is given and known, the inquiry is monological. In the conversations that go with the concept-mapping task, we can see the dialogical forces operating principally while students are talking among themselves. But, when the teacher is present—though not always—talk becomes oriented towards a monological conception of the language around the quantum nature of light. The teacher presents and represents this monological voice of science, a dogmatic worldview, which generally puts away with the carnival sense of the world. Yet, this is not always the case, for the teacher is present when students talk about other things, joke with each other, and the students talk in a carnival manner oriented toward the teacher. In the following section, I take a close look at one 'intervention', a situation where the teacher has joined the three students and remains with the group for about six minutes. It will turn out that he does not take interactive turns with students all of the time, but frequently, after having participated in the unfolding give and take, seems to take a step back listening to the unfolding conversation only to enter it at a later point in time.

On Teaching as Translating

As we watch the video in a first-time-through manner, we do not know what the teacher has in mind when he approaches the three students and when he addresses them in a way that they reify as a question. We do not know whether he has any goal other than that to engage the students at the very instant that he actually does this. All we can know is precisely as much as is available to students: the teacher's arrival at their table and the utterances he produces. All we, analysts, have available is exactly what the students have available in this situation. Equally, we do not know what the students are thinking independently of what they make available to and for one another or to and for the teacher. We do not know whether he intends to conduct an intervention. Again, all we know is what he makes available to students and, because of the recording, to any video-mediated vicarious witness.

Arriving from somewhere in the background, the teacher addresses the students about the location of WAVE ('Why would you single out wave to go on top?' [turn 145]). This is the concept name that they have just been discussing and have decided that it should be on the top of the hierarchy (Fragment 3.16). Here the teacher offers up what could be a first turn of a question–response turn. To such a question, he does not and cannot have a preformatted answer because he has not been with the group to overhear the reasons that they have been generating for the different placements. This opens an exchange, which we may gloss in this way: 'the teacher seeks students to reflect upon the relationship between wave and quantum'. The result of this extended exchange will be, though unbeknownst at this point to any participant, the organization of the top part of their concept map.

The teacher uses the verb 'single out', which may provide an indication to a particular orientation he takes. 'Wave' is singled out, and his question is about why students do so. It is singled out, which implies that there is something else to which it belongs. Miles reifies the question in uttering what can be heard as the completion of a question–response pair ('because it is the most general'). 'What about the quantum?', the teacher says in the next turn. From the Bakhtinian perspective taken and developed here, the teacher does not merely ask a question; he does so in a language that is inherently presupposed to be shared with the students. The teacher speaks *in view of a response* that in its precise nature he cannot anticipate. The utterance 'What about the quantum?', structurally and intonationally marked and offered as a question, also constitutes a social evaluation of the preceding utterance. It juxtaposes 'quantum' to the word that has been the topic before. It is a new concept name that has been entered but in the context of the other one, 'wave', that he has said was singled out. There is therefore the possibility of hearing 'quantum' as being the complement to the 'wave' in his 'question', so that we can hear 'wave' as singled out from the wave/quantum set (pair).

Fragment 4.1
```
145 T: ((coming out of background)) why would you for example
       single out wave to go on top?
146 M: because its the most general.
147 T: what about the quantum?
148 M: no, because quantum is a part of light, and wave is,
       wave is- light is a wave, and quantum is the theory of
       light;
149 K: photons deal with-
150 M: if you put this there-
151 R: isnt this the singular form of quantas?
152 T: quan:ta. yea.
153 R: so that doesnt mean that wave;
154 K: they are the same;
155 R: doesnt that ((QUANTUM)) mean that wave doesnt have a
       continuous band of energy, but just;
155 M: bundles-
156 R: but just bundles?
157 T: bundles, but we are talking about the wave or the
       quantum, the particle character.
158 K: so quantum light, i mean, its quantum and then its
       [light].
```

Miles begins his utterance with 'no' (turn 148), thereby negatively evaluating the possibility of considering quantum as the top-most word in the hierarchy. That is, he indicates hearing the teacher ask them whether quantum could go on top; and he responds decisively. As his utterance unfolds, Miles explains 'light is a wave and quantum is the theory of light' (turn 148). He concretizes the possibility in bringing together, in the same utterance, the different reasons for placing WAVE and QUANTUM differently. We understand Miles as *evolving* an utterance, for, when we participate in such unscripted everyday conversations, we do not know precisely the shape or length of our utterances. Thought and speech develop simultaneously, write both Vygotsky and Merleau-Ponty, and in their unfolding mediate each other's development. We do not know, reflectively and reflexively, what we will say until after we have said it. It is therefore more advantageous to think of the utterance as unfolding without a finished sentence in mind, so that the idea we present actually comes to life in talking, and talking contributes to the emergence and unfolding of the idea.

Ralf then repeats what he has said word-for-word before: 'the singular form of quantas' (turn 151). In the previous instance, it has been a statement. Here it is uttered with a rising intonation and the grammatical construction found in questions: 'Isn't this . . .?'. What is the function? It is also an evaluation that others may not have taken into account what he has said already, and what he therefore has to say again. The teacher takes the next slot in the sequentially ordered turn-taking routine, 'Quanta. Yea.' (turn 152). The teacher responds using *almost* the same word, 'quanta' instead of 'quantas'; and he produces an affirmation, 'Yea'. That is, like a language teacher, he simultaneously produces an affirmation and a correction. The utterance therefore embodies a contradiction, in that it both asserts the incorrectness and correctness of the preceding statement. Ralf follows up, 'so that doesn't mean that wave', but leaves the as-question-marked utterance incomplete. Yet he does reproduce the utterance with a completion when he takes his next turn at talk. In this instant, it is interesting to note that over the turns 151–153 Ralf and his teacher produce something like a late Socratic interaction with the difference here that Ralf ('the student') takes the lead and the teacher takes the role of the simpleton.

Ralf continues by querying what QUANTUM 'means', thereby seeking a translation into a form of language that describes what the term denotes. He proffers one possibility in question form, 'doesn't that [QUANTUM] mean that wave doesn't have a continuous band of energy but just bundles?' But here the late Socratic dialogue form, characteristically monological, changes over into a form that characterizes the very early forms, where the teacher now develops an idea, a statement of what they are talking about, 'the wave or the quantum' (turn 157). Ken contributes to the dialogic nature of this instant in rearticulating a possible relation between QUANTUM and LIGHT. He, as Ralf immediately before, uses the verb 'mean', but here he is the subject of the statement ('I mean') rather than some thing or situation ('doesn't that mean').

This verb, 'mean', is interesting because in each case it marks a translation. Etymologically, it may derive from the Indo-Germanic root *men-, to think, express an opinion; this root is found in many European languages where it is used in the sense of 'to intend' or 'to signify'. It is evident from looking at Fragment 4.1 that the language that these students use is English, including terms that are characteristic of settings where natural phenomena and science are at issue (in the news, sci-fi literature, science classes). The translation operates within the language and between two different expressions. We can articulate what happens in this way. A person saying 'I mean' can be glossed as saying 'I have uttered "quantum light" but I really want to say "its quantum and then its light"'. It is a self-reference of language to language. The utterance 'I mean' implies the preceding utterance and then provides an alternative expression said to constitute the 'meaning' of the former, which now is said by using different words.

At heart of the current issue is translation. If a language can (and often has to) be translated into itself then it cannot be thought (and thought of) as a self-identical entity. This is what Bakhtin refers to as the dialogic nature of the word, the core feature from which all other dialogical features spring, such as different senses, different themes, different interpretations of texts. In semiotics, the form of translation that we observe in Fragment 4.1 and throughout this as throughout all sessions is called *semiosis* (from ancient Gr., σημείωσις [semeiosis], sign, inference from sign), whereby one sign–referent relation is articulated in terms of and augmented by another sign–referent relation. This second sign is called the *interpretant*. That is, whatever the first utterance (e.g., 'quantum') denotes is taken to be the same as what the second utterance ('wave doesn't have a continuous band of energy') denotes (takes as its referent). If we were to denote this referent (e.g., an object) by R, then the relation

$$R-\text{'wave doesn't have a continuous band of energy'}$$

is grafted onto the initial relation

$$R-\text{'quantum'}.$$

The relation between the sign and its interpretant 'is an *open* relation, in the sense that there is *always another* interpretant capable of mediating the first relation'.[6] That is, semiosis is unlimited and there are an infinite number of translations possible within language itself, whereby one interpretant (way of saying) can always be replaced by another (way of saying) and then another and yet another and so on. In classrooms, the teacher plays an essential role in such translations at the heart of language itself, thereby providing for possible trajectories that translate the foreign dialect (science, mathematics) into the students' vernacular. The translation within language is made possible by the joint experience of culture and common experience, however perfect and whatever psychological process might implement it. Conversely, in having available such trajectories of multiple translations, a path is opened for students to move from a world in which their vernacular mother tongue is constitutive to a lifeworld in which objects and events are essentially 'scientific'.

In turn 155, the utterance makes a relation between the signifier 'quantum' and a description of that which it signifies, 'wave doesn't have a continuous band of energy'. The students' textbook notes (in the context of Planck's theory) that 'electromagnetic waves do not transmit energy in a continuous manner but, instead, transmit energy in small packages or bundles'. In the process of evolving their concept map, the students report the speech of others, teacher and textbooks, but in the process enact transformations when they take up what others have said and repeat it 'in their own words'. These transformations are changes in the language, some of which are more stable over time than others. At the same time, because of the absence of a corrective machinery, the statements they produce may not be consistent with physics though they are grammatically possible. Students may even agree on the specific statements they evolve in making their map, and yet these statements may not be of the type that physicists would allow in their dialect. In mathematics, the Gödel theorem states that for any mathematical system statements can be made that lie outside the system and

---

6. Paul Ricœur, *From Text to Action: Essays in Hermeneutics, II* (Chicago: University of Chicago Press, 1991), 123, emphasis added.

that cannot be assessed as to their truth-value. The students are a little bit in that situation in that they can make statements but have no way of assessing whether the statements that they make fall within or outside the scientific dialect. They will be able to make such decisions only after they are competent speakers of the dialect. The textbook and teacher offer only a limited range of possible expressions, which are extended in and through the student conversations. All of these extensions are possible from a linguistic perspective, but only some produce significations that are also allowable within the target dialect of physics. There is therefore a definite role for the teacher if the purpose of a course is monological and if students are to learn but the particular senses of words that scientists approve of.

Overlapping with and following Ken, the teacher begins, 'but when'. The teacher thereby marks the unfolding of an opposition, which, because he stops, never comes to be articulated. Instead, the teacher's stopping allows Ken to further elaborate a position: 'it's just reacting different' (turn 160). Miles and the teacher begin to speak at the same time. But, as Miles halts, the teacher maintains his turn and completes an utterance that—structurally (grammatically and intonationally—is proffered as a question, 'aren't they like two different?'. However, Miles makes a statement about what the teacher has been saying. That is, he does not produce what we would consider an answer to a question. Instead, he articulates what the teacher meant to say without doing so ('he's saying we should pop light on top and have complementarity' (turn 163). That is, what is realized here is a statement–restatement or statement–translation turn sequence.

Fragment 4.2
```
158 K: so quantum light, i mean, its quantum and then its
       [light].
159 T: [but  ] when-
160 K: its just reacting different-
161 M: [ah, he]-
162 T: [arent ] they like two different?
163 M: he=s saying we should pop light on top and have
       complementarity.
164 T: i was just [asking. ]
165 M:            [and then] wave and quantum and photon on
       the bottom, because light=s general and then this
       describes;
```

Taking the sequential turn pair as the unit of analysis, what has happened here is a reification of the teacher's utterance as a statement followed by the articulation of an interpretation (translation). To understand the dynamic of the unfolding conversation at this instance, therefore, we need to follow Miles, who provides evidence for having heard a statement. He *formulates* what he has heard the teacher doing: 'he's saying' rather than 'he's asking'. In his turn, the teacher acknowledges that Miles has heard a statement whereas the teacher articulates that he was asking ('I was just asking'). That is, the two individuals clarify the *intent* of the discursive act—linguists call it the 'illocution' or 'illocutionary act'. Miles articulates the intent of the teacher to be one of making a statement, whereas the teacher says that he merely intended to ask a question. In this instance, Miles reports, using indirect speech, what the teacher has said, but the teacher reformulates the intent as having asked a question. Here, the turn allows us to understand that the teacher hears the student as imputing to him a statement whereas he clarifies to have been asking a question. It will be an extended sequence, as part of which the teacher introduces the concept name 'phonon', walks away to his office to get a book, and then contributes further to the conversation with reference to what he has been finding.

Monological and Dialogical Inquiry

In this last fragment, we can see that the question whether lessons are monologic or dialogic in nature cannot be decreed once and for all. In the present instance, the teacher tells for everyone to hear that he wants to raise a question, whereas the student hears him as making a definitive statement. Statements are more or less authoritative—depending on a range of modifiers that the speaker can employ to weaken the locutionary force—and this is especially so when they are pronounced from the institutional position of the teacher, who both takes and is made to take this position. Questioning, on the other hand, if the answer is not already prefigured, is a fundamentally dialogical endeavor and constitutes the form of the early Socratic dialogues, where the philosopher did not already have the truth to which he would lead his counterpart in the conversation. We therefore have a different appreciation for the situation at hand: Teachers, even when they ask or intend to ask open-ended questions, may actually be heard (by students) as making authoritative statements. The monological nature of the expression is produced in the hearing rather than in the speaking.

Fragment 4.2 concludes with a new organization of key concept name. In fact, Miles utters a conclusion of a statement that has already begun, 'we should put light on top . . . and then wave and quantum and photon on the bottom' and he adds as explanation 'because light's general and then this describes' (turn 165). As previously, the teacher marks an objection ('but' [turn 166]). Yet he stops again, which allows Miles to utter what we can structurally hear as a grammatical completion of his earlier utterance ('and then this describes'), in the form of 'a certain type and this describes a different type' (turn 167). Whatever the private intentions involved, Miles, because the teacher has stopped talking, now has the space to take a turn at talk and to produce a grammatically complete statement.

This time Ken marks an objection ('but' [turn 168]). His unfolding utterance makes a statement in a question form, a statement that contrasts whatever has been accomplished previously but, because available to everyone, it is not and does not have to be repeated (i.e., it goes without saying). Ken asks whether an X-ray is the same thing, where whatever he refers to is available in the preceding utterances that rapidly recede into the increasingly distant past. The subsequent statements involving X-rays are constructed parallel to the statements about light, 'isn't X-ray a photon', which parallels the utterance 'light is a photon [quantum]'. The wave nature of light has already turned up in the conversation (e.g., turn 004), which is paralleled in the present utterance by 'X-rays like travel in waves' (turn 168). Miles confirms implicitly by stating that X-rays are involved in the Compton effect, where wave and quantum character of electromagnetic phenomena are exhibited simultaneously. Ken's confirmation by means of the affirmative 'yea' not only ascertains the contents of Miles' utterance but also establishes its congruence with his own earlier statement. At this point, the teacher takes another turn.

```
Fragment 4.3
166 T: but-
167 M: a certain type and this describes a different type.
168 K: but isnt the x=ray the same thing, isnt x=ray a photon,
       x=rays is involved in the quantum theory? x=rays,
       [like travel in waves]?
169 M: [look x=rays have to ] do with compton [effect    ]
  a K:                                        [yea like]=
170 T: =you you may you you may want to change for example, i
       dont know, those two ((QUANTUM, WAVE)) have
       complementary character or something- or something of
       that nature.
171 R: we should put this here; at the same level.
172 T: quantum, they would be at the same level.
```

The teacher utterance turns out to be both simple and complex (turn 170). It begins with a lot of hesitation as the teacher makes repeated starts before coming to the point, 'You may want to make a change'. He then proffers a quadruple hedging move. First, he prefaces a possible action of change by 'you may', thereby creating the possibility for, but not (strongly) enforcing, a change. Second, he utters 'for example', which indicates that what comes is but one possibility, an example of the kind of changes that can be made. Third, he also says, 'I don't know', which again characterizes uncertainty about what is to come, whether it is a good example or a merely appropriate example. The proffered statement then comes forth, 'those two (QUANTUM, WAVE) have complementary character'. Here, the teacher refers to the same concept names that Miles has articulated earlier as to be organized under the concept name of 'complementarity', which itself is to be organized under the concept name 'light' ('light on top'). Although there are more than 25 minutes to come before they will have completed the map, this configuration will be the one with which they end. At this point, however, they do not yet know this. The teacher ends with the fourth hedge, 'or something of that nature'. Ralf then utters a statement about what to do, namely put the second concept name at the same level as the first. The teacher names the second concept, 'quantum' and then, in repeating part of Ralf's utterance as a statement, confirms it ('they would be at the same level'). We do not know whether Ralf's use of 'should' means that he has heard the teacher saying that they 'have to' place the two concepts names at the same level, or whether they, the students, ought to place the two concept names at the same level because of what they know at this moment in time.

In this fragment, we can almost 'see' (hear) the teacher attempting to refrain from telling students how scientists organize the concepts. He uses hedges surrounding a statement, thereby opening up the inquiry by offering other possibilities. Hedges generally introduce uncertainty.[7] But the teacher is heard repeatedly as making definitive statements. That is, whatever his moves to create uncertainty and to create space for further deliberations, and therefore, for a dialogical approach, the students concretize his talk into directives for what to do and how to hear what the teacher says. That is, dialogicity is not something a teacher can simply implement. Monolingualism, here, is the monolingualism of the students, who hear one voice rather than a polyphony of possibilities. The teacher may have the intent to create an environment in which students dialogically explore ways of talking with/about new concept names and renew ways of talking with/about more familiar concepts. But the students also have a crucial part in the production of the lived curriculum. That is, if students are not part of the game of creating a dialogic inquiry, they themselves contribute to the monologic nature of school conversations when they seek single right answers.

There are definitive parallels between Jacques Derrida's concept of *monolingualism* and Bakhtin's notion of *monologic discourse*. Each term denotes the reduction of interpretive possibilities and flexibility, that is, the possibilities for words and utterances to mean differently than they say. Importantly, Derrida states that monolingualism always is a monolingualism of the other. In addition to monolingualism imposed in colonial contexts[8] 'the monolingualism of the other means another thing ... that in any case we speak only one language—and that we do not *own* it. We only ever speak one language—and, since it returns to the other, it exists asymmetrically, always for *the other*, from the other, kept by the other. Coming from the other, remaining with the other, and returning to the other'.[9] Derrida here makes a strong case for the essentially passive moment in the realization of the effect of each speech act, language returns to the other, who, through his or her speech act, completes the turn pair. However much the teacher might have intended to allow a dialogical inquiry to emerge, what is said and heard is subject to how his students complete and therefore determine the sense of what he has said. Both Derrida and Bakhtin emphasize the role of the recipient in completing just what they saying/writing has said/expressed. The teacher *does* play an agential role in setting up (projecting), in some situation, a next-turn completion, but whether the turn pair is actually completed in the intended way is out of his hands. That is, with respect to the lived curriculum we cannot just speak of teacher agency. There also is an essential, irremediable passivity with respect to the effect of what he says: It is not he but *language* that speaks. That is, the concept *agency* alone does not assist us to theorize the lived curriculum or the role of an individual in a conversation. We need a dialectical notion that includes agency and passivity as equal but complementary moments, for every a form of agency inherently includes the passivity of the body that is involved in producing an action. This notion,

---

7. Wolff-Michael Roth and David Middleton, 'Knowing What You Tell, Telling What You Know: Uncertainty and Asymmetries of Meaning in Interpreting Graphical Data', *Cultural Studies of Science Education*, Vol. 1 (2006), 11–81.

8. Such as when in my own context, the boarding schools for Canadian Indians not only did not allow the aboriginal children to speak their native tongues but severely punished them when they did.

9. Jacques Derrida, *Monolingualism of the Other or The Prosthesis of Origin* (Stanford, CA: Stanford University Press, 1998), 40.

this *one* phenomenon, I denote by agency|passivity[10], which means that there is no agency without passivity, and there is no passivity without agency. The two are the different sides of the same coin.

Problems Differentiating Relations between Categories

In the concept-mapping task, students organize concept names and, by the same token, classify the corresponding entities. It is immediately evident that higher-order categories emerge when there are several lower-order entities that a category entails. In Fragment 4.4, the essence of the question is how photons and quantum relate. Without further background understanding, this is a difficult question to resolve, especially because the students' textbook uses the two terms alternatively. How does one get variation in students' language if they cannot draw on precedence, which they, as I show in the previous chapter, transform in direct and indirect speech, and thereby make it more familiar talk? How does one distinguish the generality of concepts (categories), if there are only two words currently available, which are used (nearly) identically in the students' main source of reference? That is, if one has only two category names P and Q, does category P include category Q? Does category Q include category P? Are category Q and P co-extensive? Or are category P and Q mutually exclusive?

Unbeknownst to the students here is the fact that all photons are quanta ($P \rightarrow Q$) but the reverse is not true, not all quanta are photons. This is the key statement that places the two concepts at different levels in a category system. But neither in the course as prescribed by the curriculum nor in the textbook is there any mention of additional quanta that are not photons. It therefore does not surprise that part of the conversation turns around the question about how to relate the two concept names. Again, it is helpful to think about learning in terms of language and learning to speak a language (dialect) rather than in terms of concepts that are somehow encoded in the brain. For if one understood concepts even in the case of there being only one example, then two concepts can be related. The students' trouble therefore would be ascribed to—as one can find examples of in the conceptual change literature—to some problem in the conceptual understanding of students. If, on the other hand, we think of knowing as linguistic competence, then limited experiences in encountering correct forms of speaking and writing propositions immediately provides a rational explication of the fact that the students wrestle with finding an appropriate way of ordering and linking two or more closely related concept names.

A key issue in the current state of the unfolding conversation is the status of quantum with respect to photon. The previous fragment has ended with a teacher statement that the two terms at hand 'would be at the same level' (turn 172). We open the next

---

10. To create dialectical notions, I use the Sheffer stroke '|'. It corresponds to a logical NAND (not and) operation. If, as in the instance of agency and passivity, we have two mutually exclusive terms, that is, they are alternately true or false, the resulting statement agency|passivity—which can also be written as 'NOT (agency AND passivity)'—is always true precisely because it embodies an inner contradiction.

fragment with this statement. Miles begins his utterance with the demonstrative adverb of time, 'then' that indicates an inference and subsequently produces an inference (turn 173). The resulting statement may be glossed in this way: 'if the concepts you are talking about are at the same level, *then* put light at the same level, too, because they are the same thing'. The social evaluation is immediate, as the teacher announces an opposition to come ('but'), and then articulates the question, 'these two aren't the same thing, are they?' (turn 174).

Fragment 4.4
```
172 T: quantum, they would be at the same level.
173 M: then put light at the same level, too, because they are
       the same thing.
174 T: but these two arent the same thing, are they?
175 R: why, why are they in the same level, because-
176 T: why?
177 M: why wouldnt they?
  a K: these travel in the form of photons. not photon is
       quantum.
178 R: but quantum and photon are the same.
179 K: there is different types of photons, and photons are
       like particles.
180 M: photon has a discreet energy and quantum is just saying
       travels in bundles so they are the same thing.
       basically.
181 K: but its general. this ((QUANTUM)) is general; this
       ((PHOTON)) more detailed.
182 M: a little more exact.
183 K: okay, yea, i guess.
```

In the teacher's utterance emerges a question where there first is a statement. Such a configuration, where a statement is followed by the query 'are they?' (heard as a query because of the rising intonation), may have different functions. First, it may be heard as a marker of uncertainty, where the listener hears the speaker to be less certain about something than the original statement might lead on. The construction expresses uncertainty such as in the utterance, 'this isn't true, is it?' In fact, as the comma in the transcription suggests, there is a slightly rising inflection at the inside of the utterance, but the rise is not as strong as one would associate with a question. The statement 'these two aren't the same thing', with a rising inflection, may actually itself be heard as a question—depending on the sensitivity of the listener to the upward inflection. If the statement is heard as a question, it is still open whether it also may be heard as a rhetorical question, produced by a teacher interested in making his students stop and reflect. Yet how the statement is heard in *this* situation and how it mediates *this* conversation, can only be found by looking at and listening to the next (several) turns.

Ralf begins by indicating that he is addressing the statements about the concept words that are to appear at the same level. In fact, he repeats an earlier teacher utterance (turn 172) almost identically, but prefaces it with the interrogative 'why', and then suggests the beginning of an answer 'because'. But he stops short of a completion. The teacher follows up, 'Why?' Miles offers up an answer, but it is in the form of a question, 'why wouldn't they travel in forms of photons?' (turn 177). The first part can be heard as asking for evidence that refutes the statement embodied in the preceding utterance. Ken elaborates the relation, 'they travel in the form of photons'; and he adds what the relation is not, 'not photon is quantum' (turn 177a). We can hear this parsing of the sound stream—because there is a brief pause after 'not' and then an emphasis on 'photon'—as 'we cannot say "photon is a quantum"'.

In his turn, Ken uses the verb 'travel'. This verb has been used before, but in the context of waves (Miles, turn 093; Ken, turn 168) and electrons that constitute matter waves (Ralf, turn 140). Ken thereby produces a variation of language, employing the verb in the context of another entity, photon, which is related, as he states, to the quantum. This utterance than varies the theme of a type of particle that can be used to describe a phenomenon. Miles responds to Ken by directly addressing the two concept names that end Ken's turn, quantum and photon, making a case for the two names to be at the same level. Ken disagrees, and, before articulating the content of the disagreement, flags the difference by means of the conjunctive 'but' that participants generally use to introduce a contrast. He then produces a characterization of the two concept names in question, and he does so in predicative speech, whereby the terms are actually not articulated but marked with a pointing gesture. Miles adds, 'a little more exact', which Ken hears as a different description of the relation that does not put the hierarchy in question ('okay, yea, I guess' [turn 183]). This entire fragment therefore shows that the nature of the entities denoted by the names 'quantum' and 'photon' still is unsettled, although they are already at issue at the very beginning of this session. We see cases of public predicative thinking that use phrases such as 'is general', 'is more detailed', and 'a little more exact' to associated things in the material world, here, slips of paper inscribed QUANTUM and PHOTON. In this instance, thought, which is both collective and individual, is very much in the process of evolution, moving fast, predicatively. In the next fragment, then, the students mobilize the names of famous scientists to make their case.

Mobilizing the Voices of Scientists

In Fragment 4.5, Max Planck and Albert Einstein are said to have said certain things; the grammatical form is indirect speech. Miles asks his peers whether they understand the difference, and then quotes Planck as having said 'quantum' (turns 184, 186). He continues with a connective implicative 'and then', followed by the mobilization of another eminent scientist, Albert Einstein, who specified the quantum as having discrete energies. Ralf, speaking simultaneously, twice affirms, 'yea' and 'that's right' and completes his utterance in synchrony with Miles, 'discrete energy'. We do not know whether the two scientists actually said *this* or whether they said something *like* this. It is important in the present instance that Ralf not only produces affirmatives but also utters the same words 'discrete energy' simultaneously with Miles. It is an indication that they are (literally) aligned, that they produce the same word/idea publicly, and they produce it at the same time. This simultaneity is an indication of the temporal

Fig. 4.1. The three students teacher are fully focused on and involved in discussing the precise hierarchical relation of QUANTUM and PHOTON. The teacher observes and listens attentively.

alignment, of their *participative thinking*, and their conjoint attention to a public rather than private thought. It is not merely the same form of consciousness but the same form of consciousness that comes to play simultaneously.

```
Fragment 4.5
184 M: do you understand the difference, cause [planck said]
185 T:                                          [quantum is ]
186 M: quantum, and then
       [einstein said it has discrete energy   ]
187 R: [yea, thats right, but discrete [energy]].
```

All the while students are talking, the teacher has been standing on the other side of their table (Fig. 4.1) watching, and listening to, them. Intermittently, he has contributed. Most recently (turn 185), he appears to have made the attempt to make a statement, but, overlapping with Miles who takes a turn at talk, he stops again. Now the teacher begins, overlapping the very end of the overlapping turns of Miles and Ralf. Unbeknownst to all and perhaps even to himself, the teacher is going to enter a new concept name. Because, as Vygotsky says in *Thought and Word,* words emerge from thought and thought becomes itself through words, we cannot know whether the word is present in the teacher's consciousness at the beginning of the utterance or whether it emerges together with the utterance. For understanding the movement of this conversation, however, this question is irrelevant. It is the presence of the word that brings a new resource into the conversation, where any participant, student or teacher, can mobilize it in subsequent speech acts.

In turn 191 of Fragment 4.6, the teacher introduces to the conversation the new concept name 'phonon'. At present, he merely states the existence ('there are also phonons'). In my first analysis in 1991, it had not dawned upon me that this move could be a potentially complicating one for the unfolding conversation in the context of another term, 'matter waves'. Phonons are coherent vibrations within a solid-state crystal, that is, waves created by the correlated movement of many atoms or molecules. On the other hand, the term 'matter wave' is used to refer to the fact that a material but subatomic particle, such as an electron, proton, or neutron, behaves under certain conditions like a wave. That is, much as light, originally thought of in terms of a wave, behaves under certain circumstances in ways that requires thinking of it in terms of a particle, elementary *particles* have to be thought of as waves. The momentum p of such a particle ($p = $ m·v) can be directly related to its wavelength much as the wave of light can be related to the momentum of a photon (light as particle).[11] There is therefore a possibility of confusing the debate, because a solid-state crystal constitutes matter. But the waves *in* matter, phonons, are of a very different sort than matter waves, which are associated with, and used to model, the interaction of individual particles with matter.

Fragment 4.6
```
187 R: [yea, thats right, but discrete [energy]].
188 T:                              [photon] is a light
       bundle, because you also have [phonons   ]
189 R:                              [but planck] gave a
       certain energy to that quantum, because he said its h
       times f
190 M: but it was [einstein-      ]
191 T:            [its ultimately] its photon that have this
       energy, but there are also [phonons;   ]
192 R:                            [but he used] quanta and
       then just einstein said its a photon, so its almost
       exactly the same.
193 M: but no, einstein added something to it, too, like added
       something; ((turns pages of the book, pause)) i can=t
       remember what it was. ((Teacher walks away, heads
       toward his office))
194 R: work function.
195 M: here=s the compton effect.
196 T: ((returns with a book in his hand)) see, the thing is,
       you=ve got more quanta than just photons, then quantum
       would be more general.
197 M: its gotta go up by x=rays.
198 K: right over here.
199 M: just-
200 K: like this, right over here.
201 R: i still think we should put this one on top.
202 M: but this one talks about the wave duality, and then we
       talk about the duality and then we talk about the
       duality over here.
```

---

11. Physicists construct this relation by equating the kinetic energy of the particle ($E = p^2/2m$) with the energy of an electromagnetic quantum ($E = $ h·f = h·c/λ), where m is the mass of the particle, f is the frequency of a wave, λ is its wavelength, h is Planck's constant, c is the speed of light, and c = $f\lambda$.

What is relevant to the development of this conversation is that neither Ralf nor Miles take up the addition of the new term. Ralf mobilizes Planck for his purposes to articulate a contrast ('but') and Miles, also in a contrast (where it remains open which statement he objects to), invokes Einstein. Overlapping with the latter, the teacher states 'photons have this energy'; he thereby revoices Ralf's statement but replaces concept name 'quantum' with that of 'photon'. Again, the teacher repeats|transforms in modified form his earlier statement, 'but there are also phonons' (turn 191). We can literally see and hear Ralf resist. He uses the contrastive 'but', which prefaces the statement that '"he" used quanta'. He then adds that Einstein 'just said' that 'it' was a photon. Using the inferential conjunctive 'so', he then states that 'it's almost exactly the same'. Here the two adverbs 'almost' and 'exactly' suggest differences that are ever so slight making the same but preventing them from being *precisely* the same. Miles disagrees, not only evaluating the preceding utterance by beginning with the contrastive conjunction ('but') but also by adding the adverbial negative 'no'. He then strongly asserts that 'Einstein added something to it' by repeating the latter part, 'like added something'. But he formulates not remembering at the moment 'what it was'.

We understand what happens here when we consider the language used in the students' textbook. It uses action verbs to articulate the work that the scientists have done. Thus, in addition to more formal ways of describing the quantum nature of light, we find in the textbook expressions that ascribe articulations to Einstein and other physicists. These include 'Einstein knew about . . . made the radical proposal' bundles of energy 'he called photons'. 'He proposed . . .' 'Einstein used his . . . theory . . . to explain . . .. He predicted . . .. He reasoned . . ..' That is, when students employ expressions such as 'he [Planck] said', 'he used quanta', 'Einstein said . . .' they in fact paraphrase what they had been reading during the previous weeks in their textbook chapter. They utter these paraphrases not only with intention—when they propose a link—they also use them as a statement of matters of affair when they talk without choosing the words. In Bakhtin, we read about how the words of others are evaluated, refracted as they are being taken up again in the speech of others, who ironize them. In the present context, the reported speech comes from authoritative sources, or, rather, the authoritative nature of the source is both produced and reproduced in the statements. The reported speech is to maintain its authoritative tenor, which precisely enters the dialogue through the attribution of the statement to a particular person known to have been an authority in the field and whose name is associated with the particular effect or phenomenon.

In Fragment 4.6, the verb 'remember' is used. Etymologically, it derives from the same root as 'to mean', the Indo-Germanic root *men-, to think, and the Latin (Umbrian) prefix re-, back, again. This verb—or an equivalent expression like 'I'm [might be] thinking back' (turns 327, 328)—is used repeatedly in this conversation and mobilized for different purposes. The teacher uses it once to encourage students to make present again the content of an earlier unit, where students did experiments that point to the wave character of light (turn 088). Ken uses the verb three times, in each case asking his mates to make present again another part of their conversation (turns 453, 463) or the subject matter content of the unit that is coming to an end with this concept-mapping session (turn 274). Miles uses it five times, once to ask his peers to think of how they had 'screwed up' the placement of LIGHT during a previous session (turn 021). In three instances, he uses it in the negative form to state that he cannot remember, that is, make present again some fact or instance (turns 049, 193, 307). Finally, in turn 386, he formulates a non-continuation of a statement as 'trying to remember exactly'.

In these situations, the verb actually has particular pragmatic functions. When it is used in the positive, then an individual not only asks others to recall or make present something again but the speaker also asserts the facticity of what is to be remembered. Facts obtain a normative force. Thus, for example, Miles asks his peers to make present again that in placing LIGHT on the top they 'screwed up'. He in fact asks them to remember that they screwed up, and this screw up consisted in the placement of LIGHT. The verb therefore is mobilized to bring into the present and make salient something that has occurred at another time and to bring it to bear on the issue at hand as an irremediable fact. Thus, when one student asks another to remember something, it is making reference to having heard or read or talked about something before. It is referring to speech, their own or someone else's. The speaker constitutes something as factual, as having really happened, something that is present to him at the moment, and that he now wants others to make present again as well. On the other hand, saying that one does not remember allows a person to make a statement all the while co-articulating why the statement remains incomplete or why the normally required evidence cannot be provided. The statement thereby becomes vulnerable, because the absence of remembering some situation delimits the degree to which it can be taken as factual.

Expanding the Range of Available Concept Names

In an earlier section of this chapter, the teacher introduces the concept name 'phonon'. But the differentiation of language to allow category relations has not yet happened. At the time of turn 193 and just after uttering the word 'phonon', the teacher leaves the group, but the students do not appear to pay attention. They continue the debate about the relation between quantum and photon. At the beginning of turn196, the teacher returns from his office that joins the classroom near the students' table. He has a book in his hand, open, apparently searching for something, Ralf briefly looking up at the book in the teacher's hands, though the Miles and Ken have not yet oriented toward him (Fig. 4.2). Without a social evaluation on their part, we cannot know whether they are conscious of his actions or not. Having returned to his former position next to the computer and in front of the threesome, he utters a statement about phonons (turn 203). In this instance, the teacher, evidently having read something in the book and still looking into the book, talks about the existence of 'phonons'. He points to the book that he has just brought to the setting, evidently pointing to some place within it (off-print, turn 203). This is a form of action similar to the one that students produce above when they bring the voices of eminent scientists to bear on the issues at hand—support from an authoritative source.

Fragment 4.7
```
203 T: ((points to a page in the
       book, all three students
       orient toward it *)) you
       also have phonons which
       are elastic waves, which
       are quantized, but its an
       elastic wave in matter,
       its not like, its inside a
       crystal, but the molecules
       they can move
```

We do not know the teacher's intention, whether he is uncertain about the concept, whether he wants to confirm the existence of phonons for himself, or whether he seeks to convince the students whose textbook does not mention phonons. The teacher points to but does not say what kind of book he has brought, so that this is not an aspect in and of the situation that mediates the conversation. By pointing to the book, the teacher is reporting what there is, phonons, without actually saying that another authoritative person, the writer of the book, is saying it. It is a reference to what can be said generally. It is similar to the students' use of '*They* are saying . . .', a form of articulating that something can be said in this or that way. As the next turn shows, Ken is taking up the newly introduced concept name, indicating that there is or should be an inference as indicated by the implicative conjunctive 'so' (turn 204). The teacher begins to speak, then stops. This provides Ken with a slot in the sequential order of talk and thereby the opportunity to continue: 'is a form of quantum energy' (turn 206). His statement completes the marked implicative statement, which, once completed, says 'a phonon is a form of quantum energy'. The teacher hears it precisely in this manner: 'that's right' (turn 207).

Fig. 4.2. The teacher returns from his office located behind the door next to the students' table.

Fragment 4.8
```
204 K: so phonon,
205 T: move-
206 K: so a phonon is a form of quantum energy;
207 T: thats right.
```

Ken is producing a statement of what they can say to be saying in the map. He is also reporting elements of the preceding teacher utterance, now in his own words by converting 'which are quantized' into 'is a form of quantum energy'. Each pair of concept names with a verb between them is something that they will have said, and which they prospectively articulate as something that they can say, want to say, or will be saying in and through the concept map. In this way, the students fold language back onto itself, because they have this discussion in language, used to produce the statements of which the concept map consists. Ken also produces a statement that offers the possibility to contribute to the differentiation necessary for settling the issue about the similarities and differences between the phenomena named 'quantum' and 'photon'. If there are not only photons but also phonons that come with quantized energy, then 'quantum' would be the more general category and 'phonons' and 'photons' are specific instances. Whether these considerations bear on the differentiation in *these* students' language remains to be seen.

There is an interesting aspect concerning the language at and the addition of the concept name phonon. This concept name is not generally found in high school physics textbooks. But it is one that has been in university textbooks for decades. Here it is a term that enters the conversation of high school students and their teacher, and therefore opens up the possibilities for its own reproduction not only in this high school physics course but also within society more generally. In fact, the very moment of its production and entering into the high school conversation constitutes a repetition and transformation of the concept name within the culture more generally. Phonon discourse remains alive and renews itself each and every time someone uses it. As soon as a concept name has come out of fashion, that is, once nobody uses it any longer, this aspect of the idiom dies and constitutes a resource mainly for historians. Thus, the concept names 'flogiston' or 'ether' are of historical interest only, remaining in use for mainly ideological didactical purposes to show how powerful science really is in getting rid of wrong ideas.

Ken affirms again the preceding teacher statement 'yea, that's it' (turn 208). The teacher adds to what has been said ('and'), making a statement about 'wave' being more general than 'light', and Ken responds that this is the reason for it being on top (turn 209). Ken utters what turns out to be simultaneously an affirmation, an implication, and a statement.

Fragment 4.9
```
208 K: yea; thats it,
209 T: and wave is also more general than light wave.
210 K: thats why we have it on top. ((points to slip))
211 T: wa- okay; but these two ((WAVE, QUANTUM)) would be at
       the same level; what i mean, if you have waves you can
```

```
        have water waves surface waves you can have a sound
        wave;
212 K: oh, yea, i understand.
```

The teacher has said that 'wave is more general than light wave', to which Ken's utterance is an implication, 'that's why' (turn 210). He states a fact 'we have it on top'. And in making a positive, conjunctive implication ('that's why')—where the teacher's statement is the premise and his assertion of a fact is the consequence—he thereby affirms the positive evaluation the statement receives in public. Following a false start ('wa- okay'), the teacher utters 'but'; and he thereby marks a contrast. He follows up with the statement that 'these two', waving his right hand and index finger over the two paper slips on which are imprinted QUANTUM and WAVE, 'would be at the same level' (turn 211). He translates his own statement, 'what I mean', and then, hand waving above WAVE, adds 'if you have waves, you can have water waves, surface waves, you can have a sound wave' (turn 211). That is, the teacher utters a sentence in which the concept name 'wave' comes to be differentiated as he repeatedly articulates the word each time associated with another noun. Thus, he produces the structure 'noun + "wave"', which, in the English language, can be heard as the specification ('surface wave') of a more general category 'wave'. Here, he practically achieves the articulation of a hierarchical relation between a wave and different forms in which it comes. Differentiation and categorical subordination lie at the heart of the task itself. The teacher thereby provides precedence, a case that may serve as a resource for modeling the formulation of other cases. Most importantly, this pertains to the difference between quantum, on the one hand, and the different quantum phenomena that exist, on the other hand, including photons and the phonons he has just introduced. However, whether the students recognize this addition as a resource remains to be seen. How they might be using it after recognizing the concept name as a resource for action is yet another issue, which can be resolved only empirically. Fragment 4.9 ends when Ken formulates understanding what the teacher has been saying, 'Oh, yea, I understand'. We can say little about what this implies and only further conversation will reveal, to participants and analyst, the extent and depth of this understanding. There are instances where it is understood that the listener understands and there are instances where the listener indicates understanding, and there are possibly instances where the listener thought to understand when this in fact is not the case. Of all these alternatives, only those are of interest to me (in my endeavor of theorizing conversations) that participants actually mobilize for one another in and through the praxis of concept mapping.

Evolving Distinctions

In the previous sections, we see the problem that arises for learning a language (dialect) when the learners have no precedence for distinguishing category names from the things that these denote. Do photons include quanta? Or do quanta include photons?

Can the two concept names be used synonymously? In the present instance, the teacher attempts to help by introducing another quantum phenomenon. But to do so, he presents the concept name 'phonon' and articulates its content as 'waves in matter'. This adds not only new possibilities for talking the idiom but also has the potential to open a can of worms, as there is the possibility for a new confusion to emerge, between 'matter waves' and 'waves in matter'. Electromagnetic waves do not need a material carrier to propagate.[12] This ambiguity is a direct consequence of the fact that not words are related to the world but the structure of language (and therefore consciousness) as a whole corresponds to the structure of the world in human experience. Words and world are the woof and weft that make the cloth of life, which disappears in the attempt of separating the two types of thread that make the mesh.

There are different forms of phenomena that can be theorized in terms of waves, but, from a physics perspective, these are quite different. The waves on a pond are very different in kind than light waves. Thus, using the same concept name 'wave' for quite distinct phenomena not only provides opportunities but also constraints to learning the idiom of physics, that is, to learning to speak physics in and through speaking physics. Differentiation in and of language is not a simple problem, because of the constitutive relation between making differences in the world and having the cultural tools to mark differences, linguistically or otherwise. Thus, it has taken a long time until scientists themselves began to differentiate between, and thereby came to get a handle on, heat (an energy) and the temperature of a substance. Today scientists talk about the temperature as 'a measure of the average kinetic energy of particles in a substance' and heat (energy) as 'the total energy in a substance'. Moreover, it is not only heat and temperature that need to be distinguished, but also entropy, which is a measure of order within a substance. Thus, as we know from daily experience, we can boil and boil a kettle of water but the temperature stays the same. The heating simply evaporates the liquid water. Meanwhile, the temperature of the substance does not increase until the water is evaporated. Historically, therefore, a single language concerning heat phenomena subsequently differentiated into an idiom that includes three concept names: heat, temperature, and entropy. Together with this differentiation in the discourse, scientists began to heed different phenomena, heating a substance, its temperature that increased as a consequence, and the heat-requiring evaporation of a substance at constant temperature.

. . . In Talking

When students learn to speak the physics idiom, they are often in some situation where they do not have experiences with the phenomena that the language articulates. They live in a world where the phenomena do not exist, just as I lived in a world

---

12. At one point in the history of the field, physicists upheld the hypothesis that there was some substance, the 'ether', which would be the carrier of electromagnetic waves, until in 1887 an experiment by Albert Michelson and Edward Morley provided evidence that no such carrier was involved in the propagation of light.

without the church that only recently came to enter my consciousness (see chapter 2). The phenomena exist only in and as of their competence in using the language. In the present instance, too, students have to begin making distinctions where they do not have experiential counterparts to the concepts they use. The textbook and the teacher talk provide them with a limited set of examples for enacting such talk. But listening to a foreigner speak a language does not make someone a competent speaker of the language. I know from personal experience of having spent three months in a French immersion classroom—where students were in their eighth year of taking all subjects (other than English) in French—that even the best students had not developed beyond some rudimentary discursive competencies when compared to native speakers of French of the same age.

The repeated returns to the difference between 'quantum' and 'photon', and the repeated returns to the relation between these two terms and 'light' and 'wave' suggests an unsettled issue of linguistic differentiation. Students question or tell each other how to distinguish two terms without apparently coming to an agreement about how to articulate this difference. This is also the case concerning the relation between 'wave', a concept name that can be used to understand the phenomenon of light and that of matter (e.g., electrons), and the energies associated with such waves. By talking about waves that are not quantized in the context where the topic is the quantum nature of light, the teacher possibly has thrown a monkey wrench into this conversation. This is so despite the fact that he offers a way of differentiating waves that are not quantized (water, surface, sound wave; Fragment 4.9, turn 211) from those that are, which therefore may constitute a resource for evolving a differentiated language about wave phenomena. In the following fragment, Ralf repeats one of the concept names that the teacher has previously uttered 'sound wave'. Given that the whole conversation is about the quantization of energy of a range of phenomena that can be understood as wave or as particle, it comes perhaps not as a surprise that Ralf would ask about the energy of sound waves. Moreover, Ralf articulates an inference or even causal relation ('because') between the fact that a wave has a frequency, on the one hand, and energy, on the other hand (turn 213). He has already stated the relation between frequency (f) and energy (E) twice before (turns 136, 189), which, for quantized wave phenomena, is expressed in the equation $E = h \cdot f$, where, where h denotes Planck's constant.[13] The teacher affirms and therefore provides a public and positive social evaluation: 'it does, it does'.

Fragment 4.10
```
213 R: doesnt the sound wave also have energy, because it has
       a [frequency]?
214 T:   [it does; ] it does;
```

What has happened here, then, is that Ralf has repeated a concept name that the teacher has uttered previously; and he produces a phrase in which the concept name comes to be linked to something he has said before. The linkage is produced via the concept name 'frequency', which is a characteristic of all waves. All waves also have

---

13. For a wave, the energy is proportional to the square of its amplitude, that is $E \propto A^2$.

energy. However, the extension that Ralf produces by relating the equation valid for quantum phenomena to sound waves, which are macroscopic phenomena, thereby is not valid, because the latter are not quantized. That is, the whole purpose of talking about quantized phenomena has evolved historically only when scientists became interested in understanding matter at scales not normally directly available to our senses. And in that range, all the rules governing macroscopic phenomena that are accessible to our senses no longer are true.

In this instance, we also note a phenomenon that is crucial in relations generally but in teacher–student relations more specifically. The question poses itself in this way: How can teachers help students if they also have to be able to comprehend the students' understanding at this moment? If the teacher were to think in terms of conceptions and conceptual change, he would have to engage in an analysis of what Ralf has said, extract and abstract from the language deployed a possible conception, then respond in terms of the conception that he has constructed in the process. This, however, as any teacher knows from practical experience, is an impossible feat to accomplish when there is no time out to reflect. In the real-time unfolding of the lived curriculum, teachers cannot stop and think about what model or structure our interlocutors have in their mind. This would take an immense amount of work and time, which would be of the same order as the time required for science education researchers to produce an analysis. We know that teachers do not have hours or days for doing such an analysis. They have to act and relate to students in real time, right here and right now. Moreover, praxis shows that science teachers generally and in some instances the present teacher specifically do not wait even for a second. Sometimes, also seen in the present transcript, they even begin to speak while students are still completing their turn at talk.

In Fragment 4.10, the teacher talks even before the student has completed the utterance that can be heard as the opening of a question–response pair. The teacher responds to *this* question, even without having had the time required if he had been processing and interpreting information that the student provided in talking. It is well known that to grasp even a simple figure in a conscious way, more than a second is required for entering the information into consciousness and consciously interpreting it. How then can it be that the teacher—or for that matter any one participant—understands another participant without the amount of time passing that cognitive science says it takes to process information? How can it be that responses often begin before the preceding utterance has been completed?[14] Bakhtin provides an answer to this 'problem of understanding': Understanding in real time is possible because of what he variously calls *authentic active comprehension* or *participative thinking*. The problem exists because the utterance specifically and the conversation more generally evolves, and 'only an active comprehension allows us to capture the theme, for a creative process cannot be seized other than by a process that is itself creative'.[15] In fact,

---

14. Perceptive readers might notice that the problem arises precisely with the questions that presuppose language to be information, a view, though possible and suitable in some circumstances, does not capture the phenomenon of language as language.

15. Mikhail Bakhtine [V. N. Volochinov], *Le marxisme et la philosophie du langage: essaie d'application de la méthode sociologique en linguistique* (Paris: Les Éditions de Minuit, 1977), 146.

in active understanding the response is already contained in a draft form. That is, speakers and listeners do not just attend to words, or utterances, they attend to the situation as a whole. The utterance is part of the whole, the theme, the world-language mesh. What speakers and listeners appear to track are changes in the situation as a whole and therefore, the evolution of the theme. In fact, those transcribing videotape or audiotape of poorer quality, with a lot of other noises, know that it is the practical understanding of the theme that allows us frequently to hear a word. Others, unfamiliar with the setting, may only hear a sound but cannot hear the word that the sound is intended to vehicle.

Ralf then continues to make his case by reiterating the relation between quantum and energy (Fragment 4.11, turn 215). In his utterance, 'quantum' is predicatively specified *as* 'a form of' energy, and then, by means of an implicature ('because'), that is, it is set equal to energy. The resulting content of his statement gains clarity in a gloss: 'quantum is energy because it's a form of energy'.[16] The teacher announces a contrast 'but', and then specifies in what the contrast exists, 'at that level sound energy is not quantized'.

Fragment 4.11
215 R: so quantum because its a form of energy it is energy;
216 T: but at that level sound energy is not quantized.

In Ralf's utterance, we observe a reporting of previous teacher talk ('sound wave') cobbled to other aspects of the current conversation, which students have previously talked about. The utterance, spread over turns 213 and 214, brings together the sound wave and energy, links wave to the quantum character (as they have done it earlier), and then relates the result to the energy of (in) the wave. Ralf thereby articulates an extension of the existing language: Sound exists in the form of a wave, and, because waves have quantum character, he infers a statement about the energy of sound waves. Inferring here means making language speak what it has not yet said in this conversation. Physicists do not accept the truth of his statement. Clearly the teacher does not accept this way of talking in the turn he takes, and in so doing, in his social evaluation. But just prior to it, there is nothing in the situation that would have contradicted the possibility of this way of talking. This way has been a possibility; it clearly has, and Ralf realizes this possibility in a concrete way. Because it is possible, it should not surprise science educators that the utterance actually comes to be realized. It is only subsequently—in and through the social evaluation part of the turn pair—that we find out about the problematic nature of the statement.

In his turn at talk, the teacher uses many of the words that Ralf also uses, but he does so in a different way. This is not unlike when young children learn to speak and parents correct them, or when foreigners acquire a new language and have others who correct their words, tenses, pronunciations, and so forth. Ralf's utterance sets up a category relation: quantum is a form of energy. In the same way that we point to a tree

16. In this gloss, I actually make use of the same phenomena that I write *about*, that is, I use translation and transformation to make the gloss say what Ralf's utterance is saying without actually doing so, that is, in different words.

and say 'this is a tree', that is, denote the *special case* by using the category name, Ralf's utterance articulates 'quantum' as a special case of energy. The teacher's utterance, on the other hand, employs the adjective 'quantized' and thereby, in the adjectival use, articulates an *attribute* of energy. In Ralf's language, quantum is a special case of energy; in the teacher's physics idiom, it is an attribute of energy. This difference—as small as it might sound to the unfamiliar ear—is, to paraphrase Robert Frost's poem *The Road not Taken* and Gregory Batson simultaneously, precisely the difference that makes all the difference.[17] This is the sole instant in the entire conversation that sound waves are being talked about and thereby constitute the topic of talk. In essence, its pertinence or rather non-pertinence has been established here and there. There is no purpose or reason of coming back and building it into the map. This shows us how language affords slippage. This slippage can be generative, but it also can lead into dead ends with respect to learning to talk like insiders.

. . . In Meta-talking

In talking, we do not merely use language to get a job done, such as when, in a recent remodeling project, I asked my helper 'Give me the hammer, please' or, in a projective way, 'the hammer!' We also talk about talking and the content of this talking, such as when I explain to my helper, a recent Chinese immigrant, the use of the English language and the permissibility of using predicative expressions without loss of politeness: 'when I say "the hammer!", I really mean to say "give me the hammer, please"'. Close analyses of everyday classroom talk shows that students, as much as people in the culture as a whole, continually co-articulate *what* they are doing in addition to using talk for getting a job done. This co-articulation, or *formulating* as it is known technically, is part and parcel of the pragmatics of situated action and talk. Fragment 4.12 begins with talk that consists almost entirely of language for getting the concept map done, but, in the process and to deal with divergent ideas that evolve, also leads to the mobilization of formulations that let others know what is or has happened. Examples of such talk are when speakers tell others *what* they have been thinking while talking, what the current topic really is, what they are talking about, and that they are looking at one thing rather than at something else.

The preceding talk, though we might impute very positive intentions to the teacher, may have actually created further possibilities to produce language inconsistent with physics (rather than the desired physics language). Ken articulates one such possibility in the next turn (Fragment 4.12), as he states that 'wave' should be super-ordinated to 'quantum'. 'No, no, both of them', the teacher objects (turn 218). 'They should be equal', Miles adds, and, after Ken utters the word 'quantum' twice, continues, 'but

---

17. I am actually blending here the voices of two authors in my own to produce a statement embodying my own intentions. Such a blending of different voices in a third is another characteristic of the possibilities of language, also observable in the very process by means of which students produce this concept map, evolve ways of speaking, and learn physics.

you let the wave duality, and then part of the wave duality, and they are both equal, they deserve equal status' (turn 221).

Fragment 4.12
```
217 K: the wave should be over quantum because,
218 T: no no both of them.
219 M: they should be equal.
220 K: quantum quantum-
221 M: but you let the wave duality and then part of the wave
       duality and they are both equal they deserve equal
       status.
222 K: i thought because waves were generalized; that thats a
       particular detailed description of the sort of waves we
       are dealing with. thats why i,
223 M: no. waves is one way of describing light; and quantum
       is another way.
224 R: but there are more waves than there are quanta, because
       for [example, ]
225 M:      [but if we],
226 R: sound is a wave; but its in matter; not quantized;
227 M: no i know; but we are not talking about what one is
       more; we are talking about equal status.
228 K: but we are looking on this sheet; it says wave -wave
       and thats all it says; it doesnt say light wave.
229 M: yea i know; but thats what we are defining though.
230 R: yea but we can also do it like this, and say that light
       and x=rays are waves.
```

The mobilization of the contrastive connective 'but' announces an oppositive orientation to the issue. There is a duality, and 'wave' and 'quantum' deserve equal status in this duality. Ken then takes a turn in which he refers to what he has been thinking before (as indicated in the past tense of 'I thought'), that is, while saying 'the wave should be over quantum'. His explication of the preceding thought|speech articulates 'wave' as something general and all the different waves as 'particular detailed descriptions of the sort of waves they are dealing with'. In this, he evolves nothing but implications from the previous teacher talk—he makes language itself speak. Language provides resources that not only can be copied but also can become material for making inferences. The teacher has articulated different wave phenomena (sound, surface, water) and has differentiated quantized phenomena from other wave phenomena. One does not have to have a mental model, framework, or conception to repeat the teacher's language and to draw inferences from his utterances. All a student needs to have is the competence for drawing inferences from previously articulated speech fragments.

Miles disagrees ('no' [turn 223]) and then relates both of the contested terms to light, each being 'one way of describing light'. Ralf, too, expresses opposition, although, while he is speaking, we do not yet know who feels spoken to, 'there are more waves than there are quanta' (turn 224). He begins to provide a reason, overlapped by Miles who himself utters a disagreement ('but if we'). In talking, Miles lets everyone present (and any analyst watching the tape) know that he is the one that Ralf opposes.

Ralf provides his example, which repeats some of the words and a phrase that the teacher has used before (turn 216), without the use of direct speech. He first articulates 'sound' as 'wave', then suggests it to be in matter, and then comes to a completion in predicating 'sound' with the expression '[it's] not quantized'. Again Miles objects ('no'), and acknowledges that he knows something, which, because of proximity, is what Ralf has stated. He first repeats the opening part of Ralf's utterance, but negates it: 'We are not talking about what one is more'. Miles then formulates what they are really talking about: 'equal status'. Ken weighs in, marking what is to come as a contrast ('but'). He suggests that they are looking at the paper slips ('sheet') and that 'it says wave'; he repeats, 'wave' and elaborates, 'that's *all* it says'. He finishes uttering 'it doesn't say "light wave"' (turn 228).

We do not yet know, at the level of the conversation, who has been spoken to, and which ideas are being opposed. We can almost hear a rhetorician, who, by pointing to the evident and by means of repetition, attempts to convince his audience. We can hear it as a plea to focus on wave and are notified only in the end what we ought to distinguish it from: 'light wave'. Miles takes the next turn, produces an affirmation with the adverbial 'yea', and then acknowledges being in the know ('I know'). He thereby accepts the status of what the previous speaker has said as being the case: it is true. Miles marks the objection to come, 'but', and then states 'that's what we are defining' and completes with another adverb ('though'). In its placement, in what comes to be the end of the utterance, this adverb reinforces both the emphatic statement and the preceding, already-marked contrast. Ralf, too, approves ('yea') but immediately states a contrast to come ('but'), in which he states that they can also organize the concepts in a different way ('say that light and X-rays are waves' [turn 230]). 'Wave' thereby comes to be the superordinate category, which includes not only the different forms of waves (light, X-rays) but also something else. As electromagnetic waves, both also are phenomena that exhibit the wave–particle dualism at the center of the current debate.

In this situation, Miles articulates what they are not (and ought not be) talking about and then reports what it really is that they are talking about. This 'what' is the referent in the current context, the content of their talk, as reported by Miles. Ken then reports what the sheet says ('wave') and what it does not say ('light wave'). Ken reports speech, 'It says wave' and articulates what is not written, 'it doesn't say light wave'. Miles suggests that he knows this but that their job (here reflexive language) is to define the terms. Ralf adds that they can link both X-rays and light to the concept of wave. Here we have a whole discussion about wave and its relation to other terms and in the process of this discussion, the language used comes to be transformed.

In this exchange we find clues for how students' language of physics changes in talking. Students explicitly or implicitly use the language that has come from the other, sometimes directly, sometimes indirectly. When they use indirect speech, attributed or unattributed, they transform language as such. 'In each epoch, in each social circle, in each small world of family, friends, acquaintances, and comrades in which a human being grows and lives', Bakhtin writes, 'there are always authoritative utterances that set the tone—artistic, scientific, and journalistic works on which on relies, to which one refers, which are cited, imitated, and followed'.[18] This is why the unique speech experience of each individual is shaped and developed in continuous and constant interaction with the utterances of other individuals. The appropriation process is more or less creative but always expressive of others' words. But the words of others are not simply reported: In their new articulation they carry with them an evaluative tone. With and through this evaluative tone, we tend to assimilate, rework, and re-accentuate the speech of others in our own speech. In so doing, speakers singularize a general possibility of language. Whether it is a possibility that will last is a function of social and societal processes that go beyond this particular instance (classroom context).

Formulating what students are doing is an integral part of the doing itself. 'We are (not) talking about' (turn 227) is in present tense. Here, Miles formulates what they are doing, 'talking', and what the topic of this talk is. Ken, too, formulates what they are doing: 'looking on this sheet'. Moreover, Miles is not just defining, as in '[WAVE, QUANTUM] they should be equal', but also formulating what he does as 'that's what we are defining'. He raises talk to a different level: it is talk about talk and talk about the topic of a stretch of talk and what they are doing in talking. This form of talk is used pragmatically to organize the unfolding process itself, as it highlights the real topic to be discussed and distinguishes it from other things that they could have talked about, perhaps in a different context, but which is not the purpose of the conversation at hand. The paper slips and the larger sheet of paper onto which the contents of the slips, once organized, are to be transcribed are present in the situation and present to their talk. These, too, may be quoted as saying something. This talk is not distinguished from other talk in the unfolding stream of talk. Both are part of the situation, both bear on the event. There is also a future orientation where Ralf suggests what they can do and say, that is, 'light and x-rays are waves'. What they are going to say will be in and through the concept map, which is a different form of saying what they currently do. What they can do thereby is implicitly characterized as something else: it also involves the work of doing the saying they ultimately do. The finished concept map, therefore, will be an account of the mapping session as a whole, and it will, in part, be a literal account (when the link and what has been said are identical).

How a Teacher Intervention Ends

'I have a meeting across campus in five minutes', my colleague says and, without allowing me to respond, walks away, leaving me alone in the hallway. Face-to-face meetings always end at some time. But they generally do not just end. Members to the meeting do work to end the event in progress. Here, the colleague is not just telling me that he has a meeting. He is telling me something else. What is this something else? If he had just left without saying a word, abruptly turned and disappeared, I might have

---

18. Mikhail Bakhtin, *Speech Genres and Other Late Essays* (Austin: University of Texas Press, 1986), 88.

thought of him as rude. He might have thought that I could think of him as rude. In saying 'I have a meeting across campus in five minutes', he actually provides me with sufficient material to evolve a fuller explanation of why he is leaving rather suddenly. From personal experience I know that walking across campus takes at least 10 minutes. If he really has to get to a meeting (he might have merely uttered an excuse), he will already be late. It might have been that he did not watch his time and now realizes that he is too late. I might even feel guilty for having held him from getting to the meeting in time. The point is not what the precise inferences are that I make. The real point is that he, in uttering that he has a meeting, provides legitimate reasons not only for ending our conversation but also for ending it rather rapidly. It is a legitimate reason and making his rather sudden departure plausible. This is not influenced by the fact that he might not have a meeting at all. There might be some other reason: He may want to meet a person for an extramarital affair, or he may simply want to leave because he finds me boring (or for any other reason one might think of). In such a case, this legitimate reason, though not corresponding to what happens thereafter, might actually be better for me, especially if these other reasons for leaving could be used to construe a negative evaluation of myself.

Whereas many everyday situations are actively brought to an end, and this process of bringing the situation to an end takes work, there may be situations that differ. We have already seen that the teacher leaves the group to get a book without saying a word. He joins the group to listen, perhaps contribute to the conversation, and leaves, again without uttering a word. Just saying that the teacher does not engage in doing the work of leaving or joining because he is in a familiar situation with familiar individuals is an insufficient explication. I do, for example, explain to my wife why I get up from watching the recorded evening news: 'just getting a bottle of wine'. Depending on the circumstances, she may stop the recording until I return or continue playing them, for example, after I say 'I am tired, I am go to bed'. Unless the members to the situation provide us with a formulation or explanation themselves, we can only speculate how the institutional relations themselves mediate the beginning and ending of situations typical of schooling, including 'interventions' in 'student-centered activities'. The present six-minute intervention does come to an end below when the teacher leaves after being involved intensively for several turns in a sequence. He leaves after one of the students, Miles, makes a statement consistent with and summarizing the teacher's preceding contributions. The teacher leaves and the students continue. There is no more and no less to the ending: as if it were the way in which *these* kind of situations do end in practice. Before this happens, however, a few more turns remain to be taken.

As the conversation continues, Ralf and Ken articulate (in Fragment 4.13) propositions that they could use, a form of talk materialized in the appearance of a stable concept pair-link.

Fragment 4.13
```
231 K: they can travel in waves.
232 R: and they are quantized.
233 M: nea, i like it as we had.
234 R: and they travel in photons.
```

This entire concept-mapping session is about what can be said and how the concept names provided can be linked up together to say something as a whole, a theory, and about evolving an ordered way of making the conceptual domain hang together. With the concept names one proposition at a time, the students are evolving a language, an idiom, making decisions about which concept names are more inclusive than others and expressing inclusivity by means of propositions. This idiom, however, is embedded in a more extended language that also includes the tools for bringing the statements about, for coordinating the work, for ascertaining that they 'are on the same page', and so on. The language in the emerging concept map is an index to and, in being its result, a description of the conversational work that leads to the final map as a whole. But whereas it is possible to derive from the work done the concept maps that students will have produced at the end of the lesson, the reverse is not possible. We cannot take the final concept map and derive from it the work that has gone into its evolution; and we cannot recover the language that has allowed this concept map to emerge. The work and the concept map form a pair that in a formalized way can be expressed as 'doing [constructing a concept map]', where the brackets enclose a practice and the 'doing' denotes its work complement. In this work, the teacher has an essential part to play, even though the final map will be attributed to the students.

In the next fragment, a key issue turns out to be the organization of the terms surrounding or involving COMPLEMENTARITY, which currently does not have a place. Miles makes another proposal that points to his preference for something they already have had (turn 235). Ken announces a contrast ('but'), followed by what we can hear as a question (because of the intonational and grammatical marking): 'where should this on come in?' (turn 236). While speaking, Ken simultaneously holds up the paper slip on which is imprinted COMPLEMENTARITY (turn 236). He proposes, in the form of a question, a solution, 'should we scrawl this across?' and, simultaneously, places COMPLEMENTARITY across several terms in the existing hierarchy. All three suddenly burst out in a brief and contained laughter before Ken continues to articulate, 'the complementarity has to go somewhere'. Miles immediately provides a positive evaluation, 'yea, that's why I liked it'. The moment is significant in two ways, a reason for me to discuss it in greater detail in chapter 8. First, Ken provides a solution to the difficult issue at hand: how to place LIGHT, WAVE, and QUANTUM, how to produce the related statements, and how to include in this relation another term, the one central to the unit, 'complementarity'. Second, Ken's solution proposed in the form of a question, 'should we scrawl this across' and his placement of COMPLEMENTARITY in a for concept mapping non-habitual way, is greeted by all three with laughter. It is a joke. Shall we place COMPLEMENTARITY in a way that is clearly against the rule of concept mapping? By means of a joke, understood and communicated to each other as such, the unusual configuration breaks open the stalemate and offers the possibility for another approach to their problem. The laughter frees them, if only for a moment, from the seriousness of their involvement in the task. I return to this issue in chapter 8.

Fragment 4.14
```
235 M: the way we had before.
236 K: but then, where does this one ((COMPLEMENTARITY)) come
       in? should we scrawl this across? ((places
```

COMPLEMENTARITY across 3 other slips; all three burst
out in brief laughter)) the complementarity has to go
somewhere.
237 M: yea thats why i liked it; because we=re gonna use it;
then we could put the wave down.
238 T: then quantum a::nd wave have to be side by side;

The breaking open of possibilities is announced in the comment Miles makes following Ken: 'because we're gonna use it, then we could put the wave down' (turn
237). The teacher also agrees, providing a conjunctive 'then', which also marks an
implication, before uttering the proposal for an organization, 'quantum and wave have
to be side by side' (turn 238). The utterance is not proposing a form of language but a
hierarchical ordering outside of a statement that shows how the concept name is related to other concept names. But more importantly, he says 'have to be' rather than
simply 'are', turning the 'then' into a strong implication that follows from Ken's proposal. That is, the advance has been made possible in and through the student-
generated talk; and the teacher, in a Socratic manner, simply serves as a midwife to
help the idea come to the world in its full splendor. Both agreement and possible ways
of continuing the mapping process emerge from this tiny but critical instance.

Miles agrees (turn 239), and the teacher continues in providing a rationale ('because') for his preceding statement, 'because the complementarity principles' (turn
240). The teacher confirms ('that's right' [turn 242]) Miles' summary 'they have
equal status' (turn 241). Ralf asks what 'quantum' 'means'. In this instance, the
teacher talks about what something means, perhaps implies, which is not articulated in
the thing itself. Here the current theme is the quantum, and Ralf has asked what the
term means.

Fragment 4.15
239 M: yea.
240 T: because of the complementarity principles.
241 M: they have equal status.
242 T: thats right.
243 R: does quantum mean its- um a particle- a wave
[or a particle?]
244 M: [we had it right] before.
245 T: that means that it is a particle.
246 R: and then we could say that energy is like particle;
247 T: no, it has particle character, its bundled, like, like,
like a piece of mass. see it says ((points to the book
in his hand book)) particle like entity or quantum;
which- a photon; but you can like; but you also have
phonons.

Central to Bakhtin's idea about how language reproduces and renews itself rests on
the phenomenon of referring to the speech (writing) of others by using direct and indirect speech. In writing, quotation marks are used to set apart the author's text from the
text it quotes. When the quotation is made as indirect speech, other markers about
what has been quoted have to be used. Or rather, historically, people have used means

Fig. 4.3. A speaker 'air quotes', thereby bringing into speech the resources developed for quoting in written texts.

that distinguish a voice from the voice it is quoting, and written language has introduced quotation marks as a means to make a similar distinction. In speaking, quotation marks do not generally exist, unless a speaker 'air quotes' (Fig. 4.3), that is, brings a feature characteristic of written speech into discourse by means of hand and finger gestures.[19] But this written feature cultural-historically emerged later than the use of direct speech quotation. What then is the manner by means of which speakers, when necessary, make it known that they begin and end a quote? That is, our question is 'How do we know, while listening to someone speak, when the (in-) direct quote ends?'

In Fragment 4.15, the teacher directly attributes something being said to the textbook. He says, 'see it says' and then he articulates what 'it' says. How does a hearer know which part of his speech is to be taken as a quote and which part is his own? The same problem will arise again almost immediately, when, in Fragment 4.16, Ken says what example the teacher is 'giving' them and he continues to say what 'Ralf was saying' (turn 252). In each case, an attribution is made to others, as distinct from something that is to be attributed to the speaker. It is therefore important to know how the audience parses the speech, pragmatically, which allows it to make the distinction between quoted speech and actual speech. When the attribution is to an authority, then it is important to know precisely what is not attributable to the authority, because this is the content more easily contradicted, critiqued, or attacked.

One way in which speakers make the distinction is by prosodic means that come together with relevant grammatical means (Fig. 4.4). Thus, the teacher marks off the quoted text grammatically in the beginning, 'see it says' (turn 247). He thereby *projects* that the something to come is a quote. At this point we do not yet know at what point he begins to quote, but we hear (and see in Fig. 4.4) that in the next instant, the

---

19. In some disciplines, scholars literally read papers, indicating the beginning and end of a quote verbally, e.g., in saying 'begin quote' and 'end quote', respectively.)

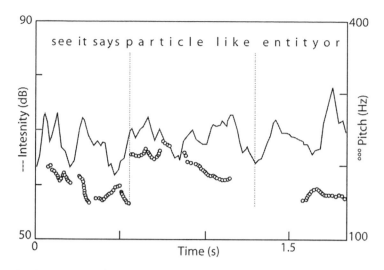

Fig. 4.4. Markers that a quote is beginning include shift in pitch register, speech rate, and grammar.

pitch increases in and with the production of 'particle'. The speech rate slows dramatically, as the distances between the letters show. The pitch slowly falls back to the level where it has been with the utterance of 'says'. The statement 'see it says', articulated with a falling pitch, can itself be heard as coming to an end, thereby marking intonationally a grammatical unit, 'see', point to the text, and 'it says'. The verb here is in the transitive form requiring an object, and this object provided is marked off with a sudden change of pitch and at a much slower speech rate. The same happens when Ken quotes Ralf. Sometimes small pauses between formulating that someone or something is quoted further sets the beginning of the directly or indirectly referenced speech apart, allowing the latter to be more distinguishable. Equally, we see the downward slope in the pitch of the quoted speech, which eventually comes to an end like a statement does. This end-point is generally followed by a pause that precedes a new beginning, often further marked by an upward jump in the pitch register again followed by a falling pitch. That is, even though speakers do not consciously attend to the modulation of their pitch, they use it in such a way that it allows listeners to make required distinctions without articulating these distinctions in so many words (which would make the text really cumbersome).

Fragment 4.16
```
248 K: yea, i know thats why quantum should be over-
249 T: quantum is over-
250 K: but thats-
251 T: i really dont know, because you are talking about light
       and x=rays.
252 K: but because you=re giving us that example with phonons,
       then thats like ralf was saying, that waves also have a
       lower detailed description within itself and thats why
```

```
it should be above quantum. because quantum is only a
subdivision of
[wave. no.]
253 T: [but then-]
```

Here, Ralf is quoted as having said something and that is why they should do something (turn 252); the teacher is reported as having entered the example of the phonon. So there are two levels. And again, we have a shift from quoting Ralf, one the one hand, to what needs to be done in the present context, on the other hand. In Fragment 4.16, the students go a few more times back and forth, and both Ken and the teacher raise objections using the opposition-marking conjunctive 'but'.

In Fragment 4.17, there are three predicative contributions before Miles makes a longer statement. He uses formulations to mark off the topic from what they do not and should not care for, and then articulates 'complementarity' as the real issue ('we are concerned about'). He immediately draws implications for the way in which WAVE is placed and where they 'need it'. He adds a rhetorical question: 'otherwise where are we gonna put it?'. He thereby highlights an especially pressing problem when considering where they are 'gonna put it' when they 'get down here?' The teacher takes the next slot in the sequential order of turns. But he does not speak to what Miles has marked off as the topic. Rather, he addresses a rule ('idea') of concept mapping, which is that 'you don't have the same word at two levels' and he provides a reason, 'because otherwise you are skipping levels with the same concept' (turn 256). Miles begins with a negation ('no'), but this time not to mark difference. Rather, he follows with 'I know'. He knows that what the teacher says is the case, and no, he is not attempting to cross levels. He explicates that the word could be in one of two places ('both here and here'), that it makes sense to have it in either place ('it makes sense'), and then specifies that 'it needs to be here' while pointing to the top part of the arrangement before them. While he is still talking, Ken begins to utter what turns out to be a statement equivalent to what Miles is saying simultaneously, 'leave it up here' (turn 259). The teacher projects an implicature ('in this case'), and then specifies where WAVE has to be placed (turn 260). He walks away, and the students continue.

Fragment 4.17
```
253 T: [but then-]
254 M: because if its-
255 R: for example-
256 M: light=s a wave, but we dont care for that particular
       concept map what we are concerned about is the
       complementarity and therefore we need the wave down
       here. yea, we could put it up here, but we dont need
       it. but we need it here, otherwise where are we gonna
       put it, we get down here and-
257 T: with the concept map you also have the idea that you
       dont have the same word at two different level because
       otherwise you are skipping levels with the same
       concept.
258 M: no, i know, but you could put it both here and here and
       it makes sense, but it [needs to be here.]
```

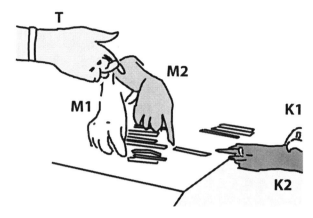

Fig. 4.5. Successive hand placements that go with and specify 'here'. M1 and M2 are Miles' hand position, T the teacher's, and K1 and K2 are positions of Ken's left hand.

```
259 K:                     [okay, leave it up] here.
260 T: in this case, it needs to be here;
  a K: alright then.
```

An interesting issue in this fragment is the disambiguation of the adverbial 'here'. It is another problem of disambiguation—like the one concerning the distinction between speech and reported speech—that speakers solve without problem, which nevertheless means that work is involved. But this work of disambiguation is hardly ever made salient in the literature on learning science. In this fragment, the adverb appears nine times with associated placement of hands and fingers (Fig. 4.5). Here, I take a closer look at its use in turns 258, 259, and 260. 'Here' is an index used for proximal entities. For Miles, who sits sufficiently close to be able to touch any location within the emerging map, 'here' and the placement of his finger fall together. 'Here' is wherever the finger rests, so that in the first instance, 'here' is lower (M2) than in the second instance, where it is at the top of the hierarchy (M1). In the third instance, the hand is placed again at M2, precisely where WAVE 'needs to be'. While he is speaking, Ken's hand rests in a place marked by K1. When he speaks, he moves his hand forward so that it comes to rest near the place that Miles has already marked in space (K2, M2). At the same time, he says, 'leave it up here'. From where Miles sits, 'up' is further away from him. Thus, 'up' from Miles' perspective is at M1 relative to M2. But by the movement of his hand forward and its subsequent retraction when he is finished talking, Ken makes relevant a placement near where his hand comes to lie, that is, closer to Miles though 'up' is near his hand and close to where Miles already has indicated. This hearing is further supported by his uttered agreement, 'okay', and the positive evaluation that comes with leaving the status quo rather than changing something.

The third speaker in this instant is the teacher. He is a little farther away and cannot touch the table and paper slips without moving. He thrusts his hand forward, which previously was out of the frame, and points. But from where he stands, M1 is closer to him and, according to the research findings about the use of the proximal 'here' (relative to the distal 'there') it should be the named position. On the other hand, he is too far away to be able to say that he is pointing to one rather than the other position; and he is too close to employ the distal 'there'. However, the question is not only his physical distance, but also the temporal distance with respect to the previous utterances. Both Miles and Ken have employed the same index 'here' with associated finger pointing. They have marked being in agreement about the placement of WAVE. In repeating the indexical while not marking a contrast—to point to a 'here' that is different from the 'here' of either Miles or Ken—the teacher is thereby confirming that the already agreed-upon destination of 'here' is the 'here' he supports. That is, in repeating the word 'here' he confirms the previously uttered instances of 'here' rather than contrasting them with a 'there'.

After this exchange, the teacher walks away and goes to another group. Rather than doing further work of bringing an episode to an end, which therefore is an episode only in as far as it is marked by the change over from his absence to his presence and vice versa, the teacher leaves. This points us to the fact that encounters in the setting are habitual rather than other forms of encounter where the mutual engagement and disengagement requires additional verbal work to be accomplished in and by means of sequentially ordered turns. More extensive research on this phenomenon is required, for we may observe many instances in school where students do not ask a teacher for permission to interrupt another conversation but simply do interrupt.

Teachers and Dialogicity

In this chapter, I feature a lengthy exchange between students and their teacher. There are only four groups of students in this class, so it is not surprising that he would have the time to spend such an extended amount of time with one group. He spends approximately equal amounts of time with all four groups. Ethnographic evidence shows that rather than chopping this time into short segments, he spends lengthy amounts of time with each group unless some pressing issues in another group encourages him to end an interaction and to attend to the needs of other students. We see that the exchange begins as the teacher approaches the group and directly asks members about the relative placement of WAVE with respect to other concept words. He joins without further ado, without any further articulation of what is happening and why. The 'intervention' ends in the same way. The teacher simply steps back and walks away in the direction of another group. I contrast this with the general practices that begin and end face-to-face meetings. If this behavior does not offend, and there is no indication in this recording that it does, then it may just be that in this kind of setting, leaving without doing the work of leaving observable in other settings is acceptable. In fact it may be superfluous, because joining and leaving a group is a constant and repetitive form of events in classrooms so that an {intervention} becomes a matter of course.

I bracket the term 'intervention' because there is no evidence that the teacher or students treat *this* or *such* events *as* interventions. Such exchanges make what are expected, normal, everyday, and mundane forms of schooling, at least in contexts such as the present, where the students tend to come from families with considerable incomes, dominated by a middle-class ethos. In this transcript, there are no instances where students from other groups call the teacher's attention. But in the database more generally, there are such events. Generally, the students, too, though they enact the work of getting the teacher to attend to them and their needs, do not generally do the work of 'polite' interruption and change in membership (joining, leaving).

This {intervention} begins when the teacher asks students for an account of the placement of two concept names. We do not know what he thinks or intents other than what he makes available to the students. It may also be that expressing any such intent would destroy the dialogical approach that he has declared to practice in his classrooms and that we see him attempting to realize in his teaching praxis. In any event, the very query for an account of the concept name placement makes this placement salient: language points to something and thereby brings it into existence in and for the purposes at hand. In this, there may actually be an asymmetry, whereby the problematic issue from the perspective of the person asking for such an account is favored over querying other aspects of work that appear to be unproblematic.

At heart of the relational work throughout the fragments shown is the differentiation of key words. This differentiation occurs at the textual level, because the domain is inherently inaccessible, though students previously have conducted laboratory experiments on the wave nature of light where they have seen the photoelectric effect. But as a whole, the examples of ways of talking and talking about the relevant phenomena have been limited. Thus, although there are numerous quantized phenomena, even entire fields concerned with such phenomena—as apparent from their names quantum mechanics, quantum chromo-dynamics, and quantum electrodynamics—in the students' textbook the expressions linking the concept name to other concept names are limited.

Similar difficulties pertain to the phenomena themselves that the concept names are used to set apart as natural phenomena to be described and theorized. At the microlevel, momentum and energy are quantized. But students not only have limited opportunities to encounter and speak the language of quantum physics, but also they have even fewer opportunities to engage in experiments that require quantum explanations. It is not surprising therefore that distinguishing between related concept names does not come easy. In other words (and more appropriate for the language-orientation in this book), differentiating the use of words in phrases does not come easy. In this chapter, one can observe some of the work involved in producing such differentiation on the parts of all members to the setting.

One aspect of this work lies in the introduction of additional concept names, denoting additional phenomena. Such a proliferation allows students to understand that one term constitutes a category name and another is the name of a sub-category, it names one of the elements of the more general phenomenon. This is the case, here, with 'quantum' and 'photon'. The first refers to any entity that cannot be further divided and constitutes the elementary multiple, that is, a quantum phenomenon does not come as a continuum but only in multiples of the basic unit. The energy of entities such as photons or phonons is one such phenomenon; the momentum is another such entity; and the spin of an electron is yet another.

In addition to introducing a new concept name, which denotes another kind of thing within a larger group, is only one way in which differentiation may occur. Another way in which differentiation occurs comes with the increased articulation of utterances with the same words. Some of these come to be acceptable by other members and others do not. That is, students learn to differentiate statements that are allowable and others that are not within a particular topic that the idiom makes possible. But although such new expressions and statements are easily generated, a process that we expect to occur within a Bakhtinian perspective, we cannot expect that students are already in a position of making the social evaluations that scientists would make to separate possible from impossible statements within the idiom. They will be in that position only once they already master the idiom as a whole. That is, linguistic variation is inherent in the phenomenon of speaking, but the selection between the forms of utterances produced requires something more. It requires the competencies of being a member in the community, a state that students may attain at some point down the road, but a state in which they are, qua learners, inherently not at the moment of this conversation.

I show that differentiation occurs not just at the level of talking that goes with producing the map but also at a meta-level, where the talk is about the process itself (see Fig. 3.3). Importantly, although the adjective 'meta' frequently is used to suggest that the process so described occurs over and above its associate process that is not thus described—such as in the contrast of physics, body and matter, and metaphysics or in the contrast between analysis and meta-analysis—the meta-level here is merely a shift in topic. Meta also has, according to the *Oxford English Dictionary,* the sense of marking change, transformation, permutation, or substitution. Here this is precisely what I describe, a change in or substitution of the topic.[20] When students talk concepts—and thereby bring the concept-mapping session into existence—they use language to make thematic subject matter relations. When they formulate what they are doing as part of the previous process, they make this process itself the topic of their inquiries. These formulations, as I show, have particular functions. Here, they contribute to the project of differentiating the language of mapping and the language of the map itself. Formulations moderate how the work is to be done, mark the real topics from other possible topics of talk, mark the real focus of the session versus other possible foci, and so on.

Pertaining to the teacher, he often uses formulations to mediate the nature of the statements he makes. Thus, he frequently formulates what he has said such as to make it more uncertain, including the questions he asks (students and perhaps himself). He thereby provides the conditions where the inquiry can become more dialogical. We also see in this session evidence that students hear him speak authoritatively, even in situation where he formulates 'just to be asking a question'. It is *their* monolingualism that reduces a potential dialogical inquiry to the monological nature of science. That

---

20. This substitution is one of the core concepts and ideas in the work of Derrida. See, for example, Jacques Derrida, 'La différance', in *Tel Quel: Théorie d'ensemble* (Paris: Seuil, 1968), 41–66.

is, the teacher alone cannot make a classroom more dialogical, because the lived curriculum is always the outcome of a collective effort in which students and teacher have to collude.

One of the implications we can draw from reading of Bakhtin and his concept of dialogism is the difference between the traditional pedagogical intention and true dialogism. In his *Problems of Dostoevsky's Poetics*, it is quite clear that dialogism and dialogicity do not necessarily mean conversation. These students are members to a conversational setting, but such a conversation is subject to be dominated by the monologic voice of science. The intent underlying science courses is not to make students develop *any* form of language. No. At all levels of schooling, beginning with ministerial guidelines down to the planning books of teachers, students are to learn science content in the way articulated in the guidelines. It is the same kind of content that students are tested on in in-house examinations, provincial examinations, college entrance examination, international comparison tests (TIMMS, PISA), and high-stakes tests. Not assisting students to be prepared for these tests means playing with their futures. Teachers subscribing to a Bakhtinian perspective on learning therefore may find themselves in the quandary, where they want to foster dialogic forms of inquiry in a context that requires outcomes consistent with the monologic language and genres of standard science.

How can we change education generally and content-focused subjects more specifically to make them more dialogical? Perhaps focusing on everyday issues, allowing students to engage in forms of activism where there are multitudes of approaches relevant, including a multitude of concerns, forms of disciplinary knowledge, and forms of participation. As students deal with pertinent issues, they would find themselves in a context within which they could truly explore societally and educationally relevant issues in a dialogical manner. One of my projects, where seventh-grade students engage in environmentalism by choosing their forms of participation, foci, ways of proceeding, and forms of representation to the public constitutes a context suitable to practice individual and collective development in a dialogic way, that is, change and learning through the interrogation of ideas. This interrogation does not have to stop because it is a form of participation in the world not delimited by the hours and buildings of formal schooling. Environmentalism is an ongoing endeavor in this municipality

In such a context, the role of the teacher changes. My role as teacher no longer consists in pushing particular 'science competencies' but in allowing students to develop together with their ideas, interests, competencies, and so on. There is a focus on the development of the collective, which makes possible, and is made possible by, individual development. The educational aim is to allow students to become competent in participating in a conversation where there are multiple languages at work, those with origins in ethics, science, sociology, philosophy, law, humanities, and so on. The key competencies to be developed relate to the ability to participate in new idioms that are themselves instances of heterogeneity and multiplicity, forms of language and culture in which change is inherent and therefore the norm. We, educational researchers and theorists, already observe linguistic and cultural change occurring around us. But our theories are still focused on structure and stasis, stable conceptions and conceptual frameworks, rather than on the inherently changing languages that allow us to talk to each other even though we come to same settings with very different backgrounds, (linguistic) competencies, and interests.

There are new roles for teachers who embrace dialogic inquiry, but these new roles need to be enabled by the structural relations that others, at the school board and ministerial level, are better placed to call into question and thereby to change. As is, an individual teacher may choose to subvert the system momentarily, allowing students to inquire dialogically—because, for example, it might support their sense of understanding—and then prepare them for the crucial examinations near the end of the school year and within a short period of time. My experience-based expectation is that students develop such a tremendous linguistic competence in the field (subject matter) that getting them ready for (public) examinations or high-stakes testing becomes relatively easy. As a teacher, I have never worried about whether my students would learn however much we spent on engaging in inquiries other than those that one might find in a traditional physics classroom—including repeated discussions about epistemology and the relevance of the subject matter knowledge at hand to understand the nature of knowledge and students' own learning.

In this chapter, we also encounter a number of phenomena central to the production of face-to-face encounters generally and to learning more specifically. One of these phenomena concerns quoting others—including historical authorities in the field, a teacher, and a textbook—by means of direct or indirect speech. Because the speaker quotes, that is, uses his voice to bring a second voice into play, markers may have to be produced to allow listeners to distinguish between what is attributable to the authority and what is attributable to the current speaker. The two different sources may be important when students debate two alternative possibilities of acting, and the voice of authority might then weigh more on the matters at hand than the voice of the current speaker. I show that speakers have available means that allow marking the transition within the voice from speaking for itself to speaking for someone other. I show that at the transition point, we might find prosodic changes in the pitch register, pitch trends, and speech rate. Other markers may be grammatical, and these may interact with the prosodic markers. Thus, speakers may formulate that they are going to quote (e.g., 'Einstein said'), which may be followed directly what the physicist is attributed to have said or followed first by 'that' before articulating the direct or indirect quote. Here, 'Einstein said' might be associated with the falling pitch characteristic of a statement followed by a jump in the pitch register that marks the beginning of the attributed statement. When the attribution includes 'that' as in 'Einstein said that', the grammatical marker is even stronger, for the 'that' more readily projects the anticipated and anticipatable quote.

Finally, an important competency required in face-to-face encounters is the disambiguation of indexicals. In this chapter, I provide an example of 'here', which is used nine times within three turns at talk, but which orients the audience and speaker to different things and locations. Generally a marker of proximity, I show that proximity may be temporal and ideational rather than spatial, such as when the teacher's 'here' really is distal with respect to where he currently stands. But the 'here' repeats a student's immediately 'here', and in this repetition and temporal proximity can be heard as supporting the students' latest indexical target rather than any of the preceding ones. The situation itself provides resources for the members to the setting to hear precisely what is there to be heard.

5

The Body as Expression

Talking is generally taken to be a process, as I show in chapter 2, by means of which speakers render their private thoughts public. Speaking is thereby reduced to the translation of a cognitive framework or propositions from some internal representation into language by means of which the internal becomes external. This dichotomy of inside and outside also exists among those Western scholars who apparently subscribe to Lev Vygotsky's approach. In the previous two chapters, we see, however, that there has to be more to speaking and (participative) thinking for a simple speech event such as a classroom conversation to take place. The concept of the *theme* points us to the role of the setting as a whole, which allows individual words and utterances to take on a specific from several possible forms of dictionary sense. That is, we come to think of communication-in-situation. In situation, however, individual speakers take up positions, and their entire body becomes a gesture, a form of expression. In speaking, my body therefore is not an object, but the locus in which the drama of the world, which itself contributes to constituting, plays itself out and I loose myself in this drama. Thus, I hold it with Jacques Derrida that language and everything else that makes our life are inextricably interwoven. 'The *interweaving* (Verwebung) of language, of that in language that is purely linguistic and the other threads of experience, constitute a [woven] cloth. The word *Verwebung* refers back to this metaphorical zone: the "layers" are woven and their intrication is such that one cannot discern the woof from the weft. If the layer of the logos were simply founded, then one could lift it off and allow the appearance of the underlying layer non-expressive acts and contents. But since this superstructure acts back on the *Unterschicht*, one is obliged, from the beginning of the description, to associate to the geological metaphor a properly textual one: because cloth [tissu] means text. *Verweben* here means *texere*. The discursive is related to the non-discursive, the linguistic "layer" interlaces with the pre-linguistic "layer" according to the regulated system of a textual kind'.[1]

The traditional view of concept mapping is based on the idea that knowledge is stored in the human mind in the form of propositions. A proposition can be parsed, at

---

1. Jacques Derrida, *Marges de la philosophie* (Paris: Les Éditions de Minuit, 1972), 191.

a first level, into a subject and a predicate. The predicate decomposes into a (generally transitive) verb and another noun. Because each word can appear in multiple propositions, the theory suggests that conceptual understanding is encoded in the mind by means of frameworks that are externalized in the form of—come to find their expression in—concept maps. The concept map therefore is but an external articulation of something already present in mind and its organization therefore already prefigured. There would be then no need to ask how student groups to complete the task, which requires them simply to externalize what they know, perhaps necessitating some negotiating of differences. And this would be it. Throughout the preceding chapters we can see, however, that the life of concept mapping is much more complicated. First, students do not have a framework in mind and yet can competently participate in a task such as this. Second, there is more than negotiation at issue, because the propositions and organizations only emerge from the talk; they do not exist prior to the talk. Much of the public thinking is predicative rather than in the form of propositions, in the form that much of private thinking is said to take. As a consequence, and in contrast to the fundamental idea on which (individual) concept mapping is based, the videotapes show students in the process of *talking propositions into existence* before students can take this or that stand with respect to them. Their talking the conceptions thereby precedes the development of the conceptions that the talking is taken to presuppose.

Although I initially bought into the official theoretical explanation of mental organization, I (as a teacher) soon found that even individuals with some familiarity in a subject matter domain struggle in the process of constructing a concept map. But I continued to suspect that concept mapping might be a good tool for learning when *groups* of (rather than individual) students are presented with the task. Underlying the use of the technique does not require accepting the theoretical framework that has led to its invention. Rather, I have viewed concept mapping as an interesting task context where the product does not represent the content of the mind but rather constitutes an emergent artifact produced in and through collective work. As a high school teacher, I have been interested in enabling exchanges between students and providing a specific goal for orienting their conversations in and through which the maps came about. I have come to realize over the years that the concept-mapping task also has a reflexive component in that not only do students get to talk science, as they do in other tasks, but also they make the very language of science the topic of their talk. Language not only is a tool for doing things, like designing an investigation and executing it, but also it is the material (object/motive) itself. In this situation, language thereby functions as a tool that comes to operate upon itself.

An interesting aspect of collaborative concept mapping—a direct implication of my approach—is that the organization of the imprinted paper slips is only the first stage. The students move the paper slips about and discuss possible ways of connecting them. Eventually they end up with a spatial organization of these paper slips. But what they do not yet have in final form are the links, because these have only been talked about but have not yet been inscribed on paper. New issues might emerge in the process of producing the links and linking words. In this chapter, I present aspects of communication while students are in the final stage in the production and evolution of the spatial organization of the map, which the students transcribe when they are done.

In chapter 6, I therefore follow the students in the process of finalizing the map, which occurs when they draw the actual lines that connect pairs of concepts and as they settle on the connecting word that together with one of the concepts constitutes the predicate that specifies another concept.

In the process of accounting of this last section of the first part of the session before the three students come to an agreement that they have arrived at a suitable spatial organization, I focus on other aspects of the communicative process and of the work by means of which the arrangement of concept names comes about. In saying that this is the final part of the establishment of the spatial organization, I do not intimate that there is a determinate process at work that makes this part of the session recognizably the end. Rather, bringing this part of the session to an end is itself part of the work of mapping and how students bring off this work is itself worthy of attention. The students themselves do not know when this end will be, though they know that they are to complete the entire task within this lesson. Thus, both students and teacher make reference to the amount of time that is left, thereby orienting students to a moment of closure. In this chapter, we observe Miles making the comment that they have about ten minutes left. This, therefore, is an instant where we see that language goes beyond the science idiom. Students are in the fullness of life, with the full resources of language, though generally repressing or suppressing most of it. Settling when they have come to an end and orienting toward an end is itself a form of work to be accomplished in and as part of the session.

The nature of the talk in the concept-mapping sessions changes as it unfolds. As I initially reported 15 years ago, taking an analyst's perspective one observes phrases that roughly fall into four groups: (a) phrases that make reference to the global hierarchy of the concepts (e.g., 'Light is the most inclusive and should be on the top'); (b) phrases referring to a local hierarchy (e.g., 'Wave goes above quantum'; (c) phrases that simply expressed proximity (e.g., 'these three concepts go together'); and (d) phrases that expressed a clear relationship (e.g., 'Matter waves undergo diffraction'). At the time, I show that the frequency of organizational statements expressing one of the four categories changes over time. Comparing what I called a successful and an unsuccessful group—based on the individual students' retention of what they had done and learned in their group over a longer period of time—one can see that both groups were concerned initially with relations of proximity and global hierarchy (Fig. 5.1). The students from the group that retained the results of this lesson for a longer time showed a consistent concern for local hierarchies. The less successful group exceeded the other group in the relative frequency of phrases that merely expressed proximity.

Repetition and Difference: A Second Return

Reading through the transcripts from the concept-mapping sessions, we cannot but notice the constant repetitions of words, phrases, and parts thereof. In the classical view, repetition means making something that is self-identical, the same. Repeating is

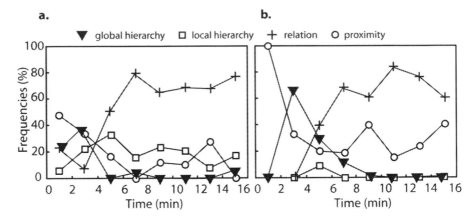

Fig. 5.1. Relative frequencies of statements making reference to global hierarchy, local hierarchy, proximity, and clear relationship in a successful group (a) and in an unsuccessful group (b).

thought to be a central feature of the reproduction of practices specifically and all of culture more generally. 'Repeat after me' and 'do as I do' are characteristic ways of talking in which teachers, while 'teaching', express the pedagogy for the reproduction of cultural practices. But if pure repetition were to be the case, we would not be able to observe the continuous evolution of cultures, which, in fact, has been accelerating in recent decades. To get to an appropriate theory of knowing and learning in and of a culture, we therefore need a different way of thinking about repetition.

We already see in the previous chapter that there must be more to repetition. If a teacher were to respond to a student query 'what do you mean?' by saying exactly the same words in the same sequence, the learners might complain saying that the teacher just repeated himself rather than really teaching her for understanding. This is precisely what I observed in a study of a lecture-oriented physics course in Brisbane, Australia. So exactly the same is not an option for repetition. Teaching therefore always also means translation, which might mean, for different students, ever-new ways of articulating the subject matter, using new and different sentences. There is at work a continued translation of the language at hand into another such version of itself. But saying precisely the same words again covering the whole utterance or part of the utterance may itself have important functions in teaching and learning. In a noisy laboratory session, with vacuum pumps running and other devices creating interferences with actually hearing another person, 'What did you say?' may be followed by the precisely same words that have already made a previous utterance. Such repetition, which has a specific function repairing a problem emerging from the presence of noise, would not give rise to suspicion. What other functions of repetition might there be and what are their function?

The following fragment, which continues the conversation precisely at the point where it ends in the previous chapter, begins with Ken making a proposal for the arrangement of the concept names at the very top of their hierarchy. Nobody actually names the words that they are moving about but take knowing these for granted. Ralf

objects, but softens the objection by using the modifying 'I don't think' before proposing his solution. Miles, too, moves a paper slip and suggests that 'they (QUANTUM,
WAVE) should be equal', 'this should be'. Ralf, talking at the same time as Miles, repeats the words, 'this should be, this should be' (turn 264). Miles cedes and Ralf continues, 'the Compton effect is', but Miles simultaneously counters, 'no, no, there'
(turn 266). Ken also weighs in, calling Ralf's name repeatedly and louder than normal,
'Ralf, Ralf, Ralf' (turn 267), and while so doing, moves out of his chair leans across
the table and in front of Ralf, then squarely gazing the former into his face (see offprint, turn 267). As Miles and Ken stop talking, Ralf continues by himself, thereby
completing the utterance that the other two have been overlapping repeatedly. Ken
utters another agreement/opposition, 'Yea but' and then states that 'it' 'is off' (turn
269). He utters Ralf's name yet again, 'Ralf', and then continues, 'what we were doing with complementarity'. What is not so clear from the transcription—limited because of the amount of space in a single line and for marking overlaps—is the fact that
Ralf begins to overlap Miles, who eventually cedes. Ken also begins to talk, but he
then halts until after Ralf has finished talking before voicing his opposition ('yea but')
that what Ralf proposes 'is off'.

Fragment 5.1
```
261 K: if this is more so have it like that;
262 R: i dont think that x=rays and light should be up here.
263 M: they should be equal [not on this should be  ]
264 R:                       [this should this should]
265 R: [the compton effect is    ]
266 M: [no no there,             ]
267 K: [<<f>^ralf; ^ralf; ^ralf;]>
       ((*))
268 R: exactly the same level.
269 K: yea but its off; ralf; what
       we were doing with
       complementarity,
```

   Ken's prosody is of interest. The voice analysis program shows that he utters Ralf's
name with 8 times the normal speech intensity (9 dB difference). The word is uttered
rapidly and sounds more like 'raf' than like 'Ralf'; and the pitch rises and falls again
within the short utterance. It is almost like a bark: 'raf', 'raf', 'raf'. With Merleau-
Ponty, we might rethink speaking as constituting a verbal gesture, which produces
itself in a certain setting common to the interlocutors. It is a verbal gesture because I
know my body only through living it, which means that I take up the drama that is
played out in the situation and because my bodily I is co-constitutive of the event, in
my body itself.[2] Thus, we literally see Ken take up position as he moves forward and

---

2. Maurice Merleau-Ponty, *Phénoménologie de la perception* (Paris:Gallimard, 1945).

thereby positions himself opposite to Ralf who, in his previous position, has been to Ken's right; and Ralf himself has been oriented slightly to his right and toward the top right part of the emerging organization in front of them. It is not, therefore, that Ken utters Ralf's name for a total of four times, as a computer would indistinguishably print the name four times or, as it appears on this line, four times the same, and therefore without difference. But in and through his body, Ken expresses a position; and this position is not the same as Ralf's: it is in *op*position to Ralf. For the other to recognize, he has to listen, and Ken, through his entire body, communicates the insistence of his call on the other.

Here we have a repeated articulation of Ralf's name. Ralf speaks, overlapping others, without stopping. Ken addresses Ralf, again, and again. Ralf continues as if he does not hear, and Ken repeats so that Ralf can hear that he is called upon. Ralf does not respond to Miles or Ken. Uttering his name repeatedly thereby becomes a call, 'Ralf, listen'. But Ralf continues, as if undeterred. 'Ralf, Ralf', Ken calls again. It is here that he comes out of his chair (see offprint in turn 267), moves into Ralf's field of vision, turns his head, and squarely addresses Ralf, 'yea, but it's off'. He calls again on Ralf to attend to what he is saying, 'what we are doing with complementarity'. With each utterance of the name, the call becomes more insisting. That is, although the sound pattern can be recognized as yielding the name of the other student, with each addition, we hear the insistence increase. This is further emphasized in and by Ken's movement, which increases the intensity of the call for attention.

In this instance, Ken is not just spilling words as a computer might spill words onto paper by means of a printer. On the contrary, there is evidence that the body is not just a vehicle but also the very content of the expression. When Ken calls upon Ralf three times, he does so with an eight-fold increase in speech intensity, much more rapid production of sound, and a distinct rise and fall of the pitch. He moves forward and gets right into the visual field of Ralf and thereby 'into his face'. It is therefore in and through his body that opposition and urgency come to find their expression. It is not that Ken has to think about how to change his voice and about moving his body forward. Rather, he moves as part of his implication in this world, which he both produces and is subject to. The theme governing the moment is co-expressed in purely bodily (as opposed to 'mental') form. It is not, too, that a mind has to plan this expression beforehand, the theme is both expressed in and evolves by means of the bodily involvement.

The second repetition in Fragment 5.1 has a similar function but is much less intense. Miles reproduces Ralf's preceding 'should', which Ralf, in his turn, repeats again twice. Ralf continues to talk and both Ken and Miles object, though in different ways. Their social evaluation is an objection, but it comes in different ways. Ralf's name is uttered again in turn 269, naming the specific addressee of the conjunctive contrast ('but'), and its function also is to say something like, 'listen, Ralf, listen to what I am trying to say'. Here, then, we have two forms of multiple repetitions. Our question has to be, 'What is the function of these repetitions, if, according to Bakhtin, the same word, though it has the same dictionary sense and therefore is repeatable, never marks the same theme?'

Has all this insistence paid off? The next fragment begins with Ralf expressing agreement ('I know' [turn 270]), thereby providing positive social evaluation to the preceding call for attention to 'complementarity'. Ken's own utterance 'that's why' signals that he hears Ralf to agree. Ralf again employs the conditional 'should' to express an expectation of what has to be done, or rather, where COMPLEMENTARITY is (not) to be placed in the hierarchical arrangement emerging before them. Miles addresses himself to Ralf, again by using the name of the latter thereby increasing the degree of insistence that we can hear and experience. Ralf has but reiterated his previous position and shows no indication that he is going to follow the solution that Miles and Ken now favor: subordinating QUANTUM and WAVE to COMPLEMENTARITY.

Fragment 5.2
```
270 R: i know;
271 K: thats why,
272 R: it shouldnt be here; it ((COMPLEMENTARITY)) should be
       under waves.
273 M: ralf; because you can put wave there and you could put
       it there but it doesnt need to be here; you have light
       as a heading and we dont loose a thing in the concept
       map. but we have it when we dont put wave here. we are
       totally left without half our-
274 K: we could say, dealing with the subject matters of light
       and x=rays and then go into further detail. actually-
       when you think about it, light is a detail of wave, but
       wave is also a particular aspect of light. cause
       remember; that light isnt just waves, now that they=re
       saying that there is quantum physics, so thats just a
       detailed explicit expression of light waves and x=rays.
```

Miles explains to Ralf that because 'wave' can take alternative positions in the arrangement does not mean that it 'needs to be' in one place or the other. That is, Miles hears Ralf as being bound—'should' in the sense of 'ought'—to one of the two. In fact, Miles articulates that they have a choice of where to put the concept name. He further explains that they do not 'loose a thing' with the alternate arrangement, especially because of LIGHT taking the top position. He completes with another articulation of possibility, and then begins to specify what would happen if they did not place COMPLEMENTARITY in the way he proposes ('we are totally left without half our . . .'). Ken then further expresses possible ways of thinking about the map as it is unfolding beneath their hands. He, too, articulates alternative ways of placing WAVE ('light is a detail of wave, but wave is also a particular aspect of light'). He then calls on Ralf to remember, and articulates the very purpose of the chapter they just studied, 'light isn't just waves' as they have learned during a previous unit dealing with the wave character of light, but 'now they are saying that there is quantum physics'. He concludes— using the adverbial conjunctive 'so'—'that's [WAVE] just a detailed expression of light waves and X-rays' (turn 274).

Going over both preceding fragments allows us to hear both (a) Ralf's reluctance to move away from the idea about the organization that they 'should' implement and (b) his peers' calls for him to listen and then to articulate more extensive reasons for going with their proposal of placing COMPLEMENTARITY. Here Ken may be quoting directly or indirectly when he calls his interlocutors generally and Ralf in particular to 'remember': 'light is a detail of wave' and 'wave is a particular aspect of light'. Ken asks others to remember, something someone or something has said, 'light isn't just waves' followed by a statement about what *they* are saying. Here we need to understand remembering not as bringing into consciousness a self-subsistent aspect of the past, but as a push into the horizon of the past until 'the experiences that [the memory] denotes are as if lived again in their temporal setting'.[3] Ken uses the word 'that', which, according to Bakhtin, often introduces indirect reporting of speech, that is, he is reporting the speech event in which he has taken part and thereby lives again this past.

In the following fragment that continues the conversation, we observe again instances of repetition. These indicate particular concerns for how to organize one term and the region about it. The repetition thereby constitutes a form of stabilizing the topic for a moment before the conversation goes on and takes another concept name and its surroundings as the topic. 'Planck's constant' appears in turn 277 and is repeated twice in the following turns, and then again in turn 283. Similarly, and overlapping with the articulation of utterances with 'Planck's constant', the articulation of 'Compton effect' occurs in turn 280, when Ken asks his interlocutors to 'wait' and, thereby, to turn their attention to this concept word. Ralf then utters the name of this concept twice in turn 288, for which Miles produces a predicate 'it frees electrons', a statement which he invokes again in turn 295. In the meantime, the 'photoelectric effect', too, enters to conversation and becomes its topic in turns 290, 291, and 292. Just as Miles has announced, there are then three concepts that have to be and, here are, considered together because they 'go together' (turn 295).

Fragment 5.3
```
275 M: both are waves, so we leave it.
276 K: so we are gonna organize the rest of this? where are we
       gonna?
277 M: plancks constant, threshold frequency,
       [plancks constant, electron].
278 K: [plancks constant involves ] everything; threshold
       frequency,
279 M: these three concepts go together (.) or that goes
       everywhere electron; this involves frequency; so,
280 K: wait; does compton effect [involve, ]
281 R:                           [threshold] frequency.
282 M: is the [compton effect ] the one where they try,
283 K:        [this deals with]-
       the plancks constant too; that goes [under-  ]
284 R:                                     [you know] what?
285 K: like if you can go somewhere up here;
286 R: these basically make up the kinetic energy.
287 K: yea where we have the-
288 R: compton; the compton effect is,
```

---

3. Merleau-Ponty, op. cit. note 2, 30.

```
289 M: it frees electrons; high energy x=rays,
290 K: the photoelectric effect also ejects electrons;
291 M: so put it down here, in between the two.
292 K: no this is for the photoelectric effect
293 M: sorry; i thought that was
294 R: they eject electrons,
295 M: but the [compton effect also],
296 R:            [but they have      ] to have
       [the kinetic energy].
297 M: [no, its gotta go  ] between the two because they both
       eject, they both need the threshold frequency.
298 K: these both need a threshold frequency?
299 R: okay, but you also have to have
```

In this fragment, the students arrive at articulating similarities between the concepts of the 'Compton effect' and the 'photoelectric effect'. In fact, their textbook likens the two effects as interactions of electromagnetic waves with matter, though the waves in the former effect are X-rays and in the latter effect are in or near the visible spectrum (i.e., 'light'). In both cases, electrons are ejected from the materials with a certain amount of energy. However, only in the case of the photoelectric effect does the textbook talk about threshold energy, which is not the case in the Compton effect, because any binding energy is surpassed by several orders of magnitude by the energy of the X-ray photon. The verb 'eject' is not one that is frequently found in students' vernacular, as shown in the videotapes collected while I taught in this school. But here, the term appears. The language surrounding the verb 'eject' thereby can be traced right to the textbook. However, another verb used in the textbook ('emit') is not used here. The relationship between the textbook language and students' language therefore is not causally linked—as some constructivist scholars interested in 'learning pathways' have expressed in the past the relation between curriculum materials and learning.

The use of the adverbial conjunctive 'because' is interesting, as it can (a) express a causal relation or provide a rationale for acting in one rather than another way or (b) enter evidence from somewhere else, not from the text but from the experiment or a description thereof. In the present instance, Miles suggests that THRESHOLD FREQUENCY 'gotta go between' the PHOTOELECTRIC EFFECT and the COMPTON EFFECT, 'because they both eject, they both need the threshold frequency'. Here, the first of the three concept names is proposed to be superordinate, because of something else. This something else has to have a more secure foundation than the proposal itself, for otherwise it cannot be taken as a rationale for doing what is proposed. In the present instance, Miles suggests that the two other terms *both* eject (electrons) and 'they *both* need the threshold energy'. That is, because there are two things, on the one hand, and one concept name is part of both, the singular entity is suggested to be higher up in the hierarchy—just as Immanuel Kant proposed categorization to work. Thus, 'the lower concept is not contained in the higher, because the former actually contains more than the latter. But the lower concept is lower, because the higher concept also contains the epistemological ground of the former'.[4] Despite their experimental and external dif-

---

4. Immanuel Kant, *Werke III: Schriften zur Metaphysik* (Wiesbaden: Insel-Verlag, 1956), 529.

ferences, there is something, according to Miles, common to both. It thereby becomes
the organizing principle.

Ken repeats Miles' utterance almost exactly, 'these both need a threshold frequency' (turn 298). Why would he? Does he not merely produce a gratuitous duplica-
tion? But repetition is not gratuitous. We generally do not contribute to conversations
gratuitously. Rather, repetition has a function, which derives from the pragmatics of
the situation.[5] Here Ken utters the phrase again. He does so with a rise of the intonation toward what comes to be the end of the utterance. We can hear this as a question,
and in fact, we can hear astonishment: 'So they both need a threshold frequency?'
That is, Ken, although he is on Miles' side concerning the current arrangement of the
concept names, here questions the evidence Miles has used to argue for a particular
arrangement of concepts.

In uttering 'Okay', Ralf articulates agreement with what has been said, yet then
produces the contrastive conjunctive 'but'. This therefore both mediates the 'okay'
and allows him to state in which respect the previously articulated content is insufficient. Here he begins to suggest what else they 'have to have'. Ken proposes
'Planck's' (turn 300), and Ralf then states—while pointing to PLANCK'S CONSTANT
and THRESHOLD FREQUENCY—that 'these two multiplied together is the energy of the
photon' (turn 301). Ken does not contradict or express reservation but—using the conjunctive 'and'—inherently suggests that what he says is added to what previously has
been said. Here, the 'I think' is a form of evaluation of a preceding statement-like utterance. It qualifies its certainty as a statement, contrasting thereby, for example, the
kinds of statements in which famous scientists are linked to particular utterances, reported indirectly from the textbook in more or less fidelity. Miles employs the same
conjunctive without mediating contrast, and Ken adds to the discussion by beginning
with 'and' that they can find the 'work function'. From a physicist's perspective, this
is precisely the case, as the threshold frequency of a photon supplies exactly the
(minimum) energy required to release the electron from the material ('work function').

Fragment 5.4
```
299 R: okay, but you also have to have
300 K: plancks
301 R: these two multiplied together is the energy of the
       photon;
302 K: and these go under here like this and thats all
303 M: and then we can just draw arrows like this
304 K: and with the threshold frequency, thats where you find
       the work function and then diffraction, diffraction
       should go under this. i think. because they both can
       diffract off anything.
```

Here, three turns begin with the conjunctive 'and', which can be employed to express that what follows in the clause is to be taken side by side with, in addition to,

---

5. Saying that there is a 'reason' for the repetition may overstate the issue, for, as we see above, the
repetition may not be consciously produced but may arise from the way in which a person takes position.

and along (together) with what precedes. That is, the repeated deployment of 'and' by different speakers thereby articulates not only that they add something but also that there is a fundamental agreement about the acceptance of the current state of affairs to which speakers can add because there is nothing to contest about the previous statement. It is an articulation of the common ground that they have achieved and continue to elaborate. In using 'and' in this way, repeatedly and in consecutive turns, the participants to this event not only reproduce the collective agreement but also elaborate, concretize, and therefore further transform it. Here again, repetition does not mean 'the same'; or rather, the 'it', in taking the same form, differs.

The events in this section also provide us with clues about how to understand communication in ways that differ from the traditional sender–receiver (interpreter) analogy that dominates much of current thinking about learning (e.g., in science lectures where professors 'want to get the material across'). Thus, there is little evidence that students stop, take time out to make the words of others the object of their reflection, engage in the effort of reflectively understanding or interpreting what others have said, and then construct a response. The give and take is so fast, often overlapping, that any model of the reception and interpretation of information would fall short. Some research in the cognitive sciences has shown that even in the case of very simple perceptual entities, such as the objects in the computer game Tetris, would require much more time to process than players are actually observed to take. The processes therefore cannot be understood as if players first perceived information consciously, interpreted it, and then used the results of the interpretation to 'construct' an action. Such a discourse therefore is entirely inadequate to think about and theorize learning through information processing.

Embodiment and Communication: Take One

Thought and expression, Merleau-Ponty writes in a manner entirely consistent with Vygotsky and Mikhail Bakhtin, are not independent entities but are constituted simultaneously. 'Thought, in the speaking subject, is not a representation, that is to say, it does not posit explicitly objects and relations. The speaker does not think before speaking, not even while he speaks; his speech is his thought. In the same way, the listener does not construct concepts on the basis of signs'.[6] Rather the expression, as we see in the previous section, is an entirely bodily act that occurs in situation that the speaker's and listener's bodies contribute to constituting. In speaking, we do not take consciously control over words, especially not when the conversation is engaging and animated. It is in, with, through, and by means of Ken's bodily productions (intonations, sound heard as words), his bodily movements, that his thinking *and* his position on the topic come to be articulated and come to be about. Speakers take up positions in the world, always and already shot through with thematic unity, and this world is itself partly constituted in and through the positions that the bodies take and therefore

---

6. Merleau-Ponty, op. cit. note 2, 209.

concretize among other possible positions. Such taking a position changes the world of the listener, whose body participates in the same way in the constitution of the world common to the interlocutors. In communicating, speakers and listeners do not translate ready-made thought into external representations but *they accomplish the thought itself*, which exists in, for, and through the situation as such, including their bodies. Thought, therefore, is not something internal but exists in the world to be accomplished together by the members to a situation and for bringing about such an accomplishment itself. Bakhtin refers to this as *theme*. In this section, I provide a first set of examples that support this description, already consistent with the analyses provided in the preceding parts of this book.

In the video offprints provided in this book, we can see the organization of the imprinted paper slips develop on the tabletop before the three students' eyes. Miles and Ralf are seated such that the top of the hierarchy is further away from them, the bottom closer up. Ken is situated to, and contributes from, the left side (from the position of the students). The concept map is not constituted merely by some abstract terms that students are asked to organize, as this might be the case if we merely think of propositions encoded in students' minds. Rather, there are real imprinted paper slips that are part and constitutive of the world that they together inhabit. The written words are as much part of the material as the sounds that we can hear—and that are transcribed—as words. It is in, with respect to, and constitutive of this world that the students move and orient themselves. There is no evidence for, and no need to be, thinking of students as producing a parallel world in their minds, a world that might be said to be meta-physical and to consist of concepts that are applied to this world. Their talk and the world they inhabit are enmeshed as the woof and weft in the shirts that they wear. That is, they inhabit the language in the same way that the language inhabits them.

The previous fragment ends with the production and transformation of their common understanding. The students now orient toward different paper slips. Miles is looking into the book when Ken moves a pair of slips in front of him and to the bottom right of the existing arrangement. Ralf takes the book from Miles and begins to rifle through it. At first, Miles states not knowing where to put these paper slips, which Ken acknowledges. Miles then glances at the book, back at the organization in front of him, and then moves the two slips (DE BROGLIE WAVELENGTH and MATTER WAVES) from where Ken has placed them around the bottom part of the map and to a level about midway up (Fig. 5.2). He says, 'I think that goes up there, but I want to check in the book if they go like that'. He adds, 'I am not certain about that' (turn 307).

Fragment 5.5
```
305 M: ((Ken moves MATTER WAVES and DE BROGLIE WAVELENGTH to
       bottom right and in front of Miles)) i dont know where
       where put this back in.
306 K: okay;
307 M: that should, wait ((Ralf turns pages in the book; Miles
       takes a glance at the book, then begins to move slips
       from the bottom right to the top left of the hierarchy,
```

Fig. 5.2. Miles moves the two concept names in an arc away from him around some other concepts and up toward the top.

```
Fig. 5.2)) i think that goes up here but i want to
check in the book if they go like that probably like
this, but i am not certain about that. whats pair
production, i can=t remember.
```

In this instance, we not only see sense marked all over the situation but also Miles orienting toward it in a way that comes to be articulated in multiple ways. First, before he actually moves the pair DE BROGLIE WAVELENGTH and MATTER WAVES, he gazes at the book as if he wanted to look something up. He is physically orienting and turning his head toward the book. He later articulates uncertainty ('I think that goes up there'), for the removal of which he 'wants to check in the book if they go like that'. In the meantime, he has moved the concept name away from him to end in a position diagonally about halfway up the hierarchy from where he has taken them. It is therefore not just abstract concept names that need to find place in some abstract hierarchy, but there is actually a physical arrangement and the paper slips find their place in it. The conceptual arrangement of the names and the physical world of the students are one. Moving the paper slips requires Miles' body, so that he can lean forward and move his arm for DE BROGLIE WAVELENGTH and MATTER WAVES to end in the place that he articulates these as belonging to. There is no separation noticeable between some ideal (metaphysical) world up there in lofty spheres, consisting from purified ideas and concepts, and a physical world down here, where the students move paper slips with words. There is no indication in any instant in this entire session that there is a separation between the physical world containing traces on paper and sound, on the one hand, and a metaphysical (transcendental) world entirely consisting of abstractions, on the other hand. Rather, sound-words and ink-trace-words are part of this world that they inhabit and constitute. Language (already material in its production) and the material world to which it refers are inextricably interwoven such that knowing the former inherently means knowing to get around the latter. There is no longer a difference between a practical understanding of language and a practical understanding of the world that these students inhabit.

The physical organization of the imprinted paper slips parallels a conceptual organization of the words. The propositions that the three students produce by proposing a verb to link two nouns also will be part of this physical world that they inhabit and constitute with their bodies. This world subsequently is repeated, inscribed on the sheet of paper and also exists as a combination of sounds that students repeat and modify until they settle upon as a suitable combination. Each combination attributes one or more predicates to each concept, or, at least, has concepts that co-constitute a predicate. Producing a statement that makes part of the conceptual hierarchy therefore takes physical work. The material work and its ideal complement irreducibly go together. Uttering a statement of and about the hierarchical relation between two concept names is possible because the students already know, in and through their bodies, how to move entities into physical proximity and hierarchical relations.

In the following fragment, we observe the indistinction between (a) the material world containing imprinted paper slips, which can be manipulated and moved about, and sounds produced by means of the vocal cords and (b) the purported transcendental world of concepts and ideas, on the other hand. Thus, Miles talks about 'put[ting] high energy in' and Ken utters words that we hear to reflect a physical organization. In turn 313, Miles suggests that the electrons 'should go below here' and 'right here'. He thereby unmistakably talks about the physical placement of the slip on which ELECTRONS is imprinted.

Fragment 5.6
```
308 R: creation of matter; ((reads))
309 M: oh; by putting high energy in; high energy-
310 K: diffraction (.) no diffraction is under the compton
       effect; because remember, the x=rays when you put them
       through.
311 M: um (.) are they diffracted around the photon?
312 K: yea; and then the lower frequency x=rays photons come
       through;
313 M: but thats why we need threshold frequency too; because,
       no electrons should go below here; it should go right
       here.
314 K: i dont know where this-
315 M: okay; down there (.) cause if these two dont have (.)
       okay;
  a K: (???) ((Puts finger to forehead, as if getting sweat,
       then drawing on table))
  b M: i get some so i can draw a diagram; ((takes some sweat
       of his forehead and "draws" lines between slips on the
       table))
316 K: ((laughs))
317 M: see if,
318 K: we gonna need compton effect to see diffraction; we
       gonna-
319 R: is conflicting;
320 K: so thats- right there ((goes through book)) that
       describes it see it diffracts; ((shows drawing of the
       compton effect))
```

Fig. 5.3. Ken points to and moves his finger toward a drawing representing the Compton effect, as seen on the right.

```
321 R: no thats momentum- ((pause)) knocks it out ((his finger
       moves from material to the right)) because,
```

In this situation, Ken utters 'we gonna need Compton effect to see diffraction' (turn 318). This is an ambiguous phrase, because it could be describing an event in the world of which he provides a description. But it also could be the proposal for a proposition to be entered in the semantic network. That is, in addition to the material words that appear in the form of sound and as ink traces, students move about the paper. Any conceptual hierarchy thereby is produced by entirely material behavior. The spatial organization is one that develops with respect to the students, and with which they entertain proximal ('here') and distal relations ('there'). The differently inscribed paper slips go 'below' and 'above' some other slip or slips. That is, there no longer is a difference between any conceptual and material worlds: the two are one and the same. Moreover, there is no evidence that the students keep the structure unfolding before them in their minds. The structure is materially present and therefore does not have to be made present ideally. Whenever students need to consult the structure, they simply look. It is in this one world that the students orient themselves and each other, marking, re-marking, and remarking sense.

All the while students are talking Ralf leaves through the book. At the very end of Fragment 5.6, just after the word 'Compton effect' has been uttered, Ken points to an image in the textbook (Fig. 5.3, right). It, too, is constituted by a set of ink traces, and it is part of the inhabited material world. It does not, in the first instance, constitute a sign for something else. It is an ink trace in and of this world, contributing to the constitution of the latter. The image is integrated into the world in and as ink trace, but it is also integrated as something that points students to something else not directly accessible to their senses. But in being material, it can be pointed to and is part of their world. Again, any distinction between the conceptual and the material is erased, as

Ken points (Fig. 5.3, left) to the image of the Compton effect (Fig. 5.3, right) all the while uttering 'that describes it, see it diffracts' (turn 320). That is, in one and the same utterance, itself a material aspect constitutive of their world, Ken traverses the conceptual and the physical spaces, integrating the thing being described in the image and the image itself. That is, there is no longer a distinction between the communication between the three students and the material world that they point to directly and ideationally. All distinctions between knowing their language, which describes the world at hand and the conceptual world of physics, and knowing their way around this world are erased. We do not communicate with representations but with, paraphrasing Merleau-Ponty, speaking human beings who inhabit and constitute a world together with us, and who differ in exhibiting their particular styles. Our lifeworld always and already is endowed with thematic unity and our embodied communication, in dialectic communicative production, marks, re-marks, and transforms the themes and significations of words, and, therefore, the material world. In the following section, I take a closer look at the differentiation of language that occurs as students engage in comparing and categorizing drawing on analogies. Images themselves, in being made present again, are transformed, likened to other images, and all of this not at some conceptual level beyond this world but in the practice of seeing and remembering.

Ken makes a statement about subordinating 'pair production' to the 'Compton effect'. Ralf responds by uttering what we might hear (because of intonation and grammar) as a question, 'what does it say'. Rather than articulating what it says, Ken verbally and gesturally points Ralf to a particular place on the page ('we go it right here'). A long silence ensues, broken by Ralf who utters, 'but does it say anything about the Compton effect?' Part of the students' effort in bringing a concept name into their language consists in describing what the thing it names is about. That is, students can produce a description of events said to occur in the natural world and then name this event total, for example, 'Compton effect'. Or they may simply point to a diagram depicting the experiment. Pointing then is a special form of quoting another person, who is, enacted by a pointing gesture to the diagram, mobilized in the argument for the student much as he would using a direct (verbal) quote. That is, saying that someone has said something and quoting the person directly and pointing to a diagram in a textbook both may serve the same function in students' conversation. In his turn, Ken points to a diagram in the textbook to underscore his point, 'see it diffracts', which supports his earlier point about a relationship between the Compton effect (Fig. 5.3) and the fact of being enabled to see diffraction. That is, by pointing others to some aspect of the world, which thereby becomes salient, Ken brings this thing pointed to into his expression, allowing it to speak for itself, but doing so in a context entirely framed by his own voice.

In the last turn of Fragment 5.6, Ralf makes available a negative evaluation of the preceding contribution not only saying that 'momentum' is involved and that the electron is knocked out but indeed moving his right index finger from the 'thin metal foil' (Fig. 5.3, right) toward the right, enacting with his finger a movement that parallels the one we see depicted in the diagram. The moving finger appears to increase the communicative force of Ralf's contribution, because the momentum is undeniably available in the momentum of his finger. That is, one part of Ralf's body moves, and this movement, created by the body, is one that exhibits an iconic relation to the movement depicted, stylized, and represented on the page. Here again, the 'knocking out' and the movement that the 'ejected electron' undergoes ('kinetic energy') exist in the parallel and simultaneous world of body movements. It is not that the two worlds are different, as the image and Ralf's index finger are present to them in the world. They can be perceived. They are present as objects and therefore are objectively available to all members to the situation. But simultaneously, the moving finger and the diagram with respect to which it moves, and with which it forms an integrated whole, also refer to something else, something that physicists make an independent realm of and for itself, a realm of metaphysical, objective truth. But this something else only exists in and through the material embodiment of speakers, listeners, and their world the spectacle of which they witness in and with their bodies.

Comparing, Differentiating, Categorizing and Making Analogies

Textbooks present massive amounts of diverse content and yet provide only a small number of examples for the possibilities of deploying any one word together with other words. It is therefore left to students to figure out whether certain phrases they evolve make sense or not. We already see in the preceding sections and chapters, that the students featured here, despite their subsequent successes at the university and in life generally, struggle with finding propositions that connect the terms. As teacher, my own use of concept mapping as a teaching–learning tool—which, to recall, requires students to link all major concepts words found in the same chapter—emerged from the recognition that textbooks provide few if any opportunity for students to talk about connections between many of the concept words within and between chapters. It is not surprising that some learning scientists have used the term 'knowledge in pieces' to refer to their observations that students do not inherently make connections between different vocabularies that they have come to be exposed to in school. Thus, the Compton effect, which the three students discuss for an extended amount of time, can be talked about as a phenomenon whereby electromagnetic radiation (X-ray photons) interacts with matter. In the students' textbook, there are other phenomena in which electromagnetic radiation interacts with matter (Fig. 5.4). But there is no connection in the textbook that would use a common language to describe and compare these phenomena, though the book does provide a bulleted list in which the terms appear. But differentiating means that establish both similarities and differences, resources for evolving an idiom suitable to talk about the diverse phenomena simultaneously, are not provided in and by the students' textbook. Moreover, unless explicitly addressed, such a common idiom hardly ever is the goal of instruction concerned with chapters and units, immediately tested following their 'coverage', rather than with the 'big picture'.

The following fragment begins with turn 318 because, upon hindsight, we may conclude that the Compton effect as topic-organizing idea has its origin precisely here. In Fragment 5.7, we observe Ken evolve an utterance in which the Compton effect

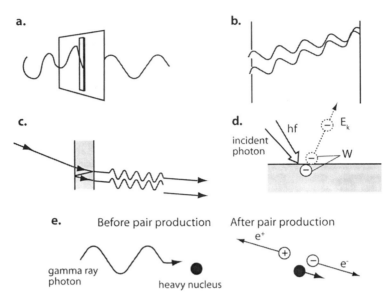

Fig. 5.4. Drawings similar to those that the students have seen in their textbook featuring waves that interact with matter and change their path. There are surface similarities with the drawing of the Compton effect. a. A wave interacts with a polarization filter. b. A wave is diffracted at a double slit leading to interference patterns. c. A light wave is refracted and partial reflected inside a medium, which explains an interference phenomenon on the right side. d. In the photoelectric effect, an incident photon is absorbed, its energy being used to free (W) and to give kinetic (movement) energy to an electron. e. In pair production, an electron and a positron are created from the energy released by a decaying gamma ray photon.

comes to be related to 'diffraction', one of the concept names that they have included in their conversation only once before (between turns 061 and 069). Now, in these last several turns, the concept name has become a topic again. In response to Ralf, Miles suggests that they need 'diffraction', and Ken queries the former (turned toward him) whether 'that', the Compton effect they are pointing to, 'isn't a form of diffraction'. As can be seen from the reproduction of other images that appear throughout the students' textbook (Fig. 5.4a–c), there are images similar to that depicting the Compton effect (Fig. 5.3, right), similar in that they all feature (a) an incident light wave that interacts with matter and (b) an exiting light wave. Miles does not appear to address Ken's utterance, asking instead about the organization of electrons with respect to threshold energy, that is, asking about an organization that uses the language of the photoelectric effect. But this effect is not depicted in the book using the incident light in waveform but as an arrow (Fig. 5.4d). That is, the textbook images, too, do not exhibit similarities. We should not be surprised therefore if the students do not evolve an idiom common to the different phenomena, that is, a language suitable for talking about, comparing, contrasting, and evaluating the three phenomena on the same plane.

Fragment 5.7

```
318 K: we gonna need compton effect to see diffraction; we
       gonna-
319 R: is conflicting;
320 K: so thats- right there ((goes through book)) that
       describes it see it diffracts; ((points to drawing of
       the Compton effect; Fig. 5.3, right))
321 R: no thats momentum- ((pause)) knocks it out ((his finger
       moves from material to the right)) because,
322 M: so we need this for diffraction; electrons, photons,
       threshold frequency; they dont (??)
323 K: ((turned toward Ralf)) isnt that a form of diffraction
       by doing that?
324 M: do you agree with electrons being down below threshold
       frequency?
325 R: ((inaudible))
326 M: because they need the threshold frequency- no electrons
       are like they have to be otherwise nothing.
327 K: diffraction goes (.) i might be thinking back to the
       nature of light.
328 M: i=m thinking back to double slits.
329 K: yea; exactly;
330 M: but its gotta something to do with- its to do with-
```

Miles continues by providing an explication using the conjunctive 'because', which introduces clauses that propose reasons for what is stated in the preceding clause: 'because they need threshold frequency'. But he appears to answer himself, 'no', utters something about electrons, and then finishes in uttering 'nothing' (turn 26). Ken returns to the issue of diffraction and explains, 'I might be thinking back to the nature of light' (turn 327); and Miles, in making an assertion pertaining to the same topic, produces agreement, 'I'm thinking back to double slits' (turn 328). Ken, in turn, transforms the situation by producing further agreement ('yea, exactly'); Miles follows him, insisting that it has to do with 'something' else, although he does not articulate this 'something' here. He introduces the statement with 'but', which both signals agreement and that there is something missing.

We see here that the students talk about the Compton effect in terms of 'diffraction', talk that they then elaborate further in terms of what they have seen and learned in a preceding chapter about light and its wave nature. Although the students' textbook does not provide explicit linkages between the different topics—i.e., talking about all phenomena at the same time highlighting similarities and differences between the topics—the images available in different parts of the textbook suggest at least some (conceptual and iconic) similarities. These similarities may be of a surface type with substantial differences at the conceptual level. Thus, in Figure 5.4d, we see an articulation of the photoelectric effect, another phenomenon that the students talk about, which also constitutes the interaction of a photon with matter. In this instance, the photon is from the visible spectrum, that is, it is also called 'light'. Here, the energy of the photon is entirely absorbed to release an electron from the surface of a metallic substance; and the electron takes up any remainder of the energy as kinetic energy (energy of motion). When the energy of the photon is just sufficient to free the electron but not enough to give it additional energy for moving away, physicists speak of its frequency as 'threshold frequency'.

Pair production is yet another interaction of electromagnetic radiation, here the interaction of a gamma ray photon with matter (Fig. 5.4e). In this case, the photon is destroyed and its energy is used to create a pair of new particles (e.g., an electron and a positron), the remainder going to the kinetic energy of the created particles and of the heavy nucleus. There is a threshold effect as the energy of the gamma ray photon has to be equal or greater than that required for producing the two particles.[7] That is, in all three instances—the Compton effect, the photoelectric effect, and pair production, an incident photon (i.e., an electromagnetic wave) interacts with matter. In the process, it is either completely destroyed or changed into another photon, the remainder of the energy being taken up to release an electron and giving it energy or to create new particles. Because the initial photon (electromagnetic wave) is changed, its energy changes so that all three cases can be classified as phenomena of *inelastic* interaction with matter.

Inelastic interaction (scattering, absorption) with matter is not the only form of interaction. There is elastic scattering as well, including diffraction at a double slit (Fig. 5.4b), refraction and interference when a beam of light is partially reflected inside material and then superposes constructively or destructively with the remainder of the beam (Fig. 5.4c), or in polarization (Fig. 5.4a), when part of a light beam is filtered out (absorbed) so that the remainder of the light beam (electromagnetic wave) has only one orientation (polarization). In all of these instances, the frequency (wave length) of the electromagnetic radiation (energy of the photon) is not changed, which is but another way of saying that the interactions are elastic. Elastic interaction can be compared to a perfectly bouncy ball reflecting back from a wall or from the ground, or when a billiard ball bounces off a wall or off another ball without loosing a bit of its energy (i.e., the ideal case).

The question now is how students can truly learn, that is, evolve a language such as the one I evolve in the preceding paragraphs for describing these phenomena, when they do not have appropriate and suitable (role) models. Fluency in speaking such a language is equivalent to saying that they can over and over again say, 'I mean', and then articulate yet another way of making some statement. Analogies, whereby one effect or phenomenon is compared to another based on similarities at the conceptual level is one way of sorting through subject matter and to derive a language suitable for describing and distinguishing multiple phenomena. In analogies, two situations are similar in some structural aspect but differ substantially in other aspects. For researchers of the evolution and use of analogies, a main concern lies with 'deep structure', that is, similarities at a conceptual level that are often not available and even contradicted at the 'surface level'. For example, in one study of German tenth-graders studying chaos theory, my colleagues and I investigated students' self-generated analogies.

---

7. Albert Einstein's equation that relates mass and energy ($E = m \cdot c^2$) is needed, because it is used to relate the energy of the photon ($E = h \cdot f$) to the total mass created ($2 \cdot m$). Because the particles have a given mass, the energy (frequency) has to be equal to or larger than some threshold, given by the frequency that is just sufficient to create the pair.

The students see a pendulum swinging above two magnets change the plane in which it swings, which gives rise to a comparison with Foucault's pendulum that they have seen in the physics museum in Berlin. Here, the surface level similarity is deceiving, because in the chaos pendulum, the changing plane of swing is said to be caused by the shape of the combined magnetic and gravitational field, whereas in Foucault's pendulum, the effect is brought about by a rotation of the earth and a constant plane of swing of the pendulum. That is, whereas the two phenomena look similar (the same) at the surface, their scientific explanations ('deep structure') are very even radically different. But there is a contradiction: When they come to some subject matter, students only have the surface available so that they, as part of the instruction, have to bootstrap into seeing deep structure where they have only surface structure available to them. This is but another repetition of the learning paradox in a new form.

In the next fragment, the students continue to search for ways of relating concept names with a first attempt to further specify 'diffraction'. Ken asks Ralf to 'look in the back of the book' to find the pages where 'diffraction' is treated as the topic but then pulls the book toward himself (turn 333). Miles articulates the situation as one that requires them to have more than one book (turn 334). Ken, instructing the others to 'organize' the map 'to make it look more normal' and turns to the back of the book.

Fragment 5.8

```
331 K: with what ((pause)) what do you say, diffraction?
       diffraction; look in the back of the book; what pages
       are the first-
332 M: lets get,
333 K: its right here. ((Pulls the book away from Ralf and
       toward himself.))
334 M: we need more than one book.
335 K: <<instructing the other two>here; organize so that it
       looks normal; looks like,> ((turns to the book,
       searching))
336 M: do you agree they ((Points to MATTER WAVES and DE
       BROGLIE WAVELENGTH)) should go up here?
337 K: diffraction four ninety two ((turns pages)) yea; double
       slit; guys; doesnt that look a little similar? ((shows
       Ralf the page he has found.))
338 R: now but momentum doesnt have anything-
339 M: its just a collision;
340 K: momentum diffracts;
341 M: the only thing is; may be; the electrons passes close
       to a photon; then bends around;
342 K: pair production doesnt- isnt that the compton effect?
a   M: uh; so much sweat.
b   K: guys, pair production goes under the compton effect;
       bring it under,
343 M: what does it say?
```

He lets his peers know what he searches and finds in the index: 'diffraction, four-ninety-two'. Turning to the page, he sees a diagrammatic representation of the double slit experiment (Fig. 5.5b), and then asks his peers, 'doesn't that look a little similar?'

Rather than directly addressing and thereby evaluating what Ken has asked, Ralf again brings up 'momentum' suggesting that it 'doesn't have anything'. Miles comments, 'it's just a collision' (turn 339), thereby collocating 'momentum' and 'collision', two concept names that can be used to talk about the Compton effect. Ken brings together two concept names involved in the Compton effect, 'momentum' and 'diffraction', here in its verbal form (turn 400). He does not thereby state, though, how these words might appear in a statement together with 'Compton effect', where one of the terms takes the place of the subject and the verb and the other term predicatively specifies this subject. Miles evolves the description of an event in which both an electron and a photon participate, and something 'then bends around' (turn 341). Grammatically, it would be the electron that bends. Ken proposes to organize 'pair production' below the 'Compton effect', but he does not provide either a verb to form a predicate or a reason for why the second term should be subordinated to the first (turn 342b). I end this fragment with Miles' request to find out what 'it', that is, the textbook, says and continue the analysis of the subsequent talk oriented toward the textbook in the next section.

At heart of the interaction here is the Compton effect, around which the students evolve a language that subsequently will be captured, in part, in the appropriate organization of the concept name within the concept map as a whole. In this effect, both the ejected electron and the photons are articulated in terms of momentum. This allows an explanation of the phenomenon, because the momentum of the incident photon is transferred to the momentum of the exiting photon and to that of the ejected electron. Because of one of the major conservation laws of physics, the momentum of the incident photon has to equal the sum of the photon and electron momentums after the collision. But how to express and talk about these relations is what the students are working on right here. The textbook shows numerous equations featuring the energy of the photons and electron involved, how to derive momentum, the equation for relating the momentum of the electron to the momentum of the exiting photon, and, therefore, to its frequency or rather wavelength. But readers of the textbook are not provided with a lot of conceptual language that brings together the different terms into statements.

Despite considerable discursive work and perusing the book, looking up in the index and finding relevant pages, the three have not (yet) come to a conclusion about how to organize the map around COMPTON EFFECT or, for that matter, around (in the vicinity of) PAIR PRODUCTION. They also have not yet clarified the relation these two concept names have with PHOTOELECTRIC EFFECT, which also describes the interaction of photons with matter and which, like the other two phenomena named, involve electrons, though in different ways given the different energies of the incident photons. The key issue then is the evolution of an idiom that is about, and can be used to relate, different phenomena that are not specifically linked in the students' textbook. A traditional approach to knowing and learning might suggest that each of these physical phenomena is presented in the textbook. Students are supposed to 'construct' an 'internal representation'. They could then compare the representations of the three phenomena and relate them. This relation could then be spilled like beans in and through their talk. But a language approach reasons differently, for language is not something represented in the head that is then spilled like one spills beans from a pot. There are only few scholars left who argue, with the early Noam Chomsky, that grammar is innate. Instead, cognitive scientists working with artificial neural networks have shown that it is entirely possible for a system to learn the grammar of a language simply by being exposed to the language. That is, one learns grammar together with the words and the semantics by participating in the use of language. We do not learn how to speak by taking grammar like a pattern with empty slots and fill them (mechanically) with words from a lexicon. In fact, those who do learn a language in this way, more often then not, literally do not know what they are talking about. There is evidence that students who only know the dictionary definition of a word will tend to place it inappropriately; and grammar itself is a contingent achievement directed toward and in service of the purposes at hand. It turns out, in fact, that learning rates of artificial neural networks increase if the 'attention span' (short-term memory) of the neural network is increased from small values to those more typical of adult speakers. That is, the network learns proximal relations before more global relations are understood. This, too, is what we see in concept mapping where students develop the idiom bottom up, one link at a time, rather than having a completed conceptual framework that they impose on the task.

Most relevant to our present discussion is this: Whereas craftspeople know what they are supposed to construct, students caught in the learning paradox cannot know what they need as vocabulary before succeeding in speaking a language in which the vocabulary has a place. As I point out earlier, the philosopher Richard Rorty has developed a nice way of talking about this situation. The craftsperson selects tool in the construction of the final product to leave his knowledgeable hands. Students, on the other hand, to paraphrase Rorty, much like Galileo, Yeats, or Hegel, are typically unable to make clear exactly what it is that they want to do, here, implement a specific organization of the concepts involved. They do know not it before developing the idiom in which they actually succeed doing it. They do not know how to relate two or more concept names such as 'Compton effect' and 'pair production' until after they actually evolve the idiom that is co-extensive with their success. Their formulations make possible the relation between the concepts before them, and the relationships they arrive at come with the transformation of the language that they have started out with. 'Uttering a sentence without a fixed place in a language game is . . . to utter something which is neither true nor false . . . This is because it is a sentence which one cannot confirm or disconfirm, argue for or against. One can only savor it or spit it out. But this is not to say that it may not, in time, *become* a truth-value candidate. If it *is* savored rather than spat out, the sentence may be repeated, caught up, bandied about. Then it will gradually require a habitual use, a familiar place in the language game'.[8] In the present situation, therefore, being successful in a part of the world, here the physical and ideational concept map unfolding before the students' eyes, and knowing the language concerning the concepts, do become indistinguishable once a habitual use has developed.

---

8. Richard Rorty, *Contingency, Irony, and Solidarity* (Cambridge: Cambridge University Press, 1989), 18.

Visual and Auditory Presencing

We are in and constitutive of our world with our bodies. Our bodies are also both centers of agency and, as bodies among other material bodies, subject to the agency of others, that is, marked with an essential and irremediable passivity. Our material bodies mark physical positions in the world, which, because no two material bodies can take the same position, also mark unique and singular perspectives on the world. Each position therefore comes with *dis*positions, *sup*positions, and *presup*positions, thereby marking the *pro*positions we produce. Each position also marks space and breaks its symmetry. We view the world from the perspective of and given with our position, and how we view the world is mediated by our historically and culturally constituted dispositions, suppositions, and presuppositions. All of this provides us with resources to make present sense and theme of the instant of speaking. That is, in visual and in auditory ways, we *presence* the world shared with others. Our bodies are resources for moving about and interacting in and with a world, which comes into being, as lifeworld, with specifically human characteristics. The lifeworld—or, to use another term that philosophers and semioticians sometimes use, the *Umwelt*—of a dog or bird living in the same part of the material world looks different. There are very different resources in the world that are, such as in the case of smells, radically different for a dog and a human being. [9] Our unique relations with the world that we act in and enact also gives rise to *pre*positions, words that indicate our relation with the world: 'in', 'on', 'under', or 'above'. We further indicate relative positions using 'shifters' or indexes such as 'here', 'there', 'these', or 'those'. Even without words, our positions give rise to particular forms of relations in and with the material world and with others. We point, we move our bodies, we gesture iconically; and with each movement we mark and re-mark sense so that others can, and do, remark it.

In the concept-mapping task, the students first and foremost structure the world around them. This world includes paper slips with words imprinted on them. Their task is to produce a hierarchical arrangement where the physical locations express and constitute conceptual relations. 'Up' is more inclusive and 'down' is more specific and less inclusive. Words that come to appear at the same level are also conceptually of the same order. Space therefore is marked relative to some origin, which, as the video offprints show, is the position of Miles and Ralf at the table. Up means away from their body, and down means close to them. Up means higher-order category, more abstract, and down means a lower-order category in the hierarchy, a more concrete entity. Their bodies therefore become the reference with respect to the conceptual organization of the lifeworld aspect, here the emerging concept map. The words, repeatable and recognizable ink traces and sounds, are part of this intersection, co-presence, and collocation of material and ideal worlds.

---

9. This is why European phenomenological philosophers distinguish between body and flesh, the latter being endowed with senses to make sense, thereby distinguishing human beings from mere material beings. It is Galileo rather than Descartes who brought about the split between the body and flesh, as he wanted to make the world independent of our senses. See Michel Henry, *Incarnation: une philosophie de la chair* (Paris: Seuil, 2000).

At the beginning of the task, the students do not know what they will end up with. They are not in the position of masons, who have plans for the homes they built, selecting tools that they need for specific jobs so that the homes they actually built look like the ones that they had envisioned (planned) to be building. Because they already know what the outcome will be, masons also have an image with which to compare all the intermediate stages their project takes. It is because they have this image that they can *intend* to construct. And they are in a position that allows them to *pre*-position all the materials and tools that are required in the job. But it is impossible to form such an image without knowledge of the thing to be constructed. The students who are members to the present situation therefore are not in the same kind of situation. They are not, therefore, in a position to *construct* anything in the manner of the mason or carpenter or whoever else participates in making the home exist in the way it was envisioned on paper (in the mind) beforehand.

The students in fact are in a *radically* different position, because they have to come to produce something the nature of which they will know only when they actually have completed it, the material and conceptual organization of a set of paper slips imprinted with words. Beginning with the vernacular that they are familiar with, to which the words on the paper slips are added, the students organize the world and organize the relevant idiom at the same time. The result will be that when they are done, knowing the idiom and knowing their way around this world that they created (without having an initial plan) are co-extensive. The world surrounding the students, the one that they constitute for the task, also includes other things; and the students act such as to make other things (e.g., the textbook) a constitutive part of the world in which they act. In the previous section of this chapter, we already see that the students produce and refer each other to images that appear elsewhere in the book. They point to particular parts of the text. Students also ask each other to 'remember' something, which, in the sense of rememorating (*re*-, again + **mem*-, to think + *ate* [to make noun form]), inherently makes a past situation or event present in the present to be mobilized as an objective fact supporting a statement or position.

In essence, therefore, students, in and through their bodies (e.g., in pointing, gesturing, speaking) mark something in their setting to make it part of and present in their conversation that constitutes collective consciousness. Or they ask others to remember, which, etymologically, also means making something mindful again. That is, both pointing to an image or paragraph in the textbook and asking someone to 'remember' both are ways in which an aspect of the world is marked and re-marked to be re-marked and therefore marked and re-marked by others as well. These are ways of producing repetition and difference simultaneously, as the very fact of marking comes to be significant and thereby contributes to the dialectic of production of signification. The word stem 'mark' comes from the Indo-Germanic root **mereĝ*-, boundary, edge, a demarcation that produces marks as signs of something else. My phenomenological inquiries reported elsewhere show that the perception of boundaries and the areas they enclose require movement, involving the whole body or of the eyes or head alone. [10]

---

10. Wolff-Michael Roth, 'Phenomenological and Dialectical Perspectives on the Relation Between the General and the Particular', in *Generalizing from Educational Research*, edited by Kadriye Ercikan and Wolff-Michael Roth (New York: Routledge, 2009), 235–60.

Marking, re-marking, and remarking are mediated by our positions and require agential movements of our bodies (or parts thereof, like the eye) that something bring into our lifeworld that was not part of collective consciousness in the conversation before.

In this situation, Ralf brings a piece of text from their textbook into their conversation by indirect speech in the present of the language itself. Here, Ken has available both an original and the way in which Ralf repeats and refracts what is written in the textbook and as pointed directly to. Fragment 5.9 begins with the last line of the preceding fragment, where Miles asks what 'it', the textbook, 'says' with respect to the topic at hand. In uttering 'we got it right here' (turn 344), Ken orients his peers to the book in his hand, where they 'got' the 'it' that they are looking for. Ralf, however, asks whether it says anything about the Compton effect. That is, whereas we might have assumed that 'it' refers others to the Compton effect, the topic of talk in the preceding utterances, Ralf makes problematic whether the 'it' that Ken announces to have 'here' actually pertains to the Compton effect that they have been talking about over the last several turns.

Ken says 'it's exactly the Compton effect', but Ralf, even though the word appears twice on the textbook page, evaluates it as inappropriate ('no, it's not'). He then articulates an alternative of what 'it' is and simultaneously, after turning the page, points to a specific place in the textbook. He moves the tip of his thumb along the phrase 'Five main interactions are possible' uttering 'It's just the five main interactions' (turn 347).

Fragment 5.9
343 M: what does it say?
344 K: we got it right here,
345 R: (4.0) but does it say
        anything about the compton
        effect. ((turns toward the
        book in Ken's hand, *))
346 K: ((Ken is looking for
        something in the book
        ((Ken points to a part on
        the page where the term
        'Compton Effect' is
        printed)) its exactly the
        compton effect. ((Turns to
        another page))

347 R: ((Ralf turns the page,
        points to the sentence
        'Five main interactions
        are possible', *)) no its
        not; this is just the five
        main interactions.
348 K: is that positive? oh wait;
        have you checked it for
        diffraction,
349 R: no; there is no
        diffraction there.

```
350 M: okay; we got ten more
       minutes.
351 K: matter waves can be
       diffracted.
352 R: yea.
353 K: matter waves can be
       diffracted; but there is
       two things-
354 R: they can also go into
       compton effect here or for
       the properties of the
       compton effect; ((Moves
       his finger along in the text, *))
```

In and by means of his gesture Ken makes a statement and 'quotes' the textbook in support, pointing to the relevant place. He emphasizes each word, thereby providing an additional resource that constitutes the authoritics both of the book and of Ralf's voice that is using the textbook text for his own intentions. He brings this part of the textbook to bear on the present conversation by pointing and thereby marking and re-marking a part of the textbook so that Ken also may remark it, that is, see it as the sign that it has been marked to be. Simultaneously, he provides an evaluation. In uttering 'it's just', he marks the presence of the statement and, simultaneously, that it is not precisely what they are looking for at the moment. On this page, they find 'just' the five interactions but not the information Ralf has been asking for earlier ('does it say anything about the Compton effect?').

As Ken before him, Ralf points to and alternately moves his thumb and finger along in the text while he is reading. He thereby makes available the fact of his reading, that is, engaging in an act of direct speech. His gesture attributes the speech to someone else, here the textbooks, but it is in and for his own task that he reads the text, and he does so not only for himself but also for the benefit of the others. Here, by reading and by following the text read with his thumb, Ralf brings the voice of the other (textbook) into their conversation. As the textbook, it is also a voice that is more authoritative than any one of their own voices. Moreover, because Ralf follows the text with his finger so that every member to the situation can see that he is literally repeating the words of this authoritative other, he provides his own voice with a greater degree of authority. These are the words *of* and *from* the other, here appearing *in* the voice of Ralf, with his inflections and intonations, for the present purposes, which are not only his own but also those of the collective task as well. This utterance remains uncontested as Ken goes on to look for something else. In both instances, therefore, attributing a stretch of talk to others has a specific function. It lends greater authority to the speaker by exploiting the authority of the source. In the previous instance, this authority is the textbook, as can be seen in the fact that Ralf's statement goes unchallenged even though the word 'Compton effect' is printed twice, just as Ken suggests. But Ralf also provides an evaluation of what the text constitutes in its entirety: 'just five interactions'. This contrasts a or the pertinent statement that they require at this instant.

Ken asks the others to wait as he returns to the page with the five interactions, 'have you checked it for diffraction?' (turn 348). But Ralf responds with an adverbial 'no', and then elaborates, 'there is no diffraction there'. Checking the textbook, we can affirm that the word 'diffraction' does not appear on the page. Miles, turning around and looking at the clock, notes that they have 'ten more minutes'. Neither Ken nor Ralf react noticeably. Rather, the former returns to the issue of diffraction noting that matter waves are subject to this phenomenon.

As I note above, the textbook does not provide a language that students could use to integrate talk across the various phenomena of photonic interaction with matter. It does in effect list five ways in which photons interact, but the texts in the bullets that follow simply reiterate (summarize) what has been said before thereby failing to articulate, for example, the different energy ranges of photons involved and to name (classify) the types of scattering (diffraction) as elastic or inelastic. The five interactions appear as independent facts rather than as subject to some generative principle that would subordinate them to a common language. The common idea expressed in and through the words and diagram is one of the possibilities in language as such, not just in the language of science. In this way, the theme can be other than any single sense affirmed in and by science. The students mobilize the words and diagrams of the textbook for their own (individual‖collective) intentions and even before they absolutely master these themselves. They mobilize them in the here and now. But their intentions themselves are subject to the task, designed by their teacher as part of the overall activity of schooling that this lesson realizes. The students, although they do not or may not know the motive of the lesson, nevertheless have to take it up to learn what the teacher has articulated in his lesson plan.

As they continue, Miles touches one of the paper slips while uttering a statement without actually articulating the concept name 'quantum' that is inscribed as QUANTUM on a paper slip. His utterance can be understood only if we insert the word—the physical instantiation of which he touches—into the verbally articulated statement, 'should we put "quantum" below photons?' (turn 359).

Fragment 5.10
```
355 M: okay; lets move-
356 R: oh no, diffraction-
357 M: lets move.
358 R: diffraction can be explained by the quantum theory.
359 M: thats good then, oh wait; should we put ((QUANTUM))
       below photons?
360 R: yea.
```

In this instance, the concept name is printed on the paper slip but it becomes an integral part of the communicative move nevertheless. The teacher printed the concept names on paper slips and cut them out; these are mobilized here in the students' task. Moreover, in the utterance the teacher's word is entering the talk of the students, who impose their own inflections (intonations). The attribution is no longer signaled, as it is when a student attributes a word or an image to someone else. It is both in the world and in their conversation. There is no more difference between what is inside the students' heads and what is between them. The word is not even produced by a student, it just there, present in the world, marked, re-marked (again), and therefore remarkable, re-markable, and remarked. In this world, the book, too, is a material object in which there are resources that the students, by means of their bodily orientation and gestures, mark for and thereby make re-markable by their peers.

In the fragment that follows, students continue to organize the field before their eyes in terms of *pre*positions that are learned through metaphorical extensions of lived experiences in a material world with a body that is the key reference point because of the position it takes up and that becomes constitutive of the world. Indexes such as 'up there', 'pull down', 'put it under', 'where', and 'here' all are heard relative to the bodies of the speakers and are the predominant relations with the salient aspect of their lifeworld before their eyes. That is, if we want to use the discourse of body and mind at all, then we have to say that the mind has come to embody the world as it engages with the world that has come to embody the mind (in the structures that the students impose upon it).

Fragment 5.11

```
361 K: matter waves goes up there under compton effect.
362 M: and pull down everything a little bit
363 K: ((Ralf and Miles 'organize' the slips)) doesnt matter
       waves- matter waves is just another way of saying
       quantum waves? and,
364 R: no; diffraction of matter waves;
365 K: which can occur with matter waves; just put it under
       diffraction.
366 M: under diffraction?
367 K: where does the damn, does this go?
368 M: right under matter waves.
369 K: here we go.
370 M: starting joining it-
```

In addition to the verbal indices, the students both point and act upon the artifact that is emerging in front of them. Pointing generally is recognized as a sign, but prior to being a sign, gestures may have been hand and arm movements that have changed the world and then, in the course of development, dropped the work-related function. In the transition period, a hand and arm movement may have both work and semiotic function, only the latter of which will remain or, when replaced by verbal indices, even they may be dropped from communication.[11] Thus, in turn 307 and the associated video-offprint, we see Miles move two paper slips from a place close to him around some other paper slips and 'up', but 'below' some other concept names. That is, with his work, he has organized the world around him, and this structure he achieves comes to organize his talk/thought about the concept names. These movements (which bring about a change in the position of the slips and therefore of the imprinted concept words) also, and simultaneously, signify. Moving a word from the

---

11. Wolff-Michael Roth, 'From Epistemic (Ergotic) Actions to Scientific Discourse: Do Gestures Obtain a Bridging Function?' *Pragmatics & Cognition*, Vol. 11 (2003), 139–68.

bottom to a place higher up in the hierarchy also has semiotic function: It 'means' that the word is to be arranged at a place that signifies its nature as a more integrative and more abstract concept (category). In moving the slips around so that horizontal relations and vertical alignments come about not only moves the paper slips, but also can be seen as producing a more orderly arrangement in and of the project in progress. In fact, without that the students specially notice it, the result of their physical and discursive work is a slowly emerging order. And *this* will be their accomplishment once they will have come to a point where they recognize that what they have is 'it', that is, the conceptual order that they were asked to arrive at without knowing what this order might be. The work is not just cumulative, pulling together and organizing preexisting elements, which here, would be the propositions that they evolve by predicatively modifying subjects with other given subjects and verbs of their own choice. Each decision creates new resources and a new state of affairs so that both process and product are emergent phenomena that could not have been predicted on the basis of elements that knowledge construction workers could have pre-positioned and then employed as they move along in their task.

The integration of gestures and work-related movements may be easily intelligible, as may be their transition. But this may be less so for the transition and integration to words, which, in their nature and shape, have nothing to do with the things they denote. However, we already see in the chapters and sections to this point that two forms of the word come to be treated the same: the ink traces on paper slips, for example, in the form of QUANTUM and the sound that is heard as 'quantum'. The problem of integration of the different modalities and how the switch occurs from one to the other, or, as some theories hypothesize, the work that happens in the brain to move between different coding mechanisms, appears to me to be a pseudo-problem. It is a pseudo-problem if we take the approach that both Bakhtin and Vygotsky have advocated, namely to move from element analysis to unit analysis. Unit analysis allows us to understand the whole situation—as does cultural-historical activity theory that has been worked out from the precepts that Vygotsky stated—as the integrative and integrating unit. Whereas there may be an iterable sense that stays the same across situation, the theme of an utterance is singularly tied to the instant and situation. Movements, gestures, sounds, body positions and orientations, relative distances and movements all are but part of the situation and the participants orient to the theme rather than to dictionary definitions of the sense that this or that word have.

This argument is further sharpened and brought to the point by thinking about how much time an act of interpretation takes if one has to (a) represent something internally, (b) then subject it to mental processes, and (c) finally come to understand what a particular thing we see or hear means. This would take so much time that we would be forever behind trying to understand the minutest aspects of reality let alone a little part of it such as the speech of another person. However, if interlocutors track events in the world, the events themselves keep track of information, which therefore does not have to be manipulated in the individual mind. This is what I understand Bakhtin to express with the idea of *participatory thinking*. This form of thinking is possible only if human subjects are incarnated (enfleshed) rather than are governed by a calculative mind that produces abstract, that is, detached (symbolic) thought in which 'we are simply no longer present in it as individually and answerably active human beings'.[12] Being in our actions and being/constituting our lifeworlds are central to an understanding of who we are. It is also important to an understanding of how we and our students act so tremendously efficient in the everyday world.

The following fragment contains more of these forms of communication, in which the respective speaker assumes that the other two participants know and understand what is being communicated without express articulation. That is, each speaker presupposes the participative thinking of others so that what we observe and hear is in fact the trace of their collective thinking. Each person not only talks to and for the other but also, in turn, monitors what others say and communicates his understanding that the presupposed participative thinking is still on track. This practical understanding concerns the situation as a whole, the thematic unit, rather than the words alone. When the assumption of understanding can no longer be taken for granted, such as in the exchange concerning the location of work function with respect to threshold frequency (turns 381–386), then members to the setting actively orient to dealing with the absence of mutual understanding.

Fragment 5.12
```
371 R: we have to connect this one here (.) this one with this
       one-
372 M: you start joining on top- the top we agreed upon- down
       to photon-
373 K: yea; okay.
374 R: you have to connect this one here; this one;
375 M: plancks constant with,
376 R: this one with this one.
377 M: threshold frequency with photons.
378 R: these two with this one here; and thats the energy; we
       need the kinetic energy;
379 M: i connect this one for you.
380 R: no this one.
381 M: work function energy goes below threshold frequency.
382 R: why?
383 M: because the threshold frequency ah no the work
       function;
384 R: isnt that one equation?
385 K: okay; wait.
386 M: wait. work function should be below threshold frequency
       cause the two are related and i just- trying to
       remember exactly
       ((Teacher has joined and watches and listens to them.))
387 R: these are related here ((hand near THRESHOLD FREQUENCY,
       PLANCK'S CONSTANT and WORK FUNCTION)) and this one
```

The mechanism for raising the question of the ongoing alignment is simple, as shown in Ralf's one-word interrogative utterance 'why?' (turn 382). Miles utters, 'because', thereby beginning the completion of a query–response sequence. But follow-

_____

12. Mikhail Bakhtin, *Toward a Philosophy of the Act* (Austin: University of Texas Press, 1993), 7.

ing a subject ('threshold frequency'), he utters an interjection of regret ('ah'), moves to name another subject, and then stops. Ralf asks 'isn't that one equation?'. Ken first accepts and then asks to hold over. Miles, too, asks others to 'wait' and then states that 'work function should be below threshold frequency cause they are related' (turn 386), but, as he announces adding something, he formulates trying to remember exactly. In stating that he is trying to remember 'exactly', he in fact formulates uncertainty about what he has been saying and the extent to which it conforms or is correct.

From the standpoint of physics, the work function simply is the energy required to release an electron from the surface of a metal, that is, the amount of work required to move it out of the potential well (trough) in which it finds itself. The minimum energy W required for this release is supplied, in the photoelectric effect, by a photon, which, according to Planck, has an energy that can be expressed as $E = \text{h}\cdot f$, where h is a (i.e., Planck's) constant and f the frequency of the light wave corresponding to the photon. That is, at the threshold, the energy of the photon equals the work W required to release the electron, that is, $W = \text{h}\cdot f$. When Ralf states in a questioning tone, 'isn't that one equation', then it might have been this equation, which is featured in his textbook. In turn 383, Ralf, while his hand moves near the three paper slips containing PLANCK'S CONSTANT, THRESHOLD FREQUENCY, and WORK FUNCTION, suggests that 'these are all related here'.

In the meantime, the teacher has joined them. Ken utters with a rising intonation, 'Hey Doc, does diffraction have something to do with matter waves?' (turn 388). The teacher begins his turn at talk by uttering an affirmative ('yea') and then reproduces the words that the student has offered up. The teacher's utterance exhibits a descending inflection, thereby marking the utterance as a statement. In the student's use, the words are used and ordered to produce a hearable question, and in the teacher's voice, it becomes an affirmation of the relationship between the two terms. The teacher not only affirms the relationship but also provides an example of a proposition that links the two in the form 'matter waves' 'can be' 'diffracted'.

The teacher has been asked, and responds to a question about the relation between two terms. It is a question not posed at the level of the inquiry, but to someone who is in an institutional position associated with this knowledge. The teacher does not hesitate for an instant, but immediately responds. He elaborates and gives a specific name to the experiment that is to show the relationship of diffraction and matter waves. More so, although he is asked as the teacher ('Hey, Doc'), he enhances the authority of the response by pointing toward the book (offprint, turn 392). By pointing to the book, he allows students to understand that they can find out about the experiment should they have forgotten. The authority of the voice therefore comes to be doubled. The pointing here again makes use of space, though the specific place in the book cannot be indicated because of the distance. But this distance also opens up the space of authority, spanned between the teacher who has earned a doctorate, and the textbook, which is the reference for curricular purposes.

Fragment 5.13
```
   ((Teacher has joined and watches and listens to them.))
387 R: these are related here ((hand near THRESHOLD FREQUENCY,
    PLANCK'S CONSTANT and WORK FUNCTION)) and this one
```

388 K: hey doc, does diffraction ((Points)) have something to
       do with matter waves? ((Points))
389 T: yea; matter waves can be diffracted.
390 M: we put that right here;
391 R: yea.
392 T: germer and davisson
       experiment. ((Gestures in
       direction of the book, *))
393 M: we put this like that
       then-
394 R: okay, and because this
       screws everything up, just
       put it here and link it-
395 T: yea, you can link it.
396 K: what about plancks constant?
397 T: ((turns toward class)) <<f>we have about ten more
       minutes so try to figure> ((walks away))
398 K: okay guys, complementarity do i put it right? i mean,
       wave and quantum, i put right here.

When the teacher and students point to a diagram or text in the book, they mark
existing resources so that others can re-mark and remark them, thereby rendering their
pertinence salient (i.e., remarkable!) in and to the present instant. But gestures may
also be used to mark heretofore-empty space where something might or ought to happen or appear. The gesture then has a prospective quality. Thus, as soon as the teacher
leaves, Ken calls on others ('Okay guys') and then proposes how part of the configuration in front of them ought to be transposed onto the sheet that lies before him and
where he, indicated by the pencil in his hand, projects to produce a pencil drawing
(turn 398). The sheet of paper that is to hold the ultimate, pencil-drawn map is oriented in landscape format with respect to Ralf, Miles, and the organization of the paper slips (see video-offprints in turns 392 and 398). Ken first points to
COMPLEMENTARITY, then to a spot on the paper (right below where his hand is in turn
398), returns to COMPLEMENTARITY, then back to the sheet, where he now spreads the
thumb and index finger and places them on the paper. The line that we can think of as
connecting the two, the thumb and the index finger, is parallel to the top of the paper,
the hand being placed about 20% downward from the top (see offprint in turn 398).
Here, the projected conceptual organization of COMPLEMENTARITY, QUANTUM, and
WAVE is made present at this instant to the others in the form of a repeated pointing
gesture, initially with one finger, then with the double index involving index finger
and thumb. The two body parts together not only suggest two placements, but also
suggest precise relations, parallel with respect to the top edge of the sheet and side-by-
side. The overarching term, COMPLEMENTARY, has already been placed and is
ephemerally present at a location previously but prospectively indicated by the single
pointer. Ken then orients toward copying the arrangement onto the sheet, whereas
Miles and Ralf continue to talk about the relation of concept words. As Fragment 5.14
shows, they disagree: Miles repeatedly expresses both agreement 'I know' and disagreement 'but'.

Fragment 5.14
```
398 K: okay guys, complementarity
       ((points to
       COMPLEMENTARITY)) do i put
       it right? i mean, wave and
       quantum, i put right here.
       ((Gestures, *))
399 M: yea, side by side.
400    (4.8) ((Ken begins to
       write on the sheet,
       transcribing the words
       from the organization))
```

```
401 R: we have to erase that ((pause)) electrons- electrons
       are like this here; ((Ken writes, Ralf and Miles
       continue to talk, Ralf looks into the book))
402 M: electrons; it has to be; no because look if they dont
       meet the minimum threshold frequency; ((pause)) they
       dont meet the threshold frequency in either cases, no
       electrons are freed. and this is-
403 R: electrons are related to all of those here.
404 M: i know, but-
405 R: its even related to this one here.
406 M: i know, but it has to be, they have to meet the minimum
       threshold frequency, in either of those cases no
       electrons can escape.
407 R: but still; you have to connect it to this one; this
       one; this one;
408 M: but how do they relate to de broglie?
409 R: this is matter; so its matter waves; photoelectric
       effect knocks out electrons;
410 M: and pair production?
411 R: and compton effect?
412 M: knocks out electrons;
413 R: yea; <<authoritatively>collides with electron? which
       means that it is a wave; a matter wave; and pair
       production produces electrons. we should put it right
       here- and they have to,>
```

Ralf speaks with an authoritative intonation and Miles begins to question Ralf about what essentially are implications of the arrangement he is proposing. The authoritative voice does not go lost on Miles, as I extensively show and discuss in chapter 8, where Miles calls him 'Führer' and then (playfully?) accuses him of racism despite their long-time friendship before and for over a decade now thereafter.

Fragment 5.15
```
414 M: all be related;
415 R: they have, [they all have to],
416 M:             [put matter wave ] down too;
417 R: not at the same level; because they=re kind of
       interaction; its a sort of wave;
418 M: it should be a little higher;
```

```
419 R: yea just put down.
420 M: here-
421 R: and then work function;
423 R: we have to connect-
424 M: we should put pair
       production; switch these-
425 K: does pair production
       concern electrons?
426 M: yea; all of these;
       ((Interlude about racism))
427 K: okay guys; connect all
       these; we gotta do it
       pretty fast.
428 M: okay, we=re done doc.((*))
422 M: i dont know where we can arrange for that; we gotta
       connect x=rays and compton effect;
```

In the course of turns 422–426, Ralf and Miles make some adjustments, which will have been the last ones made to the physical organization of the concept words before their eyes. While Ralf and Miles go back and forth in a part of the transcript that I originally referred to as "Interlude about racism" in the typed transcript, Ken finishes writing the names of the concepts onto the 11-inch-by-18-inch sheet approximately maintaining the same spatial arrangement and relative physical distances. Ken continues to transcribe and Miles and Ralf talk about the relations between several pairs of concepts. When Ken erases something and blows the crumbs away (turn 426), three of the paper slips fly through the air, which Ralf picks up and replaces. Ken comments, 'still a racist guy', and then Miles teases Ralf about being a racist. Although I had recorded this part by hand from the videotape into my first hand-written transcript, I had not included it in the next transcription into machine form, in part because I thought about it as 'an aside'. Today, I understand that 'aside' differently, and present an extensive analysis and contextualization in chapter 8. After that 'aside', Ken having completed the transcription and showing it to his peers, Miles addresses the teacher with an undramatic 'we're done, doc'.

The end to this part of the session, announced as such by Miles, has come all of a sudden. Watching the videotape again, in real time and from a first-time-through perspective, does not give me any clues for predicting even an instance prior to his announcement that the end of the task as Miles articulates it at this instant has come. There is no other announcement, no conversation between the three about having finished. There is no reflective comment in which the students might have stood back and thought about what they have achieved *as an achievement*. All of a sudden what they currently have in their hand is recognized as a finished product. That is, if they had a conception in their mind that had been externalized, they would have had indicators beforehand that they were coming close to the end of the session. They would have known and likely made available to each other that little more is to be done. On the other hand, in emergent product this is not possible, because the final result can be denoted as such only after it has happened.

Coda: Body and Positionality

In this chapter, I articulate the central role that our bodies play in the constitution of the lifeworld, which both surrounds us like a habit and which we inhabit. Our bodies mark the positions that we take in the world and singularize in and through our practical engagement. Communication generally and language more specifically constitute the conceptual taking of a position in a world of signification that accompanies our physical position in a social and material world. The material and the ideal dimensions of life are not separated entities, so that the ideal somehow would require efforts to be anchored or grounded in the material. There is but one world and the material and ideal aspects are but two of its constitutive moments. In this world, categorical behavior and language are but two, mutually constitutive and mutually presupposing forms of behavior that cannot be reduced to each other. The term 'world' should not be taken as a manner of speaking: 'it means that the "mental" or cultural life borrows from natural life its structures and that the thinking subject has to be founded on the embodied subject'.[13] Throughout this chapter, I provide plenty of evidence for how the spatial organization around the students and the conceptual organization that they produce are interleaved with the language that they have at hand and develop. In the process, they talk about conceptual relations and thereby evolve new forms of talking without consciously attending to the creation of new forms. They mobilize the world perceptually available, rememorate events past, organize their material and conceptual worlds in and through the mobilization of their embodied agency and, as a result, evolve an artifact that they recognize after the fact as the end result of their work.

As part of organizing a world and orienting within it, students use language. This language is not independent of the social and material relations that they are exposed to and constitute. The flesh is the central organizing point and force: It is in and through the flesh that life realizes and senses itself. As body, it cannot but take a position, a position that no other body can take. This, then, is the essence of positionality, which is associated with features characteristic for our interaction with the world, our *dis*positions, *sup*positions, and *presup*positions. The way of being in the world, and especially the way in which we orient, gives rise to the *pre*positions we use and to the *pro*positions that we make. More so, the *pre*positions, by means of metaphorical extension, come to be transferred into other discourse domains so that our bodily experiences in a material world come to characterize the conceptual experiences in an ideal and idealized world.

---

13. Merleau-Ponty, op. cit. note 2, 225.

6

On Finalizing

In the three foregoing chapters, I articulate the work that takes the students from a pile of paper slips inscribed with concept names to an organized arrangement. But this arrangement does not constitute a map, just as white sheet of paper with dots and city names does not make a traveler's road map, or rather, not a very useful one. Without the roads between cities, the traveler does not know how A is connected to B, and whether the road to C is a direct one or whether some other towns have to be traversed on the way. In the same way, words on the large sheet of paper do not make a map. Even if there were lines, these would only indicate *some kind of* connection but would not specify the *nature* of this connection. An analogy on the road map might be the differentiations of highways from Interstates, byways, gravel roads, or mere footpaths. Words alone mean nothing; words in the vicinity of other words mean nothing. Sentences are the primary vehicles of signification, because they specify both a subject and elaborate it by means of a predicate—at least with respect to stand-alone texts that can be read by a non-present reader. It is in this that the concept map constitutes part of an idiom that is radically different from, though overlapping with, the language that students speak while producing the map. The educational opportunity of a task like concept mapping derives from the fact that it brings together into one event the use of situated conversation and the production of a text that has to function separated from the world in which it is produced.

The distinction between the two forms of text is important, but frequently not appreciated and theorized in the educational sciences. Thus, I am not aware of any major theoretical framework that suggests how the relation between the two forms of language can be theorized and what the transition points and mechanisms are in the actual practice that leads students from speaking a language (dialect) to writing this language (dialect). Discourse refers to a world, the world of the speaking subjects that are constitutive of and members to a situation. Dialogue refers us to the situation common to the interlocutors. Thus, I hold it with Paul Ricœur, who writes that the 'situation in a way surrounds the dialogue, and its landmarks can all be shown by a gesture, by pointing a finger, or designated in an ostensive manner by the discourse itself through the oblique reference of those other indicators that are the demonstratives, the adverbs of time and place, and the tense of the verb. In oral discourse, we are saying, reference is *ostensive*'.[1]

Written discourse, however, no longer has the immediate world as its context. This does not mean that the written text no longer has a reference. Together with being freed from the ostensive reference, the written text also is freed from its limits. The referent of the written text no longer is the situation of interlocutors, both surrounding and being produced by them, but the world projected by the nonostensive references of all written texts. This world is, in some circles, referred to as *intertext* and the relations different texts maintain are intertextual. Intertextuality leads to a situation where '[t]o understand a text is at the same time to light up our own situation or, if you will, to interpolate among the predicates of our situation all the significations that make a *Welt* of our *Umwelt*. It is this enlarging of the *Umwelt* into the *Welt* that permits us to speak of the references *opened up* by the text—it would be better to say that the references *open up* the world'.[2] That is, pertaining to the present case, students work to produce their concept map, which will have to be a standalone text that others can read and understand independent of their conversational situation. For example, the teacher has to be able to read the maps for science content independent of the presence of the students, independent of their conversation only part of which has come to be embedded in the map, and independent of their reasons and reasoning to produce the map in this rather than another way. That is, students are asked to produce a text that opens up the world of all texts all the while they are situated in their lifeworld that they can directly and ostensively reference. There always are both intertextual and intratextual relations, including the texture that makes this world.[3] Producing the concept map therefore constitutes this juncture between two different worlds that exists because the two worlds are collocated. It is this collocation of the two contexts—the discourse and the writing—that allows students to evolve their ultimate text. Here, then, we have one condition that gives the bootstrapping procedure a way out of the learning paradox.

In the course of this chapter, the three students come to end of their task, not so much because there is some natural end inherent to their work but because of the temporal constraints of the institutionally defined end of the lesson (i.e., the bell). Already they work past the end-of-lesson bell to be able to supply every line linking a pair of terms with a verb. They know that there is little time left for doing this part (Miles has already noted some time ago that they have only ten minutes left), and there is an air of hurriedness about this part of the concept-mapping session. In a sense, therefore, they are asked to finalize their task. *Finalization* is a key concept in Mikhail Bakhtin's work, because it is associated with those discourses that are monologic in nature. In a dialogical situation, ideas continue to speak to one another such that one response begets a second, which begets a third, and so on to infinity. Finalization means that

---

1. Paul Ricœur, *From Text to Action: Essays in Hermeneutics, II* (Chicago: University of Chicago Press, 1991), 148.

2. Ricœur, op. cit. note 1, 149. *Welt* is the German world for 'world', whereas *Umwelt* is the world surrounding and recognized by the (here human) being, which in other instances may also be referred to as 'lifeworld'.

3. Mikhaïl Bakhtine, *Esthétique de la création verbale* (Paris: Éditions Gallimard, 1984).

there is an end-point, a perspective, that is or can be the final word on an issue. In the education of the sciences, this final word is the language of science itself, not in the way it is enacted in scientific laboratories but in the way it presents itself in textbooks. This textbook presentation constitutes the canon. Students' work generally is judged with respect to this canon. This is also precisely the point where social constructivism and even other attempts to theorize science learning falter: As long as science and scientific discourse become the end-point, the situation as a whole strives toward finalization, and therefore, according to Bakhtin, is monological—*one* (Gr. μόνος [monos], alone, single) kind of idea or idea system (Gr. λόγος [logos], word, reason)—rather than dialogical. The essence of dialogism is this: 'the crossing and intersection, in every element of consciousness and discourse, of two consciousnesses, two points of view, two evaluations—two voices interrupting one another intra-atomically'.[4]

With respect to the concept-mapping task, the conversation is potentially open to the future, as long as there is not one final answer that is used as the yardstick to evaluate the outcome of students' work. As soon as there is, there would only be one voice left, which is the measure of the process as a whole and the product that it leads to. Pragmatically, however, there will be end-points, given, for example, by the fact that the school day is organized into lessons tightly coordinated with the school clock. Students do not have the leisure to work until they come to a point that whatever they have is all they *can* achieve but rather they have to work under the constraints of the organization and come to an end under the given conditions. This inherently gives an element of unfinishedness to the task. A second dimension of openness comes from the fact that although the individual concept names can be connected only in some ways, there are more ways than those realized in the two physics courses for organizing the map as a whole—even though scientists like to say that there are a small number of ideas that fundamentally organize their field, such as evolution in biology or the conservation laws in physics.

Absence of a Finalizing Function

At the end of their session, and therefore at the end of this chapter, students will have arrived at a completed map (Fig. 6.1). But at this instant they do not yet know (a) whether the structure of the organization they have arrived at will also be the one they will end up with, (b) what the particular form of the connections will be, or (c) what connecting lines they will have drawn and labeled. That is, once Ken has transcribed all the names onto the sheet, the task, 'is not finished', as the teacher says, but requires pencil lines between concept names and (auxiliary) verbs to produce simple statements. That is, there is yet an absence of a finalizing function in and of the discourse. External constraints, the institutionally declared end of the lesson, are as much or

---

4. Mikhail Bakhtin, *Problems of Dostoevsky's Poetics* (Minneapolis: University of Minnesota Press, 1984), 211.

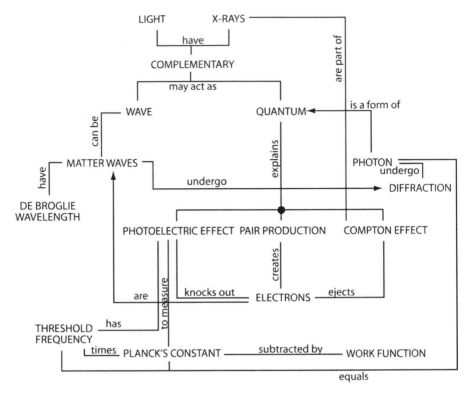

Fig. 6.1. This repetition of Fig. 1.2 shows a facsimile of the concept map as it looked when Ralf, Miles, and Ken had completed just following the bell that terminated the lesson.

more determinant of the end of the mapping session (and therefore, determinate of the final result that the students hand their teacher), as is the realization that they end because *this* is what they are capable of doing at this instant. This lack of finalizing function exists despite the fact that the students have sought recourse to the teacher and textbook to derive solutions concerning the particular shape and nature that any individual link should take. But neither the teacher nor the textbook provides a finalizing discourse for the map as a whole, telling students specifics to be arrived at. This open-endedness tends to be the case whenever there are tasks with multiple solutions and where there are, as the teacher will describe, 'no right answers' but rather 'many sensible and intelligible solutions'. We can hear the teacher's resistance to provide finalizing answers and to 'simply ask questions' as attempts to keep the situation dialogical, that is, inherently open, rather than monological with a single answer at the end.

I reproduce the final map (Fig. 6.1) at this point not to tell the story of its creation in a teleological manner, that is, to take the end result and placing it as the reason into the process of its creation. This I would not be able to do in any event because all evidence from the conversation points to its contingent and continued emergence. Rather, I produce it here at the beginning of this chapter as an advance organizer for the reader, who therefore can evolve a sense of all the different moves that are reasonable but abandoned in the end. Or rather, the reader will arrive at a sense of how much terrain the students will have covered by the time they arrive at something that they will call their final result. But they can only call it their final result after having arrived at the conclusion that whatever they have in hand is suitable for being a result that they may submit to the teacher as the accomplishment of this lesson. The real point of the present analysis is to highlight and understand the conversation about the map in its unfinalized form, which leads, in the participating two physics courses to different solutions of the same problem. These different solutions are quite different maps that integrate the concept names of the chapter, and therefore, are maps that summarize its content in a strongly structuring and structured form.

The part of the session in which the three are singularly concerned with drawing lines and inscribing verbs next to them begins here with Miles' comment that they are done, which receives negative social evaluation from the teacher 'no, no', who then articulates the connections to be 'the most important thing' (turn 429). Ken has begun to hand the sheet to the others, and Ralf, while the teacher still talks, picks it up together with the pencil that Ken is handing him. There appears to be an agreement, reached without words: Ralf is going to do the lines and verbs, which he orients to as the event unfolds. Miles says that this was 'what [he] was telling Ralf just minutes ago', but the teacher does not rejoin and, instead, continues elaborating on the issue of the connections, without, however, finishing the statement (turn 431). That is, what could have been heard as an accusation or a blame has not been taken up and evaluated by others and therefore stands alone without its (recognizable) mark on the unfolding conversation and therefore on its history. Miles suggests, moving from the bottom right in a big loop upward in the hierarchy, the production of a link from X-rays to Compton effect. The three students continue with the same form of abridged, predicative talk that they constituted their conversation to this point.

Fragment 6.1
```
428 M: okay, we=re done doc
429 T: no no the connections are the most important thing.
       ((Ken has copied the organized concept words, Ralf now
       takes over to make the connections between the terms
       and the connecting words.))
430 M: thats what i was telling ralf just minutes ago.
431 T: i think thats what makes the difference between a,
432 R: complementary;
433 M: no x=rays go to compton
       effect; draw a big loop;
       ((*))
434 R: should we link this?
435 M: no; x=ray goes to compton
       effect.
436 R: no we have to first got to
       find the words.
437 M: ah the words.
438 K: lets link them all and
       find the words.
```

```
439 M: ((LIGHT and X-RAYS)) possesses complementary and-
440 R: <<forcefully, impatiently>complementary is just, you
       just have to decide which one is useful.>
```

Miles articulates a predicate, 'possesses complementary', but Ralf responds impatiently, 'complementary is just', an alternative formulation that does not leave room for what Miles has proffered. The fragment ends with a forcefully and impatiently delivered 'complementary is just, you just have to decide which one is useful' (turn 440). Here Ralf mobilizes the language of others for his own intention. It is in the form of indirect speech, no longer attributed to anyone. It is a translation as well, because he tells us the sense of complementarity in other words, a description of what it refers us to or what one has to or can do—you have to decide which image (wave, quantum) is useful for describing the matters at hand. We hear and see clear indications in his intonation and rhythmic beating with his hands that he is impatient with Miles concerning the relationship of complementary with the other concept names. Ken then proffers another predicate: 'have complementarity' (turn 441). Ralf offers another term, and Ken, with a raising pitch 'asks' whether they should not use this term; and Miles produces a statement of agreement. Ralf writes 'have' on the two lines that join LIGHT and X-RAYS to COMPLEMENTARITY (see Fig. 6.1). The students now orient toward the next two concept names down in the hierarchy, QUANTUM and WAVE. Ken hurries Ralf on: 'connect quickly'. Leaving out 'complementarity', Ralf proffers a predicate, 'can either act as a wave or a quantum' (turn 446).

Fragment 6.2
```
441 K: oh, have complementarity.
442 R: ((inaudible))
443 K: have?
444 M: sure.
445 K: <<hurried>connect quickly.>
446 R: means that it can either act as a wave or a quantum.
447 K: yea; right; acting as,
448 M: may act; has wave or quantum;
```

Miles repeatedly utters approval, 'yea' and 'right', and again by repeating what Ken has said, 'acting as', though now in the present participle construction but with a dropped helping verb (e.g., 'is'). In so doing, the students are voicing possible ways of producing a statement. Alternatives are produced in the context of preceding possibilities, thereby qualifying them in the subsequent attempt, as a choice is made between one of them. Ken utters 'have?' with a rising intonation, which questions the use of this verb relating LIGHT and X-RAYS to COMPLEMENTARITY. Here the repetition of the words is implied, though not enacted. The hearing might be glossed as, 'Should it really be light and wave *have* complementarity?' The social evaluation immediately ensues, 'Sure', which we may gloss as, 'Sure, this is what it should be'.

In the instants that follow, Ken repeatedly urges his peers to 'remember' (turns 453, 463), 'remind [somebody]' (turn 461), and to 'do not forget' something (turn 461). He thereby marks some event or phenomenon in the past as one to be rememorated and to be taken into account in their present actions. The thing to be rememorated therefore is both past and present, but, in its explicit articulation, has the function of holding others to account for what already has achieved factual status. The past is explicitly brought to bear on the present. It is the present of the past that comes with rhetorical force. The students then begin what will turn out to become an extended exchange (right into Fragment 6.6, turn 505) concerning the way in which photons and matter waves are to be predicatively specified including the concept name 'diffraction'. This predicative specification, in fact, carries all the weight of the subject matter, for the subject could be anything that it merely names, whereas the predicate makes statements to be what or how the subject is. There are numerous subjects that can fill the slot of x in the statement 'x causes diffraction', but it is the predicate 'causes diffraction' that tells us what the world is about. 'Grating', 'double slit', 'single slit', 'surface atomic layer', and so on are but some of the things about which the predicate makes an intelligible and to physicists acceptable statement. This, then, gives us a new perspective on the concept map in its finished form. Because it is read from top to the bottom (unless there is an undesirable instance where an arrow head is used to read a link upward), each concept name higher up is predicated by means of a verb and a concept name further down in the hierarchy. This is the case until, at the very bottom, we find terms that are not further specified predicatively but *serve as the ground* for everything else above. These words therefore are part of language that grounds. The difficulty in this particular concept-mapping exercise therefore arises from the fact that none of the concept names refers to things that students are familiar with in their everyday world, so that at the outset any concept name is as good as any other to serve in and as this foundation. This is precisely the origin of the trouble in which we have seen the three students while deciding whether to organize the map using 'light' or 'wave' as the top-most concept name.

From the debate concerning the relation of QUANTUM and WAVE, the three students move to diffraction when Miles introduces the concept name (turn 466) in the context of linking PHOTON ('photon') to other concept names. In this instance, Ralf says 'photon is a form of', and thereby articulates what they should 'say', prospectively, and without mentioning the word 'say': 'do diffraction' and 'undergo diffraction'. The second word is already present and available to them in their perception. It does not have to be uttered again.

Fragment 6.3
```
449 R: okay;
450 M: join x=rays;
451 K: but then you gotta join wave and quantum; because it-
       they interact;
452 M: they dont,
453 K: yea remember, thats why we put them besides each other.
454 M: no
455 R: they dont interact
456 M: [they have quantum and photon     ]
457 R: [they=re different kinds of waves]
458 K: yea, yea
459 R: this is different kinds
460 M: x=rays to compton effect, do that now
```

```
461  K: we dont forget cause you can remind him
462  M: ((inaudible)) i figure because when i get to the
        bottom-
463  K: has; because remember, it has photon;
464  R: photon is a form of;
465  K: is form of;
466  M: diffraction of photon; and then we get diffraction.
467  K: ralf; may.
468  R: do diffraction; undergo diffraction;
```

When language is thought in a static manner, then learning means acquisition of this language so that students can use it. It is literally acquisition (Lat. *acquīrĕre*, to get in addition), as students get it from the surrounding culture in addition to what they already master. This is the sense in which scholars often use Bakhtin in saying that the students learn to use language 'for their own intentions'. But a lot of the transformations of language we observe occur in and with the language that students already use, that is, the vernacular that they are familiar with from before and outside of school. Moreover, they would not be able to acquire the new idiom if there was not already the possibility for speaking it. That is, there exists an inner contradiction in that they do not yet speak the new idiom, but they are at the very cusp of doing so, its possibility already inscribed in their present state where they are not yet able to speak/understand it. It is not that students acquire en bloc a new way of speaking, but their language changes slowly as new but already possible elements come to be integrated as reported speech and increasingly become independent of the original source. Hearing both precedes speaking and is implied in speaking, both on the part of the listener and the speaker. Speakers always also hear themselves and check whether others hear what they hear themselves saying. If the other's response suggests that there is a difference, speakers then are likely to engage in remedial action to remove the difference between hearing what others appear to have heard and what they heard themselves say.

Much of the language we 'acquire' in the course of our lives, we do so without being conscious of it. It is not so that we intentionally operate on language, but we use the sounds in the way they have come to us. We do not consciously 'construct' new language, but we simply participate in speaking it. We say 'howdy' or 'how do you do?' without consciously thinking about acquiring and using it for our intention. We simply begin using these expressions in the way and at times that we experience others in our surroundings to be using them. We also take on the intonations and accents of others, which thereby come to be reproduced but with a difference.

In the next fragment, the students evolve an extended exchange over the question of how to connect MATTER WAVES and DIFFRACTION. At this point, the concept name 'diffraction' is inscribed immediately below PHOTON, which we find at the same level as MATTER WAVES (Fig. 6.1). Whereas the normal rule is that a concept map is to be read from top to bottom, exceptions are permitted when necessary. We see in the following exchange that even without talking about the exception as exception, and therefore exhibiting the openness of the discourse, the students proffer either term as the subject to be specified by means of a predicate including the other. That is, even though the students have arrived at an ordering in which the normal procedure would be to make 'matter waves' the subject to be predicated by 'diffraction', alternative solutions are proffered in which 'diffraction' takes the place of the subject and 'matter waves' are part of the predicate.

Fragment 6.4
```
469 K: photons do diffract;
470 R: ((mumbles, inaudible))
471 M: and then,
472 R: we have to connect this here.
473 K: connect, just draw a straight
474 R: yea, but
475 K: how, no matter where you go;
476 M: matter waves do diffraction.
477 K: can affect,
478 M: anyway-
479 R: we shouldnt put- we should put it- because we also have
       different;
480 M: we=re not getting marks for neatness.
481 R: ah-
482 K: can we connect the waves to diffraction?
483 R: we can connect it to all.
484 K: can alter matter waves; put can alter;
485 M: diffraction can alter; affects; diffraction affects;
486 R: can alter?
487 M: [affects.]
488 K: [affects.]
489 R: diffraction affects matter waves?
```

In this situation, we have the emergence of a new way of saying something involving the concept names 'diffraction' and 'matter waves'. Ken first utters 'can alter' as the connective verb. The following utterance, which also constitutes the social evaluation, first repeats the word but then substitutes another one, 'affects'. Miles repeats the verb. Ralf utters 'can alter?' with a rising pitch, as if he said something like 'should we use "can alter"?' First Miles, then Ken utter 'affects' with a decreasing pitch, indicating statement-type utterance. We might hear it as 'let's use "affects"', and the repetition we can hear as, 'Yes, I agree, let's use "affects"'. Ralf confirms this hearing by uttering the statement as a whole, 'diffraction affects matter waves', but also questions (hearable in the raising pitch) whether this is the way the connection should be. Miles then confirms (turn 490), and Ken elaborates further (turn 491). But this is not the way in which the proposition ultimately will be noted, as a glance at their final result confirms (Fig. 6.1). Rather, it will be a transformed way in which the subject and predicate are exchanged, 'Matter waves undergo diffraction'. It is another translation at the heart of language, a self-quoting that transforms the language in and through use.

It is in this way that we use language to produce the sense of agreement that people walk away with from such instances. The speech is a shorthand form of the kind that Vygotsky describes inner speech to be. In a situation such as the present, predicative speech increases the speed with which the issues at hand can be discussed. Because they all are present to the situation, there are many resources at hand to be marked by means of ostension; and anything said will contribute to the collectively realized *participative thinking*. In this situation, the concept names specifically and the entire arrangement more generally constitute other aspects of the communicative event. They are both signifier and the context that dialogically exchange to produce the *theme*, the significance of the said in *this* context. That is, whereas Vygotsky only writes about how thought and language develop in parallel, each a process on its own, subordinated to a process that integrates them, thought and context here are produced collectively. This brings us closer to Bakhtin, whose concept of the theme provides a unit that integrates and subordinates both the word *and* its context.

Fragment 6.5
```
490 M: yea, because they do diffract.
491 K: frequency can alter matter waves, it just means that
       matter waves can diffract- just put like can alter or
       affects; which ever one you feel.
492 R: matter waves can can diffract.
493 K: yea.
494 M: put like can; can alter or affects; whichever one you
       feel.
495 R: matter waves can can diffract.
496 K: yea.
497 M: put like, ca:n.
498 R: undergoes;
499 M: you arent going- undergo.
500 R: uh i cant write undergo, give me another word.
501 M: we gave you about six.
```

In Fragment 6.5, the conversation is explicitly about the verb that connects two other words, attributing a predicate to the present subject with the constraint that the predicate should contain 'diffraction'. That is, in the concept-mapping task, the question is not to place any predicate, 'which ever one you feel', as both Miles and Ken suggest to Ralf, but to produce a predicate given one part of it, which is one of the concept names that also appears in bold face in their textbook. Without delimiting their accomplishment one iota, the students are not in the business of evolving an *entirely* new idiom, even if this or that concept name is new to them and even if this or that concept does not yet have a referential object that it names. The referential object exists in cases where *direct unmediated discourse* is an expression of the speaker's semantic authority. The referential object does not exist in all those situations where the students articulate trouble specifying what a concept name or an expression 'means'. But unmediated discourse constitutes only the first level in a three-level categorical scheme that Bakhtin develops: *direct unmediated discourse, objectified discourse* (discourse of a represented person), and *discourse with an orientation toward someone else's discourse* (double-voiced discourse).[5]

Objectified discourse constitutes the second level, which is the discourse of someone else represented in speech. At issue no longer is the referential object of the sen-

---

5. Bakhtin, op. cit. note 4, 199.

tence—e.g., whether there is something like matter waves that undergo diffraction—but the utterance as utterance. We can see this second type of discourse repeatedly and throughout this conversation including in the following fragment, where Ken articulates what Ralf has uttered previously as compared to what he has been suggesting. Ken brings into opposition his own 'diffraction affects' (turn 491) and Ralf's proposal to use 'undergo[es] diffraction' (turn 498) or some other verb that he asks for if he 'can't write undergo' (turn 500). Here, Ken is not concerned with *what* the statements say but in clarifying who made which proposal.

Fragment 6.6

```
502 R: matter waves can diffraction?
503 M: okay; just go, undergo;
504 K: he says, i said that; i said diffraction affects; or
505 M: i know; dont worry about that.
```

In saying 'I know' and 'don't worry about that' (turn 505) Miles acknowledges that the matters are in the way just stated. In the meantime, Ralf has written the verb that Miles has asked him to inscribe, and which Ralf himself has initially proposed. The students hurry on. There is not much time left in the lesson, though nobody attends to the precise amount of time left. They begin to speak faster and a sense of urgency is noticeable in the recording. Numerous utterances now consist of verbs only, but both the subject and the second part of the predicate are given on the sheet and identified by the proximity of Ralf's pencil next to the connecting line. That is, looking at the state of the map and locating the pencil at a particular place that does not yet have a verb marks which concept names are involved, and the verb part of the predication is all that is necessary in specifying the work to be done: finding a verb that completes a statement in the subject–predicative complement. Much as in the above referred-to study on the game of Tetris, the speed of the work increases when essential aspects of it are based on their material embodiment in the world. Here, the concept words are perceptually available, as is the pencil line as soon as Ralf has drawn it, and their participative thinking can move quicker when they only have to add verb forms to what already exists before them. Because of this situation, however, we may not suppose that there is anything 'in the head' or 'in the mind' of the speakers, as the communication *clearly is distributed across the setting*. Whether and what the individual would articulate when asked to respond at length, we cannot anticipate based on the verbs they articulate, especially because in responding at length, any thought would itself undergo development.

Fragment 6.7

```
506 K: whats that?
507 M: wave to matter waves; oh quantum to matter waves.
508 K: travels in; no thats,
509 R: i think we should- is a kind of wave;
510 M: yea; these two are; matter wave is a-
511 K: quantum property; concerning quantum; concerning
       quantum- okay hurry up.
512 M: okay; ah.
```

```
513 R: why do you have ((inaudible))?
514 M: because we have,
515 R: okay; yea;
516 M: because we connect all this,
517 K: connect pair production.
518 M: well, connect them all;
519 K: ejects;
520 M: releases;
521 R: collides with electrons.
522 M: no; if we squeeze electrons these might collide which
        gives them the energy to escape.
523 K: they dont; they eject.
524 M: put eject;
525 R: why do you want eject?
```

Here, as before in the case of MATTER WAVES and DIFFRACTION, the students are testing ways of talking, forms of language that have not yet existed for them before. The language itself is not an arbiter, so they need to decide how they want to connect the two nouns, making one the subject and the other the second part of the predicate. Therefore, neither a link nor the map as a whole is finalized, and proposition may be reopened, even in cases that they have already discussed before (turns 290–297) and even though these are the terms printed with the images that explain the photoelectric and Compton effects. Even though Ken and Miles here propose the term, and even though they are pressured for time, Ralf still asks why not just one of his partners but both want this term. That is, even with the time advancing and only seconds before the school bell will sound, there is no finalizing tendency, but a continued dialogical inquiry into the precise nature of each link.

The students hurry on. At one point, Miles reminds his peers that the bell 'rang already', not in the least at a moment when the event turns carnivalistic, changing from the seriousness of science and schooling to the converse side of life. But there still is room for relativizing the task. One such situation occurs when they break out into laughter (turn 535–536) after Ralf draws a particularly long and almost exaggerated link from THRESHOLD ENERGY to PHOTON (see Fig. 6.1). Such laughter is a bodily response to something that many (educators, psychologists) would take to be a purely mental phenomenon: a joke. That is, there is time for joking even though the bell has already gone and the students know that they are working into the next lesson. Laughter is an important aspect of everyday life, but has yet to be appreciated in the educational literature generally and in science education more specifically. Because of its importance, I return to laughter in chapter 8 when articulating Bakhtin's position on the bodily principle as the integrating feature for understanding human life generally and their conversations more specifically.

Fragment 6.8
```
526 K: plancks constant; i dont know.
527 T: well, plancks constant isnt it plancks constant- that
        plancks constant relates to quantum?
528 R: yea, we want to connect it through these here.
529 K: threshold frequency is on the same level.
```

```
530 R: and to photon;
531 M: no, why is work function here, ((Bell rings))
532 K: because these here all calculations properties these
       three.
533 R: we should include kinetic energy. we should connect
       this one to this one here.
534 M: well, just connect back to-
535 R: reflected threshold frequency- connect this one- the
       energy of a photon- the threshold frequency, plancks
       constant we just connect this one here.
  a    ((draws a link from THRESHOLD FREQUENCY to PHOTON))
  b M: ((bursts out in laughter))
536 K: ralf; ((barely containing himself, with chuckle)) like
       we said; go crazy but- ((laughs))
537 R: it rang already; here=s energy; this is the energy of a
       photon,
538 K: it says has the energy of;
539 M: ha:s-
540 K: and then=ll just-
541 M: equals-
542 K: photon has the energy of-
543 R: equals;
544 M: equals energy of;
545 R: equals ((pause)) and these like multiplied together;
546 M: just write times.
547 R: and this subtracted by
548 K: what about photon and threshold frequency?
549 M: we got it; thats everything connected; its all-
550 R: we still have quantum and photon; uh; quantum here.
551 M: what do you want (.) we didnt connect these ones here
       to anything.
552 K: put photoelectric effect.
553 R: all kinds of interaction.
554 K: quantum, yea quantum interact with-
555 R: quantum explains-
556 K: yea that explains-
557 M: i dont know what the hell-
558 R: because this one knocks out this one here.
559 M: write.
560 R: it doesnt look very good.
561 T: as long as i find my way through.
562 M: <<laughing>uh=uh>
563 K: <<laughing>like like like that math period. And then
       throw it at someone.
       ((They pose for the camera with the final concept map))
```

In the end, Ralf comments on the map that has emerged before him, 'it doesn't look very good' (turn 561). The teacher utters, 'as long as I find my way through', thereby indicating that it is not the look—e.g., 'neatness', 'tidiness'— that counts but the possibility to find his way through the connections. That is, the teacher here articulates a crucial aspect of the concept map as a text that can stand on its own and that one can

Fig. 6.2. Ralf, Miles, and Ken hold up their final result to pose for the camera and, in this, declaring that they have finished.

find one's way through without the students present. Miles comments with a laughter, and Ken makes reference to a or the math lesson, where something like that can lead to having something (the work?) thrown at you. It is entirely open whether the thrower is the teacher, and whether the object is the notebook. But all three students laugh about what apparently is a joke with respect to the common experience in their advanced mathematics course.

In this last part of the session, there is no evidence that the students read out from their mind or translate some existing framework that they make available to each other. In the limit, one might have thought that they 'constructed' such a framework during the first part of the discussion, but the continued interchanges over the specific verbs and predicates suggests that there is no fixed framework present. Everything is up in the air, both inter-psychologically as intra-psychologically. Therefore it is better to think that the map as a whole and each individual proposition indeterminately *emerges* from their relation and the collaborative work that it enables. There is a continuous searching, a continuous endeavor to structure the material at hand, both the map and the language that they have brought. This language transforms as they attend to the task. Right up to the very end, Ralf writes and erases, the students proffer links and alternatives. There is no evidence that the three are looking for *the* answer but continued discussion about which among the possible versions they ought to choose. The session, therefore, is marked by dialogism and dialogical characteristics through and through. The whole process, therefore, is unfinalized and non-finalizing.

'Prior Knowledge' and Emergence

Throughout this session right to its end, we see many signs of dialogism. Particularly absent is any reference to finalization, which is a key characteristic of monologic inquiry. That is, whereas science education generally is monologic in nature, seeking to make students reproduce science in the way that textbooks, science teachers, and scientists do, the present task is open-ended to a great extent. It is open-ended although particular linkages and relations are subject to the canon of science, which thereby finalizes the way in which two concept words can be linked in predicative manner. As a result of this dialogism, the concept-mapping process and product emerge. Bakhtin discusses the work of Dostoevsky, showing how the novelist explores ideas in and through the voices of different protagonists or as different voices within the same protagonist. That is, the novelist does not choose or impose some reference that completes the characters and therefore the way in which ideas can develop. Rather, Dostoevsky allows each character to have a voice *independent of the voice of the narrator*. This then leads to the situation where narrators cannot take positions outside the hero. Allowing characters to have their own voices takes away any possibility for a position that would provide 'the perspective necessary for an artistic finalizing summation of the hero's image or of his acts as a whole'.[6] Dialogism and emergence go together and are opposed to finalization. The characters of these protagonists therefore cannot be finalized because their ideas themselves unfold and emerge. Any closure is temporary, always open to the continued confrontation of ideas.

Thinking about dialogical inquiry, as this happens here, in terms of (open-ended) *emergence* is advantageous because results cannot be predicted on the basis of what is known before students actually engage in a task. This is so even in the event that a particular student may 'monopolize the discourse' as some researchers appear to report. If someone were to monopolize a conversation, it still would not mean that the situation is monological, as long as the speaker is open to the development of ideas in and by considering alternatives and alternative voices. First, it remains to be shown how any learning (change in discourse) has been monopolized, that is, driven by the ideas that *this* so-called monopolizing student has brought to the table. Second, if we are interested in a general theoretical framework that can explain all sorts of trajectories of lived curriculum—trajectories that such sessions specifically and lessons more generally take—then it is not a very useful to have an explanation that is based on prior knowledge and knowledge/power as a priori factors that *determine* conversations. We may, for example, consider the case of Ralf.

In the school at the time of the recording, Ralf is one of the top-achieving students (in the upper 90%). Miles' grades are intermediary (around 80%), and Ken has a grade-point average just below 70%. Ralf ends the year with the second-highest grade in physics (98%) and subsequently becomes a successful engineer with a Master's degree. Ken flunks almost all courses of the first year at the university. In a situation like this one might assume that what Ralf says is what the student group as a whole will do. But this, as we see throughout, is not the case, even if, as I analyze in chapter

---

6. Bakhtin, op. cit. note 4, 225.

9, there are some intimations that others see in him a 'Führer'. Ralf contributes in exchanges with others and it is not immediately evident that he is dominating the exchanges. Quite the contrary is the case. There is evidence throughout that he contributes in substantial ways to make this concept-mapping inquiry a dialogical one. 'Prior knowledge' does not have finalizing force.

In the course of talking and transforming their talk, all three are changing, especially Ralf. Prior to and in preparation of this collaborative task in class, the students have completed a homework assignment, which asked them to map the concepts of the same chapter from which the present concept words were taken. Ralf produces a complex map, including many more terms than are in the present task. In his map, WAVE is the most inclusive term (Fig. 6.3). LIGHT is subordinated to WAVE and PHOTON, which appears repeatedly and at different levels of the hierarchy. COMPLEMENTARITY, which constitutes the focus of this conversation for a considerable period of time, is off to the right on a line following LIGHT and WAVE-PARTICLE DUALISM.

We do observe, however, links that might have the same sources as some of the initial statements Ralf has made during the conversation embodied in his diagram. For example, at one point he makes a statement about 'just five forms of interaction'. Interactions of quanta with matter and the five forms that they can take, according to the textbook, can be found in the center of the excerpt from his map (Fig. 6.3). Also, we can find the predilection for subordinating QUANTA to energy rather than considering the centrality of the wave-particle dualism that is at the heart of the contrast between the two preceding curricular units (wave nature of light, quantum nature of light). But this alignment with the textbook is evidence how language itself comes to be reproduced as its forms are taken over from others, transformed in use until such a point that the language no longer is considered to be that of the other but as something owned by the student. Continuing our investigation of Ralf's map, we note that the energy of an actual quantum—i.e., of the photon—appears on the very bottom of the map about 10 levels down in the hierarchy from where we find QUANTA and ENERGY (Fig. 6.3).

The excerpt shown here only constitutes the upper half of the map that Ralf has submitted. We can see that there are many lines, many different levels. That is, his map looks more like a semantic network or 'mind map', as these are often called in school contexts, rather than like a highly organized concept map, in which the hierarchical order constitutes a categorical (conceptual) order. Here I understand categorical order in the sense of Kant, where more abstract terms are found on top and more specific and detailed concepts more on the bottom of the hierarchy. In such a map, each higher concept name is specified in terms of concept names below it, which, according to the rules, are part of the predicate. These predicates are telling us about the world, so that the concept map as a whole *bottoms out* in our everyday familiarity with, and practical understanding of, the world. The heavily debated relationship between 'matter waves' and 'diffraction' does not exist in Ralf's map: the latter term does not figure in his map at all. WAVE and MATTER WAVE, closely positioned and directly linked in the final group map, are far apart and without direct link in the individually produced map before this lesson (it is connected MOMENTUM OF PHOTON, to the bottom right in Fig. 6.3).

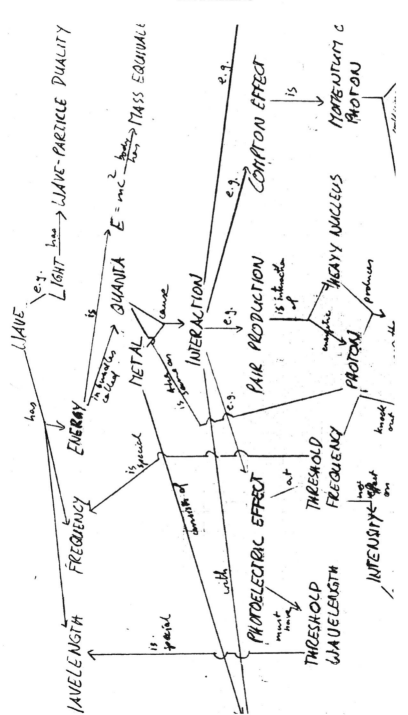

Fig. 6.3 Excerpt from Ralf's map drawn as an individual homework exercise prior to the collaborative session in class.

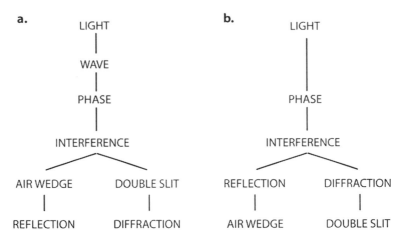

Fig. 6.4. a. The tracer configuration for the group map on the wave nature of light. b. Ralf's tracer configuration on the six-week delayed post-test.

Precisely the same can be observed in another section of the physics course with the highest-scoring student not only in physics but in the entire school, a student who subsequently goes on to study at Princeton and Yale and who shall become a successful constitutional lawyer. His homework map not only does not have a strong hierarchy, but also is organized more like a mind map, including the same concept names in different places (hierarchical levels). That is, in each of these situations, where the academically strongest students in the school have submitted their concept maps before, we see little relationship with the concept maps produced by the groups in which they participate. We observe dialogical relations as process. We also see a lot of learning (changing language) to occur, as evidenced in the differences between the propositions and organizations students produced as part of their homework and the one that they participate in producing during the group sessions.

My research shows that for many students the concept mapping sessions become forming events in their development of language on the topic, which tends to stabilize with the session and in the absence of further opportunities to talk concepts.[7] I do not have available the data on the present set of concept words. But for the preceding unit on the wave nature of light, there are videotapes and materials for several collaborative sessions, a 1- and a 6-week delayed post-test, each of which students produce on their own. In Ralf's instance, the map he and two of his peers (one of whom is Miles) produce during their second collaborative session and the map he produces on his own both on the 1-week delayed test as on the 6-week delayed test are nearly identical (Fig. 6.4), the latter two *are* indeed identical. We note that two pairs (DOUBLE SLIT,

---

7. The original research can be found as Wolff-Michael Roth and Anita Roychoudhury, 'The Concept Map as a Tool for the Collaborative Construction of Knowledge: A Microanalysis of High School Physics Students', *Journal of Research in Science Teaching*, Vol. 30 (1993), 503–34.

AIR WEDGE) of terms have changed level with the phenomena these instruments produce (DIFFRACTION, REFLECTION).

In his discussion of the dialogical nature of Dostoevsky's poetics, Bakhtin is concerned with the *finalizing* function that monologic discourse has on the shape of the product, in his case, poems, novels, plays, and other forms of literature. He uses the term monologic not to single out a monologue to be held up against dialogue. Although the two adjectives, monological and dialogical, in English pertain to the two forms of talk, monologue and dialogue, in Bakhtin's work they are used differently. The accent Bakhtin places in these adjectives is on the second parts of these compound words, the 'logic', indicating ideas and idea systems (ideologies). Thus, he shows how a monologue can be inherently dialogical and how a dialogue, when figured in a literary piece (most or all plays), may be monological when it is used to convey only one, the author's intentions and ideas. The monologic discourse knows only one correct form, which Bakhtin describes as having finalizing force. Thus, science is open to alternative ideas only while a paradigm is in formation. Once it is formulated, it is accepted as truth and is taught as such in science classrooms. The Newtonian discourse has not changed essentially and there is only one manner in which each of Newton's three laws is to be understood. Any other form of expression, any ambiguity surrounding terms such as force, energy, velocity, acceleration, position, speed, momentum, and direction is taken to be a *mis*conception, an *alternative* framework, a *naïve* conception, a *pre*-conception or whatever other euphemism is currently in vogue and not rejected because of its air of political incorrectness.

The dialogical nature of the concept-mapping sessions also leads to the dialogical evolution of thought, as speech generally and evolving speech more specifically mediate the evolving thought process. Here I make a tight link between the thinking of individuals and the thinking of collective in the theoretical notion of *participative thinking*. This conception of thought and language brings together ideas independently articulated by Lev Vygotsky and by Mikhail Bakhtin. According to Vygotsky thought evolves in a continuous dialogical relation with speech[8]; Bakhtin points us to the role of *participative thinking* as an integral feature of dialogue, where practical understanding always and already is active.[9] Public dialogue evolves participative thinking, which, because of its constitutive (dialogical) relation with individual thinking, also evolves the latter. I address this issue to a greater extent in chapter 7.

A typical example of finalizing discourse can be found in the IRE exchanges that I discuss in chapter 4 where I present and analyze an extended exchange between students and their teacher. The function of the evaluation part of this sequentially organized machinery implementing monologism is precisely to ascertain that the correct (true, right) response has been produced, where the teacher determines correctness and truth in the situation at hand. The sequential order gives the teacher the slot to make the evaluation and thereby reduces any ambiguity with respect to ways of talking science. Throughout the presentation of the concept-mapping session, with the exception of some particular instants, the conversation does not exhibit any finalizing function.

---

8. Lev S. Vygotsky, *Thought and Language* (Cambridge, MA: MIT Press, 1986).

9. Mikhaïl Bakhtine [V. N. Volochinov], *Le marxisme et la philosophie du langage: essaie d'application de la méthode sociologique en linguistique* (Paris: Les Éditions de Minuit, 1977).

And this is so until the very end, where even seconds before the students submit their artifact there are still debates about the predicates to be chosen. As the episode with the eraser to be discussed in chapters 8 and 9 shows, even a link inscribed can be erased and reconfigured. There is no right answer and the purpose is to provide students with a space within which they can in fact explore and develop language to find a suitable one. There is no finalizing function because the end result of the session is not pre-figured and the physical end of the sessions is subject to the external constraints such as the length of the lesson and the school bell that signals its end. The situation is not a finalizing one because students are doing or rather producing something that they could not have envisioned before they actually develop a language for doing so. That is, they recognize the end only after it has come, that is, the product and the language that accompanies provide the tools for recognizing that an acceptable end-point for the purposes at hand has been reached. The result and the accompanying language therefore are contingent, they are 'as much a result of thousands of small mutations finding niches (and millions of others finding no niches), as are the orchids and the anthropoids', to quote Richard Rorty speaking about the evolution of scientific language using specific creatures as his examples, the analogue in our present case would be idioms and dialects.[10] The problem for understanding the evolution of culture and language, according to Rorty, is teleological thinking, whereby a *telos* (a finalizing idea, truth or the emancipation of humanity) is attributed to and governing the history of culture. For science education, the institutionally desired telos is clear: reproduction of the 'scientifically' 'correct' answers guarantees students high grades, guarantees nations a higher rank on OECD examinations (e.g., PISA, TIMMS) than other nations. This telos makes science (and mathematics) education inherently monological, however much teachers use whole-class conversations in which students may venture their ideas. More so, the question is not students' language but its replacement by the official language. At this moment, I am not aware of any other effort than my own to explain how anything like science discourse can evolve, both cultural-historically and ontogenetically, when the very linguistic ground, the linguistic materials, and the linguistic tools available constitute *the conditions and resources* for the emergence of something *completely other than themselves*.

The telos has a finalizing function to what students have to know and how they are to communicate with respect to certain phenomena. Telos gives rise to a monological orientation, which arises when a discourse has developed that constitutes an authoritative and stabilized medium of and for ideological refraction. This conventionalized discourse dominates, and in domination, imposes *one* ideology, and thereby leads to a monological, cultured discourse. Against this discourse, 'the direct, unconditional, unrefracted word, appears barbaric, raw, wild'.[11] When words such as velocity or force are used with multiple senses, including those that Aristotle and other philosophers of the past articulated, then science educators and teachers will think of students as raw, wild, untamed, and unschooled. A child who takes talk about sunrise and sun-

---

10. Richard Rorty, *Contingency, Irony, Solidarity* (Cambridge: Cambridge University Press, 1989), 16.
11. Bakhtin, op. cit. note 4, 203.

set literally, that is, as implying a moving sun, is said to have misconceptions in his or her mind, naïve ideas, and so forth.

Contingency of collective thought and language is perfectly compatible with a Vygotskian approach, though he is concerned with the ways in which *individuals* come to reproduce culture. However, if thought and speech are thought of as processes that mediate each other via a third process, itself undergoing constant change—at all time scales, including the instant-to-instant unfolding of an event, ontological change characterizing the individual development, and cultural-historical change—then the course of development is not teleologically determined but undergoes open-ended, nonfinalizing evolution. This feature is characteristic of plot in Dostoevsky's works, where ideas are not subject to what the author thinks but, once nucleated in the novel, are allowed to develop according to their own logic and in interaction with other, contradictory ideas.

Saying that the history of linguistic and cultural development is open does not mean that the past of a word is lost in transformation. Rather, each word retains the voice of previous users, and their inflections, intonations, and sonorities are retained in as far as they have shaped the trajectory of the word. Because of the dialectic of production, which both reproduces the sound shape and transforms the senses it can take, a word changes but does not in the process forget (free itself from) the contexts in which it has been used. Thus, Bakhtin states: 'When a member of a speaking collective comes upon a word, it is not as a neutral word of language not as a word free from the aspirations and evaluations of others, uninhabited by others' voices. No, he receives the word from another's voice and filled with that other voice. The word enters his context from another context, permeated with the interpretations of others. His own thoughts find the word already inhabited' (ibid.).

Much of the confusion concerning theories of conceptions and language consist in mistaking the sound shape and utterance, which we recognize in stable ways across settings, as the word. Bakhtin, however, suggests that this is problematic: 'For the word is not a material thing but rather the eternally mobile, eternally fickle medium of dialogic interaction. It never gravitates toward a single consciousness or a single voice. The life of the word is contained in its transfer from one mouth to another, from one context to another context, from one social collective to another, from one generation to another generation' (ibid.). The stability of the word is only an illusion, for even its sound wave changes from context to context, region to region, era to era. If it were not like this, the pronunciations would not undergo historical evolutionary processes at the same time that sense undergoes changes. Yet the stability is required for anything like dictionary sense to be plausible. It is precisely in this contradiction that we need to think of the languages that students evolve as part of their schooling in subject-specific courses.

7

From the Dim Stirring of a Thought to its Formulation

In the preceding chapter, I write about how Lev Vygotsky conceives thought not as an entity related to a (cognitive) *frame*work but as a dynamic entity that evolves together with the language that articulates and shapes it. His ideas therefore are consistent the perspective that I develop in this book, itself inspired by the work of Mikhail Bakhtin on dialogism. The concept of dialogism forces us to think about evolution of thought that occurs while a conversation unfolds; the unfolding itself is a consequence and outcome of dialogism. As we know from participating in decision-making committees, the ultimate decision emerges from a dialogue of voices (ideas), which, from an etymological perspective literally means speaking (Gr. λέγειν [legein]) alternately, across (Gr. δια- [dia-]). Dialogical means a constant back and forth, a give and take among participants or participating ideas. Bakhtin therefore uses the term more frequently than the word dialectical, which, despite the same etymology (i.e., δια- and λέγειν), is heard as contrasting irreconcilable oppositions. But in both, development is evident so that the ultimate result of a dialogical (dialectical) process does not resemble any individual's voice (idea). We therefore can think the outset of such development in terms of an idea—often referred to as 'the general idea of where we are at'—in the form of a seed. This seed develops in and through talking, bringing about change in the very way participants will be talking only minutes or seconds hence. *They talk the idea into being*, and, as a result, the talking itself is changed as the idea develops. 'Let us consider', Vygotsky writes, 'the process of verbal thinking from the first dim stirring of a thought to its formulation. What we want to show is not how meanings develop over long periods of time, but the way they function in the live process of verbal thought . . .. We shall, for a while, put aside the problem of development and consider the relations between thought and word in the mature mind'.[1] Vygotsky's writing generally concerns individuals and their development. But change of language—i.e., learning—in school classrooms occurs at two levels simultaneously, at the small-group level and at the individual level. Here it may come with

---

1. Lev S. Vygotsky, *Thought and Language* (Cambridge, MA: MIT Press, 1986), 217.

some advantage if we think not only about individuals, their abilities, and the relation of thought and words in them, but also in terms of language that develops not only because of the relation between word and thought at the individual level but also because of the relation between thought and language at the collective level. In the previous chapter, I provide examples of the considerable differences that exist between Ralf's concept map that he has brought to the lesson and the one he produces together with his group mates. Quite clearly, as is evident throughout this book, repeating what someone else has said, quoting peers and teachers, transforming the language of others, paraphrasing them, and other forms of using and changing language (consciously and unconsciously) are collective processes. These processes mediate collective, participatory thinking, because of the relation between speaker and audience. This relation, too, needs to be theorized at the collective level, that is, as a social fact sui generis rather than the result of two or more people coming together.

In the present instance, we are dealing with a group of students doing the work of producing a concept map. They have come to the lesson with some language, and therefore, have to be considered, like all other members of society, as having a mind that is *mature with respect to the present position on their life trajectory*. Other than Vygotsky and other than developmental psychologists generally and Jean Piaget specifically, I am not thinking of human beings in a deficit perspective, as incomplete beings who *have to develop* in a teleological manner toward an obligatory end-point. For Piaget, this obligatory end-point of development is 'formal reasoning'. In his approach, humans are not mature and full thinkers unless they are at the highest level of formal thinking or at the highest level of moral thinking. Everything in a person's life before that is less than complete. It is merely 'concrete operational' or something of that ilk. For Vygotsky, development is a necessary corollary of participation in human activities, for he views any higher psychological function as an internalized form of previously experienced societal relation. These include the ruling relations that the feminist sociologist Dorothy E. Smith investigates, whose concerns with language are very similar to my own and, as the latter, similarly grounded in the work of Mikhail Bakhtin.[2]

Vygotsky's ideas are interesting, but perhaps too much focused, at least in the quote I provide, on the individual psychological aspects and not enough on the cultural-historical aspects of linguistic evolution. As a psychologist, he is concerned with individual development rather than with the development of the group, the self-organization that might occur at the level of language when a group of students works together such as those figuring here in this book. He does recognize the role of a teacher or other individuals, but always with respect to the development of the individual. This is also clear, for example, in his notion of the *zone of proximal development,* which Vygotsky defines in terms of an *individual's* competencies working alone versus those competencies exhibited while working with someone else, generally a developmentally more advanced teacher. A focus on collectives, on the other hand, rephrases the definition of zone of proximal development in terms of what *collectives*

---

2. Dorothy E. Smith, *Institutional Ethnography: A Sociology for People* (Lanham, MD: AltaMira, 2005).

are able to do in one context versus what they can do in some other context. Here the focus is on the collective control over life conditions and how making changes in the setting expands this control. It is this focus on the collective that I am interested in. Vygotsky is more interested in how interactions mediate individual participation, so that we obtain a development of the collective endeavor that necessarily entails a development of the individual. Any group achievement involves the productions of individuals. But the individual productions are within and for the group, that is, presuppose the group and its collective motives. Participating in a concept-mapping session means contributing in a way that *one* final result can emerge, that is, it means negotiation when there are differences.

In the previous chapter, I show how the final arrangement of concept names *emerges* after the students have already been talking for a while about and arranging these. Throughout this book, I present pertinent theoretical concepts and ways of thinking about language and its use following the *real-time* unfolding of the lesson as these students realize it. If we are interested in human experience of learning, the *moment-to-moment* unfolding of language is the only thing that we have to understand what is happening. This is so because the participants themselves do not have a picture of the final result on which to draw for organizing their work process—in the way construction workers have a pretty clear picture of the house they are making, which is similar to other houses that they have completed many times before. Rather, for the students the final result is the trace remaining of their participation and production after these have ended. Following the conversation in a step-by-step fashion does not give us, however, the bigger picture that one produces upon reflection, 'So what has happened here?' For this reason, I pull out in this chapter *all* turns in which participants utter the concept name 'quantum'. We can then think about and theorize how at the group level the relation of this word to other words evolves, and how, if so, the language involving this concept name changes.

In this chapter, I therefore present a look backward, from the perspective of where the group ends up, its final concept map. That is, I take as point of view the place where chapter 6 ends. I then look backward at particulars of talk in view of what will have been achieved when the students hand their concept map to the teacher. Already in 1991 when taking a first look at the session and attempting to understand it, my choice was the term 'quantum'. It has been subject to considerable debate within the group before the three students settle on the way it integrates with other concept names surrounding (Fig. 7.1). I then answer the question, 'How do the students get to present one concept name, here "quantum", in the network of all other concept names they end up?' This approach allows me to reflect upon the trajectory that the 'construction process' has taken from the 'first dim stirring of a thought', that about quantum, 'to its final formulation'. But, to reiterate, my concern is more with the events at the collective level, as these students talk not merely *for themselves* but also *for the other*. They do not just say what comes to their mind. What they say, they *say for others*. As we know from everyday experience, we do change our stories depending on the audience, which may consist of our children, colleagues, spouses, childhood friends, members on the sports team, or other regulars in the bar we frequent. That is, speakers make available consciousness and thought in and through speaking, which

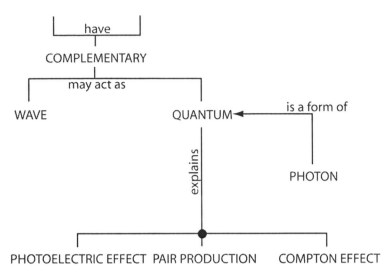

Fig. 7.1. This excerpt of the final concept map shows all connections to the term 'quantum'.

simultaneously constitutes thought and consciousness. But they always do so *for the other*, in view of the other, and in view of possible responses that provide evidence about the effect that a speech act has had. This consciousness always and already is consciousness for the other as much as it is consciousness for the self. Mikhail Bakhtin, with his concern for language and the word that bestraddles the speaker and the listener, the individual and the collective, therefore offers a suitable approach to a problem that cannot be reduced to the individual.

To reiterate, at any one point it would be dangerous to say that 'a student did something *because* . . .' and then use the final concept map as a reason. This is *not* how things happen. During the process, students do not know where they and the concept map will end up. They do not know the end result. They do not even know the nature of the idiom that they will develop, which therefore constitutes a crucial aspect of our problem: The learning paradox is at work, and students cannot make the process toward a result better if they inherently *cannot* know the end result beforehand. That is, whereas the construction workers—carpenters and masons—can and do monitor their work with respect to the anticipated outcome, the students here do not and cannot have a specific image of the outcome, and, therefore, are never in a position where they can definitively say something about the quality of their artifact or the quality of their work process. The attempt here is to deconstruct[3] and reconstruct the learning trajectory without imputing a teleological reason for the shape of the path that the evo-

---

3. The verb *deconstruct* and its associate noun *deconstruction* have received a lot of bad press, but, contrary to what many think, Martin Heidegger, from whom Jacques Derrida borrows the term, does not mean 'destroy'. In fact, Heidegger uses the term *Abbau*, which, oppositional related to *Aufbau* (construction, building), means critically taking apart without destroying the pieces. That is, a literal translation would be 'un-building' to get back to the original, etymological sense of words. See Martin Heidegger, *Grundprobleme der Phänomenologie* (Frankfurt: Vittorio Klostermann, 2005).

lution of the conversation generally and that of the concept map specifically have taken. Using the end result to explain the process by means of which it has been achieved would be a form of Whig history, here applied to classroom learning. It would also require a level of finalization and the destruction of all dialogism, for in monologism there cannot be but a single underlying logic. As soon as we admit dialogism into the picture, the development of ideas becomes unpredictable and finalization becomes impossible. Dialogism and predictable learning paths, which are possible only in monologic, finalizable systems, are incommensurable concepts.

From The Stirring of a Thought . . .

In his formulation of a thought that begins with a stirring and then develops into a fully-fledged articulation, Vygotsky places himself entirely into a history of thinking about consciousness that Georg F. W. Hegel initially articulated on an ideal level and that Karl Marx, critical of Hegel's 'idealism', subsequently developed in a materialist dialectical form. Thus, a thought undergoes a development, from an initial seed, in which its final forms are projected but not determined. Just as a plant seed does not look like the tree that grows from it, the idea in its initial form does not reflect the form of the ultimate idea emerging from it. Just as the environment mediates how the genetic material of the seed comes to express itself, so the environment mediates how the initial seed that becomes an idea develops and articulates itself. Just as an organism like a tree can change its environment to improve its own life conditions, so the idea in articulating itself in words changes the environment and therefore the developmental trajectory the idea seed takes.

Vygotsky's take on the development of thought and language is completely historical. So is the approach that Bakhtin takes, for, as he shows in all of his analyses, a particular aspect of Rabelais' or Dostoevsky's novels can be understood only within the historical development of the novel genre. Thus, Bakhtin traces the origin of the dialogism in Dostoevsky's works during the 19th century to a particular genre of the antiquity, the serio-comical.[4] This genre, which embodies the carnival principle (see chapters 8 and 9), has transformed itself into different genres through continued deaths, rebirths, and renewals in original works. This genre has its own particular logic, which continues to persist at the core that the genre as a whole undergoes over the course of the centuries. Each new concrete form that the genre takes enriches the genre itself, aids in improving both the language and the genre. In the same way, the initial thoughts that emerge at the beginning of the concept-mapping session are transformed, change, and evolve in continual death and rebirth of ideas. In this sense, Bakhtin's approach is fundamentally Marxist (dialectical materialist) in nature, embodying the very scheme in which the seed of an idea or genre leads to a continued evolution of its potential in constant death, rebirth, and renewal. If he resisted calling

---

4. Mikhail Bakhtin, *Problems of Dostoevsky's Poetics* (Minneapolis: University of Minnesota Press, 1984), 101–80.

his own approach dialectical, choosing instead dialogical, this may have been because in dialectics, the second member in the opposition is taken to be the negation of the first so that we do not have two (or more) different ideas that interact but only an idea and its negation. In dialogism the give and take between ideas leads to the cycle of death, rebirth, and renewal, which is at the heart of the carnival principle that I articulate in chapters 8 and 9 in the context of laughter and 'off-topic conversations'.

Even though the concept-mapping session is shorter than would normally be a conceptual change interview, we cannot say that students' 'conceptions' are constant. Talk, as we see throughout this book, constantly changes and evolves: what is constant is change. We cannot say that the students have no conception either, as they produce language of and about the quantum nature of light. This is a big part of the reason why I have not found the conceptual change literature helpful when it comes to the analysis of classroom talk such as the one reported here. I continue to find this discourse—i.e., the one about conceptual change—little helpful in pursuing the kinds of interests I have had as a classroom science teacher and now as a researcher concerned with the evolution of language in science classrooms. In this chapter, I trace some of the evolution of the word 'quantum' as it appears in the utterances of the three students. I use miniature maps to exhibit in diagrammatic form the hierarchical relations expressed in utterances.

In the early parts of their concept-mapping session, the three students debated above all the word itself, the 'meaning' of quantum, and how it is related to 'wave' (Fragment 7.1). On the topic of the quantum and its relation to energy, the textbook reads, '[The energy] . . . is not emitted in a continuous wavelike form, but is, instead, emitted in bundles, or packets, of energy, which Planck called **quanta**'. The students are in a situation where they attempt to evolve a language for relating different concepts but they do not yet have a language. In Fragment 7.1, we find the first few utterances from this session, where the question about the 'quantum' already emerges. For Ken, whose utterance is presented in the form of a miniature map, 'quantum' is the concept name that should organize the entire map.

Fragment 7.1
```
003 R: what is quantum.
004 K: what quantum means; are light is a
       particle instead of waves ((*))
005 R: but that is quanta;
008 K: wave and quantum are an instant;
```

QUANTUM

means

LIGHT

isn't   is

WAVE   PARTICLE

These original seeds of language evolve as the three students are working with the concept names, linking them into statements that predicatively specify one concept name after another. In the deployed language resonates what the students have heard and read during the weeks prior to this session. Thus, it is not surprising if the sequence of words that Ken utters (turn 004) resembles the sequence we find in his textbook. But he and his peers have heard and read does not exhaust the forms of combining the words they produce. And yet, how the language can be expanded, or which forms of sentences are allowable within the system is not itself available in the language. When Ken proposes a definition of the quantum ('light is a particle instead of waves'), Ralf opposes ('but') another articulation ('this is quanta'). Here, there is therefore uncertainty right down to the level whether a definition pertains to the singular or the plural of the term.

Such a 'definition' as Ken gives in response to Ralf's question is a re-articulation of 'the same' in different words, and therefore constitutes a translation. Every translation, as all translators between languages and even within languages know, constitutes both an act of treason and an act of renewal and expansion. It is by means of translations that the language evolves each and every time that a student asks what some concept name means. This is why people speaking the same language can misunderstand one another or miscommunicate: We always translate in hearing and we can always hear some utterance differently. Thus, rather than an act of treason, we may see in such translations the very possibilities of language to guarantee its own reproduction and adaptive transformation. It is by means of translations that the students actually come to get a grip on the still-unfamiliar concept name 'quantum' and its plural form quanta. That is, because different expressions can be said and are taken to mean 'the same', teachers can teach their students new forms of language, new idioms, despite the apparent learning paradox concerning how one can learn something inherently outside and beyond the horizon of currently displayed competencies.

Across the turns presented in Fragment 7.2, including those left out, Ralf articulates photon and quantum as being the same thing and quantum as being part of a wave, and specifies (translates) this articulation into quantum saying 'that a wave has not a continuous band of energy' (turn 018). Ken articulates quantum and photon to constitute different theories (turn 010) and an electron to be a particle rather than a quantum. Ralf suggests that the quantum is part of a wave, whereas Ken articulates it as a third theory next to the other two he contributes. In Ken's turn 014, the quantum is actually part of the predicate, specifying another term that is in the subject position of the statement.

Fragment 7.2

```
009 R: quantum is part of a wave and
       then, photon, photon and quantum
       is the same thing. ((*))
010 K: they are the same. no no; i am
       saying if we are going downward,
       this is going down, thats
       ((WAVE)) one, thats ((QUANTUM))
       another theory, and this ((*))
       ((PHOTON)) is the third theory,
       it goes here. ((below quantum))
011 R: quantum is part of the wave.
       ((*)
```

```
014 K: electron is a particle and not a
       quantum. ((*))
```

018 R: quantum says that a wave has not
       a continuous band of energy.
       ((*))

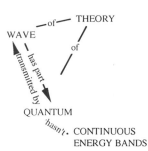

037 R: [photon and] quantum are the
       same. ((*))

QUANTUM - is- PHOTON

A glance at the full transcript with all the text that surrounds the statement shows that the he does not appear to respond to another voice, but he may be making salient something about another concept in the collection. Here this may be 'electron', as it concerns quantum and photons. That is, he introduces a new concept name and then predicatively specifies it drawing on those terms that are already part of the language they evolve. As the factual matters of a statement are given in and by the predicate, it is the subject that is thereby given a place in the language. It is the predicate that has normative force over what else might be said to exist, so that the terms on the bottom of the hierarchy constitute the concept names where everything bottoms out. Everything has to bottom out in the vernacular that we inhabit and that inhabits us, and *out of* which we do everything we do. The concept names on the bottom of the hierarchically ordered concept map, in their very position, constitute the foundation to all the concept names that appear above. It is here, therefore, where the students' vernacular ultimately comes in, because it, the vernacular, the language that they inhabit, does not require further specification. This vernacular constitutes the ground that grounds what they do, the ground on and from which, using aspects of itself as material and other aspects as tools, students evolve a language about new entities. Turn 037 is where students leave the concept name for a while.

There is then a considerable delay before the three students return to the case of the quantum and discuss its relation to other concept words. In Fragment 7.3, Miles repeats the formulation that Ralf has produced earlier in a similar way, substituting 'light' for 'wave' to produce 'quantum is part of light' (turn 148). There is then an exchange between Ralf and the teacher concerning the singular and plural forms of the concept name (i.e., quantum and quanta), and the teacher's reformulation of the relation between quantum and wave as alternates ('or').

Fragment 7.3

148 M: no, because quantum is a part of
       light, and wave is, wave is-
       light is a wave, and quantum is
       the theory of light; ((*))

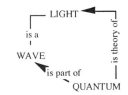

151 R: isnt this ((QUANTUM)) the
       singular form of quantas?

```
152 T: quan:ta. yea.
155 R: doesnt that ((QUANTUM)) mean that
       wave doesnt have a continuous
       band of energy, but just; but
       just bundles? ((*))
157 T: bundles, but we are talking about
       the wave or the quantum, the
       particle character. ((*))
158 K: so quantum light, i mean, its
       quantum and then its [light].
```

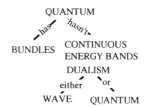

This formulation sets up the dualism of the two perspectives, 'wave or quantum' that historically preceded the development of the complementarity of the two perspectives. That is, the teacher articulates the real topic ('we are talking about') as being one in which the question is 'the wave or the quantum . . . character'. In turn 155, 'wave' is predicatively specified as not having continuous energy, and this specification is embedded in a question concerning the content of the name 'quantum'. In Fragment 7.4, then, Ken proposes an articulation that makes light and X-rays 'the same thing' (turn 168), both phenomena that can be predicatively specified as photons. Thus, in predicate logic, we can write $\exists x(x = photon) \{x|$ light, X-ray$\}$, a statement that we may gloss as 'there are x's such that x is a photon, and the set of x's in the present case consists of light and X-rays'. Gamma rays, which the students also talk about during this session, will also be part of this set, though currently only light and X-ray are salient members. The grammatical construction of Ralf's utterances place 'quantum' in the subject position, that is, as an entity to be specified by aspects of their reality that can already be taken for granted, that is, by 'the facts'. Pragmatically, therefore, the grammar of the utterance is the result of a situation where the term 'quantum' rather than something else is uncertain and therefore in need to be specified before the three students (can) settle on the content of this name and how the name fits together with the other names that make the map.

The grammatical constructions, which arise from the pragmatic issues and contingencies of a situation[5], allow us to reflect on the relation between speaking and writing science. In the writing-to-learn-science literature we observe an ambivalent relation to grammar. On the one hand, grammatical relations *are* important because they characterize what knowledge is taken as fact, what is novel, and which aspects of knowledge are more contentious. On the other hand, a quick overview of Internet sites—using '"writing-to-learn-science" and "grammar"' as terms in a Boolean search—shows that practitioners and scholarly advocates of the method suggest not to worry about grammar. There is therefore a contradiction. On the one hand, students are to learn science by writing, based on what they already know. What they already know constitutes the ground, and therefore what students can use as predicates in the specification of the new words and concept names. The present analyses therefore indicate that grammar does matter and that it, as semantics, is an achievement that the students contingently

---

5. Mikhaïl Bakhtine [V. N. Volochinov], *Le marxisme et la philosophie du langage: essaie d'application de la méthode sociologique en linguistique* (Paris: Les Éditions de Minuit, 1977).

realize under the given conditions. It does matter to these students whether 'quantum' is the uncertain term or whether it is 'photon' or 'wave'. Their utterance structures reflect these concerns, though it is more likely that these concerns are realized unconsciously rather than consciously. The grammatical concerns themselves arise from taking a position in a world, where certain aspects are given and others are novel or uncertain. Speech reflects and refracts this position in the world together with the things that make this world such that it can be taken for granted. This world is thematically organized such that new words can find a place. This, then, provides the condition that even if one speaker introduces a new word others can already understand it, because the existing significations embody the very possibility for the new way of speaking to make sense.

The different turns assembled in Fragment 7.4 and the mini-maps expressing their content further provide evidence for the existence of a language very much in search of organizing and orienting features.

Fragment 7.4

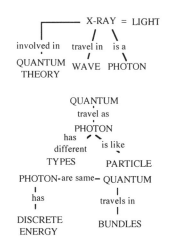

```
168 K: but isnt the x=ray the same
       thing, isnt x=ray a photon,
       x=rays is involved in the quantum
       theory? ((*)
172 T: ((WAVE)) quantum, they would be
       at the same level.
177 K: why wouldnt they travel in forms
       of photons not photon is quantum?
       ((*))
178 R: but quantum and photon are the
       same.

180 M: photon has a discrete energy and
       quantum is just saying travels in
       bundles so they are the same
       thing. basically. ((*))
```

As we scan our gaze across the different fragments presented so far, we observe that Ralf repeatedly makes statements about the sameness of 'photon' and 'quantum' (turns 009, 037, 178). Later, in opposition to a statement Ken makes about 'quantum' being more general than 'photon', Ralf suggests that these terms are 'almost exactly the same' (turn 192) and provides a reason for saying so: 'Planck gave a certain energy to that quantum . . . and then just Einstein said it's a photon' (turns 189, 192). The teacher subsequently weighs in on the question introducing the word 'phonon' and an explication of what the term denotes. Ken is the one individual who picks it up. The teacher also weighs in on the question of quantization, suggesting that sound waves generally are not quantized, speech that Ralf subsequently picks up (turn 226). Ralf also talks about X-rays as waves that are quantized (turn 232) against the ground of his very recent utterance of sound waves as a non-quantized phenomenon.

The students' use of the words resonates the textbook sentence 'the energy of light is not transmitted in a continuous wave but rather is concentrated in bundles of energy he called **photons**'. Miles takes up and employs the words from the book (consciously or unconsciously) 'quantum *is just saying* travels in bundles'. He also takes up and mobilizes another fragment, '[Einstein] proposed that the amount of energy in each of these bundles was a discrete, fixed amount'. Bringing the two forms together, he makes his own statement: 'they are the same thing, basically'. Here, we can hear the 'basically' as modifying the statement 'they are the same thing'. They are basically the same even though the two are different words. We are confronted here with the aporia of every translation possible within a language, to say something in another way. The identity of two ways of expressing 'the same' is an achievement and should not to be taken for granted.

In Fragment 7.5, the students mobilize authority figures to introduce what they have said or done concerning the term under investigation. The teacher, too, mobilizes the voice of a book to introduce a new term, 'phonon', to the discussion for the purposes, as we see in chapter 4, of assisting students to establish the relation between the concept names 'quantum' and 'photon'. Reporting someone else's voice is a highly important sociological phenomenon that can teach us much about the dialectic of language production, that is, its reproduction and transformation within a generation and across generations of speakers. This reproduction is important at the collective level, which provides us with an understanding of the stability and changes that we observe in the idiom over time. The phenomenon also allows us important inroads to the question about how individual speakers develop particular stable ways of expressing themselves about some topic. When a person, especially an influential scholar, is quoted directly, then the voice of this expert can significantly weigh on the contentious issue at hand. Less serious is the sound of the voice when it is made present as indirect discourse, because in this case, the voice of the present speaker has already infiltrated the other voice. It is heard as an interpretation of what the other person has said rather than the voice itself.

In all of the instances that follow, the speakers do not use direct speech but rather indirect speech. However, this is the same kind of indirect discourse that the textbook is using. The textbook uses verbs such as 'propose', 'hope', 'state', 'call' and 'hypothesize' to introduce the contributions physicists such as Albert Einstein and Max Planck have made to quantum theory. All of these verbs imply but do not directly quote the voice and agency of these scientists so that it comes at little surprise when students use the generic verb 'say' to attribute certain facts to these eminent physicists. Using indirect speech has important implications for the unfolding of the conversation, and therefore, because of the path-dependence of the subsequent conversation, for the ultimate concept map that results from the students' work.

Fragment 7.5

```
181 K: but this ((QUANTUM)) is general;
       this ((PHOTON)) more detailed.
186 M: quantum, and then [Einstein said
       it has discrete energy  ]
189 R: [but planck] gave a certain
       energy to that quantum, because
       he said its h times f
```

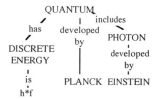

```
192 R:                 [but he used]
       quanta and then just einstein
       said its a photon, so its almost
       exactly the same.
196 T: ((returns with a book in his hand))        QUANTUM
       see, the thing is, you=ve got more        can be  can be
       quanta than just photons, then         PHOTON      PHONON
       quantum would be more general. ((*))
203 T: ((points to a page in the book)) you       PHONON
       also have phonons which are elastic         is    is
       waves, which are quantized, but its       ELASTIC
       an elastic wave in matter, its not        WAVE
       like, its inside a crystal, but the         is
       molecules they can move ((*))            MATTER
                                                    is
                                                 CRYSTAL

206 K: phonon is a form of quantum energy;       QUANTUM
       ((*))                                     ENERGY
                                                    is a

                                                 PHONON
```

    Interestingly, the teacher, too, refers to a book while introducing a new term (turns 196, 203). That is, although one might have thought that in, and because of, his institutional position, he constitutes an authority, the fact that he refers to the book defers authority to someone else. The teacher therefore places himself at the level of the students, both parties deferring authority to someone else with respect to some issue at hand. The (likely unconscious) move also allows us to better understand the kind of role the teacher aspires to in this situation: He does not act like a disseminator of knowledge but as a co-inquirer into best ways of expressing something about this particular topic. Deferring authority to the book undermines the position of the ruling relation that the traditional IRE sequence institutes between the teacher, who asks and evaluates, and the students, who respond and whose responses are evaluated. In this instance, the teacher draws on the book that he has brought to the table to introduce the concept name 'phonon' and then produces a statement that one might find in a dictionary, a definition. He is saying the same thing, but in a different way. But he also describes a situation, something that can be heard to be about the natural world, 'phonons . . . are elastic waves, which are quantized . . . its inside a crystal, the molecules they can move' (turn 203).

    In a situation such as this, we must ask how students can understand something that they have never heard before? The teacher utters a word ('phonon') that his three students have not seen or heard before. He presents it for the purposes of helping students understand that photons are but one form of quantum, a term that also refers to phonons, the periodic oscillations that can be found in crystals. That is, the teacher talks using a foreign word and phenomenon for the purpose of assisting students in talking about the relation between quantum and photon in an (for physics) appropriate manner. We can understand what the teacher does to the project of finding an appropriate idiom in which quantum has its place as providing an *explication*. The teacher explicates (Lat. *ex-*, out + *plicāre*, to fold), literally, unfolds and unpacks and therefore smoothens something (i.e., the quantum–photon relation) that has been folded and packed. By unfolding and unpacking, he makes space for the term phonon, a differentiation of quantum, which then allows the repackaging of the term to be deployed in this new, transformed form.

From the beginning of the chapter to this point, we see that there have been many utterances containing the concept name 'quantum'. Many utterances contain the concept name 'wave' and a few additional concept names. It is as if students have to find and work out appropriate ways of deploying these concept names in a variety of different utterances. They do so in the context of other concept names, where the totality of names at hand bottoms out in their experience and vernacular that serves as the ground (the bottom of the map, the ground for the bottom of the map). This allows us to understand why Maurice Merleau-Ponty suggests that 'I begin to comprehend the sense of the words by their place in the context of action and by participating in communal life'.[6] Bakhtin, too, has come to this understanding, for he writes that '[t]o understand another's utterance means to orient oneself with respect to it, to replace it in an appropriate context'.[7] We cannot determine which of the numerous senses that a dictionary provides is mobilized in a particular instant unless we know the context of its use. The specific sense of the word is completely determined by its context so that the particular theme entirely is a function of the situation of use. There are as many themes as there are contexts, though the sense is repeatable across them.

. . . to its Formulation

While participating in or following a conversation, we do not know where it will end up and what the results will be. Etymologically, the verb to converse derives from the late Latin *conversare* via the old French *converser*, to turn to and fro, to live, to dwell in and with, taking its modern sense of having a conversation only recently and most completely in English. We do not know the terrain that a conversation will cover as little as we know about the future of life. Conversations are as unpredictable as life itself. We cannot know beforehand what decisions, if any, a group of individuals involved in a conversation are going to make at the end of an unfolding conversation. I have experienced repeatedly, as a member of various committees (e.g., those that decide on tenure and promotion or those that make decisions about how to rate a funding proposal) the unpredictable trajectories and decisions of committee work. Despite my extended experience as a member of such committees, and despite my interest in and orientation to such meetings as a social scientist studying human interactions, I generally cannot anticipate at the beginning of a conversation where it will end up. And this is so *even when there are straw votes and even when members have provided preliminary assessments*. Sometimes, despite major inclinations to favor one outcome, the

---

6. Maurice Merleau-Ponty, *Phénoménologie de la perception* (Paris: Gallimard, 1945), 209.
7. Bakhtine, op. cit. note 5, 146.

committee, in and through talk, comes to an opposite conclusion. For example, I have been a member of a funding committee where both evaluators have ranked a proposal very high. In the end, the proposal was declared unfundable. It surprised me that nowhere along the trajectory of the conversation was I able anticipate the ultimate outcome, which was determined by a public vote.[8] These indeterminate outcomes of professional meetings have taught me to think differently about classroom conversations, where students clearly have no way of 'constructing' something specific. If anything, they engage in a process where they *evolve* something, a process that shapes itself as it unfolds leading to completely unanticipated and impossible to anticipate results.

Similarly, the conversations the present students have and as part of which they are to produce some outcome—a concept map, a report, some representation—cannot be anticipated. Neither they nor we know what trajectories the conversations will take or what outcomes will result from a session even if we have beforehand, as in the case of this concept-mapping session, the students' individually produced maps. Thus, as I show in chapter 6, there is very little in common between the map that Ralf, the best student in this class, has produced and the final group map that he arrives at together with his peers. This is so even though he works with two peers who have much lower GPAs than he, which some science educators might want to use to explain what happens in a session and what its outcomes are. Therefore, the decision to entitle this session as the formulation of the idea could only have come after the fact. Knowing the ultimate outcome, though, allows us to see how the formulation emerges from the previously much more heterogeneous talk.

In Fragment 7.6, the main issue worked out in the various utterances is the fact that there are different kinds of waves, some of which come with quantized energies and others that, because of their macroscopic nature ('at that level'), are not associated with quantized energies. That is, the question about the relation between 'quantum' and 'photon', the latter being only one of the quantized phenomena, is the differentiation of waves into quantized and non-quantized phenomena. This then blocks the subordination of 'quantum' to 'wave'. In the exchange between the students themselves and between them and the teacher, new forms of talking including the word 'waves' come to be worked out. Thus, as Ralf states 'X-rays are waves and they are quantized' in contrast to sound waves, which are macroscopic phenomena in matter and are not quantized (turn 232).

Fragment 7.6

```
215 R: so quantum because its a form of energy
       it is energy;
216 T: but at that level sound energy is not
       quantized. ((*))

217 K: the wave should be over quantum because,
```

8. A description of this case and a computer model for group decision making can be found in Wolff-Michael Roth (2002), 'Evaluation and Adjudication of Research Proposals: Vagaries and Politics of Funding', *FQS: Forum Qualitative Social Research/ Forum Qualitative Sozialforschung, 3*(3). Accessed February 11, 2009 at http://www.qualitative-research.net/index.php/fqs/article/view/841.

223 M: `no. waves is one way of describing`
       `light; and quantum is another way.`
       `((*))`
224 R: `but there are more waves than there are`
       `quanta, because for [example, ]`
226 R: `sound is a wave; but its in matter; not`
       `quantized; ((*))`
232 R: `x=rays are waves and they are`
       `quantized.`

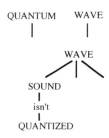

In Fragment 7.7, the teacher rejects one formulation ('no') and proposes another one to take its place. At issue here is, as I point out above, the grammar that the utterances realize because this grammar mediates the relations that the different words maintain to each other in the particular context. They also determine the relation of what is taken as known, a fact, and what is in need of specification in terms of the known. Although the grammar of speech in a conversation is contingent on the speech context, taking into account and building on what has been said and what the possible subsequent response will be, there are also semantic relations that need to be observed. The teacher's utterance immediately follows an utterance in which Ken proposes that they 'could say that energy is like particle'. Here, Ken has predicatively specified energy as something that 'is like [a] particle'. The teacher reformulates, that is, reproduces and transforms, the utterance into 'has particle character' (turn 247). Although the teacher proposes in turn 238 that the two concept names under discussion, 'wave' and 'quantum', *have to be* side by side, Ken builds on another utterance concerning the existence of quantized and non-quantized waves to make a new link that also takes into account what Ralf has said (turn 252).

Fragment 7.7
238 T: `then quantum a::nd wave have to be`
       `side by side; ((*))`
243 R: `does quantum mean its- um a particle-`
       `a wave`
       `[or a particle? ]`
247 T: `no, it has particle character, its bundled, like, like,`
       `like a piece of mass. see it says ((points to book))`
       `particle like entity or quantum; but you can also have`
       `phonons.`
252 K: `but because you=re giving us that`
       `example with phonons, then thats`
       `like ralf was saying, waves also`
       `have a lower detailed description`
       `within itself and thats why it`
       `should be above quantum. because`
       `quantum is only a subdivision of`
       `[wave. no.] ((*))`

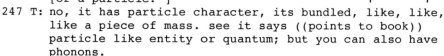

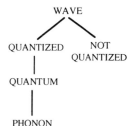

In turn 252, Ken mobilizes the voices of others—i.e., the teacher and Ralf—which prepares a ground and condition on which his own proposal 'wave should be above quantum' comes to be based. Here, Ken provides a summary of the content that Ralf has articulated rather than referring to what he has said specifically or by providing a slightly transformed repetition of his speech. In the next fragment, the transformation of an utterance has gone even further and Miles does no longer say that Ralf has said something before, but he invokes this fact only through the content of the statements that can be attributed to Ralf 'you can put wave here and you could put it there'. Addressing Ralf by invoking his name further strengthens this association between the implicit attribution in the utterance and Ralf as the source of this statement.

In the two turns of Fragment 7.8, the ultimate solution to the problem of articulating the complementarity of wave and quantum theories of certain phenomena (light, X-rays) comes to be articulated in its rudimentary form. WAVE and QUANTUM are at the same level, as the teacher has suggested some 35 turns before, and the different instantiations of electromagnetic waves (light, X-rays) are super-ordinated to the concept names 'wave' and 'quantum'.

Fragment 7.8

```
273 M: ralf; because you can put wave there and
       you could put it there but it doesnt need
       to be here; you have light as a heading
       and we dont loose a thing in the concept
       map. but we have it when we dont put wave
       here. we are totally left without half
       our- ((*))
274 K: we could say, dealing with the subject
       matters of light and x=rays and then go
       into further detail. actually- when you
       think about it, light is a detail of
       wave, but wave is also a particular
       aspect of light. cause remember; that
       light isnt just waves, now that they=re
       saying that there is quantum physics, so
       thats just a detailed explicit expression
       of light waves and x=rays. ((*))
```

But these concept names appear at the same level with respect to each other. As the excerpts in Fragment 7.10 below show, the remaining question is concerned with the precise form of the predicates that determine the concept name 'complementarity' given the nouns 'wave' and 'quantum' as the fixed constituents of the predicate. Before getting there, however, Ken raises a question about matter waves and their relation to both wave and quantum phenomena.

Fragment 7.9

```
363 K: doesnt matter waves- matter waves is just another way
       of saying quantum waves? and,
```

Ken explicitly invokes the translation involved, 'doesn't matter waves—is just another way of saying quantum waves?' Here we have the syntax of the utterances shaped by the uptake of and reference to other speakers and what the speaker himself might want to express. Repeatedly the conversation has touched upon matter waves and upon the distinction between macroscopic waves and waves that are only one of two expressions that phenomena can take. The syntax of the utterance in turn 363 is a function of the fact that it is constructed from previously articulated elements and in question form. In a similar way, the syntax of Ken's utterance in turn 252 is shaped by the preceding utterances. He cites the teacher using indirect speech 'because you're giving us that example' to construct his own argument ('because') against another ('but'). The syntax is further mediated because he also refers to what Ralf has said, 'Waves also have a lower detailed description within itself'. Together, the two aspects then allow the conclusion, 'that's why it [WAVE] should be above QUANTUM'. Ralf has said in turns 118 and 120 that 'wave should stay on he top because it's the most general'; and in turn 011, he has said 'quantum is part of the wave'. In part, of course, the talk occurs against the background of previous instructions to have a hierarchical organization, instructions repeated during the lesson: The most inclusive terms are to be 'on top' and less inclusive terms are to appear lower in the hierarchy so that the most specialized or concrete terms appear at the bottom. In Ken's utterance, Ralf's words appear in a new context now mobilized for the purpose of making his own statement. But they do not appear in the same way, syntactically or semantically. First, Ken transforms them, thereby producing a paraphrased or indirect form. The words now are mobilized in service of an intention, which is expressed in the articulation and concretization of a (vague) sense that WAVE should be above QUANTUM.

In Fragment 7.10, I assemble the remaining statements, all but one uttered during the final phase of the concept-mapping task between (a) Miles' earlier statement that they are done and the teacher's response that they are to make links and use linking words and (b) their final submission of the map that they produce in this session. During this final stage, the students seek, among others, a suitable way of specifying 'complementarity'. But although they work in and with speech, their language does not tell them how or what an appropriate predication looks like. In such a case, as the philosopher Richard Rorty proposes, one can only try and then 'spit out' all those utterances that do not taste well or seem to fit—and they do try multiple versions in many instances.

Fragment 7.10

398 K: okay guys, complementarity do i put it right? i mean, wave and quantum, i put right here. ((*))

446 R: complementarity means that it can either act as a wave or a quantum. ((*))

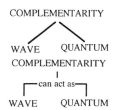

448 M: may act; has wave or quantum; ((*))   COMPLEMENTARITY
                                                                      |
                                                               ┌─may act as─┐
                                                               WAVE   QUANTUM
451 K: but then you gotta join wave and   COMPLEMENTARITY
       quantum; because it- they interact; |
       ((*))   ┌─ acting as─┐
                                                               WAVE   QUANTUM
                                                               └─interact─┘
455 R: they dont interact   ┌─ acting as─┐
456 M: [they have quantum and photon   ]   WAVE   QUANTUM
       ((*))   └─have─┘
507 M: wave to matter waves; oh quantum to   PHOTON
       matter waves.
511 K: quantum property; concerning quantum; concerning
       quantum- okay hurry up.
527 T: well, plancks constant isnt it plancks constant- that
       plancks constant relates to quantum?
550 R: we still have quantum and photon; uh; quantum here.
554 K: quantum, yea quantum interact with-
555 R: quantum explains-

Although the students come to an end with this part of their concept map (Fig. 7.1), their language continues to undergo change. During this physics course, students also participate in discussions concerning nature of physics as language and write essays about the nature of light and what this tells us about the nature of knowledge. They develop a reflective discourse about physics as language, in which the wave-particle dualism and complementarity play an integral role. This language therefore is never the same, and even (and precisely because) if it were the same, it would not have the same theme. There is therefore not a definitive conclusion to this discussion, just a temporary closure that is achieved after the lesson-terminating bell has already gone and with the finished map. This final result has emerged from a continual back and forth between the speakers, a process that is literally described by the adjective *dialogical*.

The Individual: Talking and (Participative) Understanding

In the preceding two sections, I document the evolution of the map surrounding the concept name 'quantum' from its initial formulations to its final formulation. The associated diagrams (miniature maps) clearly show how, after considerably varying forms of expression, the ultimate structure relating and embedding the concepts emerges and stabilizes. In this section, I revisit in particular the issue of Ken's utterances in the light of the Bakhtinian discursive approach that I take in this book. Accordingly, language is the primary phenomenon and the talk in any situation cannot be understood by taking an individualist perspective on collaboration. The individual has to be understood and theorized in his subordination to the collective phenomenon, for anything he may say in an intelligible way is and has to be oriented toward the other, with and toward a common understanding. The collective phenomenon sui generis is the conversation; and it occurs in and with language, which cannot be reduced to the individuals who only inherited it from and who return it to the other. But it as a phenomenon in and of itself, it is a singular plural, *a singular* conversation that is constituted by *a plurality of* voices. Individual and collective understanding therefore have to be theorized out of language and conversation, that is, in their subordination to the dialogical relation, rather than as a result of individual intentions.

One of the great themes of this book is the learning paradox, which, as discussed in the early chapters, educational theories generally and constructivism and conceptual change theories more specifically have not solved. In reproducing themselves, these fields and theories also reproduce the ideology of learning as individual intentional activity that can be planned beforehand with different grain sizes at the various levels of educational hierarchies. Of course, there is nothing dialogical about science education conceived as the transmission of the authoritative language of science; and this has been partially the case in my own classrooms despite the fact that at the time of the study I have been implementing. Throughout this book I exhibit evidence for the great degree of openness to dialogicity embodied in this lesson. But this lesson is contextualized by other aspects of the course that places students in the position of conducting their own research without specific end results to be arrived at.

There is a contradiction, however, because ultimately, these students and their parents want the teachers of this school to prepare their sons for university entrance examinations or Advanced Placement courses. This teacher, too, has as his aim helping students to produce the 'correct' answers on external tests and examinations. This becomes quite clear in interviews conducted at the time, during which students say quite specifically that they understand and can buy into the social construction of the sciences and into open inquiry in their classrooms.[9] They talk about how much they enjoy the pedagogy employed in the physics course. But, they also talk about the fact that at the end of the day, what counts are not their predilections and understandings of the nature of science that will get them into the program of their choice at one of the elite universities. This is why they want to be taught 'the right answers' and 'how to get to the right answers'.

When I first looked at these videotapes, my own theoretical discourses were lying somewhere between the positions taken by (a) individual constructivism a la Ernst von Glasersfeld and (b) social constructivism as I have come to understand it through reading the literature in the social studies of science including such authors as Karin Knorr-Cetina, Bruno Latour, and Steve Woolgar. At the time, the constructivist literature has had a profound influence on my thinking. But it also confused me, as is evident in the following quote from the article in which I presented an argument for the social construction of knowledge in school science classrooms based on the analysis of concept mapping. Readers notice how the constructivist idea of individual knowl-

---

9. This becomes quite evident in a study that investigates the articulated epistemologies, on the one hand, and students' thoughts about open inquiry and learning, on the other hand. See Keith B. Lucas and Wolff-Michael Roth, 'The Nature of Scientific Knowledge and Student Learning: Two Longitudinal Case Studies', *Research in Science Education*, Vol. 26 (1996), 103–29.

edge maintains an uneasy relationship with the idea of the discursive process that I am in the process of theorizing. One notices also a very un-Vygotskian idea about the relationship between thinking and speaking. It should be clear by now that today I completely renounce such a position on how students know and learn.

Here, then, is what I wrote: 'Often, initial individual propositions were found to undergo modifications through the discursive process of the mapping session. There was much negotiation and shifting in individual positions before the final design of the concept map was formalized and inscribed on a large sheet of paper. For example, Kevin [Ken] proposed the complementarity of wave and quantum character at the very beginning of the activity. However, as the excerpts in Table 1 show, Kevin swayed during the discussion from his initial conception to follow Rand [Ralph] in subordinating all concepts to "wave", to his original conception, to "wave", and finally back to his initial conception, this time including the concept 'complementarity'. In part, these changes can be associated with other students' and the teacher's contributions when Kevin made explicit reference to another remark ("then that's what Rand was saying"). Other sources that may have influenced Kevin in his conception were irrecoverable because, like any participant, he externalized only a part of his thoughts. We found, however, that changes in students' ideas about a proposition were more likely to occur when the other participants resorted to longer explanations and justifications of their statements. This also means that students' conceptualizations were open to changes in structural aspects and that their understanding was not set once and for all. However, individual links may also be so fixed that, although students negotiate and agree on temporary solutions no long-term changes in their understanding of a specific proposition have been made (Roth & Roychoudhury, in press). On the other hand, the mapping activities, if done at strategic points in the course, can have long lasting effects. Interviews with both Kevin and Rand over six months after they had left the school revealed that they still remembered the overall configuration of the maps they constructed a year earlier'.[10]

In the first several sentences of this quote, I write that students produced 'individual propositions', which underwent 'modifications through the discursive process'. Subsequently, Ken is said to have 'swayed during his initial conception to follow Rand in subordinating all concepts to "wave", to his original conception, to "wave", and finally back to his initial conception, this time including the concept "complementarity"'. ('Table 1' in the quote is equivalent to Fig. 7.2.) Ken therefore is said to have a conception, and this conception is said to change or is articulated differently. It is not quite clear from this quote how a conception, which, as conceptual change theorists point out, is a stable feature of mind, could change so rapidly. The changes then are attributed to other participants in the setting, students and the teacher. I have struggled with this inner contradiction in conceptual change: How change can be so rapid and how can students talk if there is no structure at all. These contradictions have led me to search for a better way of characterizing knowing and learning in science.

---

10. Wolff-Michael Roth and Anita Roychoudhury, 'The Social Construction of Scientific Concepts or The Concept Map as Conscription Device and Tool for Social Thinking in High School Science', *Science Education*, Vol. 76 (1992), 531–57, 541–43.

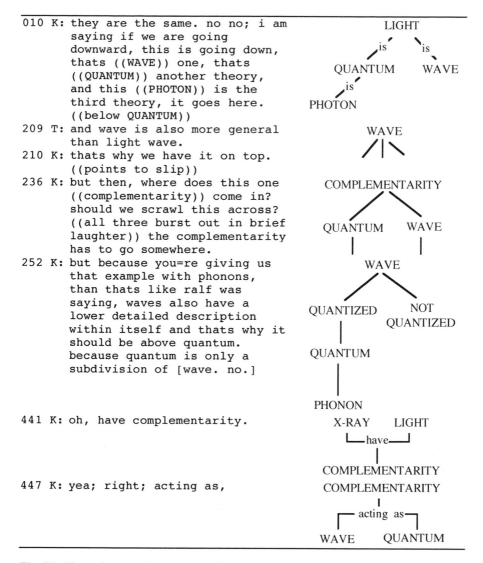

010 K: they are the same. no no; i am
       saying if we are going
       downward, this is going down,
       thats ((WAVE)) one, thats
       ((QUANTUM)) another theory,
       and this ((PHOTON)) is the
       third theory, it goes here.
       ((below QUANTUM))
209 T: and wave is also more general
       than light wave.
210 K: thats why we have it on top.
       ((points to slip))
236 K: but then, where does this one
       ((complementarity)) come in?
       should we scrawl this across?
       ((all three burst out in brief
       laughter)) the complementarity
       has to go somewhere.
252 K: but because you=re giving us
       that example with phonons,
       than thats like ralf was
       saying, waves also have a
       lower detailed description
       within itself and thats why it
       should be above quantum.
       because quantum is only a
       subdivision of [wave. no.]

441 K: oh, have complementarity.

447 K: yea; right; acting as,

Fig. 7.2. The 'trajectory' of QUANTUM in Ken's utterances and actions.

The next statement is notable because it exhibits a form of thinking about the relationship between thought and language that still is prevalent in education generally and in science education specifically. The text says, 'Other sources that may have influenced Kevin in his conception were irrecoverable because, like any participant, he externalized only part of his thought'. Here, Ken is said to have some thoughts, only part of which are articulated. That is, what Ken says is articulated as a *direct* reflection of at least part of his thoughts. There are not independent processes of thinking and speaking that intersect, as the sociocultural and cultural-historical position of Vygotsky has it. Rather, there are thought and mind on the one side, and talk—at least if not constituting a lie—is a *direct* (mirror) reflection of this thought. Talk is an embodiment, an external re-presentation of the thought, a representation of thought. This thought itself is an (internal) re-presentation of something presented previously, a representation.

The text then introduces 'students' ideas' without theorizing how ideas are related to the conceptions of the preceding sentence or to the 'individual propositions' that students are said to have uttered. The text also does not articulate how 'students' conceptualizations' are related to their ideas, though the structure of the sentence—which begins with the words 'This also means' suggests that the thing pointed to by 'this' is near because 'this' is an indexical of proximity—refers to something in the preceding sentence. The conceptualizations are then presented as something that is open to change and students' understanding is presented as flexible rather than as set. Finally, 'students' understanding' is presented as something that differs from a proposition—a statement in the concept map such as 'COMPLEMENTARITY acting as WAVE'.

The uneasy relationship between (prior) knowledge, on the one hand, and students' talk, on the other hand, is also evident in the following quote: 'These considerations illustrated that the construction of a concept map during which students have to negotiate the future, taken-to-be-shared knowledge is not straightforward. In the discussions, prior knowledge interfered with the construction at hand. During a previous concept mapping activity, the students had discussed extensively light as a wave phenomenon. At that time, one of the major issues was whether light or wave should be the focus of the concept map. Also, during the present activity the teacher introduced to the discussion the fact that there are many wave phenomena. The introduction of this additional information did not facilitate the students' construction of the complementarity node'.[11] Whereas this text recognizes the perhaps contingent or dialectical nature of available language and structures and the task at hand ('the construction . . . is not straightforward'), it is not clear what 'prior knowledge' is, how it expresses itself in talk, how it mediates talk or knowledge produced, and how it relates to the 'additional information' made available.

A field note written during the initial analysis further underscores my articulation of the issues at the time. In an instruction to myself reads in this way: 'Develop the idea of the concept map both as a representation of knowledge but also as a tool to reflect on this knowledge, and a method of engaging people in discourse about the network of concepts that make the field'. Clearly, the concept map is to be a representation of knowledge, where the 'external' nature of it is implied in the material nature of the map (which I refer to in subsequent work as 'inscription'). Not surprisingly, one champion of conceptual change uses concept maps to articulate differences between conceptual change within ontological categories (rearrangement and reordering existing concepts) and between ontological categories (radical change).[12] In the present instance, students operate with concept names, which they organize hierarchically. It

---

11. Roth and Roychoudhury, op. cit. note 10, 544.
12. Michelene T. H. Chi, 'Conceptual Change Within and Across Ontological Categories: Examples from Learning and Discovery in Science', in *Cognitive Models of Science: Minnesota Studies in the Philosophy of Science* edited by Ronald Giere (Minneapolis: University of Minnesota Press, 1992), 129–86.

may therefore appear as if all that happens is a change *within* ontological categories. But it is evident in fact throughout this book that these students discuss the very nature of the objects and phenomena involved. Thus, in this approach to conceptual change, both types of conceptual changes are observable in the concept-mapping sessions. But this is not the point of contention that I articulate here. Rather, I propose thinking of Ken as contributing to and thereby co-constituting the concept-mapping session. It is not just that he finds himself in the session as if it were a box; and it is not as if the session only existed because of his (and his peers') actions and utterances. The session and his actions are *mutually* constitutive. The session is a bigger whole that has to be thought of as existing in and for itself; and the individual contributions are its consequence rather than its cause. There are numerous dimensions of and surrounding his talk. Thus, what he says (a) is in the context of what has been said so far; (b) is in view of the overall goal of the task, producing a concept map; (c) is uttered for the benefit of the others as much as for his own benefit; (d) is said in a language that comes with its own structural and semantic affordances and constraints; and (e) is said for others to produce effects that themselves are monitored. All of these aspects enable and constrain the individual utterance. *It is not, therefore, that Ken's individual utterances reflect the contents of his individual mind; the individual utterance reflects the setting, language, task, the moment in the trajectory, and so on as much as it reflects the individual mind.*

In Fragment 7.11, the top-most statement in Fig. 7.2 has been placed in the context of the immediately preceding and the immediately following utterance. This, too, is an extraction and abstraction of the utterance from the event as a whole, but it shall suffice for the present purposes. Ken's utterance has to be understood in its double relation to the preceding *and to the* following utterance. In relation to the preceding utterance, he responds and provides a social evaluation of what has been said. He produces an affirmation, 'they are the same'. But then he immediately retracts, 'no, no' and then restates what he is really saying. The utterance occurs precisely at the point shown in the offprint of turn 010, which shows four paper slips in the ordering tat they are shown in the transcript of Fig. 7.2.

Fragment 7.11
```
009 R: quantum is part of a wave and then, photon, photon and
       quantum is the same thing.
010 K: they are the same. no no;
       i am saying if we are
       going downward, this is
       going down, thats ((WAVE))
       one, thats ((QUANTUM))
       another theory, and this
       ((PHOTON)) is the third
       theory, it goes here.
       ((below QUANTUM)) ((*))
011 R: what about this one.
       quantum is part of the
       wave. quantum is the part
       that its the end- no. no.
```

Here, then, Ken provides an indication of his monitoring the effect of his previous speech. He utters 'I am saying . . .'. That is, he does both respond to the content of the preceding utterance, which he hears as saying something that he does not say in turn 008 ('yes I see what you mean. wave and quantum are an instant'). This turn itself is an evaluation and follow-up to something Ralf has said even earlier. What he says also is a translation, for turns 008 and 010 are not identical. In turn 010, he is saying what he was saying in turn 008 without actually saying it in this way.

He then articulates a way of organizing four concept words (LIGHT, WAVE, QUANTUM, and PHOTON). There is no reason to assume that anything, any form of structure in his mind, is preceding the utterance—which does not even name the concept words but to which Ken refers in moving the associated paper slips into a specific organization. Human beings participate in talking about science-related topics that they have never talked about before, and for which they can therefore not have elaborated (i.e., 'constructed') a personal theory, conception, or conceptual framework. But they can and do contribute intelligently and intelligibly, which questions the claims that conceptions and conceptual change research makes.[13] In the present situation, Ken tells Ralf, and therefore any actually or vicariously present third person, how to organize the concept names on the tabletop before them. His utterance 'this is the third theory' while pointing to PHOTON provides resources for implying that the other two concepts also constitute theories. In fact, he does say 'that's another theory' while pointing to QUANTUM. He thereby clearly implicates WAVE as a first theory to which that of 'quantum' is related as *an other* theory. This, then, is to be heard as a translation of what he says in turn 008 ('wave and quantum are an instant') without actually saying so. He does not specify *why* PHOTON is subordinate to QUANTUM, which is a relevant question in light of the fact that he categorizes both as theories.

With his turn at talk, Ken not only articulates some idea, but also sets up Ralf, who takes the next slot in the sequential order of speakers and who thereby completes the turn pair. In addition to articulating content, Ken's utterance therefore also has, and is articulated for realizing, specific functions. The utterance therefore is not an independent oozing of conceptual content from his mind so that others come to know its contents. The utterance has a backward and forward relation in the conversation that it both realizes and toward which it is oriented. It is but a dialectical moment that gives an inner dynamic and cohesion to the *social* phenomenon that we denote by the term 'conversation'. We cannot without dire consequence disconnect the utterance from its enchainment in the conversation as a whole.

The text of the original article on 'the social construction of concepts' suggests that Ken 'swayed' in his talk and conceptions. This claim is supported by data shown in Fig. 7.2 (to which I add here the precise line numbers from the session as a whole). We notice immediately that Ken's statements are taken out of context in all but one instance (turn 210), where the indexical nature of the turn ('that's why we have it on top') requires also listing the preceding turn. Ken takes that content up by means of an indexical reference. This presentation in the article from 17 years ago is consistent

---

13. Wolff-Michael Roth, Yew-Jin Lee and SungWon Hwang, 'Culturing Conceptions: From First Principles', *Cultural Studies of Science Education*, Vol. 3 (2008), 231–61.

with the theoretical position that what a person says is a direct reflection of what the person thinks. That is, the presentation of these utterances itself suggests the individualistic epistemology underlying that work and the theory that models thinking as an individualistic process. The miniature maps that capture the content of the utterance then are re-presentations and representations of the mental structure said and theorized to underlie the utterance.

Let us take a look at another one of the different ways of producing utterances in the course of the concept mapping session and the theoretical consequences that we can draw from them. The target utterance is turn 252. As Fig. 7.2 shows, it is interpreted in the original text as an expression of a particular conception in which QUANTUM is subordinated to WAVE. As previously, I put the turn in its immediate conversational context. The analysis shows that we indeed need to consider the larger whole from which to understand the individual utterance rather than the other way around. Thus, the turn arises in a context where the teacher offers a particular organization of 'quantum' with respect to other concepts (turn 249). Ken begins ('but that's') but does not complete his utterance as the teacher continues, 'I really don't know, because you are talking about light and X-rays' (turn 251). Even with only two words in his turn, we can hear him offer up a contrast ('but') and the teacher responds to it precisely ('I really don't know').

Fragment 7.12
```
249 T: quantum is over-
250 K: but thats-
251 T: i really dont know, because you are talking about light
       and x=rays.
252 K: but because you=re giving us that example with phonons,
       than thats like ralf was saying, waves also have a
       lower detailed description within itself and thats why
       it should be above quantum. because quantum is only a
       subdivision of
       [wave. no.]
253 T: [but then-]
```

When Ken finally has a longer turn, he evolves a statement that brings together the utterances of others to constitute a different possibility than the one he hears the teacher offer up in this situation. Ken directly refers to a previous teacher intervention (see chapter 4), where the latter has left the classroom to fetch a book and present the case of the phonon, a wave *in* matter that is also quantized. In that part of the conversation the teacher points out that matter waves, in contrast to other, macroscopic waves, are quantized. Ken also reproduces one utterance in the form of indirect speech, which he attributes to Ralf ('as Ralf was saying'). He then draws the consequence ('and that's why') for proposing how to organize the relation of the concept name to 'wave' ('it should be above quantum') and 'quantum' ('because quantum is only a subdivision of wave'). Ken speaks for the benefit of the teacher, who, in saying 'but then' not only allows others to understand that he knows he has been spoken to but also that what he is saying is somehow in contrast to what Ken has been saying. Moreover, by beginning to speak before Ken has completed his turn, the teacher also marks that he understands what Ken is saying, because it is only toward a sentence actively comprehended that he can provide an alternative to.

To produce the utterance in turn 252, Ken does not need to have thought about the topic at all—though it is likely that he has, given that he has been participating during the lessons that have made this unit. He does not even have to have developed a position of his own to produce this statement. He merely needs to be an interested participant who exhibits what can be made of the utterances that others have produced. He is in language and speaks out of this language, articulating and making available its possibilities, which is feasible without ever having thought about the content that the language will be said to be about. In fact, we might think about this situation in the reverse way: Although language speaks, as Martin Heidegger says[14], it does not do so on its own but uses Ken to realize one of its possibilities. A person thereby comes to articulate the possibilities of his language that is not his own—though it is the only one he has. Any conceptions and conceptual change expressed therefore attributable to language, making doubtful any attempt to 'eradicate' 'misconceptions'. In conversation, language speaks and it does so by realizing itself in the utterances of the participants.

We therefore do not need to presuppose any conceptions, frameworks, beliefs, or internal thoughts on the part of students (all of these are in any case inaccessible to others). What matters to the understanding of the trajectory that this conversation takes are the utterances participants produce and make available to each other. These utterances together with other forms of text (textbook, additional book) constitute resources. These resources can be used for producing new utterances and for evolving new content that has not existed before. Moreover, language itself is not only a resource but also a constraint, for it limits the number of plausible utterances, statements, and so forth that can be made and the particular forms utterances may take. Thus, the grammar of Ken's utterances is mediated by the fact that he cites others and then utters an implication that can be drawn from other utterances. In addition to using both previous utterances to produce an implication, he also draws an internal comparison between the two, seeing them as aligned: 'Because you're giving us that example with phonons, then that's like Ralf was saying'.

My field notes from that time (1991–1992) clearly show that I had not come to grips with the relation between the individual and the group—I described what happened in the group in terms of rational productions and constructions of individuals. One of these notes concerns Ken (then called Kevin) and the relationship between his 'position', 'evidence', and 'constructions': 'The dialogue also gives students opportunities to evaluate their own positions when new evidence is presented, such as when Ken examines his own construction of complementarity as entailing the hierarchical equality of quantum and wave. Because of the teacher's example of quantized and non-quantized waves, and referring to an earlier statement of Ralf, Ken proposes such a classification, and a subordination of quantum to wave'. In this field note excerpt, the assumption appears that students are reflective agents, who, in talking, give evi-

---

14. Martin Heidegger, *Gesamtausgabe Band 12: Unterwegs zur Sprache* (Frankfurt: Vittorio Klostermann, 1985).

dence of reflections upon their 'constructions'. When I look today at Figure 7.2 generally and Fragments 7.11 and 7.12 more specifically, I no longer see evidence for 'constructions' that in any case would be hidden from view if they were to exist at all; and they would be available, in any concrete case, only via the medium of language.

We may want to assume for the moment that language is an instrument for revealing and accessing structures in mind that are not accessible other than by language (Plato's shadows!). In this latter case, we need to have what physicists call a theory of the instrument. Thus, in physics, the 'true signal' from a phenomenon never is captured directly but only after it has been recorded by an instrument. The instrument characteristics modify the signal thereby giving rise to the graphs that are actually recorded. Any reconstruction of the 'true signal' requires a theory of the instrument, which, when given as a mathematical function, allows physicists to 'deconvolve' the recorded signal and thereby gain access the 'real' signal from the object. Thus, those scholars interested in making inferences about the human mind should be required to provide the theory of language they use; and they should be required to state how they deconvolve the signal obtained, that is, the utterances recorded during a lesson or interview, to obtain the signal that would have been emitted by the phenomenon itself.[15] To date, such a theory does not exist so that much of what we read about the existence of mental structures has to be taken as unsupported claims.

'Learning Pathways' and the Concept of Emergence

There is a presupposition in education that learning can be preplanned. The very practice of teacher planning books and curriculum guidelines are built on this presupposition. The planning books and curriculum guidelines are thought to constitute something like maps that specify learning trajectories or learning pathways. In the very early stages of my career as a science teacher, I have noticed that what precisely students learn *emerges unpredictably* from their interactions with their peers and with the materials they use and the material investigations that they conduct. Even with increasing experiences during a successful teaching career, I have been unable to anticipate the specific trajectories students' conversations take, and each of the several conversations in the same classroom tended to be different leading to different end results. With these experiences as an experiential background, it did not take a lot for Klaus Holzkamp, through one of his texts, to convince me that the idea that learning (trajectories) can be planned is a myth.[16] That is, whatever the materials we prepare for students to engage with, we cannot plan ahead of time just *what* it is that they learn, because the form of any students' engagement is a result of the *dialectic of participation*, that is, emerges given the students' current potential for becoming, the current mate-

---

15. In technical terms, the signal h (a graph) resulting from a measurement is the convolution of the phenomenon function f by the instrument function g: $h = \int f \cdot g$.

16. Klaus Holzkamp, 'Die Fiktion administrativer Planbarkeit schulischer Lernprozesse', in *Lernwidersprüche und pädagogisches Handeln* edited by Karl-Heinz Braun and Konstanze Wetzel (Marburg: Verlag Arbeit und Gesellschaft, 1992), 91–113.

rial (e.g., bodily, social) and ideological conditions, that is, from the dialectic that I denote in the form of the dialectical unit:

agency|passivity‖resources|schema.

Here, the *resources* pertain to the given material and social structures (conditions) and the *schema* to the dispositions of the student for seeing and acting in (culturally) specific ways. *Agency* refers us to the power to act, and *passivity* to the sensitivity that allows us to receive stimuli (some of them self-generated) with our senses that give rise to the sense we make. The relationship between the moments is dialectical because if the senses are not open to be impressed (i.e., passive), the human being does not learn, and as agency engages with resources, difference is inherent because the schema never 'fit' the world. Actions therefore always arise from a dialectic relation, that is, a relation that does not *determine* the outcomes but leads to an emergence of results the specificity of which cannot be anticipated with any degree of certainty. Thus, the pathways of learning always emerge in this model and cannot be predetermined. To return to the example I offer up in chapter 2, if teachers cannot guarantee that someone like myself sees the church predominantly featuring on the road to work, then assuming I will learn something specific in a given period of time is preposterous.

An analogy from artificial neural networks transposed into everyday language may assist. Thus, the learning paths of such a network when exposed to experiences can be understood as a trajectory similar to that which a snowball may take down a mountainside. Each instant of input constitutes a bifurcation point, and one cannot predict whether the system will move left or right. The snowballs therefore take quite different trajectories, end up in different places, accumulate different amounts of snow and reach different sizes, obtain different densities, and yield different surface characteristics. Similarly, the learning and decision making trajectories, are quite different even when the starting points are nearly the same. Like any chaotic system, minor variations can have substantial effects and outcomes. This is a simple and simplistic analogy for thinking about human learning and the learning trajectories students move along. But if this unpredictable nature of the artificial neural network or of the snowball rolling down the mountainside are simplistic, how much more complex and unpredictable will human learning paths be? Just as taking a different branch leads a snowball to pick up differently packed and different amounts of snow, so participating in speaking a language leads to different amounts of 'picked-up' speech and voices, shaping the contents and intonations of individual speech.

In this chapter, I focus on the emergence of talk surrounding one particular concept name and the way this name comes to be fixed with relation to other concept names. From the presentation, it is clear that even in the instance of a single concept name, it would be difficult and even impossible to predict early on where the students will eventually end in their evolution of a language deemed suitable at the instant. What they end up with is not entirely in their hands and mouths, but to a great extent is tied to the language they use and in which they find themselves. *Emergence* therefore is a suitable concept for describing and articulating the phenomenon of learning the discipline-specific dialect concerning particular phenomena. It is especially suitable because of our everyday experience that we can never anticipate with any precision what others will say, so that we cannot anticipate what the resources will be that we take up in our responses. That is, because these are new resources, and because they return to the other colored by our own intentions, inclinations, emotions, and predilections, the utterances in any conversation become unpredictable. Dialogism therefore inherently means open-endedness and impossibility of finalization. The interesting aspect of concept mapping comes from the fact that lower-order concept words figure as part of the predicates that specify the categories that figure above in the hierarchy. Conversely, concept words are themselves specified in propositions containing subordinate concept names and suitable verbs. Further specification derives from the horizontal relations, in which a concept name may appear either in the subject position or as part of the predicate.

Emergence also is a feature that Bakhtin attributes to dialogism, whereas monologism leads to specific ends ('truths'), thereby mediating the course that a conversation takes. In his discussion of the changes in Socratic dialogue from the early writings of Plato to his later works, Bakhtin shows that the early Socratic inquiries were dialogical. The truth reached in the conversation was not yet ready made. The conversation, in which different ideas constitute counterpoints, multiple voices in a polyphonic musical piece, is not aiming toward a given truth. Rather, any truth evolves as a consequence of the conversation. In the later Socratic dialogues, truth is pre-given, and the dialogue is merely a form, a genre, for presenting the given truth to audiences. In the former case, authors themselves do not know truth beforehand just as two millennia later Dostoevsky does not know the character and ideas of a protagonist before writing. In the latter case, dialogue constitutes the simple form for expounding ready-made truths. This later Socratic dialogue subsequently degenerated into a catechism for training novices. In this latter case, Bakhtin would use the adjective monological to characterize the conversation.

Despite the shortcoming of my original research on collaborative concept mapping, there is an interesting conclusion to the study that subsequently oriented me to take a more social approach to learning and cognition. As I was analyzing the data, I realized that even with my close knowledge of the students and even though the same students may have mapped the same set of concept names before, I was not able to anticipate how the next session would run and what its results would be. This realization was captured in the following field note entry of 1991, which ultimately also entered the research article that issued from my work: 'However, there is no evidence that these histories would be similar, that is, that the same concept map would be produced under different conditions, such as different groups, different partners, or different times. Our observations indicated that the process of a map's construction was likely to be contingent upon the specific local conditions during a concept mapping session. . . . We have to concur with Knorr-Cetina's (1981) contention that "social situations constitute a reality *sui generis*, which entails constraints, organisation and a dynamics which cannot be predicted from the values which participant actors assume on a set of variables" (p. 43; italics in the original)'. I could not make sense of the data and my experiences unless I assumed that the interactions I attempted to understand would differ each and every time the 'same' task was asked of students. This clearly contradicted the kinds of research articles produced at a time where researchers, who often spent very little time in actual classrooms, talked about specific learning pathways. I did not observe specific learning pathways in the classrooms at my school and this idea, proffered by essentially constructivist researchers, made absolutely no sense to me. In the learning-pathway approach, 'learning is defined as a change in a cognitive system's stable elements' and '*concepts* are one type of stable cognitive element'[17], that is, a change in its concepts. That type of research attempts to identify the 'stable cognitive elements' in students. Whereas this might be a laudable endeavor, it does not explain the kinds of variations that occur when a close look at real classroom interactions is taken as I do here.

A key problem derives from the fact that the conceptions and conceptual change approach identifies situations, which it fixes, in a stroboscopic manner, in still images. Then, by re-animating still images in sequence in the way film re-animates still photographs on a movie reel, advocates of the approach pretend to give an understanding of cognition as it unfolds in real time to give rise to 'learning pathways'. This, of course, is a futile endeavor, because the change here is a result of an *outside* animation— similar to the movie projector—rather than a transformation that occurs from *within*. Thus, not only are the contributions each student makes historically contingent, but also the trajectories and pathways. Furthermore, no stable cognitive structures have to be present to produce the inherently changing features of language produced in the course of a session. Living language itself produces its change, from the inside, in the very fact of being spoken. What traces it leaves in individuals and how any traces may be used in future situation is itself unpredictable. Instead, we can understand learning as the process of language evolution that reveals its purposes, intents, and logic only after the language has come into existence in its full form. Thus, 'the creation of a new form of cultural life, a new vocabulary, will have its utility explained only retroactively . . . for there are as yet no clearly formulatable ends to which it is a means'.[18] It makes little sense, therefore, to suggest that the language was 'constructed' along a specific 'learning pathway'.

It is quite clear, therefore, that the language approach I evolve here is radically different from the one that conceptual change researchers take. In conceptual change theory, students are said to take on a new conception if it is intelligible, plausible, and fruitful. If we take the present evolutionary perspective (language, thought), then conceptual change researchers suggest that students will adopt a new language when it is intelligible, plausible with respect to its referential objects, and fruitful in offering descriptions for yet unexplored phenomena. But, we have to ask, how can a student explain the utility of a language before actually knowing this language? How can a student know the plausibility of a language prior to already knowing the language and the referential objects it is said to be about? Only a revisionist history of science and, parallel, only a revisionist history of learning uses end results to structure the accounts of their own becoming. Only a revisionist account places the plausibility of a concept

17. Juergen Petri and Hans Niedderer, 'A Learning Pathway in High-school Level Quantum Atomic Physics', *International Journal of Science Education*, Vol. 20 (1998), 1075–88.

18. Richard Rorty, *Contingency, Irony, and Solidarity* (Cambridge: Cambridge University Press, 1989), 55.

as an intentional object for the learning of the concept. It is for these and similar reasons that over two decades of classroom research, the conceptual change approach never has been plausible to me, let alone fruitful for theorizing learning and development.

At this point, I have not even addressed the reason generally given for a conceptual change: discrepant events. These are to provoke changes in the way students will talk about phenomena. Such events do not have to promote change. We know that physicists have been able to live for decades with discrepancies without evolving a way of talking that makes the discrepancies disappear. Moreover, physicists tended to have noted discrepancies, whereas our students, given their 'alternative theories' that should result in alternate observations, are likely making observations consistent with the original observation language rather than with the one that they are in the process of learning. One of my studies shows precisely that—students who predicted motion to be seen in a teacher demonstration actually saw motion, and those who predicted that no motion would be seen reported that there had been no motion in the demonstration. Students then use their current idiom to describe and explain their observations, mobilizing a multitude of descriptions even though the video recording shows that the observation is inconsistent with the evidence.

In the study just described, the students use everyday experiences and language as a way of responding to a task in their physics classroom. Although science educators do pay lip service to students' experience in the world, this does not translate into the theories they evolve for studying and understanding learning. When students come to the science classroom, they do not leave their lives and vernacular outside the door to engage in whatever their science teachers have planned for them, especially to engage with the subject matter in the serious ways that science educators seem to expect. They do not shed their culture only to switch into it at isolated moments during the lesson. Rather, students continue to be grounded in their everyday language, their vernacular, however much they have to repress it while attending school. It is this fullness of life that we require for a fuller understanding of learning.

In this and the preceding chapters, I follow the lead of others and, though very differently, attend to the serious side of science and science education. As I look at the videotapes from the original study again, I come to realize that this face of science is but the tip of the iceberg, everything else of which is repressed and suppressed. In the following two chapters, I exhibit aspects in this lesson that I initially overlooked, because I myself have suppressed and repressed these aspects in the past. They have come into my focus only now and with my close reading of Mikhail Bakhtin's work. Above all, Bakhtin places the material bodily principle as a regenerative force not only in life but also in language.

8

The Material Bodily Principle

In much of educational research, students do not appear as the living beings that they in fact are, with their needs—eating, drinking, eliminating, or relating to others—and worries. Rather, reading the literature on knowing and learning in science one can get the impression that students are self-sufficient cognitive engines and computing mechanisms that change their conceptions when these turn out to be no longer appropriate. Lev Vygotsky complained long ago that the classical approach in psychology, which is still in vigor today, 'makes the thought process appear as an autonomous flow of "thoughts thinking themselves", segregated from the fullness of life, from the personal needs and interests, the inclinations and impulses, of the thinker'.[1] Mikhail Bakhtin thinks along the same line and complains that 'the theoretical world is obtained through an essential and fundamental abstraction from the fact of my unique being and from the moral sense of that fact—"as if I did not exist"'.[2] There are other aspects of schooling, which educators generally do not attend to, related to 'coarse language', particular habits (including smoking), laughter, and other aspects common to human life generally but expelled from a middle-class culture specifically. Of course, there is a strong rhetorical element in school culture general: students are to learn what others impose upon them because they, like father, 'know best'. However, as Mikhail Bakhtin shows in several works and most specifically in *Rabelais and His World* and *Problems of Dostoyevsky's Poetics*, the joyful relativity of a carnival sense of life weakens and sometimes completely disrupts the monological middle-class discourses including the discourses of science. Bakhtin uses the term 'carnival' to mark the co-presence of all the contradictory elements that come to the fore during carnival: the serious and the comical, crowning and uncrowning, elevation and debasement, excesses and austerity, the bodily and the intellectual, that is, life in its *fullest* expression.

In everyday life, the carnival sense is ever present. During the weeks while I am working on this chapter, the relevance of Bakhtin's work and his descriptions of the

---

1. Lev S. Vygotsky, *Thought and Language* (Cambridge, MA: MIT Press, 1986, 10.
2. Mikhail M. Bakhtin, *Toward a Philosophy of the Act* (Austin: University of Texas Press, 1993), 9.

everyday world as carnival become very salient to me in pursuing everyday events on the world stage. During a press conference, the Iraqi journalist Mountazer Al-Zaïdi throws his shoes at the then outgoing American president George W. Bush shouting 'this is the farewell kiss you dog', an event that is recorded live. On the serious side of the event are the internment and court charges against him; there are reports that he is 'tortured and beaten'. At the same time, he is also hailed—Bakhtin might say 'crowned'—by some as a hero. Bush, the president, is uncrowned in being called one of the worst Arabic names, a 'dog', and being thrown at with something as lowly as a pair of worn shoes (itself a serious insult in the Arab world). In one instance of the carnivalization of the event, the video is played repeatedly under the title 'Bush Shoe "Terror"', thereby relativizing and mocking the sad events that has led to the destruction of Iraq and Afghanistan in the name of 'the war on terror'. Not only is the video itself viewed around the world, but also it is immediately transformed in the marketplace that the Internet and television of today constitute. At first, variants of the initial video are available online, in slow motion or with a musical (rap) score before the significations are inverted in parody over parody, as in animations that show the scene in the manner of *Matrix* ('shoes miss because everything goes over Bush's head') or as video game. In the videos, all sorts of objects are thrown at Bush, a cat, a baby, a sink, or a saxophone. In other versions, new angles have been added, for example, from a film by Austin Powers. Certainly of lesser taste but debasing, uncrowning, and therefore reflexively real nevertheless, the journalist leaves Iraq for New York to launch the shoes at the twin towers. The talk shows and late night shows pick up and mock the event in their own ways.

There is a continual development of the theme as can be seen from the fact that the movement and inversion is not limited to the Internet. But a few days after writing my initial parts of this paragraph, demonstrations in Canada occur where some protesters throw shoes at posters of Bush's face that other protesters hold up. A few weeks later, during a French-Canadian broadcast on political events, several individuals pull off their shoes, in an apparent reference to the events in Iraq, to produce an instant that brings participants and audience to laughter. That is, the serious event, with very serious consequences for the journalist throwing the first shoe, has been transformed and has transformed the cultural landscapes around the world. It is an instant of the grassroots transformation of culture and political life. Now, while editing the chapter months after the event, a sofa-sized shoe monument in bronze—with a *bush* growing where the foot would enter—has been erected and unveiled in Iraq.

In this chapter, I begin to evolve a language concerning the carnival sense of life and suggest that it is generally suppressed and repressed in schools including school science. It therefore does not come as a surprise that there are many students around the world questioning what the science fare that they are presented with in school 'has anything to do with anything'. There are, however, instances even in a staunchly conservative school such as the one where this concept-mapping session takes place, where the carnival sense of life comes into the clearing (light of the day) or seeps out of the nooks and crannies. This carnival sense, according to Bakhtin, is the very origin of transformation and change in culture and language.

Laughter, Carnivalism, and the Repression of Life

Laughter and a carnival sense of life are constitutive of human nature with particular relativizing functions both in the political and cultural arenas and around our homes. While working on the first draft of this chapter, my neighbors and I are shoveling out after a second snowstorm within two days. The jokes about 'having seen this movie the day before' and about 'being tired of re-runs' provide relief from the toil of shoveling foot-deep snow for a second and third day in a row. Equal reprieve seems to come from the occasional swear word that can be heard here and there in the neighborhood. But such laughter and the associated carnival sense of life are repressed every time some system permits only one way of understanding, one way in which language can be mobilized and understood, where what is right (conception) comes to be separated from what is wrong (e.g., *mis*conception, *alternate* framework, *naïve* conception) in very dogmatic ways. Science and science education are such endeavors that operate with what Bakhtin calls *monologic contexts*.[3] In it, language is defined in relation to some referential context, science content or competencies, or in relation to other forms of language within the same context or speech, such as when students' language is compared to standard idiom of science. The contexts are monologic, too, when educators aim at getting students to move from 'science-like' to 'scientific' discourse. The end-points of the linguistic development students are to undergo are predefined, and there are no double-voices or alternative hearings permissible.

In science education specifically and education more generally, we find scholars who draw on the concept of 'code switching' to theorize students' use of forms of language other than the one formally permitted in the classroom and school. Students then use this other code, the one they are more familiar with, to produce and reproduce forms of identity not accessible to them in the authorized language of the school. Martin Heidegger has shown long ago why the idea of language (and culture) as code makes no sense, because of the way in which language and the material world are intertwined to make the cloth of life. He furthermore suggests that any formal language has to go back to, and is grounded in, the natural vernacular in its irreducible relation with the material and social world.[4] Mikhail Bakhtin, too, gives us a very different way of understanding and theorizing language in cases of interest to educational researchers and theorists.[5] Thus, laughter, carnivalism, and the behavior of the marketplace all express the fullness of life. Schools, which work to suppress a large part of the vernacular, thereby produce situations that are similar to the societies of the Dark Ages, where laughter was suppressed and everything was focused on the church, its knowledge, beliefs, and values. Anything else was either suppressed collectively—by means of technologies that maintain ruling relations—or repressed individually. Only during special times of the year, and especially during the birth of the Renais-

---

3. Mikhail Bakhtin, *Problems of Dostoevsky's Poetics* (Minneapolis: University of Minnesota Press, 1984).

4. Martin Heidegger, *Gesamtausgabe Band 12: Unterwegs zur Sprache* (Frankfurt: Vittorio Klostermann, 1985).

5. Mikhail Bakhtin, *Rabelais and His World* (Bloomington: Indiana University Press, 1984).

sance, all people including the clergy were allowed to express themselves and their culture to the fullest. I propose, therefore, that we think about the repression of everyday culture and vernacular in analogy to the psychoanalytic concept of repression. It thereby provides us new possibilities for thinking about what happens to working-class, aboriginal, or African-American students when they reproduce the totally alien White middle-class ethos of school and repress their own forms of culture and idioms.

According to Bakhtin, laughter (carnival, the marketplace) is a special relation to reality that cannot be translated into logic. Carnival literally means the 'putting away' (Lat. *levāre*) of flesh, meat (Lat. *carne*). It was the high point of excess before Lenten, the period of fasting and penitence. Everything was allowed, and until the present day (especially in the Rhenish and Alemannish versions), kings (politicians) loose their crowns so that clowns can don them. Carnival laughter, because it always relativizes, mocks itself, self-reflexively debases and elevates itself, and subverts dogmatic seriousness. Carnival laughter does not allow, therefore, any single language to be absolutized or to congeal into a one-sided form of seriousness. When it does happen, as with science and the remainder of the human condition, then the participants in the one-sided endeavor erect a wall between what are taken to be the official approaches—certainly with some quibbles on the inside but never subversive laughter and overturn, as we can see at the present day, for example, in the struggle of scientists with the religious right in the US—and the unofficial approaches. The official language has a gloomy seriousness about it. Because language is constituted by and constitutive of the world, very different languages also characterize the official and unofficial. Just as during the Dark Ages—when the priestly cast attempted to erect a wall between the official high language, the Latin language of the altar, and the vernacular—science and scientists erect barriers between the official scientific idiom and the vernacular. In his analysis of François Rabelais' four-part novel including *Gargantua* and *Pantagruel*, Bakhtin shows how the French author inverts the seriousness and one-sidedness of the academy, the ivory tower. In his novel, for example, Rabelais subverts and derides the foremost university in the country, the Sorbonne, and its senior members, who upheld and defended orthodoxy and invulnerable divine truth.

The vernacular includes oaths and swearing, billingsgate speech, and profanities. The vernacular is full of ambiguity, wit, ridicule, and absurdity, all combined to perpetually generate and transform the old into new, continually regenerating itself while leaving a bit of itself behind. There is a continued and continual reproduction and renewal, birth and death that occur simultaneously. The vernacular is associated with anything bodily, birth and death; eating, drinking, and defecation; blood, sweat, and tears; belching and farting; procreating; anger, elation, and indifference; destruction and regeneration; and madness, insanity, and the sublime. All of these are related to the body, the physical, as opposed to the metaphysical of the pure mind that lives in the spheres and in the ether, worrying about how it is connected to the world. Readers may be familiar with the 'symbol grounding problem', the question about how a mind processing symbolic systems is (and ever can be) connected to the world. This question can only be posed in the context where knowledge is thought of in terms of symbols referring to concepts processed in a mind that has to be connected to the world that the body inhabits. Computer scientists, artificial intelligence researchers, and robotics engineers are still struggling with the problem, though some have made small advances when they allowed robots to learn while attempting to cope with reduced versions of the world. For Bakhtin, the symbol grounding problem would be a pseudo-problem that arises when thinking and language are separated from everything that is bodily connected and, therefore, generative and renewing. For Vygotsky, too, if there is not an *inner* link between emotion (inherently the result of physical, chemical, bio-chemical, and physiological bodily states) and thought, then we cannot ever get at the mutual constitution of thought and emotion, and we cannot ever understand thought as a process. The body therefore has to become thought in its constitutive relation to thought.

Although the role of the body in knowing, the 'construction' of knowledge, and in conceptual change is seldom discussed in (science) education, there is ample evidence of this role in any set of videotaped classroom lessons that I have collected over a pe-riod of two decades of research in classrooms around the world. In the past, my prin-cipal concern has been to show how physical engagement with worldly (material) things lead to gestures that have the same shape (involving same muscle groups) as the earlier lab work that students conducted. Although these movements take the same shape, the gestures have a radically different function from the earlier hand and arm movements. By means of the latter, students transform the world materially; by means of the former, they subsequently refer to and communicate about how they have trans-formed the world. In one instance, the movement constitutes *knowing how* to do something in the material world, whereas in the second case, the movement makes available a description of the transformation of the world. But what, the reader may ask, has this got to do with dialogue, dialogicity, discourse, and discursivity?

In this chapter, I provide descriptions and a theoretical framework for understand-ing the fullness of life that is expressed only in some parts of the lesson but that is the real context for the other, more serious instants of the same lesson. It is the ground that grounds anything that may be talked about and that students understand as a con-sequence of their talking. Rather than thinking of the fullness of life as a different space into which students switch before returning to the seriousness of the science lesson, I suggest that we theorize language and learning through the fullness of life and consider schooling and science as but a one-sided expression of it. By theorizing life in its fullest, much of which is repressed, we come to understand the real interests, emotions, motives and motivations that orient students in and to the world, and there-fore allows us to understand their thinking and speaking. Lev Vygotsky warned us long ago that the separation of thought, language, and other aspects of the mind in psychological theorizing is a major weakness and flaw since 'such a segregated thought must be viewed either as a meaningless epiphenomenon incapable of chang-ing anything in the life or conduct of a person or else as some kind of primeval force exerting an influence on personal life in an inexplicable, mysterious way'.[6] It is only when we return to the fullness of life, it is only when we take *it* as our unit of analysis, that we come to understand the driving forces underlying thinking, speaking, develop-ing, and transforming, that is, the real effects schooling has on the students, who both

---

6. Vygotsky, op. cit note 1, 10, emphasis added.

populate these places and constitute them. It is only when we consider the fullness of life that we gain access to motives, emotions, interests, and motivations. It is only when we consider the fullness of life that we come to understand how the body mediates praxis, leading to good days, bad (hairdo) days, and so-so days. It is only through the fullness of life that we come to understand how the body mediates our ways of being in the world[7] and, thereby, how well we do on tests, in school tasks, during interviews concerned with beliefs or conceptions and conceptual change.

There is a literature that deals with some bodily phenomena, but authors generally abstract from the body as quickly as possible. Jean Piaget teaches us about learning during the early stages of life, when the interactions with the world moved from sensori-motor to (pre-) operational to formal operational stages. The end-point of development was given: the rational human mind engaging in abstract (formal) thinking independent of the world arriving at knowledge that subsequently is brought back and applied to the world. More recently, my own gesture studies in teaching and learning show that what students know and how they know is mediated by gestures, largely of the arms, hands, and fingers. Furthermore, my recent work shows that prosody— speech rate, speech intensity (volume), pitch—is an essential part of communication that Vygotsky and Bakhtin, thinking about intonation, already introduced to their theories of language and language development. Still more recently, I have begun to realize and find instrumental means to capture, the expression of emotion in prosody and how it mediates ongoing work praxis. But what we have not had in science education, or rather, what exists still outside of our awareness, is a theory for pulling body and mind together. Or better stated, we have not yet come to a theory where body and mind are but two abstractions of a higher-order unit that sublates the dichotomies. Here, I take life and the bodily material principle to constitute this unit. It is not that there are bodily principles and mind and a shifting of learning from the former to the latter in the way that Piaget proposes it. Rather, there is an integrating and integrated principle, *the material bodily principle*, which *subsumes* mind and body and their irreducible relation. In this chapter, I move through the various expressions of the body in the interactions and articulate them as (one-sided) expressions of the larger principle, which we need to take as the unit to understand its different expressions.

Embodiment and Communication: Take Two

In chapter 5, I already present a section that provides evidence for the embodiment of communication and therefore of knowing. In this second take on embodiment and communication, I deepen the analysis as part of the overall effort of describing the irreducible nature of the body–mind unit. Although embodiment theorists provide all sorts of examples, concepts, and theories to assist educators in understanding that we

---

7. A most radical philosophical formulation of life as the organizing and grounding aspect for anything that characterizes humanity is provided by Henry, who operates with the concept of incarnation in a philosophy of the flesh. Michel Henry, *Incarnation: une philosophie de la chair* (Paris: Seuil, 2000).

cannot think concepts and about concepts in purely abstracting and abstract, that is, metaphysical ways, there has been reluctance on the part of science educators to accord the body central status in knowing. Either science educators talk in purely cognitive ways, the traditional symbol processing approach, whereby concepts are something processed in the mind but are independent of the world, which are subsequently tested for truth or viability depending on the ontological-epistemological approach of the theorist. Or science educators adopt a 'discursive' approach, and then everything is a 'construction' of language. There is no talk about the fact that without a body, no language is produced. Without the body and its needs, that is, without the body in flesh and blood, there is no requirement for a language in the first place. And there is no talk about the fact that language is but an infinitesimal, though highly important part of our ways of being in a world always and already shot through with significations and themes.

Yet it is easy to show that without other aspects of the body, which are involved in both content and process of communicative production, verbal communication alone would be impossible. The following ever-so-brief exchange exhibits the roles various bodily means have in communication, and therefore, how they mediate both the communicative process and the communicative content. When we just look at the words that listening to the sound track reveal, we do not understand much of what is happening here. (I have removed an ethnographic description to increase the dramatic effect.) Following Ken's assertion about X-rays being photons and being involved in quantum theory, we hear Miles produce a statement in which X-rays are the subject that are predicatively specified as having 'to do with Compton effect' (turn 169). This repeats, in a modified and modifying way, Ken's utterance 'X-rays is involved in the quantum theory'. Ken utters, while overlapping the last word of Miles, 'yea like'. In physically and conceptually overlapping speech, the two express and produce consensus. Just as he comes to the end of his second word, the teacher begins, repeatedly repeating himself as if starting before he actually gets started 'you, you may, you want to change', before he utters another hedge, 'for example', followed by a second hedge, 'I don't know', and then brings the utterance to a close, 'those two have complementary character or something' and then repeats and extends the last few words, 'or something of that nature'.

Fragment 8.1
```
168 K: but isnt the x=ray the same thing, isnt x=ray a photon,
       x=rays is involved in the quantum theory? x=rays,
       [like travel in waves]?
169 M: [look x=rays have to ] do with compton [effect   ]
  a K:                                         [yea like]=
170 T: =you you may you you may want to change for example, i
       dont know, those two have complementary character or
       something- or something of that nature.
```

So what *is* happening here? How has the teacher contributed, at what time, and what has he added to the conversation? We do see that the teacher 'latches' on to Ken, thereby in effect taking the next slot in the sequential order of turns, even though the

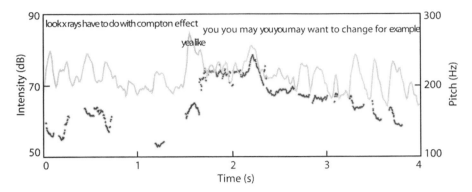

Fig. 8.1. Speech intensity and prosody in the course of three turns at talk (169, 169a, 170).

normally present pause between two speakers has not been maintained. The teacher then produces what will turn out to be several false starts and hedges. When we take not just the purified words, available in the transcription of Fragment 8.1, but also the intonation, more becomes available for hearing the interaction in a particular, singularizing way.

We immediately see that if communication were to exist in and as of language alone, we would not get very far into understanding what a conversation is about. A program such as PRAAT extracts information on the speech intensity and pitch levels (Fig. 8.1). We see that the speech intensity goes up when Ken and Miles overlap, in part due to their joint speech, in part due to Ken's louder talk. The pitch shows that the teacher first talks at over 200 Hz and then the pitch drops down to his normal range around 150 Hz. His speech is faster at first then begins to slow down. The base intensity is high at first then, visible in the lower valleys, more clearly distinguishes the words that now are noticeably separated from one another. All of the initial features, faster than normal rate, increased speech intensity, and higher pitch have been linked to situations in which two speakers compete for a turn at talk. It is as if the teacher attempted to out-compete the other speaker, not merely by beginning to talk but also by means of the other features. Of course, he does not consciously do so, as prosody is driven by conscious awareness as little as gesticulations. Once the contest is won, prosodic values return to normal. That is, just in looking at the particulars of the sound wave (the shape of which gives us the word itself), the prosody, we gain a better understanding of how the teacher has achieved having a slot in the sequential order of talk at this time. In fact, the work required to have the slot and talking itself cannot be separated, giving the conversation a particular direction and providing it with resources for continuing. We should not take such events as irrelevant, for, as noted in Robert Frost's poem 'The Road not Taken', it matters which of two paths at a bifurcation we take: 'Two roads diverged in a wood and I/ took the one less traveled by,/ And that has made all the difference'. Any instance in and of a conversation constitutes a bifurcation, and *whatever* the speech action is, it puts the conversation on a different trajectory than if someone had contributed (acted) in a different way. This is entirely consistent with the description—equally found in Bakhtin, Merleau-Ponty, and Vygotsky—of the mutual mediation of thought and language, whereby language (speech) does not constitute a mere translation of some inner thought but dialogues with the development of thought. Words make thought and thought makes words. Words and thoughts are not different things, at the individual or collective level; but neither are they the same. As I point out in chapter 5 in reference of speakers taking up a position, extemporaneously speaking individuals do not think before speaking, nor do they think while speaking, but their speaking *is* their thought.

Prosody is something that is produced together with the sound; it is an aspect of the sound but constitutes a different kind of resource than what we hear as words. Why would the embodied speaker produce this additional information? Would there not be a lot of work if the mind, were it to work like a computer using conceptions, also had to translate what it wanted to say into prosodic and other forms of information? We see here the shortcomings of a mental model approach to learning and speaking. A Bakhtinian approach that places emphasis on the fullness of life appears more promising here. If we think with Merleau-Ponty, then speaking is part of taking up a position in the world and orienting others to this position and to the worldly aspects that mark sense and theme. It is part of and arises from the interweaving of the world and language. In such taking of a position, therefore, the entire body is involved, oriented toward signification, and it produces, in various ways, markers that orient others to signification and theme. No recoding is required because, by the very fact of being embodied, the individual communicates as a *whole* person situated in and constituting the fullness of life. No re-coding between modes of representation is required for expressing information across different modalities. Rather, the *whole* body-in-situation *is* the expression of thought.

The teacher eventually makes the statement that 'those two have complementary character'. Which two? What is he talking about? What is he proposing as the organization of the map as a whole and about the relation of 'the two' in particular? Again, we need to know more about the setting, we need to have available what the members to the setting themselves have available *and use* that allows them to participate in the collective, participative thinking that currently takes place. Being physically present in and to each others' presence is one of the resources interlocutors use to mark, re-mark, and remark instantly changing sense and how it fits into the overall theme at this instant. Readers who could have been present to the situation might have observed, from the angle of the camera, that the teacher leans forward and places his hands on two paper slips inscribed QUANTUM and WAVE (Fig. 8.2). Following the teacher's movement, directed at *this* instant toward *these* paper slips (which we recognize as two) thereby makes salient *in the action* what also is available perceptually. There are two things that are, as the distal 'those' indicates, away from the speaker but that, made salient in and through the contemporaneous movement of the hand, come to be close to the speaker's hand. In various and overlapping ways, therefore, the speaker brings forth, and thereby makes available, two things.

Of course, the speaker makes salient more than merely two paper slips. In the present instant, the motive of the task is to build a concept map. Concept names are to be organized, not mere paper slips. These are but the carriers of content that really is at the heart of the present matters. The students have oriented to the emerging arrange-

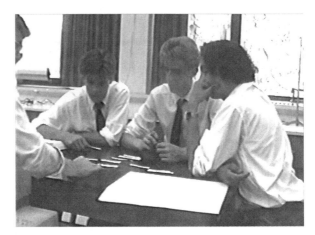

Fig. 8.2. As he speaks, the teacher moves the paper slips, and in this entirely physical action orienting the students to the conceptual content.

ment (Fig. 8.2) rather than to the speaker. Important here is *what* is said rather than that *the teacher* says it or how. In proposing an arrangement of the two imprinted concept names, the teacher orients the students to a specific topic and a specific relation to be made, especially in the parallel manner that the two slips come to find their place.

The material body, therefore, is an integral part of the collective organization of the instant, giving the teacher room to speak, and in speaking, to articulate specific content. Both facts—speaking at the instant and saying *this* rather than *that*—mediate the conversation and, because of its nature as a process that integrates itself over, on the final outcome. That is, what Vygotsky and Merleau-Ponty suggest for the thought and language (speech) of individuals, namely that they are related *processes* themselves related by a process, also and especially is true at the collective level. Vygotsky and Merleau-Ponty do not provide us with a language for theorizing this collective phenomenon, but Bakhtin does. Vygotsky ends *Thought and Language* with the comment that consciousness is not for the self but always and already consciousness for another. Language is the essential presupposed ground of, the tool for, and the object of consciousness. This end-point in Vygotsky's inquiry is precisely the central concern Bakhtin and the members of his circle work out at about the same time for collective consciousness. The word *never* is in the possession of, or owned by, an individual: it always bestrides the speaker and the listener, the writer and the reader. In so doing, it is always inhabited by individually realized but collective forms (i.e., concrete realizations, singularizations) of consciousness and, therefore, inherently is ambivalent, multiple, and polyphonic. Each word retains this polyphony of the voices of all the speakers that have articulated it before and orients itself toward the voice of the listener who will speak next.

Body and Bodily Relations

Statements such as 'Hugging and physical contact are inappropriate at school. Lunch detention will be assigned' and 'Avoid touching others. Keep your hands and feet to yourselves' belong to a type of school rule of which I find many examples during a quick Internet search. In contrast, I have many male and female colleagues who touch others as part of their communicative relations. Proper physical contact between people is a regular aspect of human relations and yet, the educational literature tends to treat in very superficial ways the physical relations between students. I say superficial but could have also said general and generalizing way. What is it that is special about the relations of and between people that mediate the very ways in which they come to communicate and what they learn? We do know that the body and its expression is involved. When Germans cannot stand another person, they actually make a connection between their appreciation of another and the sense of smell: 'Ich kann ihn nicht riechen' (I hate his odor). We do know that animosity changes what students do and, from embodiment and practice perspectives, how and what they learn. We also know that relations of friendship within a group of students changes what they do and how they do it, and therefore, what and how they learn. Students may be qualified as 'supportive' of one another, which then may be used as a reason for saying that this or that student does well. Or, a student may be described as being 'ostracized' or 'excluded', with negative effects resulting in some instances and the reverse, because of a particularly resilient 'character' in some positive development. But ultimately, all these descriptions address but *external* factors. They do not go to the heart of the matter, that is, they do not constitute an integrated principle that makes all knowing, feeling, relating, and so on a fundamentally material bodily moment.

What we really need is a theory that begins with and takes the whole life in its fullness as the unit of analysis. Such a theory can then be used to think about the effects that segregating out parts of it will have on learning, on the one hand, and on theories of learning, on the other hand.[8] For Bakhtin, the fullness of life is expressed in the material bodily principle, which, being the origin of life, includes all its contradictions and ambiguities. It includes birth and death, death and rebirth, and therefore, is a generative principle. It also has its effect on language and the way in which human beings communicate, what they communicate, and how they cope with any seriousness and oppressive relation.

In the present tapes, there is a lot of evidence that the body is involved in making the collaboration work and therefore in fixing the ideological content of the conversation. Take the following fragment, in which the students talk about how to link several of the concept names, that is, which verb to write on the future pencil-drawn lines connecting them. Ralf utters 'diffraction affects matter waves?' (turn 489), which Miles reifies as a question–answer pair by uttering 'yea' and by providing a rationale,

---

8. Henry, for example, shows how the Galilean approach, which consists in a geometrization of the world—i.e., today's scientific view of the world as independent of human senses—leads to a contradiction in that the world, to be something known, precisely requires the flesh with its senses. The Galilean approach therefore rejects and requires embodied cognition. See Henry, op. cit. note 7.

'because they diffract' (turn 490). 'Diffract', however, cannot be the linking verb as DIFFRACTION is the concept name to be linked to MATTER WAVES.

Fragment 8.2
```
489 R: diffraction affects matter waves?
490 M: yea, because they do diffract.
491 K: frequency can alter
       matter waves, it
       just means that
       matter waves can
       diffract- just put
       like can alter or
       affects; which ever
       one you feel. ((*))
492 R: matter waves can
       can diffract.
493 K: yea.
```

Ken apparently adds, 'frequency can alter matter waves', and then translates what he has said to constitute what he really meant without saying so, 'it just means that matter waves can diffract' (turn 491). He then adds a possible solution to the question which verb should link the two nouns, 'just put like can alter or affects'. The use of 'or' makes the solution ambivalent, because it allows them to choose one or the other. Ken then raises his arm, moves his hand forward and places it on Ralf's back near the left shoulder blade (see offprint, turn 491) while uttering 'which ever one you feel'. When Ralf, following the pad on the shoulder proposes to use the verb 'can diffract' (turn 492) to constitute the relation between matter waves and diffraction, Ken accepts and agrees, 'Yea' (turn 493). Here, the pad on the shoulder is an entirely physical (material) way of producing the relation between the two and to work toward decreasing tensions and thereby to make a good working climate possible. Padding Ralf on his back while discussing a problematic link between concept words has the potential to decrease any tension. It is a way of literally bridging a gulf that might have opened over the fact that they are taking different stances with respect to the verb to be chosen. Miles and Ken have provided Ralf with numerous alternatives to his own proposal, and the latter is apparently conflicted about which one to choose.

All the while Ken talks, Miles sits so close to Ralf that he touches him (see video offprint in turn 491). They are much closer in distance than that is permissible within society more generally, where he would be considered to be *within* the intimate space Ralf can claim for himself (about 18 inches or 45 centimeters). Together, they create and express being comfortable with one another, a closeness that is both physical and intellectual. This is not surprising given that they have been friends, living in the same dorm of this boarding school, and have continued to be friends following high school, attending the same university (though different programs). At the same time, this friendship comes to be reproduced and cemented in and through the physical closeness that they have.

The examples provided so far show that interactions, intersubjectivity, and participative thinking cannot be reduced to the mind alone. There are many aspects not only of life generally but also of school life specifically where one cannot make a distinction between the ideal (mental) and the material (bodily). Frustration is yet another aspect of human life where the undecidability between the ideal and material comes to the fore. In the following situation, Ralf throws up his hands while uttering 'I can't write undergo' and then asks his partners to give him 'another word'. Laughingly, Miles says, 'we gave you about six'.

Fragment 8.3
```
499 M: you arent going-
       undergo.
500 R: uh i cant write
       undergo, give me
       another word. ((*))
501 M: <<laughing>kh: kh::
       we gave you about
       six.>
```

As the video offprint in turn 500 shows, Ralf literally throws up his hands, asking his peers to give him another word, as they apparently do not want him to write 'undergo'. That is, here there is evidence for the tension between Ralf, on the one hand, and Miles and Ken ('we') on the other hand that Ken has addressed only seconds before by padding Ralf on the shoulder. We can see and hear the frustration in Ralf's voice and bodily expression. Now, we may ask, why would the debate over a *conceptual* issue lead to the expression of tension and frustration that the students attempt to resolve in bodily ways? Why would the mind go through so much effort to recode frustration to be expressed in a different channel, if he could have much more easily used words to express it? Moreover, Miles greets Ralf's question with laughter. There is something humorous about the request for 'another word' and the fact that they already have spent a tremendous amount of time discussing this link. This contradictory moment, Miles expresses in reduced laughter that comes simultaneous with his verbal response. But the situation is not just humorous and noted as such. We observe an entirely bodily reaction. Why would any being go through the trouble of making available something in a channel (bodily), when it would be much easier to report it in another channel (verbal)? It is better to think that the mind does not recode the events. The reason is because body and mind are, as already Immanuel Kant realized but never completed in his theories, inseparable. That is, where any dividing line between body and mind should lie is an undecidable question. In the fullness of life, they are but one-sided expressions of life as a whole.

These examples show that the body cannot be separated from the conduct of everyday communication. It is with laughter and bodily expressions of frustration that the walls between the official language of science and the nonofficial vernacular inevitably crumble. It is by means of bodily gestures and contacts that social relations are mediated and conflicts are reduced. This is so especially because, as Bakhtin points out throughout his *Rabelais*, these walls serve in the most important ideological sectors to separate languages. During the Dark Ages, these languages were the Latin spoken by the clergy and used at universities, on the one hand, and the vernacular that people spoke in the villages and towns.

In *Rabelais and His World*, Bakhtin shows us that the rarified intellectual world cannot explain anything, including its own transformation. Living during and producing the Renaissance, Rabelais challenges his readers to acknowledge that the medieval world has attempted to suppress the 'lower stratum' that nevertheless constitutes the generative force of life itself. Human beings laugh, eat, drink, defecate, make love, give birth, kill, and die. Often, many of these actions and associated sentiments come together: people involuntarily urinate and defecate in moments of great fear and terror; anxiety comes with trembling; embarrassment comes with red flushes; and difficult moments in life (an interview, a first conference paper, an exam) come with sweat. Moreover, the many languages that make a language cannot be understood independently of one another. Thus, the vernacular, the 'lowly language' at the time of Rabelais, has had tremendous, intrinsic value in the creation of literary forms. 'The dual image combining praise and abuse seeks to grasp the very moment of this change, the transfer from the old to the new, from death to life. Such an image crowns and uncrowns at the same moment. In the development of class society such a conception of the world can only be expressed in unofficial culture. There is no place for it in the culture of the ruling classes; here praise and abuse are clearly divided and static, for official culture is founded on the principle of an immovable and unchanging hierarchy in which the higher and the lower never merge'.[9] But transformation also comes from the ruling classes and its discourses, such as when the concept words created in some university sociology or psychology office come to infect and reproduce itself in public discourse until it has become a stable feature.

Today the same cultural forces are at work that also have transformed the Dark Ages. In the case of the throwing-shoe-at-Bush event, it is a decrowning, a farewell to a person, whom some individuals, including the rap artist Eminem, have called the 'greatest weapon of mass destruction' (in reference to what he had declared to find in Iraq). The shoe throwing event, and the aftermath in the market place of Internet and television, celebrates the political end-point, the death of Bush, and welcomes a new era in the topsy-turvy of constant laughter that does maintain the upper hand because it becomes the laughing stock of subsequent laughter.

'Concepts? No Sweat' Or 'Don't Sweat the Sweating'

So far I present gestures and prosody as two integral features of communication and then introduce other bodily aspects that are *integral* moments of the students' communication. Laughter, too, is an aspect of the bodily principle at work in human relations generally and in the relations within a classroom more specifically. In the previous section, I show how bodily expressions of humor (laughter) and frustration (throwing up hands) go hand in hand with conceptual issues of talk. That is, the body and the

---

9. Bakhtin, op. cit. note 5, 166.

mind cannot be analyzed separately in these moments of communication, and the distinction between body and mind becomes undecidable. Concerning the kind of relation the students have and concerning the understanding of what they are saying, we can also see that the bodily principles comes to the fore when *conceptual* differences are to be resolved. They are expressions of life, but also contribute to its constitution, the forms of relation students dialectically produce (reproduce, transform), and the kinds of understanding they develop from mutually understanding each other.

When students come to class, they are well rested or fatigued and sleepy, fed or hungry, tired or animated from an intense and long day at school, sweaty and tired or refreshed from the preceding physical education class (playing Frisbee in the yard during a spare period). Fever, the onset of an illness, monthly periods, changes in hormones, all are expressions of the bodily principle that not only affect us as external factors but that constitute what we are and who we are, how deeply or shallowly we participate in lessons, and how much we care about the surroundings. Although science education researchers intuitively know that these bodily states mediate students' participation in any single lesson or in schooling as a whole, our currently available theories of knowing and learning have not the slightest handle on any of these phenomena and their relation to cognition. If anything, integral features of human life, such as emotions, are theorized as *external* factors that, again if anything, are treated as diminishing cognition rather than being constitutive of it. What we need instead are theories that allow us to understand the constitutive forces that are at the origin of thought and its evolution. Vygotsky holds that unit analysis would lead us to such a theory, because it allows us to understand the dynamic system of signification that we inhabit and constitute. Unit analysis would show 'that every idea contains a transmuted affective attitude toward the bit of reality to which it refers. It further permits us to trace the path from a person's needs and impulses to the specific direction taken by his thoughts, and the reverse path from his thoughts to his behavior and activity'.[10] Merleau-Ponty, almost in the same words, suggests that affectivity and sexuality are not autonomous but have '*internal* links with the *whole acting and cognizing being*, these three sectors of behavior displaying but a *single typical structure* and standing in a relationship to each other of *reciprocal expression*'.[11] Investigating the ideal (mental) without considering how it is shaped and mediated by the fullness of life, that is, by the material body, cannot but give us inappropriate theories of (scientific) cognition.

In the lesson analyzed here, one bodily excretion, sweat, plays a central role. It repeatedly becomes the topic of talk: it is used to invert and relativize the seriousness of science talk generally and of concept maps particularly. The fact that Miles is sweating when he shows up in this class and the presence of his sweat constitute normally suppressed forms of evidence that shows the bodily principle at work. Here this principle not only comes to the fore as an off-topic issue, but also mediates the forms of participation. As the following analysis shows, it also is used in a context that relativizes the entire school context, its dress code, and the principle of cleanliness typical

10. Vygotsky, op. cit. note 1, 10–1.

11. Maurice Merleau-Ponty, *Phénoménologie de la perception* (Paris: Gallimard, 1945), 184, emphasis added.

of (upper) middle-class culture and its repression of the bodily principle. This principle has been increasingly repressed in modern times generally and in the cleanliness-
obsessed Anglo-Saxon culture in particular. (We just have to think of the TV ads that
show us 'Mister Proper', mouthwash, extra-whitening toothpaste, extra-strong disin-
fectants, etc.) With the rise of the middle class, born during the overturning of ancient
society during the Renaissance, have come an increasing sanitization of public life and
the repression of carnival principles. 'In the modern image of the individual body,
sexual life, eating, drinking, and defecation have radically changed their meaning:
they have been transferred to the private and psychological level where their connotation becomes narrow and specific, torn away from the direct relation to the life of society and to the cosmic whole. In this new connotation they can no longer carry on
their former philosophical functions'.[12] Bakhtin attributes to this suppression and repression a new monological seriousness of public life that is typical of middle-class
culture and its ideology. The body is body alone, there is no duality left, and, to paraphrase the literary scholar, *the bodily can only speak in its name*. But, as I show in this
chapter, even a private school utterly concerned with the outward cleanliness and
neatness cannot totally suppress the bodily principle, which, as I have been able to
witness, nevertheless continues to be central. That is, anything like science occurs
within the fullness of life, of which we, if we only care to look, can see signs everywhere throughout a science lesson. That is, rather than constituting another part of life
to which students return once school is over, the fullness of life is there at every instant of school life as well. It so happens that much of it—e.g., laughing, swearing,
cursing, sweating, farting, belching—tends to be suppressed and repressed in accor-
dance with middle-class sensitivities about what life constitutes. In most schools and
classes, students have to ask for special permissions if they want to relief themselves;
and women's menstrual periods are addressed in school life only in a hushed-up manner. This suppressed and repressed part of life is evident in the following episodes,
seeping from the private into the public through the cracks of a façade whose mainte-
nance requires a lot of work.

Fragment 8.4
```
028 M: i am so sweaty. ((*))
029 K: complementary?
030    (.)
031 R: complementary?
```

In this example (Fragment 8.4), Miles moves one of the paper slips (Fig. 8.3a).
When he pulls his hand away, sticks to his finger (Fig. 8.3b). His hand moves sharply
to his right but the paper slip continues to stick to his finger (Fig. 8.3c), and then eventually drops (Fig. 8.3d). Near the end, Miles turns his head, until his gaze is oriented
to the paper slip that has just fallen onto the table. He turns his hand and, squarely

---

12. Bakhtin, op. cit. note 5, 321.

Fig. 8.3. Sequence of events leading up to the mention of sweat. a. Miles moves a paper slip. b. It sticks to his finger. c. He tries to jerk it off. d. The paper slip falls back to the table.

looking at his palm (offprint, turn 028), declares, 'I am so sweaty'. As the figure also shows, neither Ralf nor Ken looks up from what they are oriented to at this instant, the concept of 'complementarity' (turns 029–031). That is, only fractions of a second after he contributes to the conversation concerning the placement of PHOTON, Miles, following the experience of the paper slip sticking to his finger (turn 028), comments on something very bodily happening to him at the instant: he is sweating. His material bodily state is articulated in the conversation and will be bridging—which we cannot anticipate but only note after the fact—the material and ideal.

Just a few instants later and without any preparation observable in the verbal part of the conversation, Miles articulates an explanation, 'because I just came back from playing Frisbee' (turn 042). But the video shows him erecting his torso after having rapidly moved his hand and finger and then looking at the sweat that apparently dropped onto the table (Fig. 8.4a). That is, we can see that he already orients toward the sweat on the table before he makes his comment. The unfolding event then is entirely about the bodily aspect of their life: Miles sweats and his sweat, especially after he swipes it with his hand (Fig. 8.4b), covers the top of the table. Ralf eventually 'complains', 'you don't have to drip all over' (turn 044a).

Fragment 8.5
```
042 M: because, i just came back from playing frisbee. ((Miles
       points to sweat; Ralf turns in his direction, Fig.
       8.4a))
043 R: look at this here.
  a M: fuck its all sweat
  b R: (???) ((Miles wipes sweat off table, Ralf punches M at
       leg, under table, Fig. 8.4b))
044 M: i just came back from playing frisbee, so i=m so tired.
       ((Ralf pulls up his shirt exposing part of the naked
       skin Fig. 8.4c))
  a R: you dont have to drip all over. ((Points to the sweat,
       Fig. 8.4d))
045 K: complementarity?
046 T: complementarity?
```

Ralf orients toward the sweat on the table (Fig. 8.4a), commenting 'look at this here'. Miles utters the coarse slang word 'fuck', which, in middle-class society is so serious that it is generally blipped out of TV shows and referred to as the 'f-word'. He

Fig. 8.4. The 'lower stratum' always is present. a. Miles swears, points to sweat. b. Miles wipes the sweat. c. Ralf pulls Miles' shirt up and off the body. d. Miles wipes his face with his tie and Ralf points to the sweat complaining that the former drips all over.

then comments, 'it's all sweat' (turn 43a). Miles wipes the sweat off the table (Fig. 8.4b) and Ralf punches him on his thigh under the table saying something with such low volume that we cannot hear it. While Miles explains that he has just come back from playing Frisbee, Ralf grabs Miles' shirt just above the belt and pulls it out from under the belt (Fig. 8.4c). Pointing to all the sweat on the table (Fig. 8.4d) Ralf comments 'you don't have to drip all over' (turn 044b). Ken utters, with rising inflection, 'complementarity', which the teacher, arriving at the table, responds to by repeating the utterance and its inflection. The sweat would come up repeatedly again ('I am swimming in sweat in this-' [turn 059]; 'uh; so much sweat' [turn 342a]), especially in one instance that will lead to a lot of laughter and that I analyze in more depth below.

In the present instance, Miles comes to class pouring with sweat. It is all over the table so that he demonstratively wipes it off using the entire palm of his hand (Fig. 8.4b). Ralf further accentuates the carnivalistic elements of the moment by pulling Miles' shirt out from under the belt (Fig. 8.4c) thereby exposing the latter's skin. Miles now is in a state completely at odds with the dress code. To sharpen the situation, Ralf then points to the sweat that is all over the table in a manner that many tender middle-class souls might find disgusting. With Bakhtin we might say that at the core of all these carnivalistic elements 'lies a profound carnivalistic sense of the world, which gives meaning to and unites all the seemingly absurd and unexpected things in these scenes and creates their artistic truth'.[13] In many schools, however, such bodily aspects and the violation of the dress code that occurs in this episode are against the dress code (e.g., 'Exposed undergarments and midriffs are not acceptable', 'pants, shirts, or blouses must not be excessively revealing'). In this school, too, students are exhorted to 'come to school prepared, *properly dressed*, on time and ready to learn', so that in this instant, the code is clearly violated.

In the present instant, the very seriousness of the science lesson generally and the task they have been asked to do specifically is undermined and relativized in and by the fact of Miles' sweating. It shows that life is more extended and encompasses more than the infinitesimal and gloomy concern with the arrangement of a few concept words. It is the fullness of life as a whole that integrates the various dimensions of human experience. To get to the singular consideration of science concepts, we have to do a lot of abstraction to get rid of everything else in life that constitutes the context and condition for the discussion of physics concepts. For Bakhtin, the fullness of life expresses itself in the carnival atmosphere of the marketplace with all of its contradictions that continually reverse and alternate the opposites of life. In subsequent works, Bakhtin extends the kinds of situations that count as 'marketplace', which now refers to any public situation where there is a passage of people. A classroom, therefore, can be understood in the image of the marketplace, a stage where the carnivalistic sense of life comes to be shared. This is especially the case when in teacher-centered courses, one or more students 'disrupt the flow of the lesson' drawing attention to what they do precisely because the monologic organization stages (makes salient) a disruption as a disruption. In the Dark Ages, when the Church repressed nearly every expression of the fullness of life, carnival and the carnivalization of official culture was a means of dealing with suppression and repression. This thought figure also is relevant to the school, where the carnival sense of life breaks through in many situations, thereby relativizing the reigning middle-class ethos. In fact, it may have an important function for dealing with the suppression and repression of the fullness of life that members of some groups within society (e.g., African Americans, working class lads) may experience as marginalization and oppression.

Carnivalization involves scandals and decrownings. In the present instance, sweating and the violation of the dress code turn the school rules upside down, relativize and exhibit them as but a particular choice that the school leaders have made in the face of other choices. Here, sweat is all over, not just in the physical education class but also in physics. The high culture of school and the conceptual purity of physics are contrasted by this other part of life, which is grounded in the body. In fact, the very dress code points to the role of the material in the ideal. Thus, googling for school dress code, I locate within seconds this interdiction: 'Clothing which is distractive, disruptive, or interferes with the learning process and/or school climate is inappropriate'. That is, clothing, which constitutes but a material and external aspect of our lives is recognized not only as having distractive and disruptive function, but also is recognized as mediating the learning process and school climate. Yet learning theorists con-

---

13. Bakhtin, op. cit. note 3, 146.

tinue to focus on conceptual issues independent of the questions about how the fullness of life enables and constrains anything that we recognize as learning process and
learning outcome. What are the inner connections in the fullness of life that express
themselves as different forms of learning and understanding?

Bakhtin shows how in Dostoevsky's novels, the social and cultural order is overturned by means of 'triumphant eccentricity', 'hysterics', 'fainting fit', 'a slap in the
face', 'scandal', and so on. 'Here everything is unexpected, out of place, incompatible
and impermissible if judged by life's ordinary, "normal" course'.[14] One of the carnivalistic elements in this school are students' violations of the dress code not only as
shown here but also when they, for example, have one bottom corner of the shirt hang
out and over the belt rather than tugged into the pants. Wearing baseball caps inside
buildings although the dress code forbids it is another way of carnivalizing the dress
code. Readers will be familiar with other aspects of dress codes and students continual
relativization of it, the wearing of pants so that the underwear is visible and the wearing of hooded sweaters. All of these are seen in many if not most schools as a forms of
behavior that undermine the social order, and, consistent with Bakhtin's writing concerning carnivalization, they constitute in fact forces that constantly question, relativize, and in some cases even overturn the ruling relations. Some time ago, when I went
to school, students still received a beating if they had done something inappropriate
and even when they came to school on Monday mornings without fresh handkerchief
or clothing. Middle-class values were thereby literally beaten into us, who were working-class children and simple country folk.

Swearing, Cursing: The Underbelly of Language

In the previous section, Miles comments on the wetness on the table caused by his
sweat 'fuck, it's all sweat'. This statement clearly is against established middle-class
values in schools around the world where statements such as 'Pupils must not use foul
or abusive language' constitute an integral part of the established and reinforced
norms and rules. It is part of the middle-class ideology produced and reproduced in
educational systems around the world on a daily basis. Yet one might ask, 'Why?'
Students themselves ask this question, such as shown in the following quote from an
Internet forum: 'No swearing. Why not? They're just words. In my opinion, f*ck is
not a bad word. Like sh*t, c*ck, and d*ck, it's merely a combination of four letters of
the alphabet to make a four-letter word. The teachers think that they're "bad" words.
Hell, they even taught us not to use them back in elementary school, and guess what
happened? I swear, and I mean, I swear like a sailor. Parents don't want their kids to
swear, but my mom uses f*ck frequently, and for some reason, I can't? That's hypoc-
risy'.[15] Swearing and cursing are integral part of the fullness of life and have the func-

---

14. Bakhtin, op. cit. note 3, 146.
15. "The SilverAce," a member in a forum concerning school rules. Accessed December 22, 2008 at
http://www.animationinsider.net/forums/archive/index.php?t-23010.html.

tion of transforming language and relativizing the cultural forms that attempt to suppress them. In this instance, the student notes that his mother uses 'fuck' frequently and yet he is forbidden to use the same word.

Swear words are regular features of life. I begin this chapter with the note that I have heard them while shoveling snow during the writing of this part of the chapter. In everyday life, even in the company of academic colleagues, I can hear swear words. They constitute an integral part of everyday life, serving numerous functions, including that of articulating, expressing, and expelling frustration. But there is ambivalence about it, a forbidden fruit that people nevertheless consume on a regular basis. In the present instance, one of the most expensive private schools in Canada with strict dress and behavior codes, where transgressions are penalized with confinement to the school grounds over the weekends, these words have a definite function and are frequently used. Bakhtin shows that swearing and cursing have been part of everyday life for a long time. They are part of the regenerative force of culture generally and language more specifically. Thus, '[a]buses, curses, profanities, and improprieties are the unofficial elements of speech. They were and are still conceived as a breach of the established norms of verbal address; they refuse to confirm to conventions, to etiquette, civility, respectability. These elements of freedom, if present in sufficient numbers and with a precise intention, exercise a strong influence on the entire contents of speech, transferring it to another sphere beyond the limits of conventional language. Such speech forms, liberated from norms, hierarchies, and prohibitions of established idiom, become themselves a peculiar argot and create a special collectivity, a group of people initiated in familiar intercourse, who are frank and free in expressing themselves verbally'.[16]

There is a curious relation of official, middle-class culture to swearing. The Oxford English Dictionary gives many examples of the use of the coarse slang word 'fuck' in many different variations. It is used not only in the literature but also by politicians. For example, then U.S. Vice President Dick Cheney told Senator Patrick J. Leahy, who questioned him about his ties to Haliburton, a company making lots of money in the Iraq war: 'fuck yourself'. Because the expression is generally suppressed, it is not surprising that rap artists have taken it up into their expressive forms as a protest against the establishment. In his protest song against then president George W. Bush prior to his second election in 2004, the rap artist Eminem has a soldier pronounce 'fuck Bush' when the latter finds out that he is sent again to Iraq. Many songs on YouTube feature comments that include this swearword. That is, swearing and cursing have been expressions of unfettered and free truth, expressions that breach common, established, normed and normalizing forms of speech. As Bakhtin points out, words that question the status quo and the hierarchical aspects of middle- and high-class society frequently come from the lower stratum. Thus, in the case of the word 'fuck' and its variations, the original sense pertains to sexual intercourse and the Oxford English Dictionary reports its use from the beginning of the 16th century. In another instance, Ken comments on the destruction of a part of the map with the interjection 'oh shit'. Here, too, the interjection, an exclamation of annoyance or disgust, derives from the

---

16. Bakhtin, op. cit. note 5, 187–8.

verb used since the 14th century for the bodily process of defecating, voiding excrement.

Even in scholarly discourse, we will not find these terms, and when one of these ('fuck') once entered my contribution to a scholarly discussion at an international conference, within a quote from a student, there was a sudden silence. Later I was warned that the ethics committee of the organization might take up the matters with me later. That is, even in our own circles, forces are at work that suppress the use of certain expressions when members do not repress these themselves. Yet there is ambivalence about the use of the word in society, for even if, *and precisely when* it is blanked out during a TV broadcast, its very existence is made salient and its continued cultural use is further enabled. Readers know that 'fuck' is used when they see on a page of printed text 'f . . .' or 'f*ck', and they even know it when the word is referred to as the 'f-word' or 'the four-letter word'. The very existence of this word is thereby reproduced and reinforced in and through negativity, asserting its existence and use in an empty word slot.

Miles uses (turn 022) another word 'to screw up' in the sense of 'to blunder', 'to make an error', which is highly ambivalent though generally acceptable in most circumstances. Ralf, too, uses the same word ('because this screws everything up' [turn 394]). The term is ambivalent because it likely emerged as a euphemism for 'to fuck up'. Indeed, 'to screw' is used as a synonym for 'to fuck', but in a changed context, it simply means to drive a screw into a wall or other material. That is, the particular sense that the verb 'screw' marks depends on the situation, where it goes with and marks the theme. And even if it is clearly used as a curse, 'screw you' may be employed seriously, in which case it might lead to physical violence, or it may be said 'in jest' and lead to general laughter. In this brief classroom episode, students articulate other words that are not normal constituents of middle-class language. Thus, in turn 331e, Miles calls Ralf a 'bastard', a term that denotes a child born out of wedlock, illegitimate, and perhaps inferior. Here, too, the bodily principle is invoked, directly referring to the renewal of life even if this happens in ways considered impure.

Other unofficial words pertain to saints, God, Jesus, and other religious objects (in Quebec schools, 'tabernak' [tabernacle] and 'ostie' [host/ie] are some favorites) and phenomena. As Bakhtin shows in the work of French-writing Rabelais, this language constitutes a questioning and reversal of established orders, ruling relations, which, in those days, were tied to the official, Catholic Church. In English, too, church- and religion-related expressions are used in swearing and appear at many instances in everyday life as unofficial expressions of the much more encompassing fullness of life normally repressed and suppressed in school.

Miles utters what can be heard as a question to his peers 'well what type' and then continues 'uh, Jesus, we should put X-rays up here with the light' (turn 34). The term 'Jesus', when not used in a religious context as a proper name, is used as (or part of) an oath, an exclamation of surprise, disbelief, or dismay.

Fragment 8.6
```
033 K: complementarity.
034 M: well what type? uh, jesus, we should put x=rays up here
       with the light, like that. should we put x=rays there?
```

```
035 R: yea, okay. work function (.) if work function (.)
       [photon and],
036 M: [we need   ] something,
```

Already before that he has used the expression off camera while talking to another group after bumping into the camera, 'Oh Jesus, is he filming us?' (turn 11a). Oaths and swear words are part of the culture of the common folk. Oaths always have been part of the unofficial form of language, the unofficial form of speech. During the Middle Age, oaths were directly forbidden. During Rabelais' days profanities and oaths (*jurons*) were colloquial forms, as they are today. Like schools today, '[t]he Church and government disapproved of the sacrilegious use of holy names, and under the Church's influence the government often condemned the *jurons*, in ordinances proclaimed by the heralds'.[17] Then, as now, they were inadmissible in and by the high culture. Yet, outside their work, even academics may use them. Religious and holy names have been among the favorite profanities since time past. Other utterances invoke the deity 'Oh god' (Fragment 8.7) or might invoke a place opposite, 'hell' (Fragment 8.8) into which someone or something can be damned (Fragment 8.9).

Fragment 8.7
```
058 R: god, what a-
112 R: god, i forgot so much.
```

Fragment 8.8
```
557 M: i dont know what the hell-
```

Fragment 8.9
```
367 K: where does the damn, does this go?
```

These examples of unofficial words show how the underside of language always is present even if generally repressed. The interesting function, of course, is that their uses not merely question the hierarchical order, the ruling relations reproduced and transformed in a production of order. Rather, in the very act of questioning and reversing, the existence of the order is actually affirmed just as the suppression and repression of the words confirms and reproduces their existence. Something can be questioned and reversed only if it exists. That is, in an interesting twist, cursing, swearing, and other forms of impermissible language affirm the very thing that they simultaneously question. This, then, is the reverse process to the one of referring to swear words in oblique but nevertheless affirming manner that I discuss above. Both middle-class accepted language and its opposite confirm their mutual existence and, in the dialectic of production, contribute to their transformation and rebirth. It is part of the bodily principle, as Bakhtin points out, to combine death and rebirth in the same act, to be generative and regenerative, to contribute to the production of life in and through itself.

The forbidden words themselves change over time. A word that questions the ruling relations most seriously at one point in time may actually be regarded as rather

---

17. Bakhtin, op. cit. note 5, 189.

innocent at another historical point in time. This means that we require a theory of language that builds in this transformation and change in the very process of its own production. Thus, James Joyce had considerable difficulties publishing *Dubliners,* a collection of short stories, because of the word 'bloody', which middle-class ears at the beginning of the 20th century heard as a reference to the menstrual cycle. Today, hardly a person worries about the use of this word. But Joyce is interesting in the present context because he may be the Rabelais of modernism, both inverting and asserting middle-class values in texts that mobilize every aspect of the material bodily principle that I list in this section and others to come: 'Boosed at five o'clock. Night he was near being lagged only Paddy Leonard knew the bobby, 14 A. Blind to the world up in a shebeen in Bride street after closing time, fornicating with two shawls and a bully on guard, drinking porter out of teacups. And calling himself a Frenchy for the shawls, Joseph Manuo, and talking against the Catholic religion, and he serving mass in Adam and Eve's when he was young with eyes shut, who wrote the new testament and the old testament, and hugging and smugging. And the two shawls killed with the laughing, picking his pockets, the bloody fool and he spilling the porter all over the bed and the two shawls screeching laughing at one another. . . . And the old prostitute of a mother procuring rooms to street couples. Gob, Jack made him toe the line. Told him if he didn't patch up the pot, Jesus, he'd kick the shite out of him'.[18] This entire quote is full of words and scenes that offended the middle class: drinking, fornicating with whores ('shawls'), attending whorehouses, talking against the Church, illicit buying and selling of alcohol ('shebeen'), laughter, swearing ('Jesus'), and slang words ('bully', 'bobby'). Yet, this excerpt, typical of the writing of Joyce, is not so far from the life of the students in the private school, who, at night, engage in many of the same behaviors equally questioning middle-class sensitivities and ruling relations as Joyce's descriptions have done nearly a century earlier. I have seen/heard students from this school return from bars and pool halls in the wee hours of the morning, smoking cigarettes and hash, engage in under-age drinking in the dorms, go skinny dipping in the lake, swear, and engage in other intolerated behaviors—only to see how all of this suppressed and repressed as daylight returned to the campus.

Seriousness and Laughter: Unity of Body and Mind

Science is gloomy and serious. All over my copy of *Rabelais* one can find highlighted text annotated by the word 'science'. This includes the following passage: 'This old authority and truth pretends to be absolute, to have an extratemporal importance. Therefore, their representatives (the agelasts) are gloomily serious. They cannot and do not wish to laugh; they strut majestically, consider their foes the enemies of eternal truth, and threaten them with eternal punishment'.[19] While reading these lines for the first time, I thought that they described science and science education quite fittingly.

---

18. James Joyce, *Ulysses* (New York: Random House, 1986), 258.
19. Bakhtin, op. cit. note 5, 212–3. An agelast is someone who does not laugh.

But facial expressions and laughter that come with talk are clear evidence of the inseparable and undecidable nature of body and mind. These features of human life point to the inseparability of the 'upper' and 'lower' strata, the ideal and the material, the bodily principle as the inherently contradictory integrating unit. Thus, when we spontaneously and without reflection laugh about a joke, clearly a stretch of discourse, something intellectual, comes with a bodily reaction. If the joke were something purely ideological, if it were nothing but an intellectual (interpretive) phenomenon, we would not understand why it is greeted with smiles and laughter, which entirely bodily actions and reactions. Laughter, according to Bakhtin, unveils the material bodily principle in its fullest; to explain laughter one must invoke the relation between the body and mind. One of laughter's functions may be to interrupt the system and state of oppression. It expresses hope, resistance, and protest. Thus, even and precisely during the gloomiest of political oppression, people joke and laugh. For Jean-Luc Nancy, laughter and pure thought expressed in speech constitute a *syncope*, the simultaneous generation of the material and ideal in humanity.[20] The syncope (Gr. συν- [syn], with + κόπτειν [kopein], to cut off), because it *simultaneously* attaches and detaches, is a suitable metaphor for understanding the relation of body and mind. The syncope marks undecidability between two seemingly exclusive phenomena, here, between the body and the mind.

During the Dark Ages, folk culture strove to defeat through laughter the extreme projection of gloomy seriousness of the Church. It did so by means of varying practices that transformed the gloom into a gay carnival monster.[21] Many of Rabelais' descriptions of the official culture of the time bear resemblance with the official culture of science, an ultra- and gloomily serious pursuit that is said to produce knowledge valued across time and locations. Official writing does not laugh, joke, or make allusions. These aspects of the fullness of human life are admitted to in informal talk but are not part of science itself. That many scientists consider others enemies of eternal truth is quite evident when it comes to certain debates, today including the one over evolution and creation or the struggle over global warming, where those not subscribing to the theory that it is 'caused by' carbon emissions are treated as heretics.[22] Laughter is inherently dangerous, because it relativizes and thereby questions the absolute truth—both the transcendental and the socially constructed ones—thereby putting all of human knowledge into perspective again. Only those who gain and profit from being in institutional positions that confer power are threatened by reversal and relativity that are associated with laughter.

Laughter in stronger and weaker form is present throughout and written all over this lesson and cannot be dissociated from the ideal (mental), as some problematic *conceptual* relation may actually be at the origin of laughter (chuckle, burst). Laughter

---

20. Jean-Luc Nancy, *The Discourse of the Syncope: Logodaedalus* (Stanford, CA: Stanford University Press, 2008).

21. Gay pride parades may have a similar function in the societies that by and large still are hostile to the equality of rights that gays and lesbians demand, for example, with respect to forming family units and raising children. Given the stance many churches take with respect to homosexuality, the analogy with the Dark Ages does not appear to be too far-fedged.

22. Freeman Dyson, a physicist at the Advanced Institute of Studies at Princeton University talks/writes about the 'holy brotherhood of climate model experts'.

emerges precisely when the very structure of the task, its very idea, comes to be up-rooted and overturned. Sample occasions include moments where students make placements of concepts that are impossible according to the rules of the game or when some simple action destroys the hierarchical arrangement and therefore the very de-terminateness of language and concept names that it pretends to depict. In some in-stances, an almost insignificant event gets everyone to laugh, a particular piece of evi-dence for the irreducible unity of body and mind. In the following fragment, Ken asks (rising intonation) 'where does this one come in?' (turn 236). He then places the paper slip across several other slips simultaneously uttering 'should we scrawl this across?' All three burst out in brief but contained laughter. Here, then, laughter arises precisely at a difficult period when the three students have an arrangement whereby LIGHT is on top of their hierarchy and WAVE and QUANTUM are located side-by-side and below the former. Ken has the paper slip COMPLEMENTARITY in his hand and asks where it is to 'come in', to which he responds, in a stroke of genius, by placing COMPLEMENTARITY across LIGHT, on the one hand, and WAVE and QUANTUM, on the other hand (see off-print in turn 236). While he does so, he utters 'should we scrawl this across?'. He thereby already implies the subsequent concept map on a piece of paper where the term would have to be literally 'scrawled across'. Without a pause, which would have permitted them to think about what Ken has said, interpret it, and then act upon it, all three break out in a brief episode of laughter.

Fragment 8.10

```
236 K: but then, where does this
       one ((COMPLEMENTARITY))
       come in? should we scrawl
       this across? ((Places
       paper slip across three
       others, *))
   ((all three burst out in
       brief laughter))
       the complementarity has to
       go somewhere.
```

Here, an unexpected solution to the question about how the concepts are to be ar-ranged provides the context in which laughter takes over before any conscious reflec-tion could have kicked in. But how can we understand and theorize this instance of human practice? Laughter is a purely bodily action. But here it emerges in the context of something that is surprising intellectually. Laughter thereby re-ties (συν- [syn-]) the body and the mind that have been separated (κόπτειν [kopein]) in successive cognitive and constructivist revolutions, and constitutes a concrete realization of the bodily principle, the *syncope*. Even the ultimate artisan of the pure intellect (Nancy calls him a or the 'Logodaedalus', the ultimate artisan of the logos, mind), Immanuel Kant, has recognized this undecidability of body and mind at the very end of his life: 'In the joke . . . begins the play of thoughts, which taken together, in as far as they attempt to express something, also preoccupy the body; and, as the mind suddenly relaxes when it does not find what it expected in the presentation, one can feel the effects of this relaxing in the body in the form of the vibrations of the organs, which contributes to the establishment of the equilibrium and has a positive influence on health'.[23] According to Kant, we laugh when hearing a joke not because we are smarter than those who do not get the joke or because of something else that our mind detects in the content of a text. Rather, laughter is an expression that anticipation suddenly evaporates into thin air. Kant further elaborates the close relationship between the body and the mind with the example when a person grows grey hair overnight because of some sorrow he (or she) experiences. In this case, too, expectation is suddenly deceived and laughter begins when the body relaxes. He suggests that a joke always implies something that deceives for an instant. When the deception comes to light, mind looks back and, in the attempt to equilibrate between expectation and its disappearance, leads to a to-and-fro movement of the organs, which externally is recognized as laughter. For Kant (in his last years), therefore, all thoughts are harmonically linked to organs in the body so that sudden shifts in mind are associated with a bodily disequilibrium and the return to the equilibrium state occurs in the form of a damped oscillation. Laughter thereby exceeds judgment and beauty.

In his analysis of laughter in Kant, Jean-Luc Nancy notes that the philosopher of the supreme thought thus came to place laughter and the sublime at the same level, he made them to be undecidably the same. Nancy raises this question: 'What if "operation"—the work and the calculation of the work, or the putting to work of the work, or even the making of philosophy into *a work*, its Darstellung or its Dichtung—was precisely Kant's *matter*?'.[24] What matters is precisely the materiality of discourse that guarantees and obliterates pure cognition. Kant places laughter at the same level as hope and sleep, purely physical-material events in which we are no longer consciousness of self, as the balance countering the difficult moments of life.

Strokes of genius, such as when a Ken solves a difficult problem but also relativizes the solution, and bodily gripping laughter, cannot be separated. They constitute a syncope, a re-joining of an undecidable belonging of the joke to the intellectual and to the material bodily strata of everyday human life. 'Laughter liberates not only from external censorship but first of all from the great interior censor; it liberates from the fear that developed in man during thousands of years: fear of the sacred, of prohibitions, of the past, of power'.[25] That is, laughter deals with both suppression, a form of external control functions ('external censors'), and with repression, an internal control function ('interior censor'). The system of repression and suppression at school, which is designed to eliminate part of the fullness of life, also is a system of oppression, which is questioned and inverted in the laughter. We might add, it liberates from the fear that might be associated with the unknown to be learned without being able to know beforehand what the new is and what it means, not only for the semantic context narrowly conceived but also for the students' life project more generally.

---

23. Immanuel Kant, *Werke V: Kritik der Urteilskraft und naturphilosophische Schriften 2* (Wiesbaden: Insel-Verlag, 1957), 436–7.

24. Nancy, op. cit note 20, 138. 'Darstellung' translates 'representation' or 'depiction', but it etymologically derives from 'to posit' (Ger. *stellen*) and 'there' (Ger. *da/r*), placing there before oneself. The German 'Dichtung' translates as 'literary work', especially as a poem (Ger., *Gedicht*), but also as an oeuvre.

25. Bakhtin, op. cit. note 5, 94.

Fig. 8.5. a. Ralf finishes drawing a long line from the bottom left all around the map to concept in the center right. b. All three 'crack up', laughing about Ralf having 'gone crazy'.

In Fragment 8.11 we find another instant where laughter overturns the order of things. Thus, Miles and Ken break out in laughter and Ralf chuckles (Fig. 8.5b) when the latter draws a long connecting arc that reaches from THRESHOLD FREQUENCY at the bottom left of the map to PHOTON, which is halfway up on the right (Fig. 8.5a). The movement appears exaggerated, and Ken provides evidence that he has seen as such: 'Ralf, like we said, go crazy but' (turn 536). That is, the line is something that is even beyond the 'go crazy' that they permitted him ('like we said'). As quickly as the event has flared up, it disappears when Ralf reminds them that the bell has gone and there are other terms to be connected. The fact that all three students break out in laughter is evidence of *participative thinking*, as only active understanding can lead to such an instantaneous, shared expression.

Fragment 8.11
```
535 R: reflected threshold frequency- connect this one- the
       energy of a photon- the threshold frequency, plancks
       constant we just connect this one here.
    a     ((draws a link from THRESHOLD FREQUENCY to PHOTON, Fig.
          8.5a, Miles smiles, Ralf smiles))
    b  M: ((bursts out in laughter, Ralf chuckles))
```

```
536 K: ralf; ((barely containing himself, with chuckle)) like
       we said; go crazy but- ((laughs, Fig. 8.5b))
537 R: it rang already; here=s energy; this is the energy of a
       photon,
```

In this instance, we might ask, what is there to laugh about? There is an apparently common understanding of and about the line Ralf has drawn, which will turn out to be the longest link of the entire concept map. In its exaggeration, the line draws precisely on the carnival principle observable in the marketplace. There, too, the principle builds on exaggerations, much like the cartoons in the daily newspaper draw their effect from the exaggerations of features. The principle leads to both 'praise' (enacting the true spirit of concept mapping) and 'abuse', both of which come from exaggeration. At that instant, it gives rise to laughter, when 'praise' and 'abuse' are torn apart and recognized in their opposition, only to be put back together in and through the laughter itself. But it is precisely dependent on the instant, for a delayed 'joke' no longer is funny. Laughter expresses the immediacy and unmediated nature of the material bodily principle at work. The exaggeration also reminds us of those that characterized the vendor announcements of the marketplace and the exaggerated aspects in television advertisements.

The material bodily principle is visibly at work whenever jokes are involved. But it is invisibly at work all of the time and throughout life as a whole. This is so especially when the joke involves the body itself, especially its secretions. Examples of this also exist in the present data. In one instance, Miles considers the relation between three concept names, one of which includes the two others immediately below it (turn 315). He looks up and gazes squarely into Ken's face. At this point and without saying a word, Ken places his left index finger against his forehead, draws it along (Fig. 8.6a), then brings his hand to the table and demonstratively draws an ephemeral line (Fig. 8.6b). While Ken comes to a close with his action, Miles smiles. He then says, 'I get some so I can draw a diagram'. He moves the tip of his right index finger across the forehead (Fig. 8.6c) and, with the sweat now on the fingertip, marks two now visible lines with the sweat linking the three earlier concepts (Fig. 8.6d). Ken breaks out into a brief cackle and laughter of low volume (intensity). Miles picks up more sweat from his forehead to draw additional lines and Ken puts his finger into the first sweat line Miles has drawn and 'smears' it about. The two students produce something humorous, as they make available to any onlooker in their cackles, smiles, and laughter (even if of low intensity).

Fragment 8.12
```
315 M: okay; down there (.) cause if these two dont have (.)
       okay; ((Draws 2 lines in hierarchical relation))
  a K: ((Puts finger to forehead, as if getting sweat, then
       drawing on table))
  b M: i get some so i can draw a diagram; ((Takes some sweat
       of his forehead and "draws" lines between slips on the
       table))
316 K: ((laughs))
```

Fig. 8.6. Jokes constitute the syncope between the material and the ideal. . Ken draws an ephemeral line. b. Ken wipes his forehead. c. Miles gets some sweat from his forehead. d. Miles makes some sweat marks on the table 'linking' three concepts in an hierarchical manner.

In this situation, we see a number of phenomena that have been at the center of Bakhtin's writings expressing dialogism. First and foremost, the students are present materially. They are not ephemeral self-consciousnesses in the process of 'construct-ing meaning' on a transcendental, metaphysical plane. Second, there is a repetition at work in the material actions: Ken draws an ephemeral line with ephemeral sweat from his forehead. Whereas Miles appears to do the same, there are differences. He uses real sweat from his forehead and produces visible lines onto the table surface. Ken's gestures are merely symbolic but Miles' lines are precisely where he has earlier sug-gested that lines should be placed. He uses sweat, a bodily excretion that in many con-texts of bourgeois society is associated with something undue. Like Ralf, who grabs Miles at his sweaty shirt and pulls it out from under the belt, Ken is not disgusted by Miles' sweat but rather puts his finger into it and smears it about. The situation is un-expected and may be considered 'gross'. Not only has Miles drawn lines with his sweat, which now appears on the table, but also Ken has touched this sweat and spread it out. This may be too much for middle-class sensitivities. But bodily excre-tions have been used to relativize the seriousness of science, science education, and of this upper-class school for well-to-do people who can afford sending their kids.

The hierarchical relations of concept names, and the entire concept-mapping exer-cise, come to be ridiculed another time when Ken, while blowing away some eraser crumbs, also makes several slips of paper drift across the table. Ken comments, 'Oh shit', and all three break out into a cackle. Here again, the unexpected blowing (he could have just swiped it off the sheet), the three drifting and displaced paper slips, the street-level comment ('Oh fuck'), and the subsequent cackle are core aspects of the carnival and carnivalistic expressions and constitutive moments of the fullness of life. These aspects normally not only go unnoticed in the seriousness of science but also are drowned out by seriousness of the social science business in which we take part and that we contribute to constituting through our gloomy approaches to research and writing. In this instance, the bodily excretions are integrated, central aspect of the communication and therefore cannot be separated from the ideal (cognitive) aspects. They both debase and bring to the fore the nature of concepts as grounded in our bod-ily experience of the world.

Integrating 'the Lower Bodily Stratum'

The material bodily principle invokes the 'lower stratum', consisting of the body gen-erally and the lower parts of the body specifically. It is an integral part of the fullness of human life, the very principle of life in its constitutive relation with death. Without the fleshly body, there are no birth and death; there are no generative forces that make life both possible and vulnerable. A phenomenology of the flesh clearly brings to the fore two *essential* correlations that emerge with this approach: 'that of the flesh and life, on the one hand, and that of flesh and birth, on the other hand'.[26] In this chapter, I

---

26. Henry, op. cit. note 7, 180.

show the material bodily principle at work both in its material and its ideal dimensions. In language (the ideal), the bodily principle expresses itself in linguistic forms—generally referred to in relevant circles as 'inappropriate' language—that counter the official, institutional, and formal forms of communication. Schools ask students, by means of school rules, to repress the use of such language and have mechanisms to suppress 'undesired' and 'undesirable' behavior. Many students experience this situation as a form of oppression, particularly students who come from non-middle-class families, such as the ones that I worked with in inner-city Philadelphia. In this private school, where students come from middle- and upper-class echelons of society—in any event well-endowed families able to afford the high fees—the oppression is not felt to the same extent, though students exhibit many behaviors countering oppression. At the same time, as a private institution, the school has an array of repressive means that exceeds that of any public school, including the curtailment of freedom during weekends (students say that they have been 'gated' when they cannot leave the school on weekends). Students may have to do physical labor imposed as punishment for transgressing school rules, for example, after they have been caught smoking. Here again, the transgression of a rule, an intellectual matter, is punished in and through the physical body. Discipline is a double-edged sword, an undecidable, the syncope of body and mind.

The most apparent form in which the students in this school revolt is in and through challenges to the dress code, by arriving in class with caps, allowing parts of the shirt hang out and over the belt, by wearing sneakers when the code requires dress shoes, and so on. Other forms of resisting oppression is apparent in the obscene language students use, though much more so when teachers are not present. (I know this, having been an assistant housemaster whom the students specially trusted.) Sexually explicit talk, going skinny dipping in the lake where it borders on school grounds (after midnight), drinking in the dorm, smoking in a grove at the edge of the school property, leaving the school grounds to play pool in the wee-hours of the morning, boys entering the dorm of female students, and other behaviors listed in the school rules as inappropriate, all question the established order. In class, much of this part of students' everyday life is repressed or the school will suppress it drawing on different forms of punishment, ranging from 'gating' (students are forced to stay on campus) to expulsion. But students may actually talk about those other parts of life as soon as they are out of the classroom or out of hearing distance with those teachers that they know will punish them.

The body is also the location where insult and injury meet when students critique and (temporarily) uncrown their teachers, particularly those who are authoritarian. I vividly remember a number of instances, where when I was a student, we precisely mobilized the material bodily principle to overturn the ruling relations and to get a kick. In ninth-grade, we had a particularly authoritarian history teacher. We played 'practical jokes' in many different ways, but I recall four in particular. In one instance, we put a used condom over the inside door handle to our classroom just prior to the history class. With disgust he realized having his hands sullied. In another, we placed thumbtacks on the chair, from which he rebounded in pain when he sat down. In these cases, we reserved laughter until after the lesson when we retold each other what had happened. In another instance, an equally authoritarian Latin teacher had a classroom door fall on him after we had unhinged it because we knew he was tearing the door open to find students that were hiding inside during recess. In another instance, we built a tower from chairs one of which was tied to the door handle by means of a long string. When the teacher jerked the classroom door open the tower collapsed chairs falling his way. In all of these instances, the 'practical jokes' were directed toward the body of a teacher, who in any case would have been very authoritarian. In and through targeting the body, the very ruling relations that these teachers symbolized were momentarily undone in the harm and disgust they were made to experience.

The bodily principle and lower stratum are constantly present in school, and scholars concerned with learning alone also repress it as an aspect of life in its fullness. What students do, how they learn, what they are interested in, why they do what they do, and so on therefore become mystified as many aspects—emotion, motivation—exist without finding proper explanations. However, precisely emotion and motivation do not come out of the subject matter itself but out of the fullness of life. There are rarer instances where a student 'falls in love' or 'becomes excited' with the subject matter to the point of being willing to abandon everything else, but even these instances cannot explain knowing and learning because, as Vygotsky and Bakhtin say, there is no theory for the internal relations that connect thought, emotion, and volition. With both scholars I think that it is in this fullness of life that we come to understand inclinations and aversions—preferring to sleep in rather than do mathematics during the first lesson or preferring to be in the physical education rather than the chemistry class. It is out of life aspirations that we come to understand students' curricular choices, such as when they want, as most students in the school of the three students, take physics to keep their options open because the subject is an admission requirement in many of the universities in the province.

The point that I make, following Bakhtin and Vygotsky, is this: We can only understand aspects of human experience and their transformation when we use the fullness of life as the unit of analysis, which provides us with the very mechanisms of understanding how change is inherent in the very life of the phenomenon. Thus, we cannot understand the dialectic of language production—i.e., its reproduction and transformation—if we do not consider language as an inherently encompassing and diachronic phenomenon that includes more than just the concept names of the discipline. 'Foul' and other 'inappropriate' language plays an important role in everyday life, especially when they allow a learner to cope with frustration and other difficult instances in school life. At this point, the words constitute something like a safety valve that allows a student to deal with a problematic issue rather than to suppress and repress it, which, following psychoanalytic discourse, will only turn out to haunt the individual at some later point in life. The inappropriate word provides an appropriate relieve to the suppressed and repressed forms of life, in the case of the students in this private school, but may be a means of dealing with the oppression that many working- and under-class students experience in a (middle-class) cultural context so different from their own. In this case, schooling is a form of oppression, because it attempts to constrain cultural others in the mold of the same, the oppressive form of homogeny of the One.

9

On Ambivalence

Over the 20 years of doing research on knowing and learning related to science and mathematics, I have disregarded—as others—conversations that are generally referred to as 'off-topic' or that use 'inappropriate language'. Despite living my early years in poverty, I have come to reproduce and renew, as part of my schooling and scholarly career, the middle-class ethos that various educational systems inculcated in me. When my high school students engaged in 'off-topic' talk, I felt embarrassed, for they did not seem to take the lessons as serious as I thought one should take physics lessons. As a teacher, I generally tolerated it, because I thought that it is a release valve for students, who might be turned off from the subject if I was too serious. I also tolerated it recognizing that life is much broader than what schools pretend it is. I knew that over the dozen years that I was teaching in middle and high school most of my mathematics education colleagues were always serious. Ambiguity, ambivalence, wit, and jokes did not fit into their ways of being. I was serious as a researcher, although as a student I was far from attentive to the lessons and lectures. I tended to pursue my own trains of thought, often dealing with different aspects of my life. We did 'stupid' things in the back of the class rather than paying attention. But I never forgot that I struggled with the subject matter, and became a better teacher because of this. Yet for the longest time I did not have a good handle on understanding 'off-topic talk', and, for this reason, I did not have a good handle on learning in school (science) classrooms more generally. For today I understand that only a framework that takes into account the fullness of life—from which we tend to abstract to get to school learning episodes as they look in the research literature—will be able to handle the complexities of student emotion, interest, motivation, and bodily states, and therefore learning and development.

Today, there are simple reasons for my recognition of the importance of using the fullness of life as the unit of analysis versus focusing on individual courses, lessons, or episodes. The latter constitute only a small part in and of students' lives. We can understand this part when we look at the whole to which it is related and which it in part constitutes. In so looking, we also understand how and why this part develops mediated by its relations to other parts of students' lives and by its relation to their lives as wholes. On the other hand, looking only at a part of life cut off from its full-ness, abstracted from the students' lives as a whole, does not allow us to understand the events and phenomena in school classrooms generally and in science classrooms more specifically. It is in these respects that dialogism, which also is the relation be-tween body and mind, has assisted me in understanding the 'bigger picture' that both constitutes cognition and consciousness and is constituted by them.

In the previous chapter I already attend to a little-studied phenomenon, laughter, and the fact that it is an inherently undecidable phenomenon. I point to the fact that Jean-Luc Nancy uses the concept of the *syncope* to theorize this undecidability be-tween body and mind that does not permit us to separate them for independent study.[1] In music, the syncope is a change of accentuation, a change of beat that is unexpected. It constitutes a displacement, a moment of disequilibrium. For this reason, it consti-tutes something like an engine that drives the music along. Syncope is when the end of one voice is heard at the same time as the beginning of another voice: the two voices are undecidable and so is the transition from one to the other. A good analogy for the undecidable is to think about a precise superimposition of the focal point of vision with the blind spot on the retina. An undecidable proposition is one that cannot be the object of a demonstration and does not submit to the logic of a single system. Double-speak is of this nature, because it belongs to different systems. Double-speak arises when the same utterances can be taken as humorous or as serious, as both hu-morous and serious, thereby expressing two different forms of truth simultaneously. Science cannot use double-speak, because this would undermine its claim to a single truth.

Mikhail Bakhtin is equally interested in undecidability and how it comes to be ex-pressed in discourse. He goes through great lengths to show how the 'lower stratum', the embodiment of the undecidable, comes to be represented in speech. In *Rabelais and His World*, Bakhtin articulates, among others, how double-speak operates as a form of critique.[2] Double-speak is produced when there are multiple voices that ap-pear in one, which allows refraction and reflection, and therefore, undecidability of official truth, humor, and critique. In *Problems of Dostoevsky's Poetics*, Bakhtin shows how in one consciousness there may be several voices, which gives rise to po-lyphony and counterpoint.[3] Undecidability derives from the contrapuntal nature of multi-voiced language. In music, the counterpoint refers to a compositional technique whereby two independent musical lines come to be juxtaposed maintaining a mean-ingful 'harmonious' relation. 'Counterpoint' is often used interchangeably with 'po-lyphony', another term in Bakhtin's theoretical discourse about language. That is counterpoint, polyphony, and dialogism refer to the same phenomenon: the existence of multiple voices that develop because of the inner tension that arises from their jux-taposition within the same exchange.

---

1. Jean-Luc Nancy, *The Discourse of the Syncope: Logodaedalus* (Stanford, CA: Stanford University Press, 2008).

2. Mikhail Bakhtin, *Rabelais and his World* (Bloomington: Indiana University Press, 1984).

3. Mikhail Bakhtin, *Problems of Dostoevsky's Poetics* (Minneapolis: University of Minnesota Press, 1984).

In *Rabelais*, Bakhtin describes how underneath all the exaggerations, the hyperboles, the gluttony, and the grotesque that mark the French author's four-part novel, there are many references to actual historical events.[4] In the discourse of the marketplace, despots and powerful individuals are ridiculed and parodied, including kings, clergy, and academics. The French author constantly mocks those who engage in a variety of practices to sustain their different institutional and societal (i.e., ruling) relations with the common people. Folk culture, using the resources of folk language and sensibilities, relativize the societal conditions through the carnivalization of language in double-speak. People, ideas, and institutions thereby become objects of ridicule and derision. That is, in contrast to the official and officially sanctioned discourses, the unrestrained vernacular retains to this day the power of the double-speak, continually open to undo ruling relations through the ambivalence that exists in the co-presence of two contradictory or oppositive but nevertheless related voices.

In the present concept-mapping lesson, an opportunity arises for the study of ambivalence, which is a marker of the fullness of life normally suppressed and repressed in school classrooms. Three times during the 38 minutes of their session, Miles, with a smile on his face, 'accuses' Ralf of racism or racist attitudes. In all three instances, the topic surfaces in the conversation suddenly and unpredictably and disappears in the same unpredictable and sudden manner. The transition itself is undecidable, a syncope. It is as if something smoldering beneath the official talk all of a sudden bursts forth into the open after seeping through the cracks of a carefully maintained facade only to disappear as quickly into the background as it has earlier made its way into the open.

We do not have available recordings of the interactions Miles and Ralf have had before and after the classroom event that might elaborate or explain what is happening. We do not have recordings of their public speeches on the topic of racism. We do know that Ralf and Miles have been friends and, at the time, are senior students in the same dormitory. The dormitory life is just part of the fullness of their individual and collective lives. As the transcriptions presented here show, we know that they have had related conversations in their dormitory as well. The three instances therefore refer us to a much larger aspect of their life together and a full understanding of the conversation would require knowing more about these other parts of their life of which the current conversation is but a constitutive part. There are also emotions, motives, and motivations at work that would have to be understood through an expanded analysis of the fullness of their life, to understand how and why the charge of racism comes to the surface here where it normally should have been repressed especially because the school rules explicitly forbid harassment. Sample behaviors that the school code of conduct lists include 'jokes or hostile comments relating to physical characteristics, ancestry or age', 'physical or verbal teasing', 'derogatory nicknames', and 'physical or sexual unwelcome contact'. But it is useful to look at the episode because it is clearly directed toward others, who do not know the background to the

---

4. Original versions of François Rabelais' texts can be accessed through a project at the University of Virginia: *La vie de Gargantua* (Gordon1542_R25) and *Pantagruel* (Gordon1542_R26t1). Project Athena out of the Université de Genève provides a marked up version of the Rabelais texts. Project Gutenberg out of the University of Pennsylvania includes an English translation.

conversation so that the speakers, in appealing to others as they do, have to articulate all relevant information as part of the three episodes.

'Ralf the Führer, Ralfy the Racist'

The following episode comes about after Miles has dropped the microphone for the back-up tape recorder in the apparent attempt to create more space for his organization of concept names. The teacher picks up the microphone and places it again on the table a bit further to the side so as not to impede with the students' work. Miles then turns toward Ralf, who has just prior to that instance uttered a statement that equates kinetic energy, on the one hand, with the product of frequency and Planck's constant, on the other hand. This has been his first utterance for a while, as Miles and Ken have taken turns at talk over the preceding ten turns. Miles then says with a smile on his face (Fig. 9.1) and subsequently pointing to the microphone, 'its like, this is like recording Ralf the Führer'. He adds, 'Ralfy the racist, now you- Ralf the racist' (turn 136a). In contrast to Miles, Ralf is serious. Using the same words 'you . . . racist', he expands the utterance by using the auxiliary verb 'are' and the superlative adjective 'biggest'. The accusation therefore not only is returned but also has become more serious: Miles is not only racist but the biggest racist of all. Technically, therefore, he does not deny the accusation but relativizes it by making the other an extreme case of his own accusation.

Fragment 9.1
```
136 R: its connected, see kinetic energy is either plancks
       constant times frequency or electrons or ((looks into
       textbook)) because kinetic energy (??)
  a M: ((turned toward teacher, who is off camera)) uh are you
```

Fig. 9.1. Joking and laughter connect the 'upper' (conceptual) with the 'lower stratum'.

```
       recording with this one? uh i didnt know ((turns to
       Ralf)) <<smiling>its like ((hand movement as if
       slapping with back hand)) this is like ((points to
       microphone)) recording ralf the führer ((points to
       microphone)) ((Miles and Ken both chuckle, Fig. 9.1))
       ralfy the racist, now you- ralf the racist.>
  b  R: you are the biggest racist here in school
  c  M: we have been discussing
       this, you=ve been
       racist
  d  R: i should=ave mentioned-
  e  M: ralf, who said- listen
  f  K: ((hand forward as
       wanting to separate
       them, *))
       <<calming>let=s go on>
  g  M: listen a sec. listen
       ((oriented toward Ken,
       throwing his hand
       forward, *)). you can
       decide on this.
       ((Sideward glance, Fig.
       9.2)) In my chapel
       speech-
```

```
  h  R: ((laughing, as in disbelief)) you are talking the whole
       hour about racist stuff. about this comment. nothing i
       have said is racist; nothing racist about it. ((looks
       at Ken)) ((Miles laughs oriented toward Ken; Ralf does
       a sideward glance to Ken, a slight smile on his face))
137 K: what is pair production up there?
```

Miles begins with a statement in which Ralf is the subject and 'the Führer' is the predicate, with the verb 'are' being omitted. 'Führer', a German word that generally has the sense 'leader' (in which case it would be written with a small letter in English), also was part of the title that Adolf Hitler used for himself. Such a charge clearly can be heard as a violation of the school code of conduct, which forbids derogatory nicknames. Of course, from an academic perspective Ralf is a leader in the school, and in discussions he sometimes either insists on his knowledge or does not easily listen to others. This is exemplified in turn 267, when Ken utters Ralf's name three times in the attempt to get the other to attend and listen. Even in the present fragment, Miles requests Ralf repeatedly to listen. Naming him 'Führer' may be heard as a charge that the latter does not easily listen. Ralf also has German ancestry and, up until the previous year, has attended schools in Germany, although, as we see below, he was in fact born in Canada. Thus, the German term 'Führer', which is ambiguous: it denotes (a) a leader and (b) *the* self-declared leader of the Third Reich with its racial politics generally and its genocidal efforts in the direction of Jews specifically, and (c) alludes to Ralf's ancestry. It is an inherently ambiguous term, with multiple allusions to race, leadership, and leadership in the utmost hyperbole of the term.

Miles responds in stating that they have been discussing this topic before turn 136c), though there is presently no indication where such discussions may have taken place. Miles thereby not only repeats the present charge but also reminds every member to the setting that the charge has been brought forward before. More so, the charge has also changed in that Miles says that Ralf has been racist. That is, no longer does Miles now use a noun to categorize Ralf but he uses an auxiliary verb and the adjective racist, which points us to instances where Ralf has exhibited concrete racist behaviors, though the specific behaviors are not referred to here. That is, he does not simply use the word as a name but he predicatively defines racism in terms of currently unnamed behaviors. Ralf, in turn, utters 'I should have mentioned' (turn 136d), thereby suggesting that there is something that he has not yet introduced. Miles, however, beginning with Ralf's name, as if imploring him to listen, then actually asks the latter to 'listen' (turn 136e). Here, then Miles asks Ralf to listen, which he would not have to do if he had a sense that Ralf was actually listening. That is, whatever it is, Miles experiences Ralf as not listening, which is part of the stereotype that comes with leaders, especially those of realizing the Führer-principle.

At this point, Ken raises his hand with his palm turned sideways as if he wanted to push a wedge between his two classmates (offprint, 136f) uttering, 'let's go on'. But now Miles implores Ken to listen, clearly denoting him by orienting his gaze and by pointing with his hand and finger toward the latter. 'Listen, you can decide on this' (turn 136g). He thereby asks Ken to decide, to make up his own mind about the matter of affairs, that is, whether Ralf is a racist or acts racist. He then begins referring to a chapel speech, a regular event at the school whereby a senior student is invited to address the entire student population during the for-all-students-compulsory daily morning interdenominational chapel service about some topic they deem salient.

Ralf reifies the denoted event as having happened in responding 'you are talking the whole hour about racist stuff'. And apparently, Miles has done so at length ('the whole hour'). That is, Miles has in fact talked about racism, as Ralf acknowledges. Ralf then insists, 'about this comment. Nothing I have said is racist; nothing racist about it' (turn 136h). Miles, orients in the direction of Ken and laughs; and Ralf turns until he gazes Ken squarely into the face, as if looking for the effect the exchange in general has had, and perhaps to request making up his mind more specifically. This is the last turn in this instance with respect to the topic of racism. We do not know its social evaluation in the conversation, as Ken makes a statement about the placement of PAIR PRODUCTION and both Miles and Ralf then continue to work on the concept map. That is, as quickly as the topic has flared up, it also disappears from the conversation. It does not, however, disappear from the reality of their lives, as we can see from the fact that racism will become the topic again at a later instant.

Throughout the exchange, Miles speaks with a voice that sounds serious. Yet at the same time, he has a grin, a smirk on his face that inverts the very seriousness with which he pronounces the charges of racism. Miles also glances sideways (Fig. 9.2), thereby literally enacting the continuous sideward glances that Bakhtin detects in the double-voiced speech of Dostoevsky's characters. Thus, for example, the protagonist in the 'Underground Man', in his monologues 'squints his eyes to the side, toward the

Fig. 9.2. Miles makes sideway glances toward an audience seated near the camera.

listener, the witness, the judge'.[5] This doubling of the voices comes from the word that makes a sideward glance and thereby becomes discourse that both conceals a hidden polemic and constitutes an internally dialogic discourse. The voice thereby is simultaneously serious and mocking, pretending to speak the truth, mocked in the second voice. Polyphony is at work right in his voice. But whereas Bakhtin has to detect any sideway glances *in* the word, we can see Miles' sideway glances literally and repeatedly in this episode. In fact, in and with the sideway glance, Miles overturns (uncrowns) his own statements, questioning their nature as stating the absolute truth. In glancing sideways with a smile on his face, he both signals to be making a joke and monitors others whether they understand it as such. What remains of the accusation therefore is only a grain of truth, some truth and some jest. This is precisely the ambivalence that Bakhtin detects in everyday language throughout recorded cultural history and captured in the various literary genres that reproduced and transformed the ancient Greek serio-comical until it is concretized and transformed again by Rabelais during the Renaissance period and, again in new and different form, in Dostoevsky's novels during the 19th century.

The episode ends with Miles' laughter and a light smile on Ralf's face while he checks Ken's own expression. In this exchange, the body plays an important part in other ways as well and thereby in producing the relation and in orienting the conversation in other ways. Thus, for example, when Ralf and Miles apparently argue over an issue that I had eliminated from my analyses when I first studied this session (in 1991), Ken brings up his hand to make his palm point sideways as if he wanted to separate the two physically (turn 136f). Hand gestures are also used to clarify the addressee of a comment, as can be seen in the video offprint that shows Miles orienting his right hand toward Ken, thereby designating the latter rather than Ralf as his addressee (turn 136g).

In this instant, the students move from one situation to the other without signaling the transition; that is, they apparently do not require a signal that a transition is occurring. The conversation is in one key at one instant and in another key in another, the

5. Bakhtin, op. cit. note 3, 237.

transition itself undecidable, and therefore syncopic in nature. The students understand and understand that others also understand that the transition has happened. They relativize the seriousness in the content of the word by means of smiles and laughter, which disrupt and undermine what on paper might be considered to be a challenge to the integrity of the other. They use each other's words to charge and counter-charge, but we can experience (hear, see) that there also is irony written over the episode. For example, Ralf's expresses irony in his comment about Miles spending 'an entire hour' to speak about racism based on a single comment (which may have been attributed to Ralf, though the soundtrack is insufficiently clear to allow a precise hearing). Irony and parody may make use of another's language but, even if the very same words are used, they are made to convey aspirations opposite and even hostile to the other. Thus, 'in the ordinary speech of our everyday life such a use of another's words is extremely widespread, especially in dialogue, where one speaker often literally repeats the statement of the other speaker, investing it with new value and accenting it in his own way—with expressions of doubt, indignation, irony, mockery, ridicule, and the like'.[6] In everyday life where there are no forces suppressing its full expression, which therefore is inherently dialogical, abuse does not only go one way. Between equals, there is a constant give and take, dialogism in Bakhtin's sense of the word. Bakhtin's marketplace can be any physical location of interest, generally where there are lots of people, and where there is a lot of come and go, such as on doorsteps, in entrance halls, in taverns, in bathhouses, or on ship decks. We can understand the 'marketplace' in general terms as a place where things are traded and where exchanges occur in a continual dialogical relation between material and ideal aspects of life and wherever others are presented who may overhear what is said. In the present instance, the carnivalistic marketplace is the classroom, co-inhabited by others (including the teacher) who can and do hear what is happening. Teasing and abuse therefore are not merely directed toward another person, the recipient of the abuse, but are also and especially so for others, the spectators to the scene. This orientation toward others, who are intended or unintended witnesses to the events, can be seen in the second of the three episodes concerning racism.

'Don't Bring in all these Technicalities'

Typical for dialogical inquiries is the nature of ideas, topics, characters, or plots to be open and without finalization. The racism issue is of this nature, which, as the episodes in this lesson show, is only temporarily closed or abandoned and can be re-opened at an instant. In this second episode concerning racism, Ralf responds to the charges. But whereas Miles continues to orient toward others as well—Ken, the group at the next table, and the teacher—Ralf is singularly oriented toward Miles, the accuser. Thus, in Miles' speech, we detect the polyphony produced for the benefit of an audience, whereas Ralf is much more serious in defending himself. His voice is

---

6. Bakhtin, op. cit. note 3, 194.

monologic rather than double-voiced. He takes the charges serious, whereas in Miles' speech the words are ambivalent. The actions and reactions of Ralf allow us to understand the issue as hearably serious, but Miles' facial expressions permit us to understand both the humorous and the ambivalent sides of the utterances.

In the present instance, the issue about racism arises again all of a sudden in the conversation but seemingly out of nowhere, in a syncopic instant, a change of tonality. However, such issues do not arise from nowhere but from some ground. The point I make here is that this ground is the fullness of life that is merely repressed and suppressed while students are in class. To understand the concept-mapping session as a learning episode, a learning pathway, we have to theorize it out of life as a whole, because only through this unit of life as a whole can we capture the interests, motives, inclinations, or dispositions of the student participants. Here, Miles leaves unfinished a statement about what some 'it' has 'to do with' (turn 330). Ken, in uttering 'with what?', makes this issue problematic. Miles initially provides a candidate response, 'diffraction', but now it is upon Ken, who earlier 'separated' his two peers, to make a reference to and predicatively link Ralf and racism. Miles immediately acknowledges that Ken has brought the topic into the conversation ('don't get Ralf's racism into that' [turn 331c]) and then articulates what can be heard as the earlier unfinished comment concerning the specific actions that the racism is supposed to consist of, 'he makes racist jokes' (turn 331c). He finishes his utterance with a statement that we can, and Ralf does, hear as a cliché: 'we know he is racist, he's German, he can't help it'. This is an explicit reference to the racism of the Nazis during the Third Reich led by Hitler, the 'Führer'. Miles, however, does not accept Ralf's framing of what he has said as a cliché and adds that the latter is 'living every bit of it'.

Fragment 9.2

```
330 M: but its gotta something to do with- its to do with-
331 K: with what? ((pause))
  a  M: what do you say, diffraction?
  b  K: ralfs racism
  c  M: dont get ralfs racism into
         this; he makes racist
         jokes. we know he is
         racist hes german he cant
         help it.
  d  R: thats a cliche.
  e  M: german racist a cliche?
         you=re living every bit of
         it; bastard. how=d you get
         into this country. ((*))
  f  R: i=m canadian.
  g  M: we let you in.
  h  R: i=m more canadian than you are.
  i  M: you,
  j  R: i was born in montreal.
  k  M: dont bring in all technicalities.
  l  K: he dreams in german.
         ((some inaudible words))
```

```
m    M: see, <<f>who> took over
        the country;
n    R: (nobody did?)
o    M: ((points to his chest *))
        WHOSE country is it.
p    R: (?)
q    M: bring that to (??) would
        you (??) to that german
        place (??) ((holds up 2
        fingers))
```

```
r    K: diffraction; look in the back of the book; what pages
        are the first-
        ((in the background, the teacher says, apparently to
        another group, 'write that down', has come closer to
        the group))
s    M: ((turns in direction of
        teacher)) we are not done
        ((pause)) ((oriented
        toward a student in a
        different group)) ((*))
        <<grinning>we just need to
        (??) undetected.
        ((laughter)) ((pause))
332  M: lets get,
333  K: its right here.
334  M: we need more than one book.
```

After calling Ralf a 'bastard', Miles then asks Ralf how he got into the country, but Ralf states that he in fact is Canadian. The issue now is Ralf's status, because others know that he has arrived from Germany during the previous year, his strong German accent of the English language being a constant reminder of his recent arrival. Miles refers to this recent arrival, 'We let you in' (turn 331g), but Ralf retorts, 'I am more Canadian than you are'. Miles queries, 'You?'; and Ralf reaffirms his earlier statement in saying that he was born in Montreal. Ralf therefore is right, he is Canadian by birth even though he has spent much of his life outside the country. Miles acknowledges that Ralf is right by articulating the preceding utterance as a 'technicality' (turn 331k).

What follows is almost inaudible. For one, both are lowering their voices. Moreover, the teacher speaks to the students in a neighboring group and that conversation drowns out much of the present exchange. But one can hear that Miles asks Ralf questions—'who has taken over the country?' and 'whose country is it?'—while pointing to his own chest (turn 331o). That is, Miles here asks what we can hear as a rhetorical question, to which he anticipates a specific answer, the one that he makes available in his hand movement to his chest 'I did' or 'we did'. But precisely in asking the question, in taking it literal rather than rhetorical, the conversation breaks open to the unanticipated, allowing Ralf to utter, 'nobody did'. That is, the question already is ambivalent because it can be heard in different ways, literally and rhetorically. Miles' implied 'I did', 'we did', or 'those of my cultural stock did' is open to contestation, though it is not taken up at that time. Even if he understands himself as British, French

Canadians do constitute the other founding culture, anchored in the constitution and in the continued bilingual nature of the nation (Canada).

After Miles makes a comment about some German place, Ken proffers the concept name 'diffraction', which has been the last one they have uttered prior to talking (about) racism. The teacher has apparently moved even closer to the group, which we can take from the fact that Miles glances upward to a person standing just outside the camera view. In response to the teacher's instruction to another group to write down what they have been talking about, Miles, too, responds by saying that they are not yet done (turn 331s). As the offprint in turn 331s shows Ralf has already turned back to the textbook. Miles turns toward the closest group of students—sitting near the camera—and, all the while grinning from ear to ear, explains that they have to do (settle?) something that would otherwise remain undetected (turn 331s). Then, following a brief pause, all three students put on serious faces and orient toward the task, that is, to the work of completing the concept map before them.

In the present fragment, we note again that Miles' delivery of the serious charges is accompanied by smiles: he grins from ear to ear and he even laughs. There is a contradiction between the seriousness of the content of his speech as Ralf hears it and its delivery. We can also hear the irony in Ken's intonation, and recognize that Miles has heard it ironically, too: he responds to Ken, 'don't get Ralf's racism into this' all the while featuring a big grin in his face. Here, the grammatical construction produces an ambivalent utterance, which we can hear as producing a serious and an ironical comment simultaneously. Adjectivally, it specifies Ralf as a racist, and therefore advances a serious aspect of the utterance, but the simultaneous grin and the inflection of the voice hearably are ironical. We see both as taking up positions, physically and ideologically, for example, in the offprints that go with turns 331e and 331o. In fact, whatever it is that Ralf has said (turn 331n) is acknowledged and completed with an apparent indignation, 'whose country is it?' That is, Miles here moves back first, drops the smile from his face, and takes up physically and ideologically a new position, one that is entirely marked by indignation. Only instances later, together with his explanation directed toward the other group, Miles again is all laughter, as if he has just completed a friendly joust.

Again, as quickly as the topic has begun, it also has disappeared. One may see and hear two different lives enacted but temporally separated. The smiles are gone and all look serious, focusing again on the concept words before them and on their task to produce a map. Some scholars think of such situations in terms of code switching between two forms of culture. Bakhtin too, in some instances, appears to suggest that there are two forms of life: 'It could be said (with certain reservations, of course) that a person of the Middle Ages lived, as it were, *two lives*: one was the *official* life, monolithically serious and gloomy, subjugated to a strict hierarchical order, full of terror, dogmatism, reverence, and piety; the other was the *life of the carnival square*, free and unrestricted, full of ambivalent laughter, blasphemy, the profanation of everything sacred, full of debasing and obscenities, familiar contact with everyone and everything'.[7] Thus far in our reading of Bakhtin we may see the justification for thinking

---

7. Bakhtin, op. cit. note 3, 129–30.

about the two different sides, especially given the distinction between the official life, paralleling schooling, and the life of the carnival square, with its parallel of students' out of school life. But our understanding may change if we that 'Both of these lives were legitimate, but separated by strict temporal boundaries' (ibid.). But the idea of the syncope, the co-presence of both aspects simultaneously and undecidably, encourages us to take a more holistic perspective, whereby the fullness of life expresses itself differently, depending on the degree of repression and suppression to less comprehensive forms. The concept of an 'in-joke'—which can be told even with the intended target present if s/he, as non-insider, does not understand—points to the fact that the fullness of life can break through even in the dullest of life instants.

In our context, of course, charging (teasing) another student with racism is illegitimate. Moreover, even in the case Bakhtin describes, an individual person does not experience leading two lives, it is the same live but during much of a life, the freedom enjoyed in the carnival context has to be suppressed. Thus, rather than thinking about Bakhtin's and our concept-mapping event as examples of code switching, I suggest thinking of it as arising from the fullness of life. The fullness of life then encompasses both (a) its serious moments, here the concept-mapping session specifically and the physics course more generally and (b) its humorous and ambivalent moments. The humorous and ambivalent moments come to be repressed and suppressed in certain contexts, such as school generally and school science lessons more specifically. They are also suppressed in other types of situations, such as university offices and meetings, though the same people participating in events that take place there may actually express the fullness of life immediately after leaving the places and events.

In the present instance, Miles has not come out as the victor, for, in contrast to Ralf, he explains what is happening, when in fact he has exhibited indignation just prior to the ending of the episode. Furthermore, he 'admitted defeat' when he designated Ralf's defense as a 'technicality'. There is in fact, however, a contradiction in Miles' charge, as he not only accuses Ralf to be a racist, as exhibited in the racist jokes that he attributes to the latter, but also makes an inherent link between being German and being racist. Ralf makes this salient as a cliché. But in and as a cliché, a generalizing remark about all Germans, Miles himself makes a racist remark. The double-edged sword of the word—its *internal* dialogism—comes back to haunt him, as it provides evidence for Ralf's earlier counter-charge that Miles is the 'biggest racist here in school'. The two voices are independent but interrelated: they thereby constitute a polyphony of voices. They are interdependent because each exists not merely for itself but precisely for the other, and each hears itself and its echo in the responses of the other, now colored with the other's intentions, emotions, and predilections.

'He Puts Words into My Mouth and Afterward He Believes in What He Says'

Dialogism is inherently open-ended; only monological speech has an ending when the single logic at work or truth has been articulated. Dialogism does not allow ideas, characters, and stories to be finalized; in monological inquiry (writing), everything is oriented toward some pre-existing truth. That is, in monological speech there is an end-point, one voice will have the final word. And this, all participants know: Students generally 'know' that teachers and textbooks are right. There is only one science, no ambivalence about it. In contrast, according to Bakhtin, non-finalization is one of the characteristics of dialogism (see chapter 6). This immediately gives a new perspective on science education, where there is indeed a *final word*. The final words constitute the established forms of science talk. There are no two radically different 'meanings' of Newton's third law or the Krebs cycle. In teacher–student relations, this monologism is at work in the sequentially ordered turn taking typical for schools, whereby teachers initiate talk about some topic, students respond, and teachers *evaluate* the response in view of the authoritative voice of science. Even with all the constructivist debate that has reigned over science education for more than two decades, students always have been expected to get the right conception, to get to the sanctified end-point of the science curriculum. Anticipating my comments in the final chapter, I say this: There are indeed ways in which we may envision students to become educated in and about mathematics, science, history, and other school subjects without a finalizing voice from the disciplines. For example, if students were to learn by engaging in societally relevant problems, such as environmental health or restoring some natural environment, they would be in a position where different fields place different constraints on what can or should be done. In this case, they would be able to enact dialogical forms of inquiry, as long as there is not the finalizing voice that scientists often employ when they intend to contribute to the solution of some problem.

Science is monological in nature. It attempts to impose its methods and concepts on everybody else, as we have observed during the George W. Bush years in the movement to support only 'evidence-based' research in education and as we can see again now in the American Association for the Advancement of Science's push for more science-based decision-making processes in Washington. In contrast to the monological voice of science, much of everyday life in a democracy is marked by dialogism, where there is not a finalizing voice that tells us what or who is right. In fact, *life itself is dialogical* (life–flesh, birth–death, reproduction–transformation, etc.) so that we cannot tell where it will lead society generally and ourselves more specifically. In everyday life, any debate can be reopened, though it may be temporarily closed because of one or the other reason. This possibility to reopen a debate is precisely what we see in the case of the accusation of racism. Above I feature two episodes around this topic, and a third one now emerges again 'out of thin air', just as unexpectedly as the two previous instances. Indeed, we see evidence in the previous episodes that there has been an ongoing debate about racism, a fact that both Miles and Ralf acknowledge. This debate has been taken into other aspects of school life: the chapel speeches. That is, the three exchanges here are but repetitions and transformations of a debate that has had its origin outside of class perhaps during some evening of their common life in the dorm. (Ken resides in a different dorm from Ralf and Miles.) But these episodes of re-emergence of the topic are not out of thin air: they are part of the fullness of life normally repressed during the official school day. But, being a moment of and appearing in the fullness of life, the students can re-enter the debate at any moment of their collective life. The issue seeps through the cracks in the façade that suppression and repression leave. We do not have evidence of other instances where they may have talked about it, but we can easily imagine that there are given the ease with which the conversations have emerged in the present context.

This points us to a way of approaching the claim that students code switch from their classroom subject matter into some other code. It appears to be more fruitful to approach the problem of discourse from the perspective of a unit that encompasses the entire life, and the conversations and language observable in particular classroom lessons—i.e., the 'scientific discourse' that we find reported in the science education literature—constitute what remains when everything else is repressed and suppressed. Only the monologism of the subject matter at hand remains in view of the researcher's or the teacher's gaze. But just as Bakhtin shows that the development of the novel genre can be understood only when we study the development of the vernacular, so the study of school science language must come from within the study of the students' vernacular. Just as the historical study of the novel does not yield the inner mechanisms that lead to its development, so the study of (mis-, alternative, naïve) conceptions does not yield the inner mechanisms of the evolution of students' competencies relative to the scientific idiom.

This third instance of Miles charging Ralf with racism, which is launched with a smirk on Miles' face, enters the conversation after Ken blows some eraser crumbs off the large sheet of paper onto which he currently transcribes the concept names in the spatial order that they take inscribed on paper slips on the table. He blows so vigorously that three of the paper slips are lifted off the table and are carried away. Ken comments on the event with an 'Oh shit' and Ralf picks up the paper slips to re-place them into the hierarchy. Miles orients toward Ken, 'Way to go big guy' (turn 426b). Ken then utters, 'still a racist guy' (turn 426c). It is not clear whom he intends to address, providing a social evaluation to Miles' comment or to Ralf's action of repairing the concept map. Miles picks up the theme but rather than presenting it as a charge launched against himself, he, with a smirk on his face, attributes the racism at issue to Ralf. But Ralf first denies that he has ever made racist comments, and thereby articulates never having enacted behavior that may be taken as evidence that he is a racist. Miles expresses indignation with a loud 'ohoho' (turn 426f). Ralf then turns the charge around, repeatedly orienting his gaze toward Ken, who is working on the transcription and does not see him: 'he is the one with racism in his talks' (turn 426g). But Ken, although he has articulated the topic first, does not look up at either Ralf or Miles. The latter then turns toward a student at the neighboring table (who is from the same dormitory), asking whether Ralf 'ever said anything racist'. Ralf, too, orients to the other student group, where one of the students laughs as Miles comments, 'not to the face'.

Fragment 9.3
```
426 M: yea; all of these;
  a   K: ((Ken blows at eraser pieces on sheet, makes a slip fly
         away)) oh shit ((Ken laughs; Ralf and Miles smile))
  b   M: way to go big guy. ((Ralf re-places the slips))
  c   K: still a racist guy;
```

d M: hey hey hey dont bring ralfs racism into this. you=ll
    bring it into these we=ll
e R: i have never mentioned any racist comments;
f M: <<f>[ohoho>]
g R: [hes the] one with racism in his talks
h M: hey feenie ((*
    orients to and calls
    a student in another
    group)) has ralf
    ever said anything
    racist? ((pause, the
    student in the other
    group laughs))
    [not to the face]

i R: [he said something] like this about our relations
j F: ((from the other group)) uh, is that a serious
    question?
k M: ralf, you guys.
l R: i hate that so much.
m M: you hate being a racist?
n R: quite a bit so.
o M: so why do you keep making these dumb comments.
p R: you accuse me of what i dont do.
q M: i can ask anyone around the school ((pause)) about ralf
    being racist
r R: first he accuses me of
    being a racist. then he
    puts words into, words
    into my mouth and
    afterwards he believes in
    what he says. and
    [he believes]
s M: [i can   ]
t R: that i said it. * (???)

u M: fï- feenie can verify my
    story. late sat- late at
    night ralf just lays in an
    totally puts in (( )) like
    classifies like every
    race.
v R: i have not done anything
    like this
x M: of course he=ll gonna be
    on the top
y R: i never do that
z T: ((comes to group)) get yourself ready
aa M: (???)
427 K: okay guys; connect all these; we gotta do it pretty
    fast.

Ralf has oriented toward a student ('Feenie') in the other group (see offprint), suggesting that Miles is saying something about their mutual relation. Although Miles has been talking with a smirk on his face, the seriousness of his utterance's content comes to be acknowledged in the social evaluations that are made available in Feenie's and in Ken's turns. The former student asks, whether Miles is asking him a serious question, and Ken calls on Ralf and then on both, as if asking them to stop it (without saying it in so many words). That is, Feenie too hears the possibility of the accusation to be serious only rather than ambiguous and double-voiced.

For Ralf, the issue has not ended. He comments, 'I hate it so much', which Miles, repeating part of the phrase, uses to mock Ralf, 'You hate being a racist?' (turn 426m). Ralf responds seriously in the affirmative, but Miles asks him why he keeps 'making these dumb comments'. That is, although Ralf has already stated that he has never made racist comments, Miles treats this issue as non-finalized, open to re-articulation. Ralf picks up precisely on the behavior that could have been observed but that he has not engaged in ('you accuse me of what I don't do'). Miles, however, appeals to the school community as a whole ('anyone around the school'). Then Ralf responds, with an interesting twist on the cases Bakhtin discusses as multi-voiced, polyphonic speech.

In Dostoevsky's novels, protagonists tend to be confronted with their own voices in the mouths of other individuals, but now they are colored by parodic and polemical intonations and semantic elements. It is this doubling of the voice that produces dialogism, polyphony, and counterpoint within one and the same voice. The fundamental process is that irony, parody, and polemics are produced by the voice that has taken up the utterance of another, returning it the original speaker with additional layers of intonation and significance. In the present instance, Ralf points us to the reverse process. He suggests that Miles first calls him a racist, then 'places words into [Ralf's] mouth' and then in fact believes that Ralf has said what he attributes to him. That is, Ralf charges Miles to attribute words to him and then to believe that these are actually Ralf's words that he returns to mock the latter. At this point, as the offprint shows, Ralf actually has oriented toward some other person (the teacher), whereas Miles still is oriented toward Feenie.

Miles, however, does not agree with this assessment. Orienting toward Feenie again, he calls him to be a witness, 'Feenie can verify my story' (turn 426u). Miles explains that late at night—when they are in the dormitory on the same floor with Feenie—Ralf is classifying every race. Although Ralf denies this (thereby questioning the truth in Miles' speech) Miles continues: 'of course he'll gonna be on top'. But Ralf denies again, 'I never do that'. The teacher, who has followed the tail end of the argument, asks students, in a mediating tone that is itself riding on the boundary between the serious accusation and the evident joke in Miles' comments, to 'get ready'. Although Miles' words taken in themselves do sound serious, insulting Ralf in ways that violate the school rules, the three continue to work together and there is no evidence that the three episodes have had an effect on their completion of the task.

Bakhtin describes and analyzes how Dostoevsky transfers words from the mouth of one person to the mouth of another, retaining the content but changing the tone and the signification. Dostoevsky thereby forces the heroes to recognize themselves, their words and ideas, in the other who has taken up their words. But these words no longer are the same, they have changed, now characterized by a different intonation, that of parody and ridicule. In the present instance, Miles talks about what Ralf presumably has said—though the latter denies having talked in the way described. Quoting some- one else using direct or indirect speech—thereby reproducing language and transform- ing it by means of the dialectic of production—works if the quote is recognized as authentic. If, however, there is a question as to whether the quote really is a quote or whether it is the speaker himself who attributes words to another is a matter that might be contested. In the present instance (turn 426p), Ralf suggests that what Miles reports him to have said are actually not his own words. Rather, Miles 'puts words into my mouth'. More so, Miles is said to subsequently 'believe in what he says', that is, that Ralf *actually* has said it. Miles hears the reversal of the attribution in precisely this way, which we see when he calls on another student as potential witness whom the present, wider audience (which includes the teacher) can ask to verify Miles' story.

Dialogism and the Fullness of Life

School subject matter language is tendentiously monologic. It is oriented toward mak- ing students speak with a serious tone the collectively accepted standard language (of science). There is but a single voice and a single tone that is acceptable, disimpas- sioned, gloomy conceptual talk. In everyday language, however, there are many voices speaking to one another, thereby relativizing and contradicting each other. Cen- tral to everyday talk is ambivalence that arises when the voice of one person reappears in the mouth of another, now colored with new tones that may express ridicule, cri- tique, polemic, and parody. Any rap lyric will show this tendency at work. For exam- ple, at this instant I am concretely thinking of the Eminem lyrics entitled 'Mosh', where all sorts of voices from the American society generally and those of George W. Bush more specifically are turned against 'This Weapon of Mass Destruction/ That we call our President, for the present', that is, against Bush himself.

In the present conversation, there are multiple voices, those of the speakers and those that speakers are borrowing from others (actually or attributed), returning them to the previous speaker, now with social evaluation, mockery, ridicule, and parody. The events make clear that the episode is not just about the two, the accuser and the accused, but that there is a third party involved. This third party—which, in turn, is Ken, Feenie, and the teacher—is called upon as witnesses to this event or as witnesses to events that have occurred at some other time and now are mobilized as evidence in support of this or that voice. Moreover, the ethical question itself is one that resides not between two—racism is not something that characterizes the relation of two inter- locutors but refers to something involving entire people—but involve a third party, the generalized other. Thus, when Ken does not look up and provide commentary and feedback, Miles and Ralf appeal to others in the classroom. In this appeal, their voices deny themselves a finalizing force and therefore truth.

The appeal to the generalized other is an interesting phenomenon in its own right, as it shows us an aspect of the nature of this conversation: It is open-ended and resists finalization. There is no ultimate authority and no right answer in the way that this is the case of teacher questions about (physics, science) subject matter. That is, in appealing to others, the students also articulate the non-finalizable nature of their debate, and this is one of the essential characteristics of dialogism.

This debate therefore has not been finalized and cannot be finalized. It can surface and resurface at any instant in time, and it does so unpredictably, as the present fragments show. The debate is part of the full set of relations that Ralf and Miles entertain. Therefore, if we, researchers, suppress, neglect, or turn a blind eye to the full set of relations, to the fullness of life, we place ourselves into a position that no longer allows an understanding of the relations in and through which students articulate their knowing and come to learn. These relations essentially mediate and leave their marks on the products, the learning outcomes. As pointed out above, schools realize that racist comments, teasing, and other forms of 'undesirable behavior' do indeed mediate student learning and they have made school rules accordingly. Unfortunately, much of educational research and theorizing acts as if the prescribed and sanctioned form of life at school constitutes an accurate depiction of the fullness of life that mediates school-based events and processes, most importantly, learning and development. In presenting this chapter, I suggest that there is more to life than what educational research portrays, describes, and reports.

Bakhtin faces a similar problematic when he tries to understand the cultural-historical evolution of literary genre that has eventually led to the emergence of the novel, which then continuously transformed to give us the different forms of the novel genre available today. He comes to the conclusion that we cannot understand the dialectic of production of the literary genres, their reproduction and transformation, if we only look at literary works. These, he suggests, specific novels are but *synchronic* images of the particular literary form of life at the instant of language as a whole. They can be likened to photographs that provide a snapshot of language at some instant in cultural history. But they do not provide an understanding of language as a dynamic, *diachronic*, cultural-historical phenomenon. The history of genres does not come alive if we play the synchronic slices quickly, one after the other, like we play a sequence of photographs quickly to yield the impression of motion (as in film, video). We do not understand in this approach the *internal* dynamic that actually produces change. For this to happen, we need an internal mechanism—dialogism—to achieve the 'peculiar *perpetuum mobile*' that leads to 'an endless dialogue where one reply begets another, which begets a third, and so on to infinity, and all of this without any forward motion'.[8] I take it with Bakhtin that it is language and life as a whole that we need to study using a sociological approach to arrive at an understanding of the historical transformations that lead to the emergence of genres and their subsequent evolution and transformation. We need to study the fullness of students' lives to understand their interests, predilections, dispositions, motives and motivations, and so on.

---

8. Bakhtin, op. cit. note 3, 230.

To understand student learning, we therefore cannot just look into this or that class-room, considering this or that voice, this or that action. Rather, we have to take the entire life of the student-within-society as the unit of analysis. There we may find emotions and motives at the very core, as constitutive moments rather than as external factors. We thereby open up an access to changes in students' interests and motivations. It is the fullness of life that provides students such as Ralf, Miles, and Ken with the resources to participate in life and thereby change the language, discourses, and genres that they are familiar with and mobilize. Although schooling constitutes in some senses a public activity, it segregates students in many ways from other aspects of the adult world of work and other forms of involvement that make everyday life. This leads to a gradual concealment of certain forms of development and to repression. Thus, 'the gradual concealing of various attributes of development, including major aspects of sexuality, is the outcome of these processes of segregation'.[9] Anthony Giddens uses the concept *sequestration of experience* to articulate how certain aspects of human experience are removed and, through institutional sequestration, concealed from everyday life. What we observe here, however, is a similar but re-fracted process, whereby young people are institutionally sequestered from the every-day life before—after a process of disciplining both mind and body, mind through disciplining the body—they are released back into the fullness of life. But this seques-tration into the disciplines occurs only part of the day, the other, repressed and sup-pressed parts of life seeping and shining through wherever and whenever we look. Part of the disciplinary gaze and monologic discourse developed in the process are a result of this sequestration, suppression, and repression.

Students from the middle classes essentially are comfortable at school, because the find there the same rituals and (discursive) practices that characterize their life at home and in leisure activities. This also is the case at this school, where students come from well-to-do homes, their parents being doctors, business people, lawyers, and so on. There is therefore not much suppression and repression necessary, no more than students are already exposed to and enact at home.[10] The discursive and relational practices of the working-class students are very different. This difference may mediate their participation such that the experience of sequestration from other aspects of their life through self-imposed repression and enforced suppression may lead to experi-ences of oppression. As Chris Emdin suggests, 'many students walk into schools and are physically and emotionally forced to subdue their "selves" and "realities" in order for schools to maintain the existent structures that ultimately function to the detriment of student engagement in the classroom. This act of subduing oneself, which is forcing one to become part of a foreign ideal that provokes discomfort at the risk of being even further ostracized from the school or the classroom, is shared by many students

9. Anthony Giddens, *Modernity and Self-Identity: Self and Society in the Late Modern Age* (Stanford, CA: Stanford University Press, 1991), 152.

10. Penny Eckert, *Jocks and Burnouts: Social Categories and Identity in the High School* (New York: Teachers College Press, 1989).

who are engaged in hip hop culture'.[11] Oppression simply is a matter of differentiated and differential knowledge/power, that one group applies to limit the chances in and control over life of others. It is a form of realizing the partial interests of the ruling class against the interests of other classes. Language is one of the means and objects in this mechanism of oppression. Using language outside the one that is sanctioned and monological undermines other practices (e.g., working-class students smoking just off the school grounds) that carnivalize official culture, including laughter. These other languages, full of ambivalence and laughter, may actually have a liberating effect.

Suppression, repression, and oppression have consequences that are little explored in the literature on learning science in schools. If much of the fullness of life is repressed and suppressed in schools generally and in science classes in particular, we have to ask how this mediates the personalities students develop? What kind of social and psychological beings do we foster? What kind of social and psychological beings emerges from the schooling experience? Some science educators may say that it is not their business to ask such questions. But then I might ask this: Whose business is the education of the young generation if not that of educators? The effects of current practices are to be born not only by individuals but by the collective as well, for all repression involves 'the transition from a first-person existence to a sort of formalism of that existence, which lives on a former experience, or rather on its memory, then on the memory of having had the memory, and so on, until only it retains only its essential form. Now as an advent of the impersonal, repression is a universal phenomenon, revealing our condition as incarnate beings by attaching it to the temporal structure of being in the world. To the extent that I have "sense organs", a "body", and "psychic functions" comparable with other people, each of the moments of my experience ceases to be an integrated and strictly unique totality, in which details exist only as a function of the whole'.[12] Repression thereby comes to be a collective phenomenon, and one that marks the collective consciousness of the entire social class.

---

11. Chris Emdin, 'Reality Pedagogy: Hip Hop Culture and the Urban Science Classroom', in *Science Education from People for People: Taking a Stand(point)* edited by Wolff-Michael Roth (New York: Routledge, 2009), 70–89, 73.

12. Maurice Merleau-Ponty, *Phénoménologie de la perception* (Paris: Gallimard, 1945), 99.

10

Dialogism, Constructivism, and Beyond

'If there is nothing like *the* language, if there is no absolute monolingualism, there remains the task of defining what a mother tongue is in *its active division* and what grafts itself between this language and that said to be foreign'.[1] This statement, which Abdelkebir Khatibi makes as part of his introduction to a book on bilingualism, has guided my inquiry into language and learning throughout this book. From the beginning of this project, I have been thinking about learning in terms of the unfolding and complexification of language, which is not homogeneous but rather, even when it concerns the idiom of a field such as physics, is always divided from within, is always non-self-identical. This is the fundamental point Mikhail Bakhtin makes in and through his writing about dialogism, which I articulate in this book as the answer to learning generally and to the learning paradox specifically. For Bakhtin, dialogism begins with the individual word. In this he makes us conscious of the fact that each utterance is doubly invaded by the voices of others rather than merely being a characteristic of the speaking subject alone: the words and their combinations carry within themselves the traces of their past usages; and at the same time, the reaction to come on the part of the addressee of the utterance already is inscribed in the utterance itself.[2]

One of the secondary intentions for my writing this book in the way it appears here has been to provide readers with an opportunity to read an analysis of a classroom conversation as it unfolds in real time and in all its aspects. All too often we are provided with abstract descriptions of classroom events peppered with a few excerpts from transcripts. We are not provided with an extended analysis of a real conversation as it unfolds in time, without time out for reflection, and without knowledge of what the ultimate outcome of the conversation is once it will have been completed. Such a perspective and analysis provides opportunities for revising and newly articulating issues concerning learning, particularly issues concerning the question of the intentional construction of 'knowledge', which both 'in pieces' and as 'framework' lie outside the horizon that separates the known (inside) from the unknown (outside).

---

1. Abdelkebir Khatibi, 'Présentation', in *Du bilinguisme* (Paris: Denoël, 1985), 9–10, 10.
2. Tzvetan Todorov, 'Bilinguisme, dialogism et schizophrénie', in *Du bilinguisme* (Paris: Denoël, 1985), 11–26.

Moreover, as I show here, essential aspects of the conversations may be lost—such as the recurrent discussion concerning racism or the swearing and cursing—to the detriment of a proper theory of changing participation, language, and forms of knowing. If we abstract the physics from the fullness of this lesson, the laughter, the sweat, the jokes, and the accusations, or the orientations and positionings, then we will never come to understand some of the concerns that make students' individual and collective lives, and therefore the reproduction and transformation of bodily states generally and emotions (motivations) more specifically.

Language: A Recursive and Generative System

For Bakhtin, the word is ambivalent, literally is of worth (Lat. *valēre*, to be powerful, to be worth) on two sides (Lat. *ambi-*). There are two alternate sides worthy of consideration. Ambivalence is the generatrix of birth and death simultaneously, and therefore of becoming and transformation. That is, a language regenerates itself at the very instant that it is spoken rather than only through the inventions of 'great poets'. At the very instant that students talk and talk about the quantum, the wave, the principle of complementarity, the language of physics comes to be regenerated. In the very act of speaking a version of English (German, French, and so on), students not merely repeat and reproduce language but simultaneously transform it. As I show throughout this book generally but in chapters 5, 8, and 9 specifically, the word also is the site of the undecidability (syncope) of the body (material, 'lower stratum') and the mind (ideal, 'upper stratum'). This undecidable moment, this syncope, because it refers us to the fullness of life, is the generative force of situated and situational change and learning. The learning paradox exists only when mind is thought of in terms of fixed, monological structures, which, as Bakhtin shows in his *Rabelais*, has led to the cultural stagnation of the Dark Ages. The present students *do* engage in a task of which they cannot know what its end result will be, which they therefore cannot aim at intentionally. They abandon themselves to the task such that, as shown in chapter 6, the end result looks rather different than the 'prior knowledge' that the students have displayed going into the session. The task and with it the concept map evolves until an instant comes where the mapmakers can and do say, 'we're done'. At that time, they also have evolved an idiom that allows them to give reason to and for the concept map and the language that they have co-evolved. Rather than requiring a conception or conceptual framework, the students evolve a language that allows them to do something that they cannot think of when they begin this task. In fact, it is the task itself that leads to the development of a language that (subsequently) allows entirely new descriptions and articulations of complementarity and its conceptual relations with wave and quantum, for example. Moreover, the new language can be used to formulate purposes (intentions) behind its own use: the language of and represented in and by the map. That is, the intention for the specific conceptual language is available only *after* the students are actually speaking it—and thus we have come full circle in our inquiry concerning the learning paradox. It is only when we speak a language that we also have the tools to formulate its purposes. We *cannot* intend it beforehand, because it gives itself together with a reason for its existence and its purposes.

Students come with a language that turns into something else that they could not have envisioned before. In the process, language turns out to have very different functions simultaneously: it is ground, material, and tool. That is, 'natural language serves persons ... as circumstances, as topics, and as resources of their inquiries, furnishes to the technology of their inquiries and to their practical ... reasoning *its* circumstances, *its* topics, and *its* resources. That reflexivity is encountered ... in the actual occasions of their [speakers'] inquiries as indexical properties of natural language'.[3] Language is the ground upon which the task is built, however 'inadequate' one may deem to be students' pre-task language. In fact, my inquiry procedurally is marked by an ethnomethodological disinterest for judgments of the adequacy, value, importance, necessity, success, or consequentiality of students' talk. The students' natural language *is the condition* for anything they do, and therefore also is the condition for—rather than the to be eradicated antithesis of—anything like the 'correct' dialect of physics. In the concept-mapping task, language also is the material that and with which the students work. It is the language in and constituting the concrete propositions that is their topic. There are concept names that they assemble into statements that contain subjects and predicates, the latter constituted by concept names and verbs. These material productions become integral part of the language itself. But students therefore do more than operate on the ground of language and use it as a material. They also use language as a tool to manage the task, its contents and its processes. It is their resource for doing what they do. That is, in this concept-mapping task, language is allowed to fold back over itself and integrate itself over. In other words, language is recursive.[4]

Recursive systems generally are complex, but the following analogy might help in understanding the way in which a system integrates itself over and becomes undecidable. A simple recursive system can be generated with the equation

$$x_t = \lambda \, x_{t-1} \, (1 - x_{t-1}) \qquad\qquad (10.1)$$

with $0 \leq x \leq 1$. The value of x at some time t is calculated from its value at time t - 1 and some constant λ. The beginning value of $x(t=0) = x_0$ lies between 0 and 1. The result is then used to calculate the next x, that is, x at time t, and so on. That is, the previous value of x comes to be multiplied by itself and then determines the next x which lies in the same domain. That is, the number x_{t-1} comes to be folded over itself (multiplication by 1 - x_{t-1}) and is projected back into the original domain where $0 \leq x \leq 1$. Another way of saying that the x was multiplied by itself is to say that it 'operated upon' or folded over itself, and then, by means of the equal sign ('=') was mapped back onto itself. For $\lambda < 3$, a number of recursions will lead to a constant x, that is,

---

3. Harold Garfinkel and Harvey Sacks, 'On Formal Structures of Practical Actions', in *Ethnomethodological Studies of Work* edited by Harold Garfinkel (London: Routledge, 1986), 160–93, 160.

4. There are some claims that not all languages are recursive, but these claims are still very much disputed. In the case of the Pirahãs, this apparent absence of recursion comes with a radically different way of conceiving reality, which allows them to live in the moment, enjoying each day as it comes, without worrying about the future and without guilt for past actions. See Andreea S. Calude, 'Pondering Grammar and God', *Science*, Vol. 323 (2009), 463.

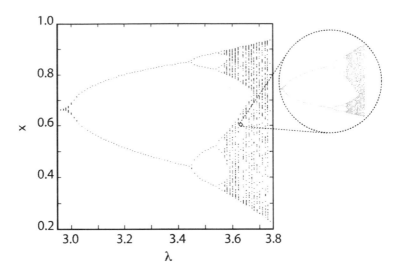

Fig. 10.1. End values of *x* for different values of the parameter λ.

there is a definite end-point to the iterations from which point on the previous *x* and the next *x* are the same (Fig. 10.1). The interesting thing is, however, that for λ > 3, there are no longer unique solutions and, as λ is increased, the number of solutions for *x* themselves becomes unpredictable. A recursive system therefore is a chaotic system, yielding unpredictably predictable outcomes: we have an idea of where it might end up but can only predict an outcome probabilistically. If we think of language in the same way, then we get a system that inherently changes as it continuously works on itself, is folded back, upon itself. But in the process language changes in indeterminate and non-deterministic ways. Readers will be familiar with the marvelous and unpredictable images that books on fractals and chaos theory publish. Conversations, so I maintain, need to be understood in a similar way as fractal and chaotic phenomena. recently became aware of another situation that might serve us as a suitable analogy. In a book that I currently edit on the embodied and cultural nature of mathematical knowledge, Laurie Edwards discusses an investigation where students use a Lego-like language to move geometric objects so that they coincide with another one at a different place on the plane. She points out that to the students, the operation is a movement of the object. For the mathematician, however, what happens is the mapping of the *x-y* plane back onto itself. To me, conceptual change researchers investigate how students change their conception in the plane of language, whereas I propose throughout this book a mapping of an enfolded form of language back onto language itself.

'How is this relevant to science education?', some readers might ask. Well, the answer should be evident by now, at this point of the book.[5] Each utterance constitutes material that enters subsequent utterances. But the former never enters the latter iden-

---

tically, or, in other words, the new utterance does not reproduce precisely and unambiguously the previous material, in which case we get something where the x at time t is identical to the x at time $t - 1$, that is, we have stasis rather than development. That is, we can think of language as reproducing itself but never identically: we are in a domain of λ where there are an infinite number of solutions and developments possible (to the far right in Fig. 10.1).

At the origin of this book, however, are not only questions of language and speaking but also some fundamental questions about learning. How can scientific talking and thinking emerge when students talk and think in pre- and un-scientific ways? How can this development occur when even the teacher talk only makes sense to students after having been translated into their natural language? How is development possible when all the students have available these very ways for dealing with new experiences, languages, and ways of thinking? In constructivist conceptual change theory, confrontation with contradictory evidence is supposed to lead students to a reconstruction. But all that students have available is their 'ur-material', their natural language (vernacular), which constitutes material, tool, and ground upon which the new ways emerge. That is, to translate this statement into conceptual change talk, there would be only 'misconceptions' as ground, material, and tools and without any remainder. The question is this: How can anything other than further 'misconceptions' emerge from this mix? This constructivist line of thinking and theorizing therefore does not take us out of the learning paradox. A second set of question concerns change. How can language change over time? Especially, how can language change from the everyday forms that students come with to their science courses to the scientific ones that the curriculum intends them to acquire as part of the schooling process? And how, in the course of history, does the language of science (education) itself change?

One of the theses that I maintain throughout this book is—following Mikhail Bakhtin and Lev Vygotsky—that the language changes *in speaking*, continuously, as students use it to deal with certain problems (which are not articulated as 'construction of knowledge'). As students engage in concept mapping, they know that they are working toward an organized arrangement without knowing what the resulting organization will be. The intention for this organization is available to them *only after they have achieved the organization and thereby the idiom that goes with it*. Students are therefore in a position that differs from the one in which craftspeople find themselves while constructing a house. The latter, knowing what the end result has to look like, have prepositioned a definite plan, tools, and materials. Even more important to me, the question about learning science is not merely a question about individual acquisition, construction, or whatever verb is used as a descriptive metaphor to denote the process. Rather, there is a problem of the *universal historicity* of the sciences themselves that is hardly addressed—if it is addressed at all—in the science education literature.[6]

One of the problems that Edmund Husserl poses during the earlier parts of the 20th century, in framing the crisis of the European sciences, is the question of the regeneration (reproduction) of the identity relation between the newly produced form of

---

6. But see my treatment of this question in Wolff-Michael Roth and Jennifer Thom, 'The Emergence of 3d Geometry from Children's (Teacher-guided) Classification Tasks', *Journal of the Learning Sciences*, Vol. 18 (2009), 45–99.

knowledge (by scientist, by learner) and the knowledge forms of the past.[7] This requires that the originally constituted practices embody the possibility of being evidently identical even under and following unlimited reproduction and transformation
in the historical unfolding of the field. Bakhtin deals with a similar problem when he
attempts to understand Dostoevsky's novels as a historical phenomenon. Bakhtin
shows that the origins of this novel form lie in the serio-comical literature already
existing at the time of the ancient Greek. This genre embodies some archaic elements
that (repeating a quote that I also mobilize in chapter 3) 'are preserved in it only
thanks to their constant *renewal*, which is to say, their contemporization. A genre is
always the same and yet not the same, always old and new simultaneously. Genre is
reborn and renewed at every new stage in the development of literature and in every
individual work of a given genre. This constitutes the life of the genre. Therefore even
the archaic elements preserved in a genre are not dead but eternally alive; that is, archaic elements are capable of renewing themselves. A genre lives in the present, but
always *remembers* its past, its beginning. Genre is a representative of creative memory
in the process of literary development. Precisely for this reason genre is capable of
guaranteeing the *unity* and *uninterrupted continuity* of this development'.[8]

Bakhtin's position on the development of language parallels his position on genre.
Thus, 'Language advances at the same time as the current [of verbal communication]
and is indissociable from it. In fact, language is not transmitted, it endures and per-
dures in the form of an uninterrupted process of evolution'.[9] This inherent capacity to
change is precisely what we need to understand how students, in the concrete practice
of their work, pull themselves out of the learning paradox, at their bootstraps so to
speak. If the word is hagiographic, if it allows one interpretation (sense) only, then it
cannot change, it does not have a reason to change because it always has already
achieved its final stage. This idea is equivalent to saying that eternal life is immobility
and death. The very advantage of the perspective on language I take and propose here
is that it not only allows learning to occur but also that speaking is in fact constitutive
of and co-extensive with change and learning.

Like Bakhtin, Husserl is concerned with the reproduction of a scientific field (he
uses geometry) through forces that are internal to the domain itself rather than external. An external explication for the tradition of a science is that its accomplishments,
knowledge, and theory are 'handed down' from generation to generation or that they
are appropriated and taken up by every new generation. An internal explication identifies structures in the very praxis of the sciences (which include, for Husserl, mathematics) that reproduces the field at the very instant it produces the field anew. Every
act of doing (thinking, speaking, experimenting) science is both a historically bounded
and an innovative creative act. We do not and cannot understand a phenomenon (scientific knowledge, science) historically if we consider it in terms of facts that come to

7. Edmund Husserl, 'Die Frage nach dem Ursprung der Geometrie als intentional-historisches Problem',
Revue internationale de philosophie, Vol. 1 (1939), 203–25.

8. Mikhail Bakhtin, *Problems of Dostoevsky's Poetics* (Minneapolis: University of Minnesota Press,
1984), 106.

9. Mikhaïl Bakhtine [V. N. Volochinov], *Le marxisme et la philosophie du langage: essaie
d'application de la méthode sociologique en linguistique* (Paris: Les Éditions de Minuit, 1977), 117.

be animated in the way that are the individual images of a movie reel. Playing the reel exhibits change, but this is only an impression of a dynamic of changes. This dynamic is produced on the outside of the images and does not, therefore, emerge from a mechanism internal to the phenomenon. That is, however inappropriate their language might be deemed, the students, in doing the concept map, in fact reproduce the very condition for the idiom of physics to reproduce and renew itself. Expression, as it were, is creative everywhere; and what is expressed is always inseparable from it. Any form of expression is a creative act; and as a creative act, it innovates as much as it aligns itself with the history of a field with respect to which the expression innovates. Thus, '[t]o give expression is not to substitute, for new thought, a system of stable signs to which assured forms of thought are linked, it is to ensure, by the use of words already used, that the new intention carries on the heritage of the past, it is in a single stroke to incorporate the past into the present, and weld that present to a future, to open a whole temporal cycle in which the "acquired" thought will remain present as a dimension, without henceforth our having to evoke or reproduce it'.[10] Moreover, speech therefore is a paradoxical phenomenon. In speaking, we attempt to join—by means of words with given numerous dictionary senses and already available significations—an intention that goes beyond itself in principle. In speaking, we modify, and, in the last instance, fix the sense of words. Therefore, the word translates itself in speaking, and inherently evolves into something that we have not intended.

As part of my original work on concept mapping, I suggested that students draw on the authority of the teacher, textbook, and student knowledge as conversational resources. Whereas this is correct to a certain extent, it does not describe the real effect that the teacher's utterances have on students' conversations. What is important to the development of the language is the paraphrasing that is at work, which itself changes language, where the question of authority is a mediating element in making the particular formulation weightier. There is no doubt that the concept map is the outcome of a collective effort involving all the students. But the students are not the sole reasons why we can see the statements students produce in the map. A more accurate way of articulating the issue might be to say that the possibilities for this concept map and the idiom that emerges with it already exist in language and *these* students realize one of the existing possibilities in *this* way, whereas other student groups realize the possibilities in different though similar ways. Language speaks, and students, in and through their collaborations on the concept-mapping task, bring about the unfolding of the possibilities that the language itself harbors. It is therefore not so much that the students that express *themselves* than that they bring to expression the possibilities of language. What we find is a recycling of forms of language that already exist, and subsequently are cycled, recycled, and renewed within each group. What the students thereby really do is this: they engage to see what language yields in and through their engagement.

---

10. Maurice Merleau-Ponty, *Phénoménologie de la perception* (Paris: Gallimard, 1945), 449–50.

Seeing (Hearing) What it Yields

In the constructivist ideology and rhetoric, students 'construct' 'meaning' and 'knowledge'—each term having to be bracketed, as the nature of their sense and referents remain to be established. More importantly, the constructivist and conceptual change rhetoric places an agential accent on the process of learning, even though we have all experienced the surprise when we realize that we have learned (discovered) something really new that we could not anticipate beforehand. If we cannot anticipate what it is that we are going to learn, if the very structure of my current knowing is inconsistent with my knowledge after the learning process, then we cannot orient toward that new structure. There is therefore an essentially passive moment to learning: the moment that has been articulated in the learning paradox. Learning has to be understood as a creative discovery process in which artists produce something that they inherently and by the very nature of the beast cannot anticipate. In an earlier work, I already begin to wrestle with this problem[11] and I further contribute here to the phenomenology of learning something that lies completely beyond the horizon of that which can be anticipated. In the present situation, I use as my starting point the phenomenology of the creative process of painting.

In painting, innovating painters make visible something that without them would have remained in the realm of the *unseen*. Whereas the invisible cannot be seen, the unseen is not seen at the moment. The unseen is not seen, like the unheard-of is not heard, and the unknown is not known. The unseen has never been seen and its existence therefore is unknown. The students who speak a language that is inappropriate from the perspective of the scientist insider does not know how to speak properly until that point when they actually speak it properly. To bring the unseen into the seen, the painter has to go to the undecidable boundary between the visible and the unseen and cross it. Feeling the way, groping in the dark, the painter brings the unseen into the light of the visible, into the clearing. The students in the concept-mapping task similarly feel around, try this word or that word without knowing the one that they will ultimately select or the one that will ultimately serve their purposes until *after* they will have selected it. They cannot see and understand the new structural possibilities until these reveal themselves, in a moment of insight, from what they have evolved. This is similar to the painter, who when sinking 'so far below the line of visibility as to find there an absolutely new visible—without exemplar, model, or precedent—none of our calmly assured spectacles of their reposed visibility would be able to guide it, nor determine what is finally going to appear—perhaps because no one is able to *see* ahead'.[12] The unseen remains unforeseen by the painter right up to the point of its appearance, when, in an instance of the syncope, the unseen has already retreated out of sight and nothing but the visible remains. Students, too, are oblivious to the ulti-

---

11. Wolff-Michael Roth, *Learning Science: Singular Plural Perspectives* (Rotterdam: Sense Publishers, 2006).

12. In this description, I follow the analysis of painting that J-L. Marion gives in a text unfortunately entitled in English 'What Gives', which is a translation of 'ce que cela donne', literally, 'that what it yields'. See Jean-Luc Marion, *The Crossing of the Visible* (Stanford, CA: Stanford University Press, 2004), 28.

mate form of the concept map and the language that goes with it right up to the moment that they place, temporarily, the final mark on the large paper sheet, their piece of art (from Lat. *ars*, technical skill). What they will have learned will remain unforeseen until the moment that the unseen makes itself visible to them. Producing a concept map and the new idiom that comes with it both in the map and surrounding the map is never the equivalent of rendering real something previously seen, something already anticipated, previously conceived and already perceived before it actually comes to the light of the day. If it were like this, then the production of new language would be, from the perspective of the speaking learner, only a reproduction of something already there. Only a monological inquiry would be required. I propose a radical alternative. In an allusion to Martin Heidegger[13], I suggest that the path to language has to be one that is laid in walking because there has been no path before. But in walking the garden-path, we do not always get to a clearing because we may be led up a garden-path.[14]

Learning something new that is not already enshrined in what I know therefore requires a mastery of letting the unseen and unheard-of burst into visibility and audibility by surprise and unpredictably. Every learner already brings this competence, this mastery, to the classroom. In creating, learners let burst onto the scene something more than the pre-delineated that they can anticipate, more than that they can desire or will. The new things that learners can do in and with language do not fill their expectations but rather something else: it fills the unexpected expectation. What they can do exceeds, is in excess to, what they can anticipate and expect. The creative act at work while the students engage in the concept-mapping task opens up a possibility that to that point was unanticipated, unthinkable, and impossible.

The language that emerges in and from the concept-mapping task, the largely unanticipated garden-path they lay in walking (talking), must itself provoke the intention that renders it visible (audible). As soon as the language exists, the intention for it emerges and becomes intelligible. Thus, competent speaking precedes its aim, which learners must bring into the realm of intentionality, since they neither do nor can expect it. This new language, which is but another English (German, French, and so on), has to note that its own previous life could not foresee it and therefore renders itself as something that cannot be aimed at. In the process of speaking, the new and unanticipated language seeps from the ground, the folds, and takes shape at the very inside of the language that does not foresee it, anticipate it beforehand. The new language arises from the ground of language, from the ground that grounds. This enables the forthcoming of the new without being able to anticipate the result.

Painters bring into visibility new forms, types that, because they are first, are archetypes. But such archetypes are not merely imposed by the painter or, in the present instance, by the language workers. These archetypes of speaking arise from language, the material and ground. Just as in painting, they arise from the outside with respect to the (knowledge) worker, the speaker and listener. In and through the concept-mapping

13. Martin Heidegger, *Gesamtausgabe Band 12: Unterwegs zur Sprache* (Frankfurt: Vittorio Klostermann, 1985).

14. Here, too, in the double-voicedness of the word garden-path, the reader can practically see the usefulness of dialogism and a Bakthinian approach to language and learning in science.

work, the new forms of language emerge from language rather than from inside the students. It is as if the language structured and traced itself on its own terms. The students are but willing hosts to whatever the language they work has to offer. The new ways of speaking suddenly emerge from the speaking of language. Language itself therefore is the canvas onto which new language appears, where it shows or rather gives itself. The curriculum in general and the concept-mapping task in particular constitute a frame—for the canvas—so that the truly new, the archetypes can triumph over the unseen by escaping from the linguistic ground. The unseen (unknown, unheard-of) still shows through, and at any one moment can become the topic, but it thereby exposes itself as the fertile ground upon which new linguistic archetypes come to be founded. The interesting thing here is that it is from language as the ground that the *new* (archetype) has appeared in an unanticipated way.

It is therefore the language that brings to life the consciousness for the new archetype and not the other way around. Language itself grants to consciousness the ability to make this crossing of the known and unknown. It also grants to consciousness the ability to climb from the unseen (unknown, unheard-of) toward the visible, known, and heard-of. In the concept-mapping task, new types of speaking emerge, and new archetypes are liberated and received. Language teaches us to be and become conscious, allowing us to see/know/hear in language itself that which we could not foresee/know/hear. Language shows itself, from itself, and for itself. To see/know/hear, in language, is to receive, since to appear is to give itself to be seen/known/heard. In building their concept map, revisable—liable to re-vision and revision—and to be redrawn at any instant, the students see what their own work yields. But they definitely are unable to anticipate what they will have seen, will come to know, and will have heard until after they have completed what they subsequently recognize to have been the last stroke. What their work yields, the new language and its intentions, *gives itself* only with the last stroke, which itself cannot be anticipated but is recognized as such only after the fact.

This discourse for learning in and through language, which I offer as an alternative to the intention-dependent 'construction' of 'knowledge', marries agency and passivity. The students have to engage in and through speaking and, in so doing, they bring forth new language, new archetypes of speaking. These they inherently could not have foreseen/known/heard. In the process, therefore, the new idiom with its archetypes *gives itself* as much as it is the result of a *creative act*, which, in its being a creative act, we inherently cannot predict. To see what it (the work of concept mapping) yields, the students have to do one more thing (step): they have to step/stand back. This is so because '"[t]o see what gives" means first of all: to stand back in order to better envisage the result of a stroke or a sketch that one has just inscribed upon the canvas. But this stepping back indicates above all that the one who has just physically put the color or lines on the surface of the canvas did not know, at the moment of effecting it, what he did, since, in order to see its effect, he must detach himself from his work, in order to learn afterward, what visible appears there. He thus admits that, despite all his work, it is not he who put in the work on the painting but the painting itself, which thus, humbly called to appear upon the occasion of the work, opens itself to the visible on its own initiative. In order to see what gives, it is thus necessary first to admit that this [que cela]—the painting—gives *itself* [*se* donne], and the pictorial act is restricted to a matter of welcome, recording and being undergirded by the support of a gift. To paint means: to await a donation'.[15] Learning above all means to await a donation, which here is a new language that language itself gives. To be a learner means this: to open oneself up to receive the donation. But the donation does not come without one's work.

Dialogism and the Discourse of Constructivism

Dialogism means that all topics come with language as a singular plural and a polyphony of voices within each word. Bakhtin thereby articulates the fundamentally dialogical nature of discourse such that anything that can be said also can be heard in multiple ways, as if different people had been saying different things. Even Immanuel Kant toward the end of his life is unable—though he does not realize it to the extent that Jean-Luc Nancy articulates the problem almost two centuries later—to construct his system of transcendental reason without 'the disjunction of places, dis-placement. The Kantian unity places itself always in plurality, and within it, discourse always forbids itself from being re-assimilated into a pure presence-to-itself'.[16] This displacement operates such that no word can be identical to itself, no word can have a pure presence to itself, and, therefore, harbors dialogism within itself. That is, the language perspective developed in this book is diametrically opposite to the way in which constructivism generally and conceptual change theory more specifically articulate language and with it its topic of knowing and learning.

In true, untransformed Kantian tradition, constructivists and conceptual change researchers do not deal with the question of language, as they generally take (theoretically, methodologically) language to be a transparent window on the (structures of the) mind. These researchers apparently do not accept the internal dialogism of the word, the very source of its polysemy, but build their entire frameworks on a medieval conception of the symbol, where the 'signifying-signified relationship is clear because of a homogenous culture'.[17] Thus, a scientific concept has only one (correct) 'meaning', and, whereas students are allowed to engage in constructive efforts, the scientists' definition of the concept is the outcome of the instructional process. There is only one sanctioned outcome, which finalizes the character of the language that students have to arrive at, unless they are willing to walk away with career-constraining low marks. That is, conceptual change researchers, despite their declared commitment to constructivism, enact the monologism of science. Any dialogue in the curriculum used from this perspective is inherently monological in the way that Bakhtin understands these terms. Kant attempts to contain the enigma of the dialogical nature of

---

15. Marion, op. cit. note 12, 44.
16. Jean-Luc Nancy, *The Discourse of the Syncope: Logodaedalus* (Stanford, CA: University of Stanford Press, 2008), 108.
17. Umberto Eco, *The Aesthetics of Chaosmos: The Middle Ages of James Joyce* (Cambridge, MA: Harvard University Press, 1989), 45.

language by invoking something like the immaculate conception as its own most (im-) proper composition. That is, conceptions are unsullied by the less than pure language required to articulate them in conversation.

One central question that remains unresolved on the part of conceptions and conceptual change research is that concerning the learning paradox. How should students, having available largely 'misconceptions' as their ground, material, and tool every come to 'construct' something that transcends the limitation of the incomplete or wrong? How—especially given the theory-dependent nature of perception—can students ever get off the ground that grounds them, their dispositions and (linguistic) practices? How can they even aim at (intent) something that lies in the dark beyond the clearing of their present possibilities? How can they get off the ground if the intention, if there were one, cannot be but framed in terms of the 'misconception'? It is not surprising, then, that the discourse of constructivism has been one of deficits, where the students' 'misconceptions' have to be eradicated through teaching sequences that begin with discrepant events and the provision of alternate, scientifically correct conceptions (or rather, to be more accurate, with appropriate concept names). The deficit perspective underlying the rhetoric of constructivism is evident in the fact that— contrary to Bakhtin's conception of the word—if there is a unique (correct) 'meaning' of a concept, then any other 'meaning' is inherently incorrect. Constructivists do not relate or see related the question of the historicity of the sciences and the ontogenetic development that every human being undergoes in everyday face-to-face interactions with others. Historical approaches (Bakhtin, Vygotsky, Husserl, Merleau-Ponty) relate all these developmental levels, for individual development cannot be thought independently of the moment-to-moment evolution of praxis and cannot be understood outside of the students' relation to the historicity of and history-producing culture.

Conceptual change researchers suggest that 'learners need to be able to make different representations of entities to make difficult concepts intelligible. Learning always involves some ways of representing information and science teachers use different representational techniques such as voice, writing, and gestures in the classroom to communicate ideas to students. Representations are ways to communicate ideas or concepts by representing them either externally—taking the form of spoken language (verbal), written symbols (textual), pictures, or physical objects or a combination of these forms—or internally when thinking about these ideas'.[18] This quote shows how in conceptual change theory, words and (external) representations are thought of as vehicles independent of thought. They make concepts intelligible. Learning involves the representation of information. And the external representations are merely entities to communicate ideas and concepts. In everyday authentic situations, however, where language occurs for the first time and is unfolding, speech does not translate ready-made thought but accomplishes it. In cultural-historical activity theory, too, thought is not simply expressed and put into words but comes into existence through speech. Conceptual change theory, as expressed in the quote, places itself in direct opposition to a phenomenological formulation of our everyday experience of how humans expe-

18. David Treagust and Reinders Duit, 'Conceptual Change: A Discussion of Theoretical, Methodological and Practical Challenges for Science Education', *Cultural Studies of Science Education*, Vol. 3 (2008), 297–328, 298.

rience themselves in being. Thus, we must recognize that thought, in the speaking subject, is not a representation, that is, that it does not expressly posit objects or relations. Speakers do not think before speaking, not even while speaking but their speech is their thought. Paraphrasing Maurice Merleau-Ponty, we might say that there is no reason to contest that the expressive operation realizes or brings about signification and does not merely translate it. It is no different, despite the appearance, for the expression of thought by means of words. Thought neither comes from the interior nor exists outside the world and words. They are, if anything at all, one and the same thing. Along the lines of Bakhtin, we might say that ideological activity, the content to be expressed and its external objectification, are created out of one and the same material, for there is no ideological activity without expression and no expression without ideological activity. This is not really something new but merely a direct consequence of the dual, internally dialogical nature of the word, which, as sign, is a relation sublating its internal contradiction between its material body and its ideological content.

In direct opposition to the framing in conceptual change theory, separate representations are not required in understanding new ideas. Thus, in the context of teacher–student relations (chapter 4), I introduce the idea that a new language already has to be known to the learner. Or, in other words, it means that learners, in some way have to have, within the horizon of their current world, the possibility for understanding a new word that they have almost but not yet in their grasp. For to 'understand the words of another person, it is clear that his vocabulary and syntax must be "already known" to me. But that does not mean that words do their work by arousing in me 'representations' associated with them, and of which the assemblage eventually reproduce in me the original "representation" of the one who speaks'.[19]

In conceptual change theory, students are asked to 'strongly' or 'radically' restructure their concepts. To do so, students have to be aware of the concepts *as* concepts and engage in a restructuring effort that they cannot intent because doing so requires the final result. What conceptual change research has not shown is (a) how the students, *with the means, grounds, and tools that they have available at the time*, do the actual reconfiguration, (b) what students' actual rather than supposed problematic is, and (c) how they bootstrap themselves out of the learning paradox that the conceptual change approach itself creates. Questions have to be raised particularly because the students may not have any structures so that they would have to bootstrap into some sort of stable system where there is nothing but chaos before (e.g., more than six alternative verbs for connecting two concept names, many of which are incompatible). Conceptions and conceptual change researchers are concerned with reaching a state of stability, the one that is consistent with the current scientific cannon. It is not (or less) concerned with the process of change and how student learning expresses something about the human capacity to learn more generally, especially as it concerns the learning of science.

I am on Vygotsky's side in thinking that mind is as much in society as society is in the mind. Any higher psychological function is external, is a form of social relation

---

19. Merleau-Ponty, op. cit. note 10, 214.

between two people before it becomes anything an individual comes to embody. This is so because 'persons, in that they are heard to be speaking natural language, *somehow* are heard to be engaged in the objective production and objective display of commonsense knowledge of everyday activities as observable and reportable phenomena. We may ask what it is about natural language that permits speakers and auditors to hear, and in other ways to witness, the objective production and objective display of commonsense knowledge, and of practical circumstances, practical actions, and practical . . . reasoning as well?'[20] Society in the mind and mind in society, therefore, are but two ways of understanding the close relationships that exist between learning, developing, and cultural-historical change: '*We become* ourselves through others. In it purely logical form, the essence of the process of *cultural development* consists precisely in this'.[21] With Vygotsky and Bakhtin I am taking a similar tack suggesting that social psychology is not situated somewhere within the person but exists, to the contrary, completely outside—in the word, the gesture, the act. There is nothing unexpressed within the human being, interiorized. Everything is on the surface, everything is in the exchange, everything is in the material, and principally in the verbal material. Conceptual change research does not take this relationship into account, for it would be forced to articulate the very 'unscientific' and 'prescientific' understandings students come with to school as a manifestation of society, and therefore, as the possible itself, and thus as an explication why students are so 'resistant to change'. It is not that the students resist to the change, it is society (culture) as a whole and its language that resist the monologizing efforts of constructivist and conceptual change science (educators). This society (culture) perpetuates and makes possible the very unscientific and prescientific ways of talking about the natural world that is so decried by the practitioners of conceptual change.

Conceptual change theory treats and theorizes what calls 'the detached content of the cognitional act [which] comes to be governed by its own immanent laws, according to which it then develops as if it had a will of its own'.[22] This is consistent with the Kantian approach to thinking about thinking, which attempted to erect a system whereby metaphysical reason constructs itself without a foundation other than reason. Such an endeavor truly takes the skills of the master craftsman, the epitome of which is Daedalus, so that it comes as no surprise that Jean-Luc Nancy refers to Kant as the *Logodaedalus*. This approach, however, comes with the danger that individual human beings in flesh and blood are squeezed out of our research. In such research, the Being is controlled by autonomous psychological laws within which emotions and motivations are no longer present. Kant himself realizes that he loses intelligibility with his terse approach, which requires everyday language that he so despises. But a passionate account of how to provide (construct) an ethnographically adequate account of events suggests that we must articulate the same hesitant and momentary contexts that the natives (students, teacher) are displaying to each other and are using to organize their

---

20. Harold Garfinkel and Harvey Sacks, 'On Formal Structures of Practical Actions', in *Ethnomethodological Studies of Work* edited by Harold Garfinkel (London: Routledge, 1986), 160–93, 163.

21. Lev S. Vygotsky, 'Concrete Human Psychology', *Soviet Psychology*, Vol. 27, No. 2 (1989), 53–77, 56, emphasis added.

22. Mikhail M. Bakhtin, *Toward a Philosophy of the Act* (Austin: University of Texas Press, 1993), 7.

concerted behavior. We have to understand that the phonetic gestures human beings deploy realize, for speakers and listeners, a certain structuration of experience, a certain modulation of existence, exactly like the behavior of the body invests the objects that surround it with thematics for others as much as for the self. This allows us to understand the Bakhtinian notion of 'theme', which is the place of the vocal gesture in the world that we experience and constitute. The (verbal, hand, body) gesture constitutes and communicates this orientation in the world, in which the individual is but one of the constitutive moments.

There are also different perspectives on the timing of change and the mechanism that underlie the change. In constructivism and conceptual change theory, changed forms of activity follow development: once the theories have been reconstructed, students will be talking about the natural world in a different way. In the cultural-historical activity theoretic approach that I take here following Bakhtin and Vygotsky, activity *leads* development. This means that engagement in activity and new forms of talking actually *precede* development. This articulation thereby brings together the idea of the zone of proximal development, which describes the difference between solo performance and performance in a collective (guided) effort, with the idea that all psychological functions exist in and as social relations. These are experienced and participated in prior to development, and in fact, circumscribe the very content that this development will have.

We also need to move away from talking|thinking about learning and cognition as if human beings were computers. Human beings do not process information and respond to input from the outside world. Our students, as all human beings, always and already find themselves in a world full of signification. But significations are not merely of conceptual nature. We find underneath the conceptual signification of words, an existential signification, which is not merely translated by words but which inhabits them and is inseparable from them. The conceptual signification is Bakhtin's signification at the lower limit (sense) and the existential signification is Bakhtin's theme. When students work together on something like the collaborative concept-mapping task, they communicate. To complete the task, they talk not only about their ideas (content) but also about the current status of the task, about what remains to be done, or about their rationale for making one move over another. In so doing, their bodily states are reproduced and change, which we see expressed in the tapes presented here as laughter, anger, protest, compassion, hurriedness, and so on. In the process, the participants in the task therefore *provide each other with a sense of the task's status*, and they provide the researcher with that sense as well. The protocols that I collected in the form of the video- and audiotapes provide evidence for the collective and intelligible reasoning that the students engage in for themselves and for others, for the attribution of sense to individual events or objects, and for their efforts in convincing one another that these objects and events involved are consistent and coherent. What we therefore witness is a collective activity where anything relevant to understanding is made available publicly, for every participant and every eavesdropper (with the same cultural competencies) to be understood.

When I did this research originally, I was writing|thinking about concept maps along the lines of theories and concepts that I had come across in literature on the social studies and social constructivist studies of science. One of the concept words in use is that of *tools for social thinking*. When I analyzed for the first time the lesson at the heart of this book, I thought about concept mapping as a 'process of construction' in the course of which the emerging concept map becomes a tool for social thinking. It takes on, or so I thought, the characteristics of sketches in design engineering which serve both as interactive communication tool and as and individual thinking tool. Like the flexibility observable in sketches, I thought that concept maps were serving in both these capacities, which allowed the two functions to overlap. I thought of concept maps as thinking tools for groups that distributed cognition across people and artifacts. Because these maps are constructed in collaboration, they serve as a means of organizing the task, its environment, and the final product. This is achieved, because the emerging structure of the map is part of a shared problem space in a double sense. First, it permits students to work simultaneously on the same problem; and, especially at the beginning of a session, strict turn-talking rules do not *determine* the interactions. Second, the emerging design also provides for a taken-as-shared conceptual space in which the participants can refer to common objects by means of words, drawings, or gestures. The participants' individual involvement is indicated by their attention to the objects and to other participants in this shared space.

Throughout this book, we see the task and its particulars, the emerging network of concept words, as a joint focus. What easily confuses the issue is that words on the paper slips and the words of language cover the same terrain. It is not accurate to say, as I have done then, that 'talk and representation are co-extensive, organized in and around the design of the emerging concept map'. Rather, an always different and heterogeneous language contributes on multiple levels in the completion of the task: material (object), tool, and ground. But it is only part object, part tool, and part ground, because all the other aspects of the world also have mediating function not only in getting this task completed but also in reproducing and transforming the participating human beings. Thus, I show how, while the students talk physics, the everyday world, with its forms of language and concerns, suddenly seeps through and emerges from the cracks in the façade of the seriousness of the official curriculum. Some educators speak of code switching when students speak in their mundane, native, everyday language, including laughter, words, double meanings, and so on, a language that the official ideology of science does not admit. This characterization is not a fruitful one because it places monologic scientific discourse and dialogic carnival language at the same level, when in fact scientific language constitutes a dialect, an outcrop of language in all its heterogeneity and hybridity more generally. This outcrop, as any technical language, bottoms out and is grounded in natural language and the world with which it is entwined. The scientific idiom changes because of its embeddedness in and confrontation with the vernacular that students bring to class rather than because of its confrontation with the material world (nature). In fact, its own claim to truth rigidifies the scientific idiom, and, once truth is obtained and ascertained, change no longer appears necessary.

At the time of the original research, I came to the conclusion that the process of mapping concepts in collaborative activity may be more important than the concept map itself. I thought that the concept map was only the final product, an expression and account of the labor that has gone into producing it. Now this is precisely the crux. We do not learn because of the products that result from our task engagement but we learn because the labor itself changes us as we engage. In labor we expend energy, which, as it is produced in our bodies also changes these bodies (including the brain) materially. And these changes are cumulative and path dependent. The traces that labor leaves subsequently mediate the ways in which we engage in other tasks, including the ways in which we speak. Throughout this book I show how students' talk changes, both at the microlevel scale of the unfolding praxis and at the longer-term scales of this task—as observed in the case of the quantum.

Reflexive Coda

I end this book on and with a reflexive note. A good theory of learning opens our understanding to the very fact of our own learning in and through research and therefore opens up an understanding of the nature of our theories themselves. We do not understand a science on the basis of historical facts. We do not understand a science at all unless we make thematic the general sense upon which anything scientific is founded. That is, to truly understand the reproduction and historical development of science, in and through its tradition and tradition-generating praxis at every single moment in time and at every single place (including school science), we have to study the enormous structural a priori that enables (makes possible) culture generally and science more specifically. Our own science—the one of science education—is but one among many in constant evolution. This evolution can be understood and theorized with the approach to language that I present here. But one paradigm has held the community much stronger in grips than any other: conceptions and conceptual change and the constructivist ideas on which it built. A linguistic framing of knowing and learning has been proposed nearly two decades ago. But there has been resistance within our field to adopt language-based theories more fully. One of the perplexing facts in the history of science education is that conceptual change research itself resists change in the face of obvious discrepant evidence. Given the empirical evidence that the conceptual change model cannot explain some very salient facts—the students' resistance to change being one—why would it be astonishing that teachers are unwilling to take up conceptual change?

The language perspective outlined here has the potential to be fruitful, as it allows us to understand the effect of translating both within a language and between languages. Thus, the difficulties embodied in internal and external translations also mediate the work of educational researchers. For example, reading philosophical and psychological texts in three languages, I realize daily the differences in translated texts, all claiming to be translations of the same source. But as I show, between language translations are concrete instances of translations that also occur inside a language, such as when we say, 'what I really mean is', and then continue to say something but in different words. In both cases, how sure can we be that the target expression (in another language, in the same language) is the same? What is it, therefore, that Bakhtin or Vygotsky have said in their native Russian? What is it that Derrida or Ricœur or Husserl have meant in their native tongues (French, German) when they wrote what was subsequently published? Does it even make sense to ask such questions given that any text may be read or heard in different ways by native speakers of the source language? Does it therefore make sense to set oneself tasks such as teaching *the* language of science in the way some educators appear to do?

In the course of presenting the analyses and theory development, I make use of the same means that I report the participants as using in completing their task. Thus, I quote other, great scholars directly or use indirect speech, thereby drawing on authorities much in the way the students do during their concept-mapping task. But I always do so in and through my own voice. In fact, I constructed this book such that the quotes no longer stand apart from my own text in separate paragraphs but blend them with my own writing. In yet other cases, the sources of my original learning have forgotten, though their mark still is in the words I use and that now have taken on an additional flavor, the one that I impose upon them. I also use multiple communicative forms, for example, video offprints that point to my videotapes in the same way that students pointing to an image in their book that they thereby make part of their discourse. In the same way that their vernacular is the ground for constituting their concept-mapping work, the language in this book is very much rooted in our everyday language—I might have been charged with using jargon had I drawn too much on the on dialects of other disciplines that I am familiar with.

I suggest implicitly and explicitly that the language perspective outlined here generally and the principle of dialogism more specifically allow us to handle a segment of our reality better than do constructivism and conceptual change theory. This, however, does not mean that I consider this work to constitute closure and finalization on the questions of learning. I hold it with Richard Rorty, who suggests that to say that one's previous language is inappropriate for dealing with some part of the world simply means that one is now, having learned a new dialect, able to handle that segment more readily. Because of the dialogic nature of language, I assume that this, our language about language and learning, too, will evolve. The new language we will be speaking some ten years from now will certainly differ, transformed by the very dialogism that it uses to theorize language and learning. It is for this reason that I can be critical of (radical, social) constructivism, because their voices are opponents to my own, allowing mine to undergo continual evolution as it engages with them. Dialogism does not mean that I have to accept or take up the alien dialects and voices, but that my own ideas and language do not seek finalization. The history of my ideas, as embodied in my own scholarly work over the past two decades, shows that there has never been a finalizing tendency in my orientation to the world, allowing my discourse and me to change. The language perspective presented here, therefore, is reflexive, in that it anticipates its own transformation, a transformation of which the trajectory cannot be anticipated. I challenge anyone to tell us how we will understand knowing and learning ten or 20 years hence. Just as we more or less abandoned the discourses of behaviorism and cognitivism (information processing), we may be witnesses to the disappearance of (radical, social) constructivism together with the emergence of new idioms more suitable to the salient problematics and sensitivities that our engagements with the world come with. We do not know what the future will bring, though we might anticipate, given our knowledge about the historical sluggishness of educational discourses to change, the changes not to be of the revolutionary type. I end with a call to an unending dialogue, for

> When dialogue ends, everything ends. Thus dialogue, by its very essence, cannot and must not come to an end.[23]

---

23. Bakhtin, op. cit note 8, 252.

Appendix

In the following I provide the institutional context and the complete transcript of the concept-mapping session. The transcript was initially prepared while I was a high school physics teacher and department head of science. For the purposes of this book I verified the entire transcript and made corrections—to the extent that the deteriorating sound on the videotape and on the audiotape allowed this.

Institutional Context

The data was collected as part of two-year study on concept mapping in my 11th- and 12th-grade physics classrooms. The student participants were enrolled either in a junior year, advanced physics or in a senior year physics course. Although generally college bound, the students from this private school in central Canada most often select business and liberal arts as their majors following high school graduation. During each of the two school years covering the study, there were three sections of the junior level course for a total of 46 and 48 students. During the same time, there were 29 and 25 students enrolled in the senior level course. The 25 senior students in the second year all came from the 46 juniors from the previous year. The seniors from the first year of the study had also been introduced to concept mapping during their junior year of study. I was the teacher for all participating classes.

Concept mapping as small-group in-class activity was scheduled regularly as a means for the students to review and organize all the concepts they had studied within a unit. These concept mapping sessions thus followed a series of activities that included laboratory experiments, reading assignments, questions, word problems, computer simulations, brief teacher presentations, and whole-group discussions. During each concept-mapping session, I videotaped one group from the beginning to the end of the lesson with a stationary VHS camera. Over the course of a school year, I followed some groups for the year to get a sense for long-term changes in the activity, but I also switched to new groups to be able to construct patterns across groups. In the first year of study, I generally videotaped students during regular class time but video-taped some groups also in specially scheduled sessions after school hours. Because of my interest in concept mapping as a classroom activity, I videotaped only in-class sessions during the second year of study.

During each such class, the students took one 60-minute period to complete a concept map containing from 20 to 35 concepts; when there was less than the full period available, the number of concepts may have been as low as 15. The concepts were always selected from the students' main textbook—class sets of two other textbooks were also available to students as resource. I took concepts that appeared in the relevant chapter of the students' textbook. The terms generally included those that the textbook authors had printed in boldface type. The concept-mapping task therefore allowed students to grapple with the unit as a whole. The theory underlying concept mapping suggests that students who demonstrate a good integration of all concepts into a unified whole understand well the topic presented in and by the textbook.

Each group received a stack of paper slips, about 1.5 inches by 2 inches in size. On each of these slips students copied the concepts on the labels from a list that I provided. In some cases, particularly during the first year of study, I imprinted the slips with the relevant concepts in advance. Before actually drawing a concept map on paper, students used these slips to place the inscribed concepts into a hierarchical arrangement and to discuss possible linkages between pairs of concepts. Once group members were satisfied with their arrangement of concept names, they used a sheet of 14-inch-by-17-inch paper for transcribing their organization and inscribing their concept map.

The students in the participating physics classes usually worked together in groups of three or four individuals. Each group began the concept mapping activity by grouping the concepts. In many groups, two, three, and even four students moved concepts at the same time, talking as much to themselves as they did to others. Through this process, they arrived at the first rough classifications of concepts into groups and hierarchies. They then went into further detail with their outline, pushing concepts back and forth, trying different hierarchical orders, arranging and re-arranging paper slips. New local arrangements constrained them to regroup the concepts from other sub-groups. Shifts surrounding one concept name often required shifts in the vicinity of others. Because the concept names were printed on paper slips that could be moved about, these frequent changes in the arrangement were done easily, much more easily than if the students had tried to draw their concept maps immediately on paper. This I had found out several years earlier while first using the technique in my science class-rooms, when I felt students were 'going nowhere' with their attempts to immediately inscribe concept names on the large paper sheets.

The student discussions generally were animated. The students proposed, talked about, negotiated, and defended their positions. In some groups, even with the preliminary ordering, students made a sketch to see a preliminary map with links before they committed themselves to a final version of the concept map.

In this book, I only draw on one concept-mapping session from its very beginning to the end. The part during which students arranged the concepts on the slips and discussed linkages and hierarchies lasted around 35 to 40 minutes (analyzed in chapters 3

Tab. A1. The concept words involved in the task

LIGHT	ELECTRONS	PAIR PRODUCTION
QUANTUM	PHOTON	PHOTOELECTRIC EFFECT
COMPTON EFFECT	WORK FUNCTION	DEBROGLIE WAVELENGTH
COMPLEMENTARITY	DIFFRACTION	THRESHOLD FREQUENCY
X-RAYS	WAVE	MATTER WAVES
PLANCK'S CONSTANT		

to 5). At this stage I tended to encourage students to copy their concept arrangements onto the sheet of paper, and to begin fixing the links that they had arrived at. The students spent the final 20 minutes of the class transferring the concept arrangement onto large sheets of paper, drawing links, and writing the linking words to form propositions (analyzed in chapter 6). Even during this phase, students talked in animated fashion, they argued and they discussed. Toward the end of the class, the students often had to rush to complete the assignment by the end of the period.

The video and audiotapes reveal little, if any side talk at all, that is, talk about topics other than those related to the concepts at hand. In the tape that I draw on for the purpose of this book, the three participating students engage in three brief exchanges that pertain to an argument that they had in their dormitory about racist remarks that someone had made. During my early work, I omitted these exchanges from the analysis. Now, after having read Mikhail Bakhtin, I have come to realize that there are important lessons that we can learn from precisely these omitted transcripts and from other aspects—including jokes and laughter—that are topics seldom analyzed and discussed in the research literature.

I complete this description with a remark on the topic of the conversation that produces the concept mapping lesson and the final concept map: the quantum nature of light. The terms that the three participating students—Ken, Miles, and Ralf—are working on putting into a concept map appear in Table A1, and a glossary of the terms that students use and talk about is provided in the next section. I chose this lesson for use in this book partially because light is a phenomenon with properties that refract the idea of dialogism. Historically, light initially had been understood and theorized as a wave phenomenon. There have been many experiments and experiences that were consistent with the wave nature of light. Thus, we understand reflection of light on a mirror or the refraction of light in a prism or lens when we think of it as a wave.

There are also phenomena involving light that we cannot understand when we think of it using the wave as a model. For example, in a photographic camera there is a light meter. This light meter is based on what Albert Einstein has come to term the *photoelectric effect*, which denotes the observation that shining light on a metal leads to an electrical current. It turns out that the intensity of the light does not matter, but the wavelength of the light (blue versus red) does. Einstein then suggested thinking of light energy as existing in packages (quanta), which are referred to as *photons*. Light therefore sometimes exhibits particle character (photon) and sometimes it exhibits wave character. The question whether it *is* a wave or particle does not get us any further. It is best, as the physicists of the early 20th century showed, to think of light in terms of the *complementarity* of wave and particle. Light, as the word in Bakhtin's approach, is non-self-identical, which leads to the fact that it sometimes expresses itself as a wave and sometimes as a particle (quantum).

Glossary of Physics Terms

The students featuring in this book are working on a concept map following a unit on the wave-particle duality of light. To assist non-physics readers, the following glossary may serve as a refresher of their high school physics course. A term rendered in italic in one text also appears as main entry.

Complementarity Physicists suggest that we can think of electromagnetic phenomena (*light*, infra-red, UV, *X-rays*, *gamma rays*) and microscopic matter as waves or as particles (*photons*, *quanta*). Which way (model) to think we choose depends on the experiment that we conduct, for the same phenomenon exhibits different properties (wave, particle). For example, to understand a camera, we require both models. To understand how light is refracted in the lenses, we need the wave model; to understand how electrons are released and give rise to an electric current that is used to meter the light, we need the particle model.

Compton Effect When *X-rays* are directed onto a thin metal film, one can observe on the other side a stream of electrons and X-rays. But these X-rays have a lower energy (frequency) and come at an angle that complements the angle of the current of electrons. This experiment can be explained when X-rays are thought of as *photons*.

De Broglie wavelength Just as electromagnetic waves exhibit particle-like, *quantized* behavior, matter (*electrons*, protons, etc.) may exhibit wave behavior. The wavelength λ (or frequency f) of such a material particle can be calculated using Einstein's energy-mass equation ($E = mc^2$) and the energy of a *photon* ($E = hf$). Because the wavelength λ and the frequency f of a wave are inversely related ($\lambda = c/f$, where c is speed of light), the mass m of a particle is equivalent to a wave of a certain frequency (wavelength).

Diffraction When electromagnetic radiation (*light*, *X-rays*) interacts with matter (double slit, grating, regularly spaced atoms in a crystal), it will change its direction and, under certain conditions, gives rise to interference phenomena when the peaks and valleys of the wave come to cancel or reinforce one another.

Electrons are material particles or clouds with a charge of -1. Their mass is very small. They are the constituents of electric current and also embody the negatively charged parts of matter.

Gamma rays are part of the electromagnetic spectrum but have even more energy (higher frequency) than *X-rays*. Under certain conditions, gamma rays behave as if their energy came in the form of bundles, that is, their energy is quantized.

Light is the visible part of the electromagnetic spectrum, which, in certain experiments, behave as if their energy came in bundles, as *quanta*. Its speed is denoted by means of the letter c.

Pair production occurs when an electromagnetic wave has sufficient energy, so that it may, upon interacting with matter, decompose and give rise to a pair of particles, for example, an electron and a positron. The waves generally fall into the gamma ray range. According to Einstein, the energy E associated with a mass m is $E = mc^2$, where c is the speed of light. The energy of the electromagnetic wave—calculated according to the equation $E = hf$ (see *quantum*)—has to be at least as much as the energy of the two complementary particles produced in *pair production*.

Phonon A phonon is a periodic and coupled movement of atoms or molecules in a crystal lattice. These movements therefore constitute a wave, which, according to the wave-particle complementarity, can also be thought of as quanta because their energy comes in multiples of a certain base quantity.

Photoelectric effect When light is shone on certain metals, one can detect an electrical current. That is, *light* is able to release *electrons* from the metal. When physicists attempt to use the wave model of light, they cannot explain the instant onset of the current as soon as the light beam is turned on. Einstein showed that thinking about light energy as coming in bundled form allows an explanation of the phenomenon. The amount of energy (work) required to get an electron just released is called *work function*.

Photon is the term for *light* that has a certain amount of energy that exists in bundled (*quantized*) form.

Planck's constant is a universal constant, generally denoted by the letter h, that appears together with *quantized* phenomena, for example, the energy of electromagnetic waves, the energy levels of electrons orbiting a nucleus, and so on.

Quantum (plural quanta) is a term that refers to the fact that some phenomena come in discrete form. *Light* can be thought of as coming in little energy packages. This way of thinking is required to understand, for example, the working of a light meter in a camera, where each quantum is thought to knock out an *electron* causing a current. Thinking of this phenomenon in terms of a light wave would lead to a contradiction: it would take a long time until the wave has transmitted sufficient energy to the electron before it could make the jump that frees it from the metal. The energy E of a quantum is calculated as $E = hf$, where h is *Planck's constant* and f is the frequency of the electromagnetic wave.

Threshold frequency is the minimum frequency of *light* required to produce the *photoelectric effect* in a given metal. If the frequency is higher, then the *electrons* released have a certain amount of kinetic energy. If the frequency is less, no electrons are observed at all. The metal might simply warm up, as can be observed from the hot body of a car left in plain sunlight.

X-rays are of the same nature as *light* but have much more energy. One can equivalently say that (a) X-rays have a much higher frequency than light, (b) each X-ray photon has a greater momentum, or (c) the wavelength of X-rays is much shorter than that of visible light.

Work function is the amount of energy (work) required to release an *electron* from a metal in the *photoelectric effect*. This amount of energy can be calculated according to $W = hf$, where f is the minimum or *threshold frequency* of *light* that produces the effect. Thus, if the particular metal were to release electrons when a beam of blue light is shone on it, then there would be nothing observed with red light, even if one were to take a powerful beam of red light and even if this powerful beam were to shine for hours, days, or months.

Transcription Conventions

The following transcription conventions have been used. They are essentially those that are common in the tradition of conversation analysis.

`((inaudible))`	inaudible text of uncertain number of words
`((mumbling))`	transcriber comment
`((05:36))`	time stamp on the video recording
`(??)`	inaudible, number of words about number of question marks
`,?;.`	punctuation marks are used to indicate pitch toward end of an audible unit: slightly rising, strongly rising, slightly falling, and strongly falling
`[photon ]` `[quantum]`	square brackets indicate beginning and end of overlapping speech
`(.)`	clearly audible pause of unmeasured length
`(5.4)`	pause in speech measured in seconds
`quan:ta`	colon marks lengthening of sound by about 1/10th of a second per colon
`x=rays`	equal sign indicates connected sound for clarification purposes; no connections indicated for apostrophe between noun and 's' in genitives or for apostrophe in shortening of 'is' to 's'.
`((*))`	Marker that matches the transcript with the video offprint provided.
`<<impatiently>complementary>`	Transcriber comment characterizing the speech enclosed in the triangular brackets.
`<<f>who>`	Forte, louder than normal speech volume.

Lesson Transcript

There are lines in this transcript that were not part of the original electronic transcript (though they were part of the original hand-written version) and analyses. Because they are out of the original sequence numbering the turns at talk, I inserted them using the letters of the alphabet to number the additional lines in the transcriptions (e.g., 011a, b).

```
001 R: plancks constant is (??) ((mumbling)); photoelectric
       effect is is pair production.
```

002 K: put that under quantum.
003 R: what is quantum.
004 K: what quantum means; are light is a particle instead of
       waves
005 R: but that is quanta;
006 K: yea; its like this;
007 R: and its quanta, its the singular form.
008 K: yes i see what you mean. wave and quantum are an
       instant;
009 R: quantum is part of a wave and then, photon, photon and
       quantum is the same thing.
010 K: they are the same. no no; i am saying if we are going
       downward, this is going down, thats ((wave)) one, thats
       ((quantum)) another theory, and this ((photon)) is the
       third theory, it goes here. ((below quantum))
011 R: what about this one. quantum is part of the wave.
       quantum is the part that its the end- no. no.
  a M: ((off camera but next to it)) oh jesus; is he filming
       us?
  b Y: yeap.
  c T: yea.
012 K: yea; its different; there is a wave theory,
013 M: ((in the background)) ?? dont worry about it.
014 K: electron is a particle and not a quantum.
015 R: no; there is a wave theory and particle theory but,
016 K: but thats only one transmitted by waves.
017   (4.42)
018 R: quantum says that a wave has not a continuous band of
       energy.
019 M: yea, this should come in front because of those- are
       also discovered first.
020 K: and this ((light)) is,
021 M: no remember, we screwed that up the last time the wave
       goes [on top.]
022 R: [wave go]es on top; thats right.
023 M: okay. photon.
024 R: in pair production are all the different things here,
025 K: they are different.
026 R: photoelectrons.
027 K: get all the;
028 M: i am so sweaty.
029 K: complementary?
030   (.)
031 R: complementary?
032 M: look around the guy
033 K: complementarity.
034 M: well what type? uh, jesus, we should put x=rays up here
       with the light, like that. should we put x=rays there?
035 R: yea, okay. work function (.) if work function (.)
       [photon and],
036 M: [we need   ] something,
037 R: quantum are the same.

```
038 M: no; this one ((photon)) should be a bit lower.
039 R: why? its the same; they are exactly the same.
040 M: this one was, this one done by planck; and this one,
041 R: yea; but this is essentially the same.
042 M: because, i just came back from playing frisbee.
043 R: look at this here.
a   M: fuck its all sweat ((Ralf turns to him))
b   R: (???) ((punches M at leg, under table))
044 M: i just came back played frisbee, so i=m so tired.
a   R: you dont have to drip all over.
045 K: complementarity?
046 T: complementarity?
047 R: was in the theory ((turns pages))
048 T: what did it have to do with bohrs principle?
       complementarity.
049 M: i can=t remember that at all.
050 R: i heard something about,
051 M: okay threshold frequency. hey- we should put the work
       function; he can=t find it; put the work function and
       threshold frequency together because they are related;
       but,
052 R: there is no energy here. ((turning pages in book))
053 M: doc, can we add terms? (1.70) doc? (0.75) can we add
       terms?
054 T: yes you can.
055 M: yes (0.40) because we want the energy? ((189.5))
056    (0.34)
057 T: energy; yea.
058 R: god, what a-
059 M: i am swimming in sweat in this- ((still turning pages))
060 K: the index, is not in it, yea; yea; okay.
061 M: we can put diffraction-
062 R: diffraction was in;
063 M: is kind of,
064 K: no.
065 R: ((mumbles))
066 M: diffraction is totally out of place, it doesnt belong
       here.
067 K: where, diffraction?
068 M: i dont think it belongs here.
069 K: no, yea, photon can diffract off all sorts of things,
       cant they?
070 T:((Coming from another group)) have you got
       complementarity?
071 K: no; its not even in the index.
072 R: concept;
073 T: what was the whole chapter, what were the last two
       chapters about?
074    (2.46)
075 M: quantum, well, the last chapter about quantum and
       photon and,
076 T: yea, and that before?
```

077 R: oh, i think that is the duality of wave.
078 T: exactly.
079 K: oh. the duality of wave;
080 T: so you are talking, complementary means that the two::,
       that wave can have both, but not both at the same time.
081 K: ah; [so thats],
082 T: [either] one or the other and complementarity
       means (.) either one or the other.
((04:22))
083 R: and you have to decide which one you want to use.
084 M: ah, okay.
085 T: yea, thats right, but it depends on your particular
       experiment
086 M: no, it should go-
087 K: no, go under light, perhaps
088 T: remember that you can show, you can do experiments that
       show wave [character.]
089 K: [are x=rays].
089 K: [are x=rays].
090 T: but the same experiment doesnt show both. ((00:05:15
       Audio))
091 K: are the x=rays proven particles, are x=rays both energy
       and particles because complementarity- if thats proven
       as energy and the particle can go over this; but if its
       not, then we go with light.
092 T: why, why, for example, do you have x=rays and light?
093 M: because they are both waves, they can both travel in
       waves.
094 T: and they are both electromagnetic waves.
095 R: thats right.
096 K: actually, x=rays;
097 R: so thats a-
098 M: yea, so have i, let me think, this electron, electrons,
       have gotta go up by the photon, no-
099 K: the electron- we=ll put-
100 R: momentum of the light, what do you think?
101 K: the electrons are,
102 M: wave, putting that over there
103 K: no; electrons are photoelectrons; so they are back
       there.
104 R: i see.
105 K: so its under photoelectric effect.
106 M: electrons, threshold frequency. whats pair production?
107 R: pair production is when,
108 K: compton effect by x=rays.
109 R: when it creates matter;
110 M: thats right, compton effect deals with x=rays that
       should be just up there. wait, compton effect is when
       it hits and it hits the electron, it hits the electron
       so the electron should be up here.
((05:50))
111 K: but there are,

112 R: god, i forgot so much.
113 M: compton effect is right there.
114 K: compton effect is just when the x=rays. its like proven
       that x=rays act like particles also, like they are
       photons. so also the compton effect says that it allows
       the lower frequency to come through.
((06:09))
115 R: this one here- and to describe light you have to decide
       with the complementarity- if it acts like a wave or- as
       matter.
116 K: and thats where- that goes to [matter wave;]
117 M: [you know what] we should
       have light on the top; have, [have wave]-
118 R: [no; wave] stays on the top.
119 M: [no, i know.]
120 R: [because its] the most general.
121 M: no, but if we have light on the top, we could put wave
       down here so we could have matter and all the way down,
       matter waves
       [we get particles]
122 K: [or we can make] our own, own [things up.]
123 R: [we can also]-
124 K: matter waves and energy waves- we can make our- a
       reason to make energy wave one-
125 R: ((mumbles)) light waves ((pause)) ((Ralf arranges))
((06:51))
126 K: because you already made the arrow up and not putting
       the wave on top.
127 M: thats what i said
128 K: so, wave is the most general, put that on top.
129 R: particle production; photoelectric effect; matter
       waves; ((reads from slips with these words))
130 M: matter waves deal with this guy- whats his?
131 K: de broglie. ((figured on the page in Ralf's book))
132 M: okay, where are we gonna toss plancks constant?
133 K: it deals with practically all of them.
134 M: its gonna be on top, because its pretty important.
135 K: under complementarity.
136 R: its connected, see kinetic energy is either plancks
       constant times frequency or electrons or ((looks into
       book, p.713)) because kinetic energy (??)
((07:33))
((07:58 interlude on racism))
  a M: ((turned toward teacher)) uh are you recording with
       this one? uh i didnt know ((turns to Ralf)) its like
       ((hand movement as if slapping with back hand)) this is
       like ((points to microphone)) recording ralf the führer
       ((points to microphone)) ((Miles and Ken both chuckle))
       ralfy the racist, now you- ralf the racist.
  b R: you are the biggest racist here in school
  c M: we have been discussing this, you=ve been racist
  d R: i should=ave mentioned-

e M: ralf, who said- listen
f K: ((hand forward as wanting to separate them, Fig.
      9.2ba)) <<calming>let=s go on>
g M: listen a sec. listen ((oriented toward Ken, throwing
      his hand forward, Fig. 9.2b)). you can decide on this.
      In my chapel speech-
h R: you are talking the whole hour about racist stuff.
      nothing i have said is racist; nothing racist about it.
137 K: what is pair production up there?
138 R: its the creation of matter.
139 K: where would matter waves go, though?
140 R: matter waves is, for example, an electron if it travels
      or even when we=re-
141 K: no, i understand now, wouldnt it be right under this?
      complementarity theory because thats like quantum?
142 M: no, matter waves deal with this guys wavelength.
143 R: make it, lets do something here-
144 M: take ends here;
145 T: ((coming out of background)) why would you for example
      single out wave to go on top?
((09:03))
146 M: because its the most general.
147 T: what about the quantum?
148 M: no, because quantum is a part of light, and wave is,
      wave is- light is a wave, and quantum is the theory of
      light;
149 K: photons deal with-
150 M: if you put this there-
151 R: isnt this the singular form of quantas?
152 T: quan:ta. yea.
((09:19))
153 R: so that doesnt mean that wave;
154 K: they are the same;
155 R: doesnt that ((quantum)) mean that wave doesnt have a
      continuous band of energy, but just;
155 M: bundles-
156 R: but just bundles?
157 T: bundles, but we are talking about the wave or the
      quantum, the particle character.
158 K: so quantum light, i mean, its quantum and then its
      [light].
159 T: [but] when-
160 K: its just reacting different-
161 M: [ah, he]-
162 T: [arent] they like two different?
163 M: he=s saying we should pop light on top and have
      complementarity.
164 T: i was just [asking.]
165 M: [and then] wave and quantum and photon on
      the bottom, because light=s general and then this
      describes;
166 T: but-

167 M: a certain type and this describes a different type.
168 K: but isnt the x=ray the same thing, isnt x=ray a photon,
        x=rays is involved in the quantum theory? x=rays,
        [like travel in waves]?
169 M: [look x=rays have to] do with compton [effect   ]
  a K: [yea like]=
170 T: =you you may you you may want to change for example, i
        dont know, those two ((QUANTUM, WAVE)) have
        complementary character or something- or something of
        that nature.
171 R: we should put this here; at the same level.
172 T: quantum, they would be at the same level.
173 M: then put light at the same level, too, because they are
        the same thing.
174 T: but these two arent the same thing, are they?
175 R: why, why are they in the same level, because-
176 T: why?
177 M: why wouldnt they?
  a K: these travel in the form of photons. not photon is
        quantum.
178 R: but quantum and photon are the same.
179 K: there is different types of photons, and photons are
        like particles.
180 M: photon has a discrete energy and quantum is just saying
        travels in bundles so they are the same thing.
        basically.
181 K: but its general. this ((QUANTUM)) is general; this
        ((PHOTON)) more detailed.
182 M: a little more exact.
183 K: okay, yea, i guess.
184 M: do you understand the difference, cause [planck said]
185 T: [quantum is]
186 M: quantum, and then
        [Einstein said it has discrete energy   ]
187 R: [yea, thats right, but discrete [energy]].
188 T: [photon] is a light
        bundle, because you also have [phonons   ]
189 R: [but planck] gave a
        certain energy to that quantum, because he said its h
        times f
190 M: but it was [einstein-   ]
191 T: [its ultimately] its photon that have this
        energy, but there are also [phonons;   ]
192 R: [but he used] quanta and then just
        einstein said its a photon, so its almost exactly the
        same.
193 M: but no, einstein added something to it, too, like added
        something; ((turns pages of the book, pause)) i can=t
        remember what it was. ((teacher walks away, heads
        toward his office))
((11:26))
194 R: work function.

195 M: here=s the compton effect.
196 T: ((returns with a book in his hand)) see, the thing is,
       you=ve got more quanta than just photons, then quantum
       would be more general.
197 M: its gotta go up by x=rays.
198 K: right over here.
199 M: just-
200 K: like this, right over here.
201 R: i still think we should put this one on top.
202 M: but this one talks about the wave duality, and then we
       talk about the duality and then we talk about the
       duality over here.
203 T: ((points to a page in the book)) you also have phonons
       which are elastic waves, which are quantized, but its
       an elastic wave in matter, its not like, its inside a
       crystal, but the molecules they can move
((12:53))
204 K: so a phonon,
205 T: move-
206 K: is a form of quantum energy;
207 T: thats right.
208 K: yea; thats it,
209 T: and wave is also more general than light wave.
210 K: thats why we have it on top. ((points to slip))
211 T: wa- okay; but these two ((WAVE, QUANTUM)) would be at
       the same level; what i mean, if you have waves you can
       have water waves surface waves you can have a sound
       wave;
212 K: oh, yea, i understand.
213 R: doesnt the sound wave also have energy, because it has
       a [frequency]?
214 T: [it does;] it does;
215 R: so quantum because its a form of energy it is energy;
216 T: but at that level sound energy is not quantized.
217 K: the wave should be over quantum because,
218 T: no no both of them.
219 M: they should be equal.
220 K: quantum quantum-
221 M: but you let the wave duality and then part of the wave
       duality and they are both equal they deserve equal
       status.
222 K: i thought because waves were generalized; that thats a
       particular detailed description of the sort of waves we
       are dealing with. thats why i,
223 M: no. waves is one way of describing light; and quantum
       is another way.
224 R: but there are more waves than there are quanta, because
       for [example,]
225 M: [but if we],
226 R: sound is a wave; but its in matter; not quantized;
227 M: no i know; but we are not talking about what one is
       more; we are talking about equal status.

228 K: but we are looking on this sheet; it says wave -wave
       and thats all it says; it doesnt say light wave.
229 M: yea i know; but thats what we are defining though.
230 R: yea but we can also do it like this, and say that light
       and x=rays are waves.
231 K: they can travel in waves.
232 R: and they are quantized.
233 M: nea, i like it as we had.
234 R: and they travel in photons.
235 M: the way we had before.
236 K: but then, where does this one ((COMPLEMENTARITY)) come
       in? should we scrawl this across? ((all three burst out
       in brief laughter)) the complementarity has to go
       somewhere.
237 M: yea thats why i liked it; because we=re gonna use it;
       then we could put the wave down.
238 T: then quantum a::nd wave have to be side by side;
239 M: yea.
240 T: because of the complementarity principles.
241 M: they have equal status.
242 T: thats right.
243 R: does quantum mean its- um a particle- a wave
       [or a particle?]
244 M: [we had it right] before.
245 T: that means that it is a particle.
246 R: and then we could say that energy is like particle;
247 T: no, it has particle character, its bundled, like, like,
       like a piece of mass. see it says ((points to the book
       in his hand book)) particle like entity or quantum;
       which- a photon; but you can like; but you also have
       phonons.
248 K: yea, i know thats why quantum should be over-
249 T: quantum is over-
250 K: but thats-
251 T: i really dont know, because you are talking about light
       and x=rays.
252 K: but because you=re giving us that example with phonons,
       then thats like ralf was saying, that waves also have a
       lower detailed description within itself and thats why
       it should be above quantum. because quantum is only a
       subdivision of
       [wave. no.]
253 T: [but then-]
254 M: because if its-
255 R: for example-
256 M: light=s a wave, but we dont care for that particular
       concept map what we are concerned about is the
       complementarity and therefore we need the wave down
       here. yea, we could put it up here, but we dont need
       it. but we need it here, otherwise where are we gonna
       put it, we get down here and-

257 T: with the concept map you also have the idea that you
       dont have the same word at two different level because
       otherwise you are skipping levels with the same
       concept.
258 M: no, i know, but you could put it both here and here and
       it makes sense, but it [needs to be here.]
259 K: [okay, leave it up] here.
260 T: in this case, it needs to be here;
  a K: alright then.
((15:52))
261 K: if this is more so have it like that;
262 R: i dont think that x=rays and light should be up here.
263 M: they should be equal [not on this should be]
264 R: [this should this should]
265 R: [the compton effect is]
266 M: [no no there,   ]
267 K: [ralf; ralf; ralf;   ]
268 R: exactly the same level.
269 K: yea but its off; ralf; what we were doing with
       complementarity,
270 R: i know;
271 K: thats why,
272 R: it shouldnt be here; it ((complementarity)) should be
       under waves.
273 M: ralf; because you can put wave there and you could put
       it there but it doesnt need to be here; you have light
       as a heading and we dont loose a thing in the concept
       map. but we have it when we dont put wave here. we are
       totally left without half our-
274 K: we could say, dealing with the subject matters of light
       and x=rays and then go into further detail. actually-
       when you think about it, light is a detail of wave, but
       wave is also a particular aspect of light. cause
       remember; that light isnt just waves, now that they=re
       saying that there is quantum physics, so thats just a
       detailed explicit expression of light waves and x=rays.
((16:48))
275 M: both are waves, so we leave it.
276 K: so we are gonna organize the rest of this? where are we
       gonna?
277 M: plancks constant, threshold frequency,
       [plancks constant, electron].
278 K: [plancks constant involves] everything; threshold
       frequency,
279 M: these three concepts go together (.) or that goes
       everywhere electron; this involves frequency; so,
280 K: wait; does compton effect [involve,]
281 R: [threshold] frequency.
282 M: is the [compton effect] the one where they try,
283 K: [this deals with]-
       the plancks constant too; that goes [under-]
284 R: [you know] what?

285 K: like if you can go somewhere up here;
286 R: these basically make up the kinetic energy.
287 K: yea where we have the-
288 R: compton; the compton effect is,
289 M: it frees electrons; high energy x=rays,
290 K: the photoelectric effect also ejects electrons;
291 M: so put it down here, in between the two.
292 K: no this is for the photoelectric effect
293 M: sorry; i thought that was
294 R: they eject electrons,
295 M: but the [compton effect also],
296 R: [but they have   ] to have
        [the kinetic energy].
297 M: [no, its gotta go] between the two because they both
        eject, they both need the threshold frequency.
298 K: these both need a threshold frequency?
299 R: okay, but you also have to have
300 K: plancks
((18:20))
301 R: these two multiplied together is the energy of the
        photon;
302 K: and these go under here like this and thats all
303 M: and then we can just draw arrows like this
304 K: and with the threshold frequency, thats where you find
        the work function and then diffraction, diffraction
        should go under this. i think. because they both can
        diffract off anything.
305 M: i dont know where where put this back in.
306 K: okay;
307 M: that should, wait ((ralf turns pages in the book)) i
        think that goes up here but i want to check in the book
        if they go like that probably like this, but i am not
        certain about that. whats pair production, i can=t
        remember.
308 R: creation of matter; ((reads))
309 M: oh; by putting high energy in; high energy-
310 K: diffraction (.) no diffraction is under the compton
        effect; because remember, the x=rays when you put them
        through.
((19:24))
311 M: um (.) are they diffracted around the photon?
312 K: yea; and then the lower frequency x=rays photons come
        through;
313 M: but thats why we need threshold frequency too; because,
        no electrons should go below here; it should go right
        here.
314 K: i dont know where this-
315 M: okay; down there (.) cause if these two dont have (.)
        okay;
  a K: (???) ((Puts finger to forehead, as if getting sweat,
        then drawing on table))

b M: i get some so i can draw a diagram; ((takes some sweat
      of his forehead and "draws" lines between slips on the
      table))
316 K: ((laughs))
317 M: see if,
318 K: we gonna need compton effect to see diffraction; we
      gonna-
319 R: is conflicting;
320 K: so thats- right there ((goes through book)) that
      describes it see it diffracts; ((shows drawing of the
      compton effect))
((00:20:20))
321 R: no thats momentum- ((pause)) knocks it out because,
322 M: we should have that in the last ball; the last
      enclosure so we need this;
323 K: ((turned toward Ralf)) isnt that a form of diffraction
      by doing that?
324 M: do you agree with electrons being down below threshold
      frequency?
325 R: ((inaudible))
326 M: because they need the threshold frequency- no electrons
      are like they have to be otherwise nothing.
327 K: diffraction goes (.) i might be thinking back to the
      nature of light.
328 M: i=m thinking back to double slits.
329 K: yea; exactly;
330 M: but its gotta something to do with- its to do with-
331 K: with what ((pause))
a M: what do you say, diffraction?
b K: ralfs racism
c M: dont get ralfs racism into this; we know he is racist
      hes german he cant help it.
d R: thats a cliche.
e M: german racist a cliche? you=re living every bit of it;
      bastard. how=d you get into this country.
f R: i=m canadian.
g M: we let you in.
h R: i=m more canadian than you are.
i M: you,
j R: i was born in montreal.
k M: dont bring in all technicalities.
l K: he dreams in german.
      ((some inaudible words))
m M: see,<<f>who> took over the country;
n R: (??)
o M: whose country is it.
p R: (?)
q M: bring that to (??) german place
r K: diffraction; look in the back of the book; what pages
      are the first-
   ((in the background, the teacher says, apparently to
      another group, 'write that down'))

s M: ((turns in direction of teacher)) we are not done
       ((pause)) we are just ((pause)) undetected.
  ((pause))
332 M: lets get,
333 K: its right here.
334 M: we need more than one book.
((22:28))
335 K: here; organize so that it looks normal; looks like,
336 M: do you agree they should go up here?
337 K: diffraction four ninety two ((turns pages)) yea; double
       slit; guys; doesnt that look a little similar?
338 R: now but momentum doesnt have anything-
339 M: its just a collision;
340 K: momentum diffracts;
341 M: the only thing is; may be; the electrons passes close
       to a photon; then bends around; ((00:23:00)
342 K: pair production doesnt- isnt that the compton effect?
  a M: uh; so much sweat.
  b K: guys, pair production goes under the compton effect;
       bring it under,
343 M: what does it say?
344 K: we got it right here,
345 R: (4.0) but does it say anything about the compton
       effect. ((turns toward the book in Ken's hand))
346 K: ((ken is looking for something in the book, ralf turns
       the page, points to a particular place p.708 and
       continues)) (?????)
347 R: no its not; this is just the five main interactions.
348 K: is that positive? oh wait; have you checked it for
       diffraction,
349 R: no; there is no diffraction there.
  a   (6) ((Ralf and Ken read in the textbook))
350 M: okay; we got ten more minutes.
351 K: matter waves can be diffracted.
352 R: yea.
353 K: matter waves can be diffracted; but there is two
       things-
354 R: they can also go into compton effect here or for the
       properties of the compton effect;
355 M: okay; lets move-
356 R: oh no, diffraction-
357 M: lets move.
358 R: diffraction can be explained by the quantum theory.
359 M: thats good then, oh wait; should we put ((quantum))
       below photons?
360 R: yea.
((24:12))
361 K: matter waves goes up there under compton effect.
362 M: and pull down everything a little bit
363 K: doesnt matter waves- matter waves is just another way
       of saying quantum waves? and,
364 R: no; diffraction of matter waves;

365 K: which can occur with matter waves; just put it under
       diffraction.
366 M: under diffraction?
367 K: where does the damn, does this go?
368 M: right under matter waves.
369 K: here we go.
370 M: starting joining it-
((24:43))
371 R: we have to connect this one here (.) this one with this
       one-
372 M: you start joining on top- the top we agreed upon- down
       to photon-
373 K: yea; okay.
374 R: you have to connect this one here; this one;
375 M: plancks constant with,
376 R: this one with this one.
377 M: threshold frequency with photons.
378 R: these two with this one here; and thats the energy; we
       need the kinetic energy;
379 M: i connect this one for you.
380 R: no this one.
381 M: work function energy goes below threshold frequency.
382 R: why?
383 M: because the threshold frequency ah no the work
       function;
384 R: isnt that one equation?
385 K: okay; wait.
386 M: wait. work function should be below threshold frequency
       cause the two are related and i just- trying to
       remember exactly
       ((Teacher has joined and watches and listens to them.))
387 R: these are related here and this one
388 K: hey doc, does diffraction have something to do with
       matter waves?
389 T: yea; matter waves can be diffracted.
((25:58))
390 M: we put that right here;
391 R: yea.
392 T: germer and davisson experiment. ((gestures in direction
       of the book.))
393 M: we put this like that then-
394 R: okay, and because this screws everything up, just put
       it here and link it-
395 T: yea, you can link it.
396 K: what about plancks constant?
397 T: ((turns toward class)) you have about ten more minutes
       so try to figure ((walks away))
398 K: okay guys, complementarity do i put it right? i mean,
       wave and quantum, i put right here.
399 M: yea, side by side.
400   (4.8)

401 R: we have to erase that ((pause)) electrons- electrons
      are like this here;
402 M: electrons; it has to be; no because look if they dont
      meet the minimum threshold frequency; ((pause)) they
      dont meet the threshold frequency in either cases, no
      electrons are freed. and this is-
403 R: electrons are related to all of those here.
404 M: i know, but-
405 R: its even related to this one here.
406 M: i know, but it has to be, they have to meet the minimum
      threshold frequency, in either of those cases no
      electrons can escape.
407 R: but still; you have to connect it to this one; this
      one; this one;
408 M: but how do they relate to de broglie?
409 R: this is matter; so its matter waves; photoelectric
      effect knocks out electrons;
410 M: and pair production?
411 R: and compton effect?
412 M: knocks out electrons;
413 R: yea; collides with electron? which means that it is a
      wave; a matter wave; and pair production produces
      electrons. we should put it right here- and they have
      to,
((27:27))
414 M: all be related;
415 R: they have, [they all have to],
416 M: [put matter wave] down too;
417 R: not at the same level; because they=re kind of
      interaction; its a [kind of wave];
418 M: [i know; get] a little higher;
419 R: and then we just put down.
420 M: here-
421 R: and then work function;
422 M: i dont know where we can arrange for that; we gotta
      connect x=rays and compton effect;
423 R: we have to connect-
424 M: we should put pair production; switch these-
425 K: does pair production concern electrons?
426 M: yea; all of these;
  a K: ((Ken blows at eraser pieces on sheet, makes a slip fly
      away)) oh shit ((Ken laughs; Ralf and Miles smile))
  b M: way to go big guy. ((Ralf re-places the slips))
  c K: still a racist guy;
  d M: hey hey hey dont bring ralfs racism into this. you=ll
      bring it into these we=ll
  e R: i have never mentioned any racist comments;
  f M: <<f>[ohoho>]
  g R: [hes the] one with racism in his talks
  h M: hey feenie ((orients to and calls a student in another
      group)) has ralf ever said anything racist? ((pause,
      the student in the other group laughs))

```
        [not to the face   ]
i   R:  [he said something] like this about our relations
j   F:  ((from the other group)) uh, is that a serious
        question?
k   M:  ralf, you guys.
l   R:  i hate that so much.
m   M:  you hate being a racist?
n   R:  quite a bit so.
o   M:  so why do you keep making these dumb comments.
p   R:  you accuse me of what i dont do.
q   M:  i can ask anyone around the school ((pause)) about ralf
        being racist
r   R:  first he accuses me of being a racist. then he puts
        words into, words into my mouth and afterwards he
        believes in what he says. and [he believes]
s   M:                                [i can      ]
t   R:  that i said it. * (???)
u   M:  fï- feenie can verify my story. late sat- late at night
        ralf just lays in an totally puts in (()) like
        classifies like every race.
v   R:  i have not done anything like this
x   M:  of course he=ll gonna be on the top
y   R:  i never do that
z   T:  ((comes to group)) get yourself ready
aa  M:  (???)
427 K:  okay guys; connect all these; we gotta do it pretty
        fast.
((29:25. Interlude about racism))
428 M:  okay, we=re done doc
429 T:  no no the connections are the most important thing.
        ((Ken has copied the organized concept words, Ralf now
        takes over to make the connections between the terms
        and the connecting words.))
430 M:  thats what i was telling ralf just minutes ago.
431 T:  i think thats what makes the difference between a,
432 R:  complementary;
433 M:  no x=rays go to compton effect; draw a big loop;
434 R:  should we link this?
435 M:  no; x=ray goes to compton effect.
436 R:  no we have to first got to find the words.
437 M:  ah the words.
438 K:  lets link them all and find the words.
439 M:  ((light and x=rays)) possesses complementary and-
440 R:  <<forcefully, impatiently>complementary is just, you
        just have to decide which one is useful.>
441 K:  oh, have complementarity.
442 R:  ((inaudible))
443 K:  have?
444 M:  sure.
445 K:  connect quickly.
446 R:  means that it can either act as a wave or a quantum.
((30:38))
```

447 K: yea; right; acting as,
448 M: may act; has wave or quantum;
449 R: okay;
450 M: join x=rays;
451 K: but then you gotta join wave and quantum; because it-
       they interact;
452 M: they dont,
453 K: yea remember, thats why we put them besides each other.
((31:01))
454 M: no
455 R: they dont interact
456 M: [they have quantum and photon   ]
457 R: [they=re different kinds of waves]
458 K: yea, yea
459 R: this is different kinds
460 M: x=rays to compton effect, do that now
461 K: we dont forget cause you can remind him
462 M: ((inaudible)) i figure because when i get to the bottom
463 K: has; because remember, it has photon;
464 R: photon is a form of;
465 K: is form of;
466 M: diffraction of photon; and then we get diffraction.
467 K: ralf; may.
468 R: do diffraction; undergo diffraction;
469 K: photons do diffract;
470 R: ((mumbles, inaudible))
471 M: and then,
472 R: we have to connect this here.
473 K: connect, just draw a straight
474 R: yea, but
475 K: how, no matter where you go;
476 M: matter waves do diffraction.
477 K: can affect,
478 M: anyway-
479 R: we shouldnt put- we should put it- because we also have
       different;
480 M: we=re not getting marks for neatness.
481 R: ah-
482 K: can we connect the waves to diffraction?
483 R: we can connect it to all.
484 K: can alter matter waves; put can alter;
485 M: diffraction can alter; affects; diffraction affects;
486 R: can alter?
((32:25))
487 M: [affects.]
488 K: [affects.]
489 R: diffraction affects matter waves?
490 M: yea, because they do diffract.
491 K: frequency can alter matter waves, it just means that
       matter waves can diffract- just put like can alter or
       affects; which ever one you feel.
((32:43))

492 R: matter waves can can diffract.
493 K: yea.
494 M: put like can; can alter or affects; whichever one you
      feel.
495 R: matter waves can can diffract.
496 K: yea.
497 M: put like, ca:n.
498 R: undergoes;
499 M: you arent going- undergo.
500 R: uh i cant write undergo, give me another word.
501 M: <<laughing>kh: kh:: we gave you about six.>
 ((33:02))
502 R: matter waves can diffraction?
503 M: okay; just go, undergo;
504 K: he says, i said that; i said diffraction affects; or
505 M: i know; dont worry about that.
506 K: whats that?
507 M: wave to matter waves; oh quantum to matter waves.
508 K: travels in; no thats,
509 R: i think we should- is a kind of wave;
510 M: yea; these two are; matter wave is a-
511 K: quantum property; concerning quantum; concerning
      quantum- okay hurry up.
512 M: okay; ah.
513 R: why do you have ((inaudible))?
514 M: because we have,
 ((33:55))
515 R: okay; yea;
516 M: because we connect all this,
517 K: connect pair production.
518 M: well, connect them all;
519 K: ejects;
520 M: releases;
521 R: collides with electrons.
522 M: no; if we squeeze electrons these might collide which
      gives them the energy to escape.
523 K: they dont; they eject.
524 M: put eject;
525 R: why do you want eject?
526 K: plancks constant; i dont know.
527 T: well, plancks constant isnt it plancks constant- that
      plancks constant relates to quantum?
528 R: yea, we want to connect it through these here.
529 K: threshold frequency is on the same level.
 ((34:54)) ((Bell rings 35:00))
530 R: and to photon;
531 M: no, why is work function here,
532 K: because these here all calculations properties these
      three.
533 R: we should include kinetic energy. we should connect
      this one to this one here.
534 M: well, just connect back to-

535 R: reflected threshold frequency- connect this one- the
     energy of a photon- the threshold frequency, plancks
     constant we just connect this one here.
a   ((draws a link from THRESHOLD FREQUENCY to PHOTON))
b   M: ((bursts out in laughter))
536 K: ralf; ((barely containing himself, with chuckle)) like
     we said; go crazy but- ((laughs))
((35:49))
537 R: it rang already; here=s energy; this is the energy of a
     photon,
538 K: it says has the energy of;
539 M: ha:s-
540 K: and then=ll just-
541 M: equals-
542 K: photon has the energy of-
543 R: equals;
544 M: equals energy of;
545 R: equals ((pause)) and these like multiplied together;
546 M: just write times.
547 R: and this subtracted by
548 K: what about photon and threshold frequency?
((36:36))
549 M: we got it; thats everything connected; its all-
550 R: we still have quantum and photon; uh; quantum here.
551 M: what do you want (.) we didnt connect these ones here
     to anything.
552 K: put photoelectric effect.
553 R: all kinds of interaction.
554 K: quantum, yea quantum interact with-
555 R: quantum explains-
556 K: yea that explains-
557 M: i dont know what the hell-
558 R: because this one knocks out this one here.
559 M: write.
560 R: it doesnt look very good.
561 T: as long as i find my way through.
((37:39))
562 M: <<laughing>uh=uh>
563 K: <<laughing>like like like that math period. And then
     throw it at someone.